ATTITUDES TOWARD
THE OUTDOORS

ATTITUDES TOWARD
THE OUTDOORS

An Annotated Bibliography of
U.S. Survey and Poll Research
Concerning the Environment,
Wildlife and Recreation

Compiled by
DENA JONES JOLMA

McFarland & Company, Inc., Publishers
Jefferson, North Carolina, and London

British Library Cataloguing-in-Publication data are available

Library of Congress Cataloguing-in-Publication Data

Jolma, Dena Jones, 1953–
    Attitudes toward the outdoors : an annotated bibliography of U.S.
survey and poll research concerning the environment, wildlife and
recreation / compiled by Dena Jones Jolma.
      p. cm.
    Includes indexes.
    ISBN 0-89950-958-4 (lib. bdg. : 50# alkaline paper) ∞
    1. United States — Environmental conditions — Public opinion —
Bibliography. 2. Outdoor recreation — United States — Public
opinion — Bibliography. 3. Recreation areas — United States — Public
opinion — Bibliography. 4. Wildlife management — United States —
Public opinion — Bibliography. I. Title.
    Z5863.P6J65 1994
  [GE150]
  016.3337'2 — dc20   94-21677
                                                  CIP

Manufactured in the United States of America

McFarland & Company, Inc., Publishers
  Box 611, Jefferson, North Carolina 28640

CONTENTS

5. ATTITUDES TOWARD WILDLIFE MANAGEMENT   *215*

Support for Wildlife Conservation *215*; Hunting as
Wildlife Management *217*; Wildlife Management
Practices *222*; Predator and Damage Control *225*;
Landowner Rights and Obligations *230*; Funding for
Wildlife Programs *232*

PREFACE

Over the past thirty to thirty-five years, Americans have become increasingly concerned about, and involved in, their natural environment. Environmental issues are favorite topics of current public opinion polling and scientific survey research. The purpose of this book is to provide a resource for librarians, students, public officials, and community activists who desire access to information about how Americans view the natural world.

This volume contains 850 bibliographic citations with lengthy annotations. The annotations vary from fewer than 50 words to over 250 words depending on the scope of the source. Whenever possible, key findings are offered from the studies. The book's emphasis is on survey findings; discussions of theory and research methodology are minimized.

This bibliography is not intended to be an exhaustive collection of all studies on the subject, but rather a review of the most important studies with enough information provided to aid users in determining the most relevant sources for their needs. Although a background in research methods and statistics is not required to use the book, readers will find a basic understanding of research terms helpful.

The scope of the book is public opinion polls and survey research conducted in the United States beginning in the early 1960s. Studies with non–American subjects are excluded except in instances where comparisons are made with American subjects. The terms "poll," "survey," and "questionnaire" are used interchangeably and no attempt has been made to adhere to the term chosen by the original authors and researchers. Surveys with national, state, and local samples have all been included, but preference has been given to national studies.

The population or universe for most of the studies is the general public or specific interest groups. Although most of the studies involve randomly selected subjects, a small number of magazine readership and organizational membership surveys are included.

Sources for the bibliography are books, newspaper and magazine articles, professional journal articles and conference proceedings, public opinion collections, and government documents. Whenever descriptions of a study were found in multiple sources, the most accessible source was chosen. Each entry in the bibliography appears only once. A study may be the subject of more than one entry, however, if the individual entries discuss different aspects of the study.

The bibliography entries have been organized by five major subject areas: The Environment, Parks and Recreation Areas, Outdoor Recreation, Wildlife, and Wildlife Management. Each subject area is further divided into subtopics. All entries are consecutively numbered by publication date. The assignment of the entries to a particular section was challenging, as many polls address multiple subjects. Users of the book should refer to the Subject Index to locate all entries related to a specific topic.

Several topics have been excluded from the bibliography: energy use and conservation, nuclear energy, noise pollution, the urban environment, and perceptions of local environmental quality. Research on human knowledge and behaviors related to the environment are not included, unless they are addressed as part of a study of environmental attitudes, beliefs, or perceptions. Each entry includes standard information about the study (as available in the original source): topics for the study, survey dates, universe or population, sample size, and survey methodology. Research sponsors are also provided when specified in the source. Information on sampling error is not included, and users are encouraged to seek this detail from the original sources.

At the conclusion of this volume, two appendixes and three indexes are offered. Appendix A provides a list of the primary sources for the bibliography. A list of state referendums and initiatives on environmental and wildlife management issues and their outcomes is presented in Appendix B. The three indexes allow users to locate sources by subject, researcher or sponsor name, and the population for the study.

ATTITUDES TOWARD
THE ENVIRONMENT

Concern for the Environment

1. "People Speak on 31 Issues." *The New York Times*, March 21, 1976, pp. 1, 17–18.

   The survey described in this newspaper article was conducted by *The New York Times* between March 4 and 8, 1976. A sample of 722 New Jersey residents responded to the telephone poll which asked them to identify what they perceived as the state's biggest problem. Environmental concerns were named by 12 percent of the sample, placing the issue third in importance behind taxes and the economy.

2. Gallup, George H. "May 2, 1974: Most Important Problem." *The Gallup Poll: Public Opinion 1972–1977*. Wilmington, DE: Scholarly Resources, Inc., 1978, pp. 257–58.

   In this poll by the Gallup Organization, college students were interviewed during January and March 1974. When asked to identify the most important problem facing the country at the time, 4 percent of the respondents cited problems related to the environment. (Multiple responses were received from some respondents.) The students indicated they felt the greatest problem was distrust in the government after Watergate. The sample size for the poll is not given.

3. McCay, Roger E.; Gansner, David A.; and Padalino, John J. *Measuring the Attitudes and Awareness of Environmental Education Camp Users*. U.S. Department of Agriculture, Forest Service, 1978, 13 pp.

   This study measured environmental awareness among school children attending education camps at the Pocono Environmental Education Center. The research was sponsored by the Center along with New York University and the U.S. Forest Service. Written questionnaries were used to solicit the children's attitudes toward pollution and the importance of having a clean environment. The students thought the hardest part of having a clean environment was getting everyone to cooperate. They also thought human health was the most important reason for having a clean environment but that most people did not protect the environment because of apathy.

4. Alaimo, Samuel J., and Doran, Rodney L. "Students' Perception of Environmental Problems and Sources of Environmental Information." *Journal of Environmental Education* 12 (Fall 1980): 17–21.

This study attempted to determine students' concern for environmental problems, knowledge about the environment, and sources of information on the environment. A survey instrument containing items on these three subjects, as well as perception of ability to solve environmental problems, was administered to 615 students in grades seven through twelve attending three schools in a suburban community of western New York. Data were collected from the students in their science classes during September 1977. Analysis of the responses to the five-item survey indicated that all of the students appeared to have a high concern for environmental problems. Most of the students, especially those in the twelfth grade, were optimistic about the chances for solving environmental problems. The students felt they had little knowledge about the environment, with the twelfth graders feeling they knew the most. Television was most often cited as the students' source of environmental information, while parents were cited least often for providing information on environmental problems.

5. Oregon Poll. *American Public Opinion Index: 1981.* Tallahassee, FL: Opinion Research Service, Inc., 1982.

In March 1981, personal interviews were performed with a sample of 654 Oregon residents by the Survey Research Institute of Salem, Oregon. The survey included one question that asked the respondents to identify the two or three most serious problems facing the state of Oregon.

6. Houston Reports. *American Public Opinion Index: 1982.* Lexington, KY: Opinion Research Service, Inc., 1984.

Houston Reports is compiled by V. Lance Tarrance and Associates of Houston, Texas. In their January and May polls, 400 Houston residents were contacted by phone and asked to identify the most important problem in the Houston area.

7. The California Poll. *American Public Opinion Index: 1982.* Lexington, KY: Opinion Research Service, Inc., 1984.

The California Poll is conducted by the Field Institute of California. In February and October, over 1,200 Californians were contacted by telephone and asked to identify the most pressing problem in their community and in the state.

8. The Merit Report. *American Public Opinion Index: 1982.* Lexington, KY: Opinion Research Service, Inc., 1984.

In this poll, 1,202 Americans were contacted by telephone and asked to identify the most important domestic issue facing the nation. The survey results were released on June 22, 1982.

9. *The Los Angeles Times* Poll. *American Public Opinion Index: 1982.* Lexington, KY: Opinion Research Service, Inc., 1984.

The September 1982 *Los Angeles Times* telephone poll asked respondents to identify the most important problem in their community, in their state, and in the nation. The sample for the poll consisted of 1,419 residents of the state of California.

10. Eagleton Poll. *American Public Opinion Index: 1982.* Lexington, KY: Opinion Research Service, Inc., 1984.

During September and October 1982, polls conducted by the Eagleton Institute at Rutgers University asked respondents to name the most important problem facing the country. The survey was performed by telephone with 1,005 (September) and 1,097 (October) New Jersey residents.

11. *Data Track 14 — Children.* American Council of Life Insurance, December 1984, 35 pp.

This survey of junior and senior high school students was conducted for the National Association of Secondary School Principals. The report gives the date of the survey as 1983 but does not disclose the sample size or the survey methodology. Results are compared with a similar survey performed in 1974. The students were questioned about their perception of the most important world and national problems. In 1974, overpopulation and environmental preservation were cited by high school students as the most pressing world problems. In 1983, nuclear disaster and the threat of World War III were of most concern to students with overpopulation and environmental problems ranking fourth and fifth. In terms of national problems, politics, unemployment and ecology took the top three slots in 1974. By 1983, concern for ecology problems had dropped to ninth out of ten major problems. (The percentages shown for individual problems indicate that multiple answers were given to the question of most important national problem.)

12. The Garth Analysis. *American Public Opinion Index: 1984.* Lexington, KY: Opinion Research Service, Inc., 1985.

Penn and Schoen Associates of New York conducted national telephone polls in February, June, and October 1984. In these polls, approximately 1,000 Americans were asked to identify the most important issues for the president to work on for the country.

13. Dallas Trendline. *American Public Opinion Index: 1984.* Lexington, KY: Opinion Research Service, Inc., 1985.

This telephone poll was conducted by the Dallas Chamber. A sample of 400 residents of Dallas County were surveyed. Respondents were asked about their perception of the importance of environmental problems in the Dallas area.

14. The Hawaii Poll. *American Public Opinion Index: 1984.* Lexington, KY: Opinion Research Service, Inc., 1985.

In February 1984, this telephone survey was conducted by the *Honolulu Advertiser* with 400 Hawaiians. Included in the survey was one question asking the interviewee to identify the most important problem for the state government to tackle.

15. Dallas Trendline. *American Public Opinion Index: 1985.* Lexington, KY: Opinion Research Service, Inc., 1986.

The Dallas Chamber sponsored the Dallas Trendline survey which interviewed 400 residents of Dallas County. Contacted by telephone, the respondents were asked about their perception of the importance of environmental problems in the Dallas area.

16. Teichner Associates Poll. *American Public Opinion Index: 1987.* Boston, MA: Opinion Research Service, Inc., 1988.

   Teichner Associates of Fullerton, California, interviewed 1,000 Californians by telephone and requested that they identify the biggest problem facing the state of California. Results of the poll were released on May 9, 1987.

17. Bowie, Liz. "Focus Shifts to Cleanup in Maryland." *Baltimore Sun,* January 3, 1989.

   The poll described in this article was conducted by the University of Maryland Survey Research Center between October 15 and November 5, 1988. A statewide sample of 1,000 Maryland residents were interviewed by telephone and asked to name the most important issue in the state. Environmental and energy issues were identified as being most important to the state by 9 percent of those surveyed, while 6 percent cited the condition of Chesapeake Bay as the most important problem. Environmental issues were rated lower than drug use and crime in importance but higher than the budget and taxes. Over three-fourths of the respondents said they favored mandatory recycling of newspapers, glass, and aluminum cans. The article also mentions results of another survey conducted by Clean Water Action in late 1987. At that time, recycling and the disposal of solid waste were given as the most important environmental issues.

18. The California Poll. *American Public Opinion Index 1989.* Boston, MA: Opinion Research Service, Inc., 1990.

   The California Poll is conducted by the Field Institute of San Francisco, California. In a poll released on March 3, 1989, 1,007 Californians were contacted by telephone and asked about the degree of their concern for protecting the environment in California.

19. Lindgren, Kristina. "O.C. Poll Shows Growing Concern for Environment." *The Los Angeles Times* (Orange County Edition), December 4, 1990.

   The 1990 Orange County Annual Survey was conducted by the University of California, Irvine's Center for Survey Research between September 5 and 21, 1990. Funding for the survey was provided by 35 Orange County public agencies, private foundations, and corporations. A sample of 1,017 adult residents were interviewed about several issues including concern for the environment and perceptions of quality of life in the future. Environmental problems pose a serious personal threat, said nine out of ten residents polled. The future quality of life is expected to be better by 29 percent of the sample, worse by 44 percent, and 27 percent foresee no change. The article includes a chart depicting responses to the quality of life question from previous polls.

20. Gallup, George Jr. "July 25: Most Important Problem." *The Gallup Poll: Public Opinion 1990.* Wilmington, DE: Scholarly Resources, Inc., 1991, p. 84.

   Interview dates for this Gallup Poll were July 19 to 22, 1990. (Sample size and methodology were not given.) When asked to identify the most important problem facing the country, 5 percent of the respondents named environmental concerns. The percentages indicate that multiple responses were accepted.

21. Gallup, George Jr. "November 6: Election Day 1990, The Mood of the Country." *The Gallup Poll: Public Opinion 1990.* Wilmington, DE: Scholarly Resources, Inc., 1991, p. 148.

  The Gallup Organization completed this poll between November 1 and 4, 1990, with an undisclosed number of Americans. Only 2 percent of the poll's respondents identified environmental concerns as the most important problem facing the country. Multiple responses were received from some individuals.

22. Gallup, George Jr. "May 4: Most Important Problem." *The Gallup Poll: Public Opinion 1991.* Wilmington, DE: Scholarly Resources, Inc., 1992, pp. 96–97.

  This April 1991 Gallup Poll included an item asking respondents to identify the most important problem in the country. Only 3 percent of those surveyed named the environment as the biggest problem. Responses are compared to results from a March 1991 poll.

23. "Industry Views Environment." *The New York Times*, May 28, 1992, p. D9.

  A nationwide survey by Leo Burnett Company of Chicago reported lower levels of environmental concerns among consumers in a February 1992 survey. The article does not give details on the sample size or methodology but does note that the February 1992 survey was the seventh conducted by the company since September 1989. The environment was the biggest concern of 40 percent of the surveys' respondents. Mandatory recycling was strongly supported by 46 percent of the sample compared with 57 percent in a survey 18 months earlier.

24. "Poll: Economy, AIDS, Schools Are Top Issues in California." UP western region newswire, October 7, 1992.

  The California Poll was conducted by pollster Mervin Field during September 1992. A statewide telephone poll of 1,067 adults revealed that Californians were more concerned about economic issues and crime than the environment. Despite that finding, two-thirds of the sample said they were extremely concerned about such environmental problems as toxic waste and air and water pollution.

25. "Teens Say Economy Top Issue in Selecting President." UP central region newswire, October 26, 1992.

  Teenage Research Unlimited conducted a survey of teenagers to measure their opinions on the importance of various issues facing the country. A total of 2,107 teenagers aged 12 through 19 years completed the survey. The issues of most concern to the teenagers were AIDS, race relations, and the environment. In selecting a president, they thought the economy, education, and the environment should be the top considerations.

Factors Influencing Environmental Concern

26. Tognacci, Louis N.; Weigel, Russell H.; Wideen, Marvin F.; and Vernon, David T. A. "Environmental Quality: How Universal Is Public Concern?" *Environment and Behavior* 4 (March 1972): 73–86.

  This article describes research that tested the relationship between concern for environmental quality and several demographic variables. The sample consisted of 141 randomly selected residents of Boulder, Colorado. All of the subjects were interviewed about their perceptions of the importance of a pure environment and their concern for specific environmental problems (natural resource conservation, pollution, power plant pollution, and overpopulation). Generally, the results revealed that younger, more highly educated people with liberal political ideology were more concerned about environmental quality issues. No differences were documented on the basis of the sex of the respondents.

27. Costantini, Edmond, and Hanf, Kenneth. "Environmental Concern and Lake Tahoe: A Study of Elite Perceptions, Backgrounds, and Attitudes." *Environment and Behavior* 4 (June 1972): 209–42.

Support for this research was provided by the Office of Water Resources Research, U.S. Department of Interior and the University of California, Water Resources Center. The purpose of the study was to describe a group of environmental decision makers in one community. A series of indepth interviews were conducted with 303 individuals active in environmental decision making for the community of the Lake Tahoe basin. Analysis of the surveys showed that individuals expressing a high degree of environmental concerns differed on a wide range of environmental attitudes and perceptions from those low in environmental concerns. Those high in environmental concerns were more likely to be better educated but with slightly lower incomes and were more likely to be professionals or governmental officials versus businessmen. The subjects with high concerns about the environment were also more likely to be liberal in their ideology and cosmopolitan in their orientation. The high concern group perceived deforestation and water quality as the most urgent local environmental problems, while the low concern group perceived traffic congestion and visual pollution as being the most urgent problems.

28. Kreger, Janet. "Ecology and Black Student Opinion." *Journal of Environmental Education* 4 (Spring 1973): 30–34.

In this article, the author describes a study of black college students' attitudes toward environmental problems. A limited sample of 28 black students at Michigan State University were asked to complete a six-item questionnaire during February 1972. Of the 28 students, only three felt African-Americans have as much interest in and concern for environmental problems as whites. Those three indicated that while they thought African-Americans may have an interest equal to whites, the interest was shown in more subtle and indirect ways. When the remaining students were asked why they thought African-Americans have less interest in environmental problems, the majority responded that African-Americans have other, more pressing concerns. Other explanations were that ecology is a white middle-class issue, ecology problems do not affect African-Americans as personally as whites, African-Americans are only interested in ecology issues that affect them, and ecological concern is used to direct attention away from social issues.

29. Knopp, Timothy B., and Tyger, John D. "A Study of Conflict in Recreational Land Use: Snowmobiling vs. Ski-Touring." *Journal of Leisure Research* 5 (Summer 1973): 6–17.

This project was conducted by the authors with support from Hatch Act funds. The purpose of the research was to compare the attitudes of snowmobilers and ski-tourers toward environmental and public land management issues. The subjects for the study consisted of 169 Minnesota registered snowmobile owners and 220 members of the North Star (Minnesota) Ski Touring Club. Mail surveys were distributed during June 1971, and responses were received from 70 percent of the snowmobilers and 87 percent of the ski-tourers. Analysis of the surveys revealed significant differences between the two groups on nine items of the environmental instrument and seven items of the public lands management instrument. On environmental issues, the snowmobilers were more likely to support the Alaskan oil pipeline, development of mineral deposits in wilderness areas, and less likely to support funding for endangered species protection. While only 4 percent of the ski-tourers thought the public should not have to pay to protect wilderness areas, 36 percent of the snowmobilers felt that way. Almost half of the snowmobilers thought a person should have the right to enjoy his own kind of recreation in any public park or forest, but only 10 percent of the ski-tourers supported that degree of recreational freedom.

30. Bowman, Mary Lynne Cox. "Assessing College Student Attitudes Toward Environmental Issues." *Journal of Environmental Education* 6 (Winter 1974): 1–5.

The purpose of this research was to test the effect of an environmental education course on college students' attitudes as to who should be responsible for environmental decision making. Data for the study were collected from a control group comprised of students enrolled in an education methods course and an experimental group comprised of students in an environmental management course. A total of 331 students in the two courses at the Ohio State University completed a pre- and post-course instrument during the spring of 1972. Analysis of the results revealed that the group enrolled in the natural resources course moved toward viewing society, and not the individual, as the determinant of environmental action.

31. Dunlap, Riley E. "The Impact of Political Orientation on Environmental Attitudes and Actions." *Environment and Behavior* 7 (December 1975): 428–54.

The Department of Sociology at Washington State University provided partial funding for this research into the impact of political ideology and political party affiliation on environmental attitudes. A sample of 237 students at the University of Oregon completed mail questionnaires during May 1970. The questionnaire included items covering the following subjects: political affiliation, political outlook (liberal, moderate, conservative), attitude toward the environmental movement, participation in the environmental movement, causes of environmental degradation, strategies for solving environmental problems, and the seriousness of various environmental problems. Analysis of the surveys demonstrated that interest in environmental issues was correlated with political ideology but not with political party. Approval of the environmental movement was significantly related to both variables. Political party and political outlook were also related to perception of causes of environmental degradation and strategies for solving environmental problems. In all cases, the relationship between political ideology and environmental attitude was stronger than the relationship between political party and environmental attitude. Liberal, Democratic students consistently displayed stronger environmental attitudes than conservative, Republican students. The author discusses results of other studies and offers an explanation for contradictory findings.

32. Buttel, Frederick H., and Flinn, William L. "Environmental Politics: The Structuring of Partisan and Ideological Cleavages in Mass Environmental Attitudes." *The Sociological Quarterly* 17 (Autumn 1976): 477–90.

The purpose of this research was to describe the relationship between political party and ideology and two measures of environmental attitudes: awareness of environmental problems and support for environmental reform. Data for the study were taken from a 1974 survey of 548 Wisconsin residents conducted by the Wisconsin Survey Research Laboratory. The research tested the effect of several variables (age, education, place of residence, political party, and liberal ideology) on the two measures of environmental attitudes. Results of the data analysis indicated no relationship between political party and awareness of environmental problems or support for environmental reform. Political liberalism was found to be associated with support for environmental reform but not awareness of environmental problems. Funding for this research was received from the University of Wisconsin–Madison Graduate School and Agriculture Experiment Station and from the Michigan State University College of Social Science and Agriculture Experiment Station.

33. Marsh, C. Paul, and Christenson, James A. "Support for Economic Growth and Environmental Protection, 1973–1975." *Rural Sociology* 42 (Spring 1977): 101–7.

The purpose of this research was to compare support for environmental controls and economic growth between two statewide surveys. Data for the study came from two mail surveys conducted in North Carolina in the spring of 1973 and the spring of 1975. Samples of 3,115 and 3,054 in 1973 and 1975, respectively, answered questions about air and water pollution controls and agriculture and industrial development. Significant differences between the two surveys were noted for all four issues. Between 1973 and 1975, support for environmental controls decreased, while support for economic development increased. The research also studied relationships among support for environmental controls and economic growth and socioeconomic variables (education, income, political ideology, and rural-urban residence). Those respondents living on a farm expressed the lowest support for environmental controls of any group.

34. Bowman, James S. "Public Opinion and the Environment: Post–Earth Day Attitudes Among College Students." *Environment and Behavior* 9 (September 1977): 385–416.

This research received funding from the Division of Basic Research of the University of Wyoming. The purpose of the study was to measure public opinion among college students toward various environmental issues. A questionnaire was administered to 325 freshmen at the University of Wyoming during September 1974. The survey instrument included questions on the students' awareness of environmental problems, opinions of causes of environmental problems, and opinion of the environmental movement. Awareness of environmental problems was also correlated with several background characteristics (residence, family income, parents' political ideology, ranch background, state residence, sex, party affiliation, and political ideology). Analysis of the surveys revealed a high level of awareness of environmental problems among the college students. A ranching background, political party affiliation, and political ideology were related to certain aspects of environmental awareness. The majority of the students felt environmental problems were caused by the public's concern for convenience and comfort over preservation of resources and prevention of pollution. Despite that finding, over 60 percent of the students thought environmental problems could be solved within the existing political-economic system. Attention to environmental problems by the news media was most commonly cited as the source of the students' environmental awareness.

35. McTeer, J. Hugh. "Teenage-Adult Differences in Concern for Environmental Problems." *Journal of Environmental Education* 9 (Winter 1977): 20–23.

In this study, results from two prior surveys were reviewed to determine if differences existed between teenagers and adults on concern for environmental problems. The two studies were conducted in 1975–76 in the Atlanta, Georgia, metropolitan area. In both studies, high school students, parents, social studies teachers, and school administrators were asked to rate or rank the importance of twelve objectives for teaching high school social studies. One of the objectives in each study dealt with awareness of environmental problems. (The sample sizes for the studies were 280 and 288 individuals.) In one study, significant differences in the ranking of the environmental objective were noted between students and parents and students and administrators. In the other study, significant differences were found between students and teachers and students and school administrators. In each case, the students ranked the environmental objective higher than the other groups. Parents ranked the environmental objective as more important than did the teachers in one of the studies. When the groups in the second study were asked to rank order the objectives, students ranked the environmental objective first, while parents ranked it fourth, teachers ranked it tenth, and administrators ranked it eleventh of the twelve objectives.

36. Hershey, Marjorie Randon, and Hill, David B. "Is Pollution 'A White Thing'? Racial Differences in Preadults' Attitudes." *Public Opinion Quarterly* 41 (Winter 1977-78): 439–58.

In this research, the authors attempted to explore racial differences in perception of environmental quality. A sample of 2,012 Florida children and teenagers in grades two through twelve were the subjects for the study. Personal interviews, which included dilemmas related to environmental issues, were conducted in late 1973 and early 1974. Some of the issues covered by the interviews were land preservation, litter, and endangered species. The instrument was designed to test the hypothesis that racial differences in attitudes toward pollution are related to socioeconomic status, years of formal education, exposure to pollution, and perceived political efficacy. Results of the study revealed differences between perceptions of environmental quality by race with African-Americans much less likely than whites to consider environmental issues important and worthy of public action. These differences remained even after factors thought to explain racial differences (such as socioeconomic status) were controlled. Funding for the research was provided by Florida State University, Indiana University, and Kansas State University.

37. Buttel, Frederick H., and Flinn, William L.. "The Politics of Environmental Concern: The Impacts of Party Identification and Political Ideology on Environmental Attitudes." *Environment and Behavior* 10 (March 1978): 17–36.

This research was supported by funding from the University of Wisconsin–Madison Graduate School and Agricultural Experiment Station and Michigan State University College of Social Science and Agricultural Experiment Station. The purpose of the study was to examine the relationship between several variables (education, age, size of place of residence, political party identification, and political ideology) and degree of environmental concern. During the fall of 1974, a sample of 548 residents of Wisconsin were surveyed by the Wisconsin Survey Research Laboratory. Analysis of the surveys revealed a significant relationship between all of the independent variables and environmental concern. (The relationship for education, size of place of residence, Democratic party identification, and liberal ideology all being positive relationships, while the relationship for age and Republican party identification were negative.) Political ideology was more strongly associated with concern for the environment among those respondents with a higher level of education. In addition, political ideology was shown to be a better predictor of environmental concern than party identification.

38. Tremblay, Kenneth R., Jr., and Dunlap, Riley E.. "Rural-Urban Residence and Concern with Environmental Quality: A Replication and Extension." *Rural Sociology* 43 (Fall 1978): 474–91.

This article describes a study designed to measure differences in environmental concern on the basis of residence. The study used results from a 1970 survey of 866 Oregon residents conducted by Louis Harris and Associates. Environmental concern was measured by responses to eight questions in the survey pertaining to pollution problems at the local and state level. Place of residence was categorized as rural area, small town, urban fringe, and urban area. Overall, 53 percent of the Oregon residents identified pollution as a serious problem facing the state. Urban residents of the state expressed higher levels of environmental concern than rural residents, especially for issues at the local level. Included in the article is a table summarizing results from nine prior studies of the relationship between residence and environmental concern. The study was supported by the Department of Rural Sociology, Washington State University, Pullman.

39. Tucker, Lewis R. "The Environmentally Concerned Citizen: Some Correlates." *Environment and Behavior* 10 (September 1978): 389–418.

The Center for the Study of Environmental Policy at Pennsylvania State University provided funding for this research. This study attempted to test the relationship among several variables (internal-external control, social responsibility, social class, age, and income) and environmental responsibility. For the purposes of the research, environmental responsibility was defined as membership in the Sierra Club or the Audubon Society in addition to nine specific environmental attitudes and behaviors. A sample of 27 Sierra Club/Audubon Society members and 139 general population members completed a written questionnaire in a group setting. The respondents were also observed making choices between soda in cans or returnable bottles and among different brands of laundry detergent. The results indicated significant differences between the environmental organization members and the general public members on all of the environmental behavior and attitude measures. Internal-external control was the strongest predictor of environmental responsibility. Income was a strong predictor only for the environmental organization sample, and age was an insignificant predictor of environmental responsibility.

40. Buttel, Frederick H., and Flinn, William L. "Social Class and Mass Environmental Beliefs: A Reconsideration." *Environment and Behavior* 10 (September 1978): 433–50.

Funding for this research was provided by the University of Wisconsin–Madison Graduate School and Agriculture Experiment Station. The goal of the study was to measure relationships between social class and awareness of environmental problems and support for environmental reform. Social class, in this study, was defined as a function of education, annual family income, and head of household occupation. In addition, the relationship between age and place of residence and the dependent variables was examined. The sample for the study consisted of 548 residents of Wisconsin surveyed by the Wisconsin Survey Research Laboratory during the fall of 1974. Results of the study indicated that education was the social class indicator most highly associated with environmental awareness and support for environmental reform. Age was also significantly related to environmentalism.

41. Buttel, Frederick H. "Age and Environmental Concern: A Multivariate Analysis." *Youth and Society* 10 (March 1979): 237–56.

This research attempted to measure the relationship between a number of variables and environmental attitude as defined by awareness of environmental problems and support for environmental reform. The following variables entered into the analysis: age, size of place of residence, education, and political liberalism. Data for the study were gathered through personal interviews with 548 Wisconsin residents conducted in 1974 by the Wisconsin Survey Research Laboratory. Age was found to be moderately correlated with both measures of environmental attitudes. Size of place of residence was the best predictor of awareness of environmental problems, and political liberalism was the best indicator of support for environmental reform. The article includes a table that summarizes the findings from six previous studies of the relationships between age and environmental concern and education and environmental concern. This study was funded by the University of Wisconsin–Madison Graduate School and Agriculture Experiment Station and the Ohio Agricultural Research and Development Center.

42. Van Liere, Kent D., and Dunlap, Riley E. "The Social Basis of Environmental Concern: A Review of Hypotheses, Explanations and Empirical Evidence." *Public Opinion Quarterly* 44 (Summer 1980): 181–97.

In this study, the authors reviewed the findings of 21 studies that included analysis of the relationships between environmental concern and eight demographic and social variables. Those eight variables were the following: age, education, income, occupation, residence, sex, political party, and political ideology. The researchers concluded that the relationships between environmental concern and three of the variables (age, education, and political ideology) should be considered empirical generalizations. Therefore, younger, well-educated, and politically liberal people could be considered more concerned with environmental issues than those who are older, less educated, and politically conservative. The article notes that the correlations, even for these three variables, are only moderate in magnitude. Included in the article is a table presenting the correlation coefficients for these variables and environmental concern documented in the 21 studies. Funding for this project was provided by the Department of Rural Sociology at Washington State University.

43. Leftridge, Alan, and James, Robert K. "A Study of the Perceptions of Environmental Issues of Urban and Rural High School Students." *Journal of Environmental Education* 12 (Fall 1980): 3–7.

The purpose of this research was to compare the environmental perceptions of high school students from urban and rural areas of Kansas. Students from four central city schools and five schools in rural communities completed surveys which included reactions to a series of color slides depicting urban and rural examples of air pollution, water pollution, waste disposal, and land use. Analysis of the surveys revealed that the rural students consistently responded more negatively to the slides than the urban students. The rural students' scores were significantly higher for the issues of urban water pollution and rural waste disposal.

44. Cutter, Susan Caris. "Community Concern for Pollution: Social and Environmental Influences." *Environment and Behavior* 13 (January 1981): 105–24.

In this article, the author describes her research designed to compare attitudes toward environmental pollution and attributes of the respondent's community of residence. Household residents in different communities in the Chicago, Illinois, area were interviewed for the study during the spring of 1976. A total of 940 adults comprised the sample. The survey data were analyzed by comparing attitudes on air, water, noise, and solid waste pollution with several social and environmental quality variables. Results of the study indicated that respondents in lower income, nonwhite communities were the most concerned about pollution. The greatest concern for pollution as a problem was found in communities with high mortality rates, high densities, low housing values, and high percentages of apartment dwellers.

45. Van Liere, Kent D., and Noe, Francis P. "Outdoor Recreation and Environmental Attitudes: Further Examination of the Dunlap-Hefferman Thesis." *Rural Sociology* 46 (Fall 1981): 505–13.

Data from a survey of visitors to a national seashore were used to test for a relationship between involvement in outdoor activities and positive environmental attitudes. During 1978, two mail surveys were administered to 478 visitors to Cape Hatteras National Seashore and 211 local winter residents of the area. The questionnaire asked respondents to indicate their involvement in outdoor activities and their attitudes toward environmental concepts. Analysis of the data found weak, positive relationships between environmental attitudes and participation in appreciative activities such as birdwatching, walking for pleasure, and photography. Negative or no relationships were noted between environmental attitudes and consumptive (fishing) and abusive (off-road driving, dune buggying, and motorcycling) activities.

46. Wysor, Martha S. "Comparing College Students' Environmental Perceptions and Attitudes: A Methodological Investigation." *Environment and Behavior* 15 (September 1983): 615–45.

This research compared environmental concerns among different groups of college students. The study was conducted with environmental studies and business students at Western Washington University. Initially, 38 environmental studies and 37 business students were asked to list places of importance to them in the local area. Interviews were conducted with 26 of the students who listed the greatest proportion of places identified by the total sample. For each of 15 standard places, the students were asked to rate the places and explain how they differed. The environmental studies students demonstrated a higher degree of environmental concern and involvement in pro-environment activities.

47. Jaus, Harold H. "The Development and Retention of Environmental Attitudes in Elementary School Children." *Journal of Environmental Education* 15 (Spring 1984): 33–36.

This study tested the effects of two hours of environmental education on the attitudes of one class of American third-grade students. A total of 49 students in two classes comprised the experimental and control groups in the 1978 study. Each student in the experimental group was administered a questionnaire of ten statements before and after exposure to an instruction program which included material on recycling, pollution, and conservation. Analysis of the surveys revealed that the experimental group had more positive attitudes toward the environment than the control group and had improved attitudes as a result of the education program. Another phase of the study retested both groups of students in 1980 to determine whether the experimental group had retained their attitudes over time. As fifth graders, the environmental attitudes of the experimental group remained more positive than the control group.

48. Horsley, A. Doyne. "A Comparison of American and Non-American Students' Attitudes on Issues of the Physical Environment." *Journal of Environmental Education* 15 (Spring 1984): 37–42.

The study described in this article compared the environmental attitudes of American high school age students with the attitudes of non–American students from ten countries. Between 1978 and 1980, questionnaires were administered to 204 American and 818 non–American students enrolled in geography and earth science classes. The questionnaire, which is reproduced in the article, consisted of 40 statements about the physical environment and natural resource issues. Results of the survey indicated that the American students held more positive environmental attitudes than did the foreign students. The responses of the American and foreign students differed significantly on more than half of the 40 items. (The non–American sample included students from the following places: Wales, England; Hong Kong; Taipei, Taiwan; New Delhi, India; Madras, India; Swaziland, Africa; Jos, Nigeria; Saint Croix, Virgin Isles; Nanking, China; and Nairobi, Kenya.)

49. Hamilton, Lawrence C. "Who Cares About Water Pollution? Opinions in a Small Town Crisis." *Sociological Inquiry* 55 (Spring 1985): 170–81.

In this study, residents of Milford, New Hampshire, were surveyed about their opinions of the chemical contamination of the town's water supply by local industries. During April 1983, 239 residents of the small New England town completed and returned mail questionnaires about the crisis. The results of the study demonstrated that the most concern over the toxic waste problem was expressed by respondents from more affluent households and women with young children. Long-time residents of the town were least concerned about the water contamination problem. Support for the research was provided by the Office of Water Research and Technology, U.S. Department of Interior.

50. Hamilton, Lawrence C. "Concern About Toxic Wastes: Three Demographic Variables." *Sociological Perspectives* 28 (October 1985): 463–86.

This research surveyed residents of two communities experiencing problems with toxic waste contamination to identify predictors of environmental concern. Data for the study were collected from residents of Williamstown, Vermont, and Acton, Massachusetts, two communities where the municipal wells had been discovered to be contaminated by nearby industrial operations. A questionnaire about concern for toxic wastes was returned by 156 and 346 members of the general public and community action groups in Williamstown and Acton, respectively. Analysis of the survey found the highest concern for toxic waste contamination among younger residents, women, and those with children under 18. This research was supported by funds from the Office of Water Research and Technology, U.S. Department of Interior.

51. Arcury, Thomas A.; Scollay, Susan J.; and Johnson, Timothy P. "Sex Differences in Environmental Concern and Knowledge: The Case of Acid Rain." *Sex Roles* 16 (May 1987): 463–72.

This research examined the effect of gender on environmental knowledge and concern. The study was based on a total of 516 interviews conducted with adult residents of Kentucky during June 1984. In order to measure environmental knowledge and concern, the respondents were questioned about the issue of acid rain. On the measure of active concern, the male respondents scored higher than the females. Male respondents in the survey also demonstrated greater knowledge about acid rain than female respondents. Data for the study were gathered by the University of Kentucky Survey Research Center with funding from the Kentucky Energy Cabinet.

52. Ostman, Ronald E., and Parker, Jill L. "Impact of Education, Age, Newspapers, and Television on Environmental Knowledge, Concerns, and Behaviors." *Journal of Environmental Education* 19 (Fall 1987): 3–9.

The purpose of this research was to measure the effect of education, age, newspapers and television on environmental knowledge, concerns, and behavior. Data for the study were collected from a telephone survey of 336 residents of Ithaca, New York, during April 1984. The survey questioned respondents about their concern for five specific environmental issues: acid rain, Love Canal (toxic waste dumping), and the pesticides DDT, dioxin, and EDB. The survey also asked what behaviors the respondents had participated in as a result of learning about the environmental issue. Results of the study showed that newspaper use was related to environmental attention, awareness, concerns, and behaviors, while television use was not related to any of the dependent variables. Education was related to environmental awareness, knowledge, and behaviors, but no significant associations were found for the age variable.

53. Mohai, Paul, and Twight, Ben W. "Age and Environmentalism: An Elaboration of the Buttel Model Using National Survey Evidence." *Social Science Quarterly* 68 (December 1987): 798–815.

This research used data from a prior major national survey to test a model of variables influencing environmental concern. In the fall of 1979, Louis Harris interviewed 7,010 Americans for the U.S. Soil Conservation Service. The survey covered attitudes toward the environment and natural resources, knowledge of conservation practices and ecology, attitudes toward government, and citizen activism. Variables included in the analysis were the following: education, political liberalism, current residence, past residence, and age. Age was found to be the strongest predictor of environmental concern, and its effect was independent of other variables thought to have a significant effect on environmental concern. Political liberalism was also a strong predictor of one of the two measures of environmental concern.

54. Eckberg, Douglas Lee, and Blocker, T. Jean. "Varieties of Religious Involvement and Environmental Concerns: Testing the Lynn White Thesis." *Journal for the Scientific Study of Religion* 28 (1989): 509–17.

The purpose of this research was to test the effect of four measures of religious experience on concern for the environment. Environmental concern was defined by response to two general environmental concern issues (use of the environment for the economy and protection of the environment) and two specific local environmental issues (concern about Tulsa air and water and concern about Tulsa waste disposal). (The article gives the actual survey items.) The following are the four religious variables: "Judeo-Christian," "conservative Protestant," "religion is important," and "believes in the Bible." Data for the study were collected from a telephone survey of 300 adult residents of Tulsa, Oklahoma, conducted in the spring of 1985. Responses to the survey indicated that "belief in the Bible" was the best predictor of scores on all four environmental issues.

55. Samdahl, Diane M., and Robertson, Robert. "Social Determinants of Environmental Concern: Specification and Test of the Model." *Environment and Behavior* 21 (January 1989): 57–81.

This study examined the role of different demographic variables in determining environmental concern. The authors developed a causal model of environmental concern composed of several variables: size of residential community, education, income, age, social welfare liberalism, and pro-regulatory liberalism. Environmental concern was defined by three variables: perception of environmental problems, support for environmental regulation, and ecological behavior. The data for the study were obtained from a 1978 mail survey of approximately 8,500 Illinois residents. After analyzing the data, the authors concluded that the model failed to explain any of the three types of environmental concern, although specific demographic variables did predict one or more of the environmental concern measures. Social welfare liberalism did not predict any of the measures, but pro-regulatory liberalism was a strong predictor of support for environmental regulation.

56. Caron, Judi Anne. "Environmental Perspectives of Blacks: Acceptance of the 'New Environmental Paradigm'." *Journal of Environmental Education* 20 (Spring 1989): 21–26.

A sample of 603 black residents of five cities in southeastern Virginia was surveyed in this research to determine whether African-Americans shared the same environmental perspective as white Americans. The author opened this article by noting that previous studies had reported lower environmental support among African-Americans. For this study, a previously tested environmental attitude instrument consisting of 12 items was used to measure environmental concern among the black subjects. All of the respondents were interviewed in their homes by black university students. Results of the interviews are compared with a previously surveyed sample of predominantly white residents of Washington state. The researcher concluded that the African-Americans in her study held an environmental perspective similar to that of whites. Years of education correlated with attitude. The presence of several neighborhood problems was also related to environmental attitude: pests, industrial plant nearby, stagnant water, excessive noise, and empty lots nearby.

57. Noe, Francis P., and Snow, Rob. "Hispanic Cultural Influence on Environmental Concern." *Journal of Environmental Education* 21 (Winter 1989-90): 27–34.

The purpose of the research described in this article was to determine if differences in cultural background affect environmental attitudes. The study was performed in two phases. A field survey was conducted with Biscayne Bay boaters and national park visitors during the summer and winter of 1986. Mail-back questionnaires were received from 69 percent of the selected Biscayne Bay national park visitors and 49 percent of the selected registered boat owners in Dade County, Florida. The instrument used for the survey was a 12-item environmental attitude scale used in previous research on environmental attitudes. The second phase of the study consisted of a telephone survey of randomly selected adults residing in the Dade County area. The same instrument minus two items was used. Analysis of the data revealed that the Hispanic respondents in the field study demonstrated an environmental awareness similar to that of the non–Hispanics in the field and general population surveys. The Hispanics in the general population study, however, indicated a strong opposition to the view of nature as being dominated by mankind.

58. Howe, Holly L. "Predicting Public Concern Regarding Toxic Substances in the Environment." *Environmental Health Perspectives* 87 (1990): 275–81.

The research presented in this article was performed by the New York State Department of Health, Division of Epidemiology. In the spring of 1986, a questionnaire was mailed to a sample of New York state residents. The survey was designed to identify predictors of concern for toxic wastes. The two most common predictors of concern as demonstrated by the study were the number of information sources about environmental issues and level of education.

59. Freudenburg, William R. "Rural-Urban Differences in Environmental Concern: A Closer Look." *Sociological Inquiry* 61 (May 1991): 167–98.

This article reports on a study designed to determine differences between people in agricultural occupations and other rural residents in concern for environmental problems. Data for the survey were gathered from residents of four communities in western Colorado which, at the time of the study, were all experiencing potential large-scale development of energy resources. A total of 597 questionnaires were hand delivered to randomly selected households in the communities and completed by one adult member of the household. The questionnaire included items on perception of the local environment, support for planning and zoning, mistrust of industry, and opposition to government regulation. The following demographic variables entered into the analysis: occupation, religious denomination, parents' education, political party, age, income, education, and church membership. With the exception of land use planning and zoning, the farmers and ranchers in the study expressed higher levels of concern for the environment than respondents in business/professional and mining occupations.

60. Armstrong, James B., and Impara, James C. "The Impact of an Environmental Education Program on Knowledge and Attitude." *Journal of Environmental Education* 22 (Summer 1991): 36–40.

In this paper, the authors describe the results of a study designed to test the impact of an environmental education program on the environmental knowledge and attitudes of grade-school students. The program, NatureScope, is an environmental curriculum supplement developed for use in kindergarten through seventh grade by the National Wildlife Federation. A sample of students from 61 fifth-grade classes and 27 seventh-grade classes in Virginia and Georgia were assigned to various issues of the NatureScope series. The students in the classes received pre- and post-tests on their assigned issue as well as on another issue for which they served as controls. In addition, students in six classes in each grade served as a pure control group. Analysis of the results revealed that only one of the four NatureScope issues had a significant effect on environmental knowledge. No significant differences were found among the attitude scores for any of the experimental or control groups.

61. Howell, Susan E., and Laska, Shirley B. "The Changing Face of the Environmental Coalition: A Research Note." *Environment and Behavior* 24 (January 1992): 134–44.

The authors of this article used data collected in a series of election surveys to study changes in environmental concern during the 1980s. An item on environmental spending was included in the 1980, 1984, and 1988 National Election Studies conducted by the University of Michigan, and responses to that item served as the basis for this study. The predictors of environmental concern analyzed were: party identification, ideology, urban residence, education, and age. Support for increased spending on the environment rose from 38 percent in 1980 to 62 percent in 1988. The researchers found, that during the 1980s, age, political ideology and party became less important as predictors of environmental concern. In 1988, education, political ideology, and urban residence were the best predictors of opinion on the environment.

62. Jones, Robert Emmet, and Dunlap, Riley E. "The Social Bases of Environmental Concern: Have They Changed Over Time?" *Rural Sociology* 57 (Spring 1992): 28–47.

This research used data from a series of national opinion surveys to track changes in American environmental concern over an 18-year period. The data used in the study were collected by the National Opinion Research Center for their annual General Social Survey which since 1973 had included an item on amount of spending for the environment. (Results from the General Social Survey are presented in other entries.) The purpose of this research was to determine whether the support base for environmental concern had broadened over the 18-year period to include a wider cross-section of Americans. Demographic variables included for analysis were the following: age, political ideology, education, residence at 16, current residence, political party, industrial sector, family income, gender, race, and occupational prestige. Results of the analysis revealed stable support for environmental spending throughout the period despite fluctuations in economic, political and environmental conditions. Highest support for environmental spending was found among young adults, the well educated, liberals, Democrats, those raised and living in urban areas, and those employed outside of industry.

63. Christianson, Eric Howard, and Arcury, Thomas A. "Regional Diversity in Environmental Attitudes, Knowledge, and Policy: The Kentucky River Authority." *Human Organization* 51 (Summer 1992): 99–108.

The purpose of this study was to compare regional differences in environmental attitudes, knowledge, and opinions on environmental policy. A sample of 624 residents of central and eastern counties in the Kentucky River Drainage Basin were surveyed in November 1989 by telephone by the University of Kentucky Survey Research Center. The interview included questions on attitudes toward water quantity and quality, knowledge of the Kentucky River Basin, and opinions on river management options. A previously developed instrument on environmental attitudes (balance of nature, limits to growth, and humans over nature) was also administered. While general environmental attitudes differed significantly between the two regions, attitudes toward pollution, knowledge about the river, and support for management options were similar for the two groups of respondents. Partial funding for the research was provided by the Research Committee of the University of Kentucky and by the Office of the Mayor, Lexington-Fayette Urban County Government.

Personal Commitment

64. Wren, Christopher. "Region Backs State School Tax and Transit Subsidy, Poll Finds." *The New York Times*, July 9, 1973, p. 28.

The Gallup Organization conducted this poll for the Regional Plan Association of the tri-state (New York, New Jersey, Connecticut) area. Residents of the three states were questioned about spending on the environment. Nearly two-thirds were willing to pay an additional 1 percent of their income in either higher taxes or prices to improve environmental quality. The article does not give the date, method, or sample size of the survey.

65. Thompson, John C., Jr., and Gasteiger, Edgar L. "Environmental Attitude Survey of University Students: 1971 vs. 1981." *Journal of Environmental Education* 17 (Fall 1985): 13–22.

The purpose of the research described in this article was to examine changes in the attitudes of Cornell University students toward environmental and energy resource issues during a ten-year period of time. Questionnaires were completed by 3,414 students in 1971 and 3,867 students in 1981 with response rates of 55 percent and 35 percent, respectively. The instrument included a section on awareness of natural resource limitations and another section on willingness to give up 35 specific materialistic items. The 35 items were sorted into the following groups: food stuff, household items, transportation, personal items, and recreation. Results of the data analysis indicated that significant differences existed between the responses to 25 of the 35 items on the 1971 and 1981 surveys. Generally, the 1981 students were less willing to give up items than the 1971 students, particularly in the areas of household items and transportation. Differences in responses were related to the demographic variables of political ideology, income, gender, and urban versus rural residence. Responses to all 35 items are presented in the article in the form of bar charts. Support for the research was provided by the Cornell Division of Biological Sciences, Cornell Institute for Social and Economic Research, and Office of Sponsored Programs.

66. "Fact-File: Freshmen Characteristics and Attitudes." *The Chronicle of Higher Education*, January 14, 1987, p. 40.

This article presents the results of an annual survey of college freshmen conducted by the American Council on Education and the University of California at Los Angeles. The sample for the study included 204,000 freshmen attending U.S. two- and four-year colleges, universities, and predominantly black colleges. Over three-fourths (78 percent) of the students agreed with the statement, "The government isn't controlling pollution." Only 16 percent, however, said that helping to clean up the environment was an essential or very important objective.

67. NBC News Poll. *American Public Opinion Index: 1987*. Boston, MA: Opinion Research Service, Inc., 1988.

This NBC News Poll was conducted with likely Republican and Democratic voters in New Hampshire and Iowa prior to the presidential primaries in those states. Between November 15 and 21, 1987, likely voters of both parties were asked about their willingness to pay increased federal income taxes to fund environmental protection. In Iowa, 54 percent of the Democrats and 41 percent of the Republicans were willing to pay higher taxes for environmental programs. In New Hampshire, 62 percent of the Democrats and 44 percent of the Republicans were willing to pay the extra taxes.

68. Cambridge Reports Poll. *American Public Opinion Index: 1987*. Boston, MA: Opinion Research Service, Inc., 1988.

Cambridge Reports, Inc., of Cambridge, Massachusetts, performed this poll in August 1987. A national sample of 1,457 Americans were interviewed in person and asked their perception of the amount of government regulation for environmental protection. The respondents were also asked whether they felt it was necessary to make personal sacrifices to protect the environment and whether they would be willing to pay higher consumer prices and accept increased unemployment so industries can protect the environment. The interviewers requested that those surveyed specify the amount of extra money they would be willing to pay for goods and services so that businesses can safeguard the environment. The sample was also asked to identify the most important environmental problem from a list that included: industrial air pollution, water pollution, damage to landscape by developers, air pollution from cars and trucks, solid waste disposal, hazardous waste disposal, ground water contamination, and nuclear waste disposal.

69. Stein, Mark. "Flawed Oranges with Fewer Pesticides Favored, Survey Finds." *The Los Angeles Times*, September 22, 1988, section 1, p. 3.

The survey described in this newspaper item was performed by the University of California's Davis Center for Consumer Research for the California Public Interest Research Group. A sample of 229 supermarket customers were shown three photographs of oranges, one of a perfect fruit and two of fruits with insect damage. Only 6 percent of the shoppers said they would buy the blemished fruit.

After being informed that the oranges showing insect damage had received 50 percent less pesticide than the perfect orange, 60 percent indicated they would be willing to buy the blemished fruit.

70. Bruskin Report. *American Public Opinion Index: 1988.* Boston, MA: Opinion Research Service, Inc., 1989.

This telephone poll was performed by H. R. Bruskin Associates of New Brunswick, New Jersey. In November 1988, a national sample of 1,000 were asked to describe their personal interest in solving environmental problems.

71. Kentucky Poll. *American Public Opinion Index: 1988.* Boston, MA: Opinion Research Service, Inc., 1989.

The Kentucky Poll is conducted by the Survey Research Center at the University of Kentucky. In this poll, a national sample of 1,200 Americans were contacted by telephone and interviewed about their support for more strict environmental regulations and their willingness to pay higher taxes to clean up the environment.

72. Dolan, Maura. "S. Californians Offer to Sacrifice Life Style to Save Environment." *The Los Angeles Times*, December 10, 1989, p. A1, 32–33.

The Los Angeles Times interviewed 2,690 Americans during November 1989 for the poll presented in this article. The nationwide sampling included a larger than representative number of residents from southern California. Included in the survey were questions about the importance of various environmental problems, willingness to make life-style changes to improve the environment, and willingness to accept tax increases to protect endangered species. Toxic wastes in the water supply and air pollution were identified as the top environmental problems by the southern California respondents. The California sample blamed the public for endangering the environment, along with business and government officials. Over two-thirds were opposed to oil drilling off the southern California coast, but the majority opposed raising taxes to protect endangered species. Over 90 percent of the California sample were willing to separate trash for recycling and give up smog producing devices and other environmentally hazardous products. In the national sample, environmental commitment was highest among residents of New England and lowest among those living in the South.

73. Times Mirror Poll. *American Public Opinion Index: 1989.* Boston, MA: Opinion Research Service, Inc., 1990.

The Times Mirror national poll was conducted for the People and the Press of Washington, D.C. Personal interviews were completed with 2,048 Americans during January 1989. Those responding to the interviews were asked if they supported increased spending for environmental protection and if they were willing to pay higher taxes to fund environmental programs.

74. Marist Institute Poll. *American Public Opinion Index: 1989.* Boston, MA: Opinion Research Service, Inc., 1990.

This national telephone poll was undertaken by the Marist Institute for Public Opinion at Marist College. A sample of 1,010 Americans were questioned about their perception of the role of the government in solving environmental problems. The respondents were also asked if they would be willing to pay higher taxes to improve the environment.

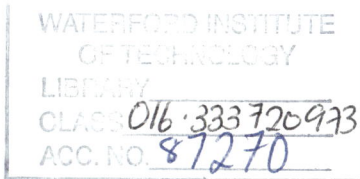

75. Dodge, Susan. "More Freshmen Willing to Work for Social Change and Environmental Issues, New Survey Finds." *The Chronicle of Higher Education*, January 24, 1990, p. A31–34.

This survey of 200,000 freshmen was conducted by the American Council on Education and the University of California at Los Angeles. The survey found that over 86 percent of the freshmen thought the government was not doing enough to control pollution. When asked about "becoming involved in programs to clean up the environment," 26 percent said it was "essential" or "very important." This percentage was 10 points higher than the response to the same question in 1986. The survey questioned students at U.S. two-year colleges, four-year colleges, universities, and predominantly black colleges.

76. Oreskes, Michael. "Poll Finds U.S. Expects Peace Dividend." *The New York Times*, January 25, 1990, p. B9.

This *New York Times*/CBS News Poll was conducted between January 13 and 15, 1990. Telephone interviews were completed with 1,557 adults from the 48 contiguous states. The respondents were questioned about their willingness to pay higher taxes to protect the environment and their opinion of federal spending on the environment. If the money would go to protect the environment, 40 percent of those surveyed said they would be willing to pay $100 a year more in taxes. When asked for their opinion on federal spending on the environment, 57 percent said it should be increased, while 4 percent said it should be decreased, and 35 percent thought spending should remain at current levels.

77. Kalette, Denise. "Poll Finds Waste Fears Are Piling Up." *USA Today*, April 13, 1990, p. 10A.

The nationwide telephone poll described in this article was performed during late March 1990 by Gordon S. Black Corporation. A sample of 850 adults answered questions about their willingness to make sacrifices to protect the environment and the importance of environmental positions in choosing a political candidate. A majority of those polled indicated they would be willing to pay 15 percent more in taxes and consumer products if waste and pollution would be reduced as a result. Fewer than half, however, were willing to pay $50 more per month for electricity to safeguard the environment. Nearly two-thirds said they would "accept a lower standard of living for a cleaner environment." The majority said they believed one person could make a difference in helping the environment. The respondents indicated they were more concerned about environmental regulations resulting in higher taxes and higher prices than they were about a less convenient lifestyle. Of various environmental problems, the sample expressed the greatest concern for hazardous waste and water pollution. Other environmental problems covered by the poll included wilderness preservation, landfills, damage to the ozone, air quality, acid rain, and rain forest depletion.

78. Robinson, John. "Poll Says 54% Willing to Pay More Taxes for Environment." *Boston Globe*, April 19, 1990, p. A22.

KRC Communications Research conducted the poll described in this article for the *Boston Globe* and WBZ-TV of Boston. During April 1990, 1,006 voters were asked whether they would be willing to pay higher taxes to protect the environment. Slightly more than half were willing to see their taxes raised for the purpose. The article does not specify whether the sample for the poll was statewide, regional, or national.

79. Rosewicz, Barbara. "Americans Are Willing to Sacrifice to Reduce Pollution, They Say." *The Wall Street Journal*, April 20, 1990, p. Al, 6.

The *Wall Street Journal*/NBC News Poll presented in this article was performed during April 1990 with a nationwide sample of 1,001 registered voters. Pollsters used geographic subgroups with sample sizes proportional to the population of the entire country. The respondents to the poll were asked their view of environmental problems and whether they supported different measures to improve the environment. Several proposed lifestyle changes received strong support from the sample: mandatory recycling (93 percent), banning foam containers (84 percent), requiring auto emission testing and repairs (80 percent), and banning disposable diapers (74 percent). Fewer of the respondents were favorable toward increasing gas prices by 20 cents per gallon (48 percent) and closing polluting factories when jobs would be lost (33 percent).

80. Dietrich, Bill. "Earth Day 1970–1990 Earthbound Priorities What's Important? Environment Is 2-to-1 'Winner' Over Economy." *The Seattle Times*, April 22, 1990, p. A8.

This article describes additional results from a poll on the environment presented elsewhere. *The Seattle Times* sponsored a Washington Poll in early April 1990 prior to the 20th anniversary of Earth Day. Elway Research of Seattle conducted the poll by randomly sampling 403 Washington adults. The poll included questions on the most important environmental problems, the need to sacrifice to solve environmental problems, and the amount of support for various proposed solutions to the problems. Air pollution, water quality, and solid waste were named as the biggest problems facing the environment of Washington. Exactly half of the respondents thought consumption would have to be reduced to relieve environmental problems, while 26 percent thought technology would be able to solve the problems. The majority supported requiring fuel efficiency and air pollution standards for cars and anti-pollution technology for factories even if higher prices resulted. The responses were evenly divided on the issue of restricting offshore drilling even if it meant importing more foreign oil and paying higher fuel prices. When asked how many additional tax dollars per year they were willing to pay to resolve environmental problems, 60 percent were willing to pay at least $100. The article notes differences in responses by age, education, income and geographic region of the state.

81. Henderson, Bruce. "Clean Environment Is Worth Cost, Effort, Most Agree in Poll." *Charlotte* [North Carolina] *Observer*, June 27, 1990.

The *Charlotte Observer* completed this survey in June 1990 with 956 adult residents of North and South Carolina. Respondents to the survey were questioned about their perception of their state's environment and their support for personal and business sacrifices to safeguard the environment. The majority of those polled felt the environment in their state was better than in most states. Approximately two-thirds indicated they thought that they could personally contribute to protecting the environment. The majority of the sample were willing to recycle, pay $500 more for a car, and pay $100 more in taxes to clean up the environment. Over 60 percent agreed that factories that violate pollution standards should be closed even if jobs are lost.

82. Ingwerson, Marshall. "On the Environment, Americans' Words Are Louder Than Deeds." *Christian Science Monitor*, August 2, 1990, p. 1.

This article presents results from a national Roper Organization poll of Americans' commitment to the environment and the relationship between attitudes and actions on the environment. On the basis of personal interviews with 1,500 Americans, the behaviors of the public on the environment were grouped in five categories: the "true-blue greens" (11 percent), the "green-back greens" (11 percent), the "sprouts" (26 percent), the "grousers" (24 percent), and the "basic browns" (28 percent). The Roper findings linked environmental action with level of income and indicated a wide gap between the degree of concern expressed for the environment and willingness to participate in solving the problems. The article also describes other results from the poll on perceptions toward environmental regulation and willingness to pay for environmentally sensitive consumer products.

83. Elliot, David. "Environment Worth the Price." *Austin* [Texas] *American-Statesman*, October 2, 1990.
    Rice University conducted this poll of 1,000 Texas residents during the summer of 1990. Those interviewed by the survey were asked their perception of the importance of environmental problems and whether they supported environmental protection measures. When asked to name the most serious problem facing their community, 11 percent named the environment. Garbage disposal and water pollution were identified as the most serious environmental problems facing Texans. Most of the respondents favored preservation of natural resources even at the expense of higher prices. Those surveyed also supported protection of endangered species despite the threat to economic opportunities. Increasing gas prices to encourage higher fuel efficiency or alternative forms of transportation was opposed by two-thirds of the respondents. A similar percentage, however, was willing to pay $200 more each year for goods to pay for new pollution controls. The majority also indicated they supported mandatory recycling and deposits on glass bottles. The article also briefly mentions results of a Texas Poll conducted in August 1990 by Texas A&M University. The poll of 1,000 Texans revealed that 4 percent of the respondents identified the environment as one of the top issues in the state.

84. "Americans Are Divided on the Environment." *The Wall Street Journal*, November 12, 1990, p. B1.
    The poll described in this brief newspaper article was conducted by the Roper Organization for S.C. Johnson and Son, Inc. Details about the survey are not provided. The survey attempted to classify Americans by five types of environmental attitudes and behaviors. Only 11 percent of Americans fell into the strong environmentalist category, while another 11 percent were described as willing to spend money, but not time, on environmental issues. Another group (26 percent) was identified as pro-environment on some issues, anti-environment on others. Nearly one-fourth (24 percent) were not very involved environmentally, because they believed most other people were not either. The largest group (28 percent) were uninvolved and believed their attitude and behavior were typical of the American public. (Other details of this study are reviewed elsewhere.)

85. Lublin, Joann S. "Creating a 'Green' Ad Campaign Risks Making Consumers See Red." *The Wall Street Journal*, December 5, 1990, p. B8.
    This article describes marketing efforts by companies to cash in on consumer interest in environmental issues. Results from two surveys of consumer response to "green" advertising are mentioned. One national survey was conducted

by Ogilvy and Mather with 500 adults. That survey showed consumers think little of ads that tout corporate donations to environmental causes but prefer campaigns describing corporate initiatives to make their manufacturing process less polluting. The second survey of 1,000 adults, conducted by Environmental Research Associates, found consumers view environmental claims as gimmickry.

86. Marist Institute Poll. *American Public Opinion Index: 1990.* Tallahassee, FL: 1991.

   Marist College's Institute for Public Opinion interviewed by telephone 1,044 residents of the continental United States. Results of the poll were released on January 31, 1990. Those responding to the survey were asked their perception of the federal government's involvement in solving environmental problems and their willingness to pay higher taxes to improve the environment.

87. Holusha, John. "So, What Is 'Environmentally Friendly'?" *The New York Times,* January 26, 1991, section 1, p. 50.

   Gerstman and Meyers interviewed 313 women in July 1990 for this nationwide consumer survey. When asked if they would pay more for a product with environmentally friendly packaging, 78 percent of the women said they would pay 5 percent, and 47 percent said they would pay 15 percent more. The percentage of the sample willing to pay 15 percent more had increased significantly from a similar study performed during the previous year.

88. Pokorny, Gene. "Earning Customer Satisfaction in a Greener America." *Electric Perspectives* 15 (May-June 1991): 40-54.

   This second article of a two-part series describes results of consumer research conducted by Cambridge Reports/Research International for the Edison Electric Institute. The study was designed to investigate consumer attitudes toward the environment and the effect of environmental issues on consumer satisfaction with electric utilities. Cambridge Reports conducted interviews with 1,250 adult Americans in September 1990. The results presented in the article focus on what environmental activities of electric utilities are seen as most important by customers.

89. Gutfeld, Rose. "Eight of 10 Americans Are Environmentalists." *The Wall Street Journal,* August 2, 1991, pp. A1, 4.

   This *Wall Street Journal*/NBC News Poll was conducted by the polling organizations of Peter Hart and Robert Teeter. A sample of 1,004 registered voters completed telephone interviews which posed questions about personal commitment to the environment and support for various efforts to protect the environment. Most of those polled described themselves as "environmentalists" and said they were willing to make fundamental life style changes to aid the environment. The majority supported various measures to improve the environment including mandatory recycling, alternative fuels, and higher fuel efficiency cars. While 67 percent were willing to pay 15 to 20 cents a gallon more for less polluting fuel, only 27 percent were willing to pay 25 cents a gallon more to encourage conservation and less driving. By a slim majority, respondents supported protecting jobs in the Northwest over protecting the spotted owl and oil exploration in wilderness areas to lessen dependence on foreign oil. But the voters sampled were not willing to allow greater offshore oil drilling.

90. "Green Consumers." *USA Today*, September 13, 1991, p. 1B.

This poll conducted by Gerstman-Meyers interviewed 318 women aged 21 to 54 years about the importance of environmental concern in making buying decisions. Results showed 83 percent of the consumers had switched product brands because of environmental concerns.

91. Manning, Anita. "Consumers Measure the Price of Going Green." *USA Today*, October 25, 1991, p. 5D.

This survey conducted for Gerstman-Meyers interviewed consumers about how their concerns for the environment affected buying decisions. A large majority of the consumers said they were more concerned about the environment than they were the previous year. Solid waste and air quality topped their list of concerns. Over half said they had decided against buying a particular product in the previous year because of the product's impact on the environment. (Other results from this survey are provided elsewhere.)

92. Bukro, Casey. "Most Americans Only Pay Lip Service to Environment, Poll Finds." *Chicago Tribune*, November 28, 1991, section 1, p. 42.

This article is based on research performed by Golin/Harris Communications and the Angus Reid Group of Canada. Researchers used results of a survey of 2,000 adult Americans to develop seven categories of environmental commitment. The seven environmental profiles are the following: young activists, community enthusiasts, ambitious optimists, mainstream followers, disillusioned survivors, hostile conservatives, and privileged bystanders. The categories with the largest percentage of members were the ambitious optimists and mainstream followers, both representing 21 percent of the public. (Other aspects of this research are presented elsewhere.)

93. Bady, Susan. "What 1992 Buyers Want in Housing." *Professional Builder and Remodeler* (December 1, 1991): 76–93.

This article describes the results of the eighteenth annual survey of home buyers and builders sponsored by *Professional Builder and Remodeler* magazine. The study was conducted in 1991 by National Family Opinion Inc. with a sample of 791 home owners. Details such as the type of survey, the selection process for the subjects, and response rate were not provided. The survey included items regarding the importance of environmental issues when considering a home purchase and willingness to pay more for energy-efficient products and options. Nearly 90 percent of the sample said issues such as saving trees and endangered species were "very" or "somewhat important" in choosing a new home. A majority were willing to spend an extra $500 for energy-efficient products to save $250 per year on heating and cooling costs. More than one-fourth of the consumers were willing to pay more for conservation options such as energy-saving water heaters, water-saving shower heads and faucets, and solar water heaters.

94. Stein, Charles. "Conservation Gets a Boost in Utility Survey." *Boston Globe*, June 9, 1992, business section, p. 12.

During the summer of 1991, residents of six New England states were surveyed about utility rates for a study commissioned by the New England Power Pool, a consortium of regional utilities. The pollster and number of respondents are not given in the article. By a margin of six to one, the customers polled said they would be willing to pay higher electricity costs to obtain power from sources that were less harmful to the environment.

95. "Recycling Popular." *The Arizona Republic*, June 17, 1992, section NE, p. 2.

Arizona State University's Morrison Institute for Public Policy conducted a study of citizens' attitudes toward the environment in April 1992. One aspect of this study is reported on in this newspaper article. The 805 Arizona residents who completed the survey were asked about their personal involvement in recycling and water and energy conservation. The residents were also questioned about other changes in their personal life-style due to environmental concerns and the effect of environmental issues on their choice of political candidates. Commitment to environmental life-style changes varied from low to moderate levels: 58 percent recycled frequently, 51 percent bought recycled products, 46 percent conserved water, 45 percent conserved energy, and 21 percent used public transportation or reduced their driving in other ways.

96. Johnston, John. "EcoEnforcers." *Cincinnati* [Ohio] *Enquirer*, July 20, 1992.

This youth survey was conducted by Peter D. Hart Research Associates of Washington, D.C., for the World Wildlife Fund. A sample of 880 youth aged 11 to 18 years and 411 parents completed the nationwide telephone survey. The youths and their parents answered questions about the importance of environmental protection and the involvement of family members in environmental issues. Both parents and youths selected protecting the environment as the most important issue that will face the country in the year 2000. More than half of the youths thought they could personally improve the environment "a lot" or "quite a bit." The youths said they most often tried to influence their parents about recycling and buying environmentally responsible products.

Environmental Protection
versus Economic Growth

97. Donohue, G. A.; Olien, C. N.; and Tichenor, P. J. "Communities, Pollution, and Fight for Survival." *Journal of Environmental Education* 6 (Fall 1974): 29–37.

This article provides a follow-up to a study presented in another entry. Residents of four communities in Minnesota were surveyed in 1970 and 1972 about specific environmental issues of concern to the residents of the area. The four communities and the associated issues were the following: Duluth (air pollution from a steel plant), Silver Bay (water pollution from a taconite processing plant), Ely (mineral exploration in the Boundary Waters Canoe Area), and Grand Rapids (control). The article reviews differences in knowledge and opinions between the two surveys and offers a more complete presentation of the specific survey items and responses than in the discussion of the original study. Over half of the residents of the control community agreed the taconite plant should not be allowed to discharge tailings into Lake Superior regardless of the effect on employment. Only 10 percent of the residents of the community where the plant was located agreed. Regarding mining in the canoe area, only 22 percent of the area residents opposed mining under any circumstances, while mining was completely opposed by between

41 percent and 65 percent of the residents of the other three communities. Willingness to pay higher taxes to eliminate air and water pollution varied between 26 percent and 57 percent for the four communities.

98. "Opinion Roundup." *Public Opinion* 3 (April–May 1980): 23.

This item is a graphic presentation of results from a survey by Roger Seasonwein Associates for Union Carbide. The survey was conducted between September 26 and October 21, 1979, with an unspecified sample. In response to the question of how environmental laws and regulations are affecting economic growth, 25 percent said they are helping economic growth, while 41 percent said the regulations are hindering growth.

99. "Landmark Survey Shows Most Americans 'Environmentalists'." *National Parks and Conservation Magazine* 54 (December 1980): 20.

This article summarizes results from a national public opinion survey sponsored by the President's Council on Environmental Quality. The study was conducted by Resources for the Future with assistance from the Roper Organization and Catril Research, Inc. Between January 26 and February 9, 1980, 1,576 adults were surveyed about their views on environmental issues. Results of the study showed that a large majority of the respondents thought of themselves as environmentalists. Solar energy was the energy source most preferred by those surveyed, while nuclear power was preferred the least. Over 70 percent of the respondents agreed that "An endangered species must be protected even at the expense of commercial activity." In general, the respondents supported environmental protection even at the expense of economic growth. (Additional results from this survey are discussed in other entries.)

100. "Environmentalists Persist." *The New York Times*, December 14, 1980, section 3, p. 1.

This brief news item mentions results of two polls on the importance of environmental protection. The Opinion Research Corporation poll found 60 percent of their sample in agreement with the statement, "Cleaning the environment is important, even if it means closing down some old plants and causing some unemployment." In the Resources for the Future poll, 42 percent of those surveyed said environmental protection was so important that improvements had to be made regardless of cost. (Other results from this study are described elsewhere.)

101. The Field Institute Poll. *American Public Opinion Index: 1981.* Tallahassee, FL: Opinion Research Service, Inc., 1982.

This poll was conducted by the Field Institute of California in August 1981. A national sample of 1,018 Americans were contacted by telephone and asked for opinions on environmental protection versus economic growth and jobs.

102. Ladd, Everett Carll. "Clearing the Air: Public Opinion and Public Policy on the Environment." *Public Opinion* 5 (February-March 1982): 16–20.

This article reviews results from several previously conducted polls: Roper Organization (September 1981), ABC News/*Washington Post* (February 1981), CBS News/*New York Times* (September 1981), and the Opinion Research Corporation (November 1981). (Other entries provide details of all of these polls with the exception of the ABC News/*Washington Post* poll.) Topics for the polls included perceptions

of environmental laws and regulations and tradeoffs between environmental protection and economic growth. In the ABC News/*Washington Post* poll, over half of
the respondents supported dropping some environmental protection regulations to
improve the economy.

103. "Study Finds Big Concern for Ecology." *Chicago Tribune*, November 10,
1982, section 1, p. 6.

The poll described in this newspaper article was performed by Research
and Forecasts Inc. for the Continental Group. The sample included 1,300 members
of the general public, 263 industry executives, and 343 members of environmental
organizations. Included in the poll were several items related to environmental
protection and economic growth. Approximately half of the general public sample
felt the nation must accept slower economic growth to protect the environment.
More than half of those surveyed indicated they would be willing to pay more for
goods and services to allow companies to clean up the environment. A majority of
the general public sample were willing to support environmental protection even
if it meant factories would be shut down or energy production would be slowed.
The article contains a graphic depicting results from three prior polls on the importance of the pollution problem. The polls were conducted by the Gallup organization in 1965 and 1970 and Resources for the Future in 1980. (The Resources for the
Future poll is described in other entries.)

104. Gallup, George H. "October 31: Public Opinion Referendum." *The
Gallup Poll: Public Opinion 1982*. Wilmington, DE: Scholarly Resources,
Inc., 1983, pp. 250–52.

This national poll of American adults was conducted from September 17
through 20, 1982, by the Gallup Organization. In one item, the respondents were
asked how they would vote on a list of hypothetical ballot propositions. One of the
proposed measures related to environmental regulations. Slightly more than half
(55 percent) of those surveyed said they opposed relaxing regulations even if doing
so would improve the economy, while 45 percent said they favored easing regulations to help the economy.

105. Capstone Poll. *American Public Opinion Index: 1982*. Lexington, KY:
Opinion Research Service, Inc., 1984.

The University of Alabama conducted the Capstone Poll in March 1982.
Five hundred Alabama residents were contacted by telephone and asked whether
they believed environmental quality must be sacrificed for economic growth.

106. Ohio Poll. *American Public Opinion Index: 1982*. Lexington, KY: Opinion
Research Service, Inc., 1984.

The Ohio Poll is conducted by the Behavioral Science Laboratory of the
University of Cincinnati. A sample of 1,336 Ohio residents were asked by telephone
to indicate their choice between environmental preservation and economic
growth.

107. CBS News/*New York Times* Poll. *American Public Opinion Index: 1982*.
Lexington, KY: Opinion Research Service, Inc., 1984.

This telephone poll was performed in September 1982 with 1,664 adults
from across the country. In the interview, the respondents were asked whether
they supported continued protection of the environment regardless of cost.

108. The Roper Poll. *American Public Opinion Index: 1983.* Lexington, KY: Opinion Research Service, Inc., 1985.

In January 1983, 2,000 Americans were interviewed in person by the Roper Organization. The respondents were asked about their opinion of the trade-off between environmental regulations and employment. They were also questioned about their personal concern for various issues including air and water pollution.

109. Gallup, George Jr. "December 16: Environmental Protection." *The Gallup Poll: Public Opinion 1984.* Wilmington, DE: Scholarly Resources, Inc., 1985, pp. 264–67.

This poll was conducted by the Gallup Organization between September 28 and October 1, 1984. The sample and survey methodology are not given. In one question, the respondents were asked to choose whether they thought environmental protection should be given priority even if economic growth might be slowed or if economic growth should be given priority even if damage occurs to the environment. Of those surveyed, 61 percent chose environmental protection, while 28 percent chose economic growth, and 11 percent had no opinion. The responses are given by sex, education, geographic region, age, and income. Respondents were also asked to estimate the extent of their concern for several environmental problems including nuclear waste disposal, industrial waste disposal, damage from oil spills, water pollution, and air pollution. Those sampled indicated that they cared a "fair amount" or a "great deal" about all of the problems with the most concern expressed for nuclear and industrial waste disposal.

110. The West Virginia Poll. *American Public Opinion Index: 1984.* Lexington, KY: Opinion Research Service, Inc., 1985.

The West Virginia Poll is performed by Ryan-Repass Research of Charleston, West Virginia. The January telephone survey asked 500 West Virginians about their willingness to relax environmental regulations to help stimulate the economy.

111. University of Pittsburgh Poll. *American Public Opinion Index: 1984.* Lexington, KY: Opinion Research Service, Inc., 1985.

The University of Pittsburgh's Center for Social and Urban Research contacted 1,767 residents of southwestern Pennsylvania in May 1984. The telephone poll asked those surveyed about their perception of environmental standards in southwestern Pennsylvania and whether they supported easing standards to improve economic conditions in the area.

112. *The Miami Herald* Poll. *American Public Opinion Index: 1984.* Lexington, KY: Opinion Research Service, Inc., 1985.

The results of this telephone poll of 760 Floridians were released on January 29, 1984. Included in the survey were questions about the following issues: concern for natural areas and parks and recreation areas in Florida, support for stronger environmental regulations even if economic growth was affected, support for higher state taxes to reduce air and water pollution, support for increased state spending for hazardous waste disposal, and support for increased state spending to purchase natural areas and beaches for state parks.

113. *Newsday* Poll. *American Public Opinion Index: 1984.* Lexington, KY: Opinion Research Service, Inc., 1985.

This *Newsday* Poll published in August 1984 included a question concerning support for environmental regulations regardless of effect on the economy. The poll interviewed 1,102 Americans by telephone.

114. Gallup, George Jr. "December 17: Environmental Protection." *The Gallup Poll: Public Opinion 1984.* Wilmington, DE: Scholarly Resources, Inc., 1985, pp. 267–70.

This was a combined U.S. and European survey conducted by the Gallup Organization. The European aspect of the study was sponsored by the Commission of the European Communities and O.E.C.D. Similar questions about environmental protection versus economic growth were asked of residents of the United States, Denmark, Italy, Germany, France, Greece, Netherlands, Belguim, Great Britain, and Ireland. (Other results of the U.S. survey are described elsewhere.) The highest support for environmental support was found in Denmark (75 percent), Italy (67 percent), and Germany (64 percent). At 29 percent, the residents of Ireland expressed the lowest level of support for environmental protection. The American respondents expressed greater concern than the European residents for four of the eleven problems (pollution of lakes and rivers, air pollution, disposal of nuclear wastes, and disposal of industrial wastes). The sample size and methodology for the survey are not described.

115. *The Houston Area Survey—1985.* Houston, TX: Rice University Department of Sociology, March 1985, 18 pp.

This poll was conducted by the Department of Sociology at Rice University with funding from *The Houston Post* and the American Leadership Forum. In February 1985, 550 residents of the Houston, Texas, area were questioned about their perception of the quality of life in the future, spending on the environment, and the seriousness of the earth's environmental problems. Approximately one-third of the sample said they thought the quality of life would be worse by the year 2000. Of those, 12 percent said the decline would be due to overpopulation, and 16 percent attributed the anticipated lower quality of life to environmental problems. Slightly more than half of the sample thought it was not possible to solve environmental problems without lifestyle changes. Over 60 percent said they opposed relaxing environmental regulations in the Houston area to stimulate the economy. A similar percentage of the sample said they supported protection of the environment regardless of its cost. The response to this question was compared with polls taken in March 1982 and February 1983.

116. University of Pittsburgh Poll. *American Public Opinion Index: 1985.* Lexington, KY: Opinion Research Service, Inc., 1986.

The University Center for Social and Urban Research at the University of Pittsburgh performed this poll in June 1985. A sample of 1,070 residents of southwestern Pennsylvania were contacted by telephone. The respondents were asked if they would support a new business in the area if it would generate 1,000 jobs but increase environmental risks. The response to the question was fairly evenly split with 48 percent supporting the new factory and 44 percent opposing it. The remaining 8 percent indicated they had no opinion on the question.

117. Harris, Louis. "Public Pessimistic About Gramm-Rudman Achieving Goal." *The Harris Survey* 8 (January 27, 1986).

This Harris Survey was conducted in early January 1986 by telephone with a nationwide sample of 1,254 adults. Nearly 70 percent of the sample voiced opposition to sacrificing environmental cleanup to lower the federal deficit.

118. Hawkes, Glenn R., and Stiles, Martha C. "Attitudes About Pesticide Safety." *California Agriculture* 40 (May-June 1986): 19–22.

This study compared the attitudes of the general public and five groups of specialists toward pesticide use and safety. A sample of 506 Californians residing in four communities (Stockton, Milpitas, Orangevale, and Concord/Clayton) completed a mail questionnaire following initial telephone contact. The specialist sample for the study consisted of an undisclosed number of elected leaders, government agency administrators, pesticide users and applicators, university scientists, and public interest group members. All respondents were questioned about their perception of pesticide risk and acceptability and asked to compare pesticide costs and benefits. The general public, public interest groups, and elected leaders all perceived pesticide risk as high and pesticide acceptability as low. The university scientists, government administrators, and applicators, on the other hand, rated pesticide use as low risk and highly acceptable. Air and water pollution were considered the greatest costs of pesticide use among the citizens, public interest groups, and elected officials. Funding for the study was provided by the University of California–Davis Public Service Research and Dissemination Service and the Agricultural Experiment Station.

119. Oakes, John B. "Back to Environmentalism." *The New York Times*, November 10, 1986, p. A23.

This editorial notes results from a *New York Times*/CBS News poll taken in early 1986. By a two-to-one margin, respondents agreed that "Protecting the environment is so important that requirements and standards cannot be too high, and continuing environmental improvements must be made regardless of cost."

120. The Houston Area Survey. *American Public Opinion Index: 1986.* Boston, MA: Opinion Research Service, Inc., 1987.

The Houston Area Survey is performed by the Department of Sociology at Rice University. In 1986, the poll interviewed 619 residents of Harris County, Texas, by telephone. The survey solicited opinions on the amount of money being spent on improving and protecting the environment. Respondents were asked whether they thought rapid economic growth is possible without serious environmental consequences. The interviewers also requested the sample to respond to the statement, "Humans are approaching the limits of the earth's room and resources." One question asked whether pollution controls should be maintained even if the economy slows and unemployment rises as a result.

121. Dunlap, Riley E. "Public Opinion on the Environment in the Reagan Era." *Environment* 29 (July-August 1987): 6–11, 32–37.

This is a summary article on public opinion of environmental issues from the early 1970s through the mid–1980s. Bar charts present results from a six poll series on the environment. Topics, dates, and the polling organizations for the featured polls are the following: 1.) support for environmental protection versus adequate energy, Roper Organization (1973-82); 2.) views on environmental laws and regulations, Roper Organization (1973–83); 3.) views on environmental spending,

National Opinion Research Center (1973–86); 4.) support for environmental quality versus economic growth, Cambridge Reports (1976–86); 5.) support for environmental protection regardless of cost, CBS News/*New York Times* (1981–86); and 6.) views on environmental protection by government, Cambridge Reports (1982–86). Cambridge Reports asked those surveyed to respond to two statements: "We must be prepared to sacrifice environmental quality for economic growth; and "We must sacrifice economic growth in order to preserve and protect the environment." The percent choosing environmental preservation over economic growth increased 20 points, 38 percent to 58 percent, between 1976 and 1986. Respondents to a CBS News/*New York Times* poll were asked to respond to a similar statement: "Protecting the environment is so important that requirements and standards cannot be too high, and continuing environmental improvements must be made regardless of cost." The percent supporting the statement increased from 45 percent in 1981 to 66 percent in 1986. The article mentions results of numerous other polls on environmental issues.

122. Times Mirror Poll. *American Public Opinion Index: 1988.* Boston, MA: Opinion Research Service, Inc., 1989.
     This poll interviewed 4,244 Americans in person during January 1988. The survey posed questions about environmental protection including attitude toward the amount of federal spending and whether environmental regulations should be relaxed to encourage economic growth. Respondents were also asked whether they viewed themselves as environmentalists.

123. Suro, Roberto. "Grass-roots Groups Show Power Battling Pollution Close to Home." *The New York Times*, July 2, 1989, p. A1.
     This *New York Times* Poll interviewed 1,497 people in a nationwide telephone survey conducted between June 20 and 25, 1989. Of those surveyed, 80 percent agreed with the statement, "Protecting the environment is so important that requirements and standards cannot be too high, and continuing environmental improvements must be made regardless of cost." This statement had been asked in *New York Times*/CBS News Polls since 1981. The article contains a graphic depicting responses to the question from seven different polls taken between September 1981 and June 1989.

124. Opinion Research Corporation Poll. *American Public Opinion Index: 1989.* Boston, MA: Opinion Research Service, Inc., 1990.
     Opinion Research Corporation of Princeton, New Jersey, conducted this national telephone poll in May 1989. A sample of 1,021 Americans were queried about their concern for air quality, water quality, and the greenhouse effect. Respondents were also asked if they would support stricter environmental regulations if the result was higher prices and lost jobs.

125. Berke, Richard L. "Oratory of Environmentalism Becomes the Sound of Politics." *The New York Times*, April 17, 1990, pp. A1, B10.
     This article presents findings from a *New York Times*/CBS News Poll of 1,515 adults conducted March 30 to April 2, 1990. The telephone poll asked the Americans sampled to give their opinions of pollution, offshore drilling, and state and federal government efforts to protect the environment. The majority supported protection of the environment even if it meant higher taxes (71 percent) or

loss of local jobs (56 percent). On the question of offshore drilling, 55 percent said the risks to the environment are too great to allow it. Approximately three-fourths of those surveyed thought the state and federal governments were doing only a "fair" or "poor" job of "keeping the environment clean." Pollution was perceived to be a serious problem locally by 42 percent and nationally by 84 percent of the sample.

126. Dietrich, Bill. "Earth Day 1970–1990 Earthbound Priorities." *The Seattle Times*, April 22, 1990, p. A1.

A *Seattle Times* Washington Poll on environmental issues was conducted during April 1990 just prior to the twentieth anniversary of Earth Day. The sample of 403 Washington residents were asked to name the most important issues facing their state (multiple answers were accepted). More respondents (40 percent) named the environment than any other single issue. Although exact numbers are not given, the article indicates that the majority supported stronger regulations and higher taxes to provide environmental protection. In addition, 85 percent of those who supported environmental protection over jobs indicated they would "definitely" or "probably" favor stricter environmental laws even if the laws threatened their own jobs. (Other results of this study are presented elsewhere.)

127. Maddux, Tom. "Real Environmental Caring Should Show in Voting Poll." *Houston Post*, June 20, 1990, p. A19.

This item is a commentary that mentions results from three polls on the environment: the Texas Poll conducted February 1990, the annual Houston Area Survey, and a nationwide poll by Cambridge Energy Research Associates in December 1989. The Texas Poll conducted by Texas A&M University interviewed 1,006 adult Texans. Almost three-fourths of the sample rated the importance of protecting the environment as at least an eight on a scale from one to ten. In the Cambridge Energy poll, 74 percent of those surveyed said they wanted an improved environment even at the cost of economic growth. The sample strongly supported higher gas mileage standards but opposed an increase in gasoline taxes. The Houston Area poll documented a similar percentage of respondents willing to protect the environment at any cost.

128. Florida Poll. *American Public Opinion Index: 1990*. Tallahassee, FL: 1991.

Florida residents were interviewed for this survey by the Institute for Public Opinion Research at Florida International University. The telephone poll reached 1,204 households and asked those responding to give their opinion of the amount of spending for parks and recreation and the environment. Respondents were also asked if they preferred higher taxes or decreased spending for other programs in order to increase spending on the environment. In a choice between jobs and environmental protection, 70 percent chose the environment. Other questions asked those interviewed to identify the most serious environmental problem in Florida and to indicate the degree of their concern for global warming. When asked the solution to environmental problems, 10 percent said technology would be able to solve the problems, while 30 percent said moderate life-style changes would be necessary, and 57 percent said major life-style changes would be required to solve the problems.

129. Florida Annual Policy Survey. *American Public Opinion Index: 1990*. Tallahassee, FL: 1991.

Between January and March 1990, 955 Florida citizens were interviewed by telephone for a survey conducted by the Policy Sciences Program at Florida State University. The survey posed questions about hazardous waste facilities including support for building such facilities and proximity to a hazardous waste disposal facility that the respondent would be willing to live. Respondents were also asked whether they thought it was more important to protect jobs or to protect the environment. Another question requested that respondents choose between "a worse quality of their own material life but a higher quality environment or a worse quality environment but a higher quality of their own material life." Nearly three-fourths said they would choose the lower material life with the higher quality environment.

130. Times Mirror Poll. *American Public Opinion Index: 1990.* Tallahassee, FL: 1991.

This telephone poll was performed by the Times Mirror Center for the People and the Press. In May 1990, 3,004 Americans were interviewed in person and 1,000 of those respondents were reinterviewed later in the year. Topics included support for increasing environmental regulations, even if employment opportunities were reduced as a result, and identification with the "environmentalist" label.

131. Talmey-Drake Research Poll. *American Public Opinion Index: 1991.* Tallahassee, FL: 1991.

In August 1991, Talmey-Drake Research and Strategy, Inc., of Boulder, Colorado, interviewed 605 residents of Colorado. The telephone poll asked those surveyed if they thought of themselves as "environmentalists." Another question asked if they agreed that "Colorado needs stronger laws protecting the natural environment, even if it endangers jobs and economic growth in the state."

132. Von Sternberg, Bob. "Antipollution Laws Aren't too Tough on Business, Most Say." [Minneapolis] *Star Tribune*, May 2, 1991, p. 1B.

In this article, results of a Minnesota Poll of 999 adults are presented. The telephone poll was conducted during April 1991 by Project Research of Minneapolis for the *Star Tribune* and KSTP-TV. Respondents to the poll were asked their perception of environmental laws and their support for relaxing the laws for retail businesses in the state. The state environmental laws were seen as "not tough enough" by 42 percent of the sample and as "just about right" by 46 percent. Only 5 percent thought the laws were "too tough." By a margin of two to one, the sample said it opposed relaxing the state environmental laws for the sake of business. Responses to this question are given by sex, age, education, income, political party, political ideology, and geographic region.

133. Petit, Charles. "Poll Finds Environment Among Top 3 Concerns." *The San Francisco Chronicle*, May 5, 1992, p. A2.

This report is based on a Gallup Poll of citizens in 22 countries, including the United States, on environmental concerns. (Other aspects of this poll are discussed elsewhere.) Topics for the poll were the following: most important environmental problems, willingness to pay to save the environment, and economic growth versus environmental protection. Environmental issues were rated as the most important problem facing the country by 11 percent of Americans. On the issue of placing blame for global environmental problems, 29 percent of Americans surveyed blamed industrialized countries, 4 percent blamed undeveloped countries, and 61 percent thought the blame should be shared equally.

134. "World Poll Finds Concerns About Earth's Health." *The San Francisco Chronicle,* June 10, 1992, p. A6.

The "Health of the Planet Survey" was conducted by the George H. Gallup International Institute for presentation at the 1992 Earth Summit in Rio de Janeiro. A sample of 1,000 citizens of 22 countries were asked questions about their concern for the global environment, perception of environmental risks to human health, and support for environmental protection. Protecting the environment was considered more important than economic growth by the citizens of all but three nations: India, Turkey, and Bolivia. The majority of respondents in 16 of the countries were willing to pay higher prices to protect the environment, and the majority of respondents in all countries thought environmental problems would affect the health of future generations. (This poll is the subject of other entries.)

135. Friesner, Craig. "Poll Shows Support for Environmental Protection." *Sierra Club Canyon Echo* 28 (July–August 1992): 3.

The research described in this article was conducted by the Morrison Institute for Public Policy at Arizona State University. (Other results from this survey are given elsewhere.) A telephone poll was conducted with 805 Arizona residents in April 1992. The respondents were asked about environmental priorities for the state, the importance of environmental protection, and their perception of the relationship between economic growth and environmental protection. The environmental issues identified as most important by the sample were air quality, water quality, and waste disposal. The majority supported a "wild and scenic" designation for the state's remaining free-flowing streams. A majority of the respondents also supported riparian protection even if there had to be restrictions on private land use in those areas. In a choice between economic growth and environmental protection, 61 percent would sacrifice growth in order to preserve the environment.

136. "Voters Rank Importance of Environment." *The Christian Science Monitor,* October 1, 1992, p. 10.

This item reviews results from a Times Mirror poll conducted by the Roper Organization during the summer of 1992. A sample of 1,200 adults answered questions about the strictness of environmental laws and environmental protection versus the rights of private landowners. Nearly two-thirds of the sample said environmental laws and regulations were not strict enough, and if forced to choose between environmental protection and economic growth, they would choose the environment. Over one-fourth (29 percent) saw themselves as active environmentalists, and an additional 52 percent indicated they sympathized with environmental concerns. Despite these findings, the majority opposed increased taxes for environmental protection, and half said the Endangered Species Act should be amended to consider the economic cost of saving species.

137. Ellison, David. "Poll: Texans Alter Views on Jobs vs. Environment." *The Houston Post,* October 9, 1992, p. A1.

A poll of 1,004 Texans was conducted during September 1992 by Rice

University's Department of Sociology and Telesurveys of Texas. Funding for the poll was provided by Margaret Cullinan Wray Lead Annuity Trust and the Texas Environmental Center. The survey interviewed residents about mandatory recycling, glass bottle deposits, and protection of the environment versus creation of jobs. When asked if a new plant employing 1,000 people should be opened even it the plant would generate significant pollution, 68 percent said no. A slim majority (52 percent) said protecting the environment should be given priority over creating new jobs. Mandatory recycling of trash was supported by 74 percent, and 82 percent favored a law requiring a deposit on glass beverage containers.

Laws and Regulations

138. Tichenor, P. J.; Donohue, G. A.; Olien, C. N.; and Bowers, J. K. "Environment and Public Opinion." *Journal of Environmental Education* 2 (Summer 1971): 38–42.

This article summarizes the findings of two polls on environmental issues conducted in 1969 and 1970 by the University of Minnesota. The first poll was performed in 1969 with adults residing along a 50-mile stretch of the Minnesota River from Osseo to St. Cloud. These subjects were asked their opinion of DDT as a pollutant and of the operation of a local nuclear power plant. Concern expressed for DDT was greater than for radioactive waste from the nuclear plant. Although two-thirds of the residents considered DDT to constitute a danger, support for banning the pesticide was not evident. In the second survey, residents of four northeastern Minnesota communities (Grand Rapids, Duluth, Silver Bay, and Ely) were interviewed about the importance of environmental issues, the Boundary Waters Canoe Area, a nearby steel plant, and a local taconite plant. Knowledge and attitudes toward the different issues varied according to the effect of the issue on the community surveyed. Knowledge of an issue was not necessarily related to support for controls. In this study, the most highly informed subjects were often the most opposed to environmental restrictions.

139. "Proposed Federal Restrictions on Society." *Current Opinion* 4 (December 1976): 124.

This monthly review of public opinion polls is published by the Roper Public Opinion Research Center. In this issue, results are presented from a poll conducted by R. H. Bruskin Associates in February 1976. The 2,582 adults who completed the national survey were asked their opinion of a federal law that would make littering a crime. A large majority (71 percent) of the respondents said they favored such a law.

140. Yankelovich, Skelly, and White Poll. *American Public Opinion Index: 1981.* Tallahassee, FL: Opinion Research Service, Inc., 1982.

The Yankelovich, Skelly, and White Poll conducted in January, May, and September 1981 included questions about environmental restrictions. A sample of 1,219 Americans were polled by telephone. The January poll asked respondents if they supported relaxing coal burning restrictions on power plants and whether they supported easing environmental standards in general to reduce costs. In May and September, the samples were asked if they favored relaxing environmental restrictions to help improve the economy.

141. *The Los Angeles Times* Poll. *American Public Opinion Index: 1981.* Talla-
    hassee, FL: Opinion Research Service, Inc., 1982.

    This poll was conducted in April 1981 by *The Los Angeles Times.* A total of
1,406 Americans were contacted by telephone and asked about support for maintaining current environmental restrictions. Respondents were also questioned
about their opinion of developing federal lands and offshore drilling.

142. "Opinion Roundup: Environmental Update." *Public Opinion* 5 (Febru-
    ary–March 1982): 32–36.

    This item graphically depicts results from several polls conducted during
1981 and 1982 on opinion of environmental regulations. The polls featured in the
roundup include the following: Louis Harris and Associates (May and September
1981), Opinion Research Corporation (November 1981), Roper Organization
(January 1974–January 1982), CBS News/*New York Times* (September 1981), NBC
News/Associated Press (October 1981), and ABC News/*Washington Post* (February
1981). Several of the polls featured specific questions related to the Clean Air Act.
Respondents to the Roper Organization polls between October 1973 and
September 1981 were asked their view of the scope of environmental laws and
regulations. In 1981, 21 percent felt regulations had gone far enough, 31 percent
thought they had not gone far enough, and 38 percent thought the amount of
regulation was about right. The responses to this question are broken down by age
and education, and the responses to a question on the Clean Air Act are given by
education, sex, and race.

143. "Stricter Safeguards Against . . ." *The Wall Street Journal,* December 30,
    1983, p. A1.

    This brief news item reports results from a Roper poll. Nearly half (48 per-
cent) of those polled felt that current laws did not go far enough in controlling environmental hazards. Details about the poll are not provided.

144. Twin Cities Area Survey. *American Public Opinion Index: 1982.* Lexing-
    ton, KY: Opinion Research Service, Inc., 1984.

    The Twin Cities Area Survey is conducted by the Minnesota Center for
Social Research at the University of Minnesota. A total of 1,068 residents of St. Paul
and Minneapolis were interviewed by telephone about government versus private
sector responsibility for environmental regulation.

145. *The Los Angeles Times* Poll. *American Public Opinion Index: 1982.* Lex-
    ington, KY: Opinion Research Service, Inc., 1984.

    The Los Angeles Times Poll conducted in August and November 1982 in-
cluded a question about the respondent's perception of present government environmental regulations. The national telephone poll interviewed 1,592 Americans
for the August poll and 1,475 Americans for the poll in November.

146. Capstone Poll. *American Public Opinion Index: 1982.* Lexington, KY:
    Opinion Research Service, Inc., 1984.

    The Capstone Poll is conducted by the University of Alabama. In November
1982, 500 residents of Alabama were contacted by telephone and asked about their
satisfaction with environmental protection programs in the state.

147. Ruberg, William. "Virginians Feel Environment in Good Shape, Poll Finds." *Richmond* [Virginia] *Times-Dispatch*, July 11, 1985.

The Gallup Organization conducted this poll for the Virginia Water Resources Research Center, the U.S. Environmental Protection Agency, and the Virginia Environment Endowment. A sample of 1,628 adult Virginians were interviewed during May and June 1985. Included in the interview were questions about perceptions of environmental regulations and the performance of government and business in protecting the environment. The interviewees were also asked their view of the most serious environmental problems in the state and whether they supported mandatory deposits on beverage containers and toxic chemical containers. Several questions on groundwater were also included. Government regulation of businesses for environmental protection was perceived as "very necessary" by 54 percent and "somewhat necessary" by 33 percent of the sample. About half of those surveyed rated the performance of industry as "fair" or "poor," while state government received a slightly better grade with 43 percent rating its performance as "fair" or "poor." Lake pollution and stream pollution were considered to be the most serious problems in the state. Nearly one-third thought hazardous waste disposal posed no problem at all, and only 9 percent viewed acid rain as a severe problem for the state. Of the respondents who had heard of the proposed "bottle bill," about 75 percent favored it. A deposit on household chemical containers also received strong support.

148. Cambridge Reports, Quarterly Opinion Review. *American Public Opinion Index: 1985*. Lexington, KY: Opinion Research Service, Inc., 1986.

In August 1985, Cambridge Reports Inc., of Cambridge, Massachusetts, conducted a poll which included several items concerning environmental regulations and offshore drilling. Personal interviews were conducted with 1,432 Americans from across the country. The respondents were asked their opinion of expanded offshore drilling, locations for offshore drilling, and the adequacy of federal regulations that control offshore drilling. One question explored the relationship between economic growth and environmental quality, and several questions related to environmental protection regulations were included. Respondents were requested to indicate what additional amount they would be willing to pay for goods and services to allow businesses to safeguard the environment. The poll also asked those surveyed to identify the most important problem in the United States.

149. Poole, Rebecca. "An Enduring Commitment." *Sierra* 71 (November–December 1986): 12.

This article presents results from a series of polls taken from 1973 through 1985 on the public's commitment to environmental issues. Graphs depict results from polls conducted by the National Opinion Research Corporation, the Roper Organization, and the Louis Harris Survey. The polls measured public attitudes toward environmental regulations (Roper), environmental spending (National Opinion Research Corporation), and the seriousness of specific environmental problems (Harris). (Details of these surveys are found in other entries.)

150. Southern California Social Survey. *American Public Opinion Index: 1986*. Boston, MA: Opinion Research Service, Inc., 1987.

This survey was performed by the Institute for Social Science Research at the University of California at Los Angeles. A sample of 1,200 residents of southern California were contacted by telephone and asked about perception of environmental protection regulations. In addition, the survey measured the respondents concern for the effects of pollution on health.

151. Walker, Tom. "Business Report: Many Doubt Industry on Environment Issue." *The Atlanta Journal*, March 10, 1990, p. F2.

The Atlanta Journal performed this poll for Ford Motor Company in 1989. A sample of 7,000 leaders in business, education, the media, government, and environmental organizations were surveyed to find out where professionals stood on the environment. (Details of the survey's methodology are not provided in the newspaper article.) Included in the survey were questions about industry's responsibility for environmental protection and cleanup and the role of government in setting environmental standards. A large majority of the leaders surveyed thought that the federal government should take the lead in setting standards. The leaders also thought that industries should be held responsible for cleaning up their own environmental pollution and that consumers would be willing to pay more for environmentally friendly products.

152. Yankelovich, Clancy, Shulman Poll. *American Public Opinion Index: 1990.* Tallahassee, FL: 1991.

Yankelovich, Clancy, and Shulman of Westport, Connecticut interviewed 1,000 Americans by telephone during December 1990. Those interviewed were asked their perception of business compliance with environmental regulations and government enforcement of regulations. Other questions concerned whether the United States should take an international role in solving environmental problems and whether consumers, the government, and industry are doing enough to improve the American environment. The survey included four trade-off questions on auto emissions, offshore drilling, industrial plant pollution, and electric power plant pollution.

153. "Environment Crimes Top Survey." *USA Today*, July 9, 1991, p. 2B.

Arthur D. Little conducted this telephone survey of 1,000 adults. (The newspaper article does not indicate the date and population for the sample.) Those completing the survey were asked their perception of the seriousness of various business offenses. Environmental crimes were considered the most serious business offenses of those listed. Over 80 percent of the sample gave the importance of environmental crimes a rank of at least eight on a scale of ten.

154. Crimmins, Jerry. "Environmentalism Surges in Poll." *Chicago Tribune*, July 9, 1991, section 1, p. 5.

The survey detailed in this article was performed by Golin/Harris Communications and the Angus Reid Group of Canada during April and May 1991. The telephone interviews, which were completed by 2,000 American adults, solicited opinions on environmental protection as a federal priority. When asked to choose between keeping environmental controls even at the risk of slower economic growth and easing up on regulations to provide more jobs, 74 percent chose environmental protection. The respondents also supported closing down factories that pollute and enacting mandatory jail sentences for repeat violators of environmental regulations. A majority of those sampled said they would be willing to pay more for gasoline, waste disposal, and "green" grocery products.

155. "America's Love Affair with Environmental Protection." *Safety and Health* 144 (December 1991): 35–37.

In this article, results are presented from a Roper Organization poll conducted for S. C. Johnson and Son, Inc. The survey, titled "The Environment: Public Attitudes and Individual Behavior," interviewed 1,413 Americans at home during February and March 1990. Respondents to the poll were asked their perception of the importance of environmental issues and their opinion of environmental laws and regulations. Of 12 national problems addressed in the poll, environmental protection ranked fourth in importance. The percent of the respondents to this poll who felt that environmental issues should be given major emphasis was 22 points higher than in a 1987 poll. This represented the greatest increase in concern for any of the 12 issues. On the issue of regulation, 69 percent of the respondents said environmental laws and regulations had not gone far enough, while only 4 percent said they had gone too far. (Other findings from this survey are presented elsewhere.)

156. Oslund, John J. "Pollution Solution." *Minneapolis* [Minnesota] *Star and Tribune*, April 20, 1992.

This telephone survey of 100 Minnesota industry senior managers was conducted for Fredrickson and Byron, a Minneapolis law firm. Respondents to the survey were asked their opinion of the effect of environmental regulations on competitiveness and different motivations for complying with environmental regulations. Of the industry managers interviewed, 47 percent said state environmental regulations had a negative effect on their company's competitiveness, while 36 percent said regulations had no effect, and 12 percent said regulations had a positive effect. As to why businesses comply, 65 percent cited potential damage to the company's image. Other reasons given were the threat of fines (50 percent), employee dissatisfaction over working for a perceived polluter (42 percent), and the possibility of legal action (41 percent).

157. Eaton, Jason. "52% Would Pay to Clean Up State's Air, Water." *The Arizona Republic*, May 28, 1992, p. B1.

This newspaper article discusses the results of a study of resident's attitudes toward the environment conducted by the Morrison Institute for Public Policy of Arizona State University. (Other results from this study are described elsewhere.) The telephone poll of 805 Arizona residents was taken in April 1992. The residents were questioned on the following issues: perception of the state's environmental quality, support for higher taxes to clean up the environment, support for stricter industry regulation, and perception of government regulation of the environment. A majority of the residents surveyed felt the state's environmental quality had deteriorated in the past five years. More than half of the sample said they would be willing to pay up to 5 percent in higher income taxes to clean up the environment. Stricter industrial regulations were supported by 86 percent of the residents even if higher consumer prices resulted, and 57 percent felt that the government was not doing enough to protect the environment.

158. Stall, Bill. "Regulations, Taxes Blamed for State's Woes." *The Los Angeles Times*, March 25, 1993, p. A1.

This article presents findings from a *Los Angeles Times* Poll conducted during March 1993 on the business climate in California. The poll interviewed 1,294 randomly selected California adults by telephone. The respondents answered questions including their perception of the most important problem facing the state and their attitude toward the amount of government regulation of business. Only 2 percent of the sample named the environment as the most important problem facing California. A majority (55 percent) thought there was "too much" government regulation of business and industry in the state. The language of this question, however, did not specifically address the type of regulation (such as environmental). When asked to choose between business concerns and the concerns of endangered species, 47 percent had greater concern for wildlife, while 44 percent were more sympathetic toward business.

Government Spending

159. "New Conservation Poll." *National Wildlife*, December 1969-January 1970, pp. 18–19.

The National Wildlife Federation commissioned the environmental survey described in this article. An undisclosed number of Americans were interviewed in person in their homes during July 1970. The interview included questions on spending for the environment, the effect of air and water pollution on personal lives, and the effect of DDT on the environment. Over half of the respondents thought the natural environment was receiving too little attention and money from the government. When asked where the money to fund environmental programs should come from, over 40 percent of the sample favored cutting national defense, the space program, and international affairs. A majority (55 percent) of those sampled said they would be willing to pay at least $20 more each year to help clean up the environment. That percentage dropped to 32 percent for $100 annually and 22 percent for an increase of $200 per year.

160. "Public Still Backs Protection of Environment, Poll Shows." *The Washington Post*, December 8, 1978, p. A3.

Resources for the Future sponsored the nationwide telephone poll discussed in this newspaper item. A sample of 1,076 Americans were surveyed during the summer of 1978 about their perception of the importance of environmental protection. Over half of the respondents agreed with the statement, "Protecting the environment is so important that requirements and standards cannot be too high, and continuing improvements must be made regardless of cost." Only 13 percent of those polled thought that too much was being spent on environmental protection, while 47 percent said too little was being spent. (Other results from this poll are described elsewhere.)

161. Lowe, George D.; Pinhey, Thomas K.; and Grimes, Michael D. "Public Support for Environmental Protection: New Evidence from National Surveys." *Pacific Sociological Review* 23 (October 1980): 423–45.

Data from the 1973–78 General Social Surveys conducted by the National Opinion Research Center were analyzed to determine trends in environmental concern. (Other entries present research based on data from this series of public opinion polls.) In the General Social Surveys, respondents were asked to comment on the amount of government spending for environmental protection and ten other national issues. Although the average mean score for environmental protection declined slightly over the six year period, the issue was ranked fourth overall in 1973 and again in 1978. Age was the best indicator of environmental concern, as evidenced by desire to increase spending on the environment, of the demographic variables analyzed (region, urbanism, age, sex, race, residence at age 16, income, industry, education, employment status, conservatism, and occupational prestige).

162. Capstone Poll. *American Public Opinion Index: 1981.* Tallahassee, FL: Opinion Research Service, Inc., 1982.

The Capstone Poll is a statewide survey conducted by the University of Alabama. In May and October 1981, 500 residents of Alabama were contacted by phone and asked questions about their attitude toward spending for the environment. Respondents to the May poll were asked if they thought more or less state money should go toward environmental programs. More state spending was advocated by 20 percent of the sample, while 14 percent wanted less spending, and 47 percent wanted spending to stay at the current level. The October poll asked those surveyed if they thought environmental quality had to be sacrificed for economic growth. Half of the sample agreed, while 38 percent did not think that environmental quality had to be given up to have a strong economy.

163. Rice University Poll. *American Public Opinion Index: 1982.* Lexington, KY: Opinion Research Service, Inc., 1984.

This Houston, Texas, area survey was conducted by the Sociology Department at Rice University. The poll contacted 412 Houston area residents sometime during 1982. Respondents were asked their perception of spending on the environment and whether protection of the environment should be pursued regardless of cost.

164. Hollander, Cohen Poll. *American Public Opinion Index: 1982.* Lexington, KY: Opinion Research Service, Inc., 1984.

This telephone poll was conducted by Hollander, Cohen Associates of Baltimore, Maryland, in October 1982. The survey contacted 800 Maryland residents and asked them their opinion of federal spending on the environment.

165. New Mexico Poll. *American Public Opinion Index: 1983.* Lexington, KY: Opinion Research Service, Inc., 1985.

Zia Research Associates of Albuquerque, New Mexico, conducted the New Mexico Poll in October 1983. A sample of 405 New Mexico residents were interviewed by telephone about their opinion of spending for environmental protection.

166. Connecticut Poll. *American Public Opinion Index: 1983.* Lexington, KY: Opinion Research Service, Inc., 1985.

The Roper Center at the University of Connecticut conducted the Connecticut Poll by interviewing 500 Connecticut residents by telephone. Included in the survey were questions about the amount of state spending on the environment and the most important problem facing the country. Results of the poll were released on March 7, 1983.

167. Houston Area Survey. *American Public Opinion Index: 1983*. Lexington, KY: Opinion Research Service, Inc., 1985.

The Department of Sociology at Rice University performed the Houston Area Survey in 1983 by interviewing 474 Houston residents by telephone. The respondents were asked their opinion of the amount of federal spending on improving and protecting the environment and whether they thought pollution controls cost more than they are worth. One question asked for a response to the statement, "Protecting the environment is so important that continuing improvements must be made regardless of cost."

168. Kentucky Poll. *American Public Opinion Index: 1983*. Lexington, KY: Opinion Research Service, Inc., 1985.

In the spring of 1983, the Survey Research Center of the University of Kentucky contacted 705 Kentucky residents by telephone. Those responding were questioned about their perception of the amount of state and local spending on environmental programs and their opinion of the strictness of environmental laws and regulations.

169. Zia Poll. *American Public Opinion Index: 1984*. Lexington, KY: Opinion Research Service, Inc., 1985.

Zia Research Associates of Albuquerque conducted this telephone poll in January 1984. The survey asked over 400 residents of New Mexico about their opinion of the amount of state spending allocated to improving and protecting the environment.

170. Maryland Poll. *American Public Opinion Index: 1985*. Lexington, KY: Opinion Research Service, Inc., 1986.

The Maryland Poll is conducted by the Division of Behavioral and Social Sciences at the University of Maryland. In this spring 1985 survey, 544 residents of Maryland were contacted by telephone and asked their opinion of the level of government that should be responsible for funding environmental programs.

171. Kentucky Poll. *American Public Opinion Index: 1985*. Lexington, KY: Opinion Research Service, Inc., 1986.

The Kentucky Poll is performed by the Survey Research Center of the University of Kentucky. In April 1985, 680 Kentucky residents were contacted by telephone and asked their opinion of state and local spending for environmental programs.

172. Connecticut Poll. *American Public Opinion Index: 1985*. Lexington, KY: Opinion Research Service, Inc., 1986.

The Connecticut Poll is conducted by the Roper Center at the University of Connecticut. In January 1985, 500 Connecticut residents were interviewed by telephone about their perception of state spending for environmental protection.

173. Zia Poll. *American Public Opinion Index: 1986*. Boston, MA: Opinion Research Service, Inc., 1987.

The Zia Poll is performed by Zia Research Associates of Albuquerque, New Mexico. In polls taken in May and October 1986, respondents were asked their opinion of the amount of state spending for environmental protection. The poll was conducted by telephone with samples of 615 (May) and 409 (October) New Mexico residents.

174. *Newsweek* Poll. *American Public Opinion Index: 1986.* Boston, MA: Opinion Research Service, Inc., 1987.

    Newsweek magazine conducted this nationwide telephone poll of 756 Americans. The respondents to the survey were asked their opinion of the amount of effort and resources the country should be devoting to solving environmental problems. Results of the poll were released on November 24, 1986.

175. University of Maryland Poll. *American Public Opinion Index: 1986.* Boston, MA: Opinion Research Service, Inc., 1987.

    In October 1986, the Survey Research Center of the University of Maryland interviewed 500 Maryland residents by telephone. The survey solicited opinions of the amount of state spending allocated to environmental programs and parks and recreation.

176. "The Public's Agenda." *Time,* March 30, 1987, p. 37.

    This *Time* magazine telephone poll was conducted by Yankelovich, Clancy, Shulman during February 1987. A national sample of 1,014 American adults were asked, "Should government spending for the environment be increased, decreased, or kept the same?" Nearly three-fourths of the sample said they supported increased spending on the environment, and only 5 percent indicated they would decrease spending for this purpose. On the question of spending for acid rain, 54 percent favored increased government funding.

177. University of Iowa Poll. *American Public Opinion Index: 1987.* Boston, MA: Opinion Research Service, Inc., 1988.

    This poll was conducted by the Social Sciences Institute at the University of Iowa. The sample included a base poll of 500 state residents with an additional nightly tracking poll of 200 to 250 residents from January 13 through February 8, 1987. Included in the poll was a question about the amount of federal spending for environmental protection.

178. Yankelovich, Clancy, Shulman Poll. *American Public Opinion Index: 1987.* Boston, MA: Opinion Research Service, Inc., 1988.

    A national sample of 1,014 Americans were queried by telephone about their view of the amount of government spending for environmental cleanup. The poll was conducted in February 1987.

179. The California Poll. *American Public Opinion Index: 1987.* Boston, MA: Opinion Research Service, Inc., 1988.

    This California Poll was conducted by the Field Institute in April 1987. A sample of 1,026 Californians were interviewed by telephone and asked about the importance of environmental protection in California. The respondents were asked their opinion of the amount of tax money spent on environmental regulations and parks and recreation services.

180. "Behind the Numbers." *Time*, September 12, 1988, p. 22.

This *Time* magazine poll was conducted by Yankelovich, Clancy, Shulman in late August 1988. The results are based on a national telephone poll of 1,474 registered voters and 1,103 likely voters in the November 1988 election. When asked if they would support a federal income tax increase to fund environmental protection, 70 percent said they would. The only two issues receiving greater support for increased spending were education and the war on drugs. The survey also asked which presidential candidate would do a better job of protecting the environment. Support for the Democratic candidate (Dukakis) was 15 percentage points higher than for the Republican candidate (Bush).

181. Consumer Research Center Poll. *American Public Opinion Index: 1988.* Boston, MA: Opinion Research Service, Inc., 1989.

In March 1988, Consumer Research Center of New York conducted a national telephone poll of 5,000 Americans. Included in the poll was a question asking the respondents whether they supported reducing spending on environmental protection to reduce the federal budget deficit.

182. The Public's Perspective on Social Welfare Reform. *American Public Opinion Index: 1988.* Boston, MA: Opinion Research Service, Inc., 1989.

This report was the result of focus groups composed of 545 residents of Philadelphia, Minneapolis, and St Paul. One item of discussion was the amount of government spending on environmental protection.

183. The University of New Orleans Poll. *American Public Opinion Index: 1988.* Boston, MA: Opinion Research Service, Inc., 1989.

The University of New Orleans contacted 835 Louisiana residents by telephone and solicited their opinions on environmental protection issues. Respondents were asked to express their concern for coastal erosion in Louisiana and their opinion of the amount of federal money spent on environmental protection. Results of the poll were released on October 26, 1988.

184. Scripps Howard Poll. *American Public Opinion Index: 1988.* Boston, MA: Opinion Research Service, Inc., 1989.

Scripps Howard of Birmingham, Alabama, interviewed 1,154 residents of 14 southern states during February 1988. Included in the telephone poll was an item concerning support for cutting environmental spending to reduce the federal budget deficit.

185. Niemi, Richard G.; Mueller, John; and Smith, Tom W. *Trends in Public Opinion: A Compendium of Survey Data.* New York: Greenwood Press, 1989, p. 79.

This reference book tracks trends in public opinion on various topics. Included in the chapter on "Taxation and Spending," are two tables presenting results from several polls on spending for the environment conducted between 1971 and 1988. Each poll asked respondents, "Are we spending too much, too little, or about the right amount on the environment?" The percentage of the respondents indicating that "too little" was being spent on the environment increased slightly throughout the 17-year period and varied from a low of 42 percent to a high of 65 percent. Sample size and the response to the item are given for each poll.

186. Black, Chris. "Poll Finds Pessimism About Environment." *Boston Globe*, April 7, 1989, p. A12.

This national survey of registered voters was performed by KRC Communication Research in cooperation with the American Political Network. Over 1,000 registered voters were asked their opinion of the amount of federal spending on the environment. Among those surveyed, 45 percent believed the quality of the nation's environment would decline in the next two years, while 22 percent said it would improve, and 31 percent believed it would remain unchanged. Westerners were less likely than residents of other regions to be optimistic about the future for the environment. More than two-thirds of the sample thought the federal government should increase spending on the environment.

187. Gallup, George Jr. "April 23: Government Spending." *The Gallup Poll: Public Opinion 1989.* Wilmington, DE: Scholarly Resources, Inc., 1990, pp. 103–5.

The Gallup Organization performed this poll for Times Mirror during late January and early February 1989. (Sample size for the survey is not given.) Respondents to the survey were asked if federal spending for environmental protection should be increased, kept the same, or decreased. Nearly half of the sample (49 percent) wanted to keep spending at current levels, while 39 percent wanted spending increased, and only 7 percent wanted to decrease spending.

188. AMA Poll. *American Public Opinion Index: 1989.* Boston, MA: Opinion Research Service, Inc., 1990.

This national poll was conducted in April 1989 by the American Medical Association with 1,004 physicians and 1,500 members of the general public. In response to a question about the amount of society's spending on protecting the environment, almost two-thirds of the general public thought the amount of spending was inadequate. Only 5 percent of the sample said society was spending too much on the environment. The poll report compares these results with responses to prior polls conducted in 1982, 1983, 1984, and 1986. Of eight issues discussed, the environment ranked third in inadequate funding.

189. Consumer Research Center Poll. *American Public Opinion Index: 1989.* Boston, MA: Opinion Research Service, Inc., 1990.

In July 1989, the Consumer Research Center of New York administered a mail questionnaire to a national sample of 400 chief executives of large U.S. companies. Included in the questionnaire was an item soliciting the respondents' attitudes toward expenditures on the environment.

190. University of South Carolina Poll. *American Public Opinion Index: 1989.* Boston, MA: Opinion Research Service, Inc., 1990.

The University of South Carolina Poll was conducted by the university's Institute of Public Affairs in November 1989. Telephone interviews were completed with 585 South Carolina residents. Respondents to the poll were asked whether taxes funding state environmental programs should be increased, decreased, or kept the same.

191. Wood, Floris W., ed. *An American Profile: Opinions and Behavior, 1972–89.* Detroit: Gale Research Inc., 1990, pp. 724–28.

This reference book presents results of the General Social Survey conducted annually by the National Opinion Research Center, a nonprofit research organization affiliated with the University of Chicago. In a subsection of the chapter on national issues, results to a question on spending for the environment are presented. Data given are from the General Social Survey from 1973 through 1989. Responses are broken down by sex, race, and age. (Other information about the General Social Surveys is presented elsewhere.)

192. *General Social Surveys, 1972–1990:* Cumulative Codebook. National Opinion Center, distributed by the Roper Center for Public Opinion Research, September 1990.

This report summarizes results from a series of nationwide polls of adult Americans conducted during February, March, and April 1972–1978, 1980, and 1982–1990. Sample sizes for the surveys ranged from 1,466 to 1,613. Separate black subsamples were included in 1982 and 1987. Results in the codebook are broken down for 1972–1982 and for 1983–1987 with other years and the results from the black subsamples reported separately. The General Social Surveys included a question on spending for the environment, with two alternative wordings, as well as a question on spending for parks and recreation. In 1990, when respondents were asked, "Are we spending too much, too little, or about the right amount on the improving and protecting the environment?" 71 percent responded "too little." The percent responding "too little" increased throughout the 19-year-period. Another version of the environmental spending question asked from 1983 on, received a similar response. On spending for parks and recreation, a majority of the sample consistently responded that the amount was "about right."

The Environment as a Political Issue

193. "Domestic Issues Top Concerns." *Current Opinion* 4 (September 1976): 92.

Current Opinion was a monthly review of public opinion published by the Roper Public Opinion Research Center. This issue includes results from a national Roper Poll conducted in June 1976 on issues of greatest concern to Americans. In one question, the respondents were asked to choose from a list of 18 issues one or two issues that would turn them away from a candidate if the candidate's stand was different from their own. Of the 2,000 adults surveyed, 5 percent chose air and water pollution as the issue that would affect their support for a candidate.

194. Gallup, George H. "August 20, 1972: Presidential Candidates' Positions." *The Gallup Poll: Public Opinion 1972–1977*. Wilmington, DE: Scholarly Resources, Inc., 1978, pp. 51–54.

The Gallup Poll presented in this entry was performed between August 4 and 7, 1972. (The sample size and methodology are not given.) Respondents were asked if they would be more or less likely to vote for a candidate who said he or she would increase spending on a variety of issues including air and water pollution. On the subject of pollution, 80 percent said they would be more likely to vote for the candidate, 10 percent indicated they would be less likely to vote for the candidate, and 10 percent had no opinion. Responses are broken down by age of the respondent. Those 50 years of age and older were slightly less likely to vote for the candidate who promised to increase spending on pollution.

195. Gallup, George H. "March 17, 1974: Views of Republican County Chairmen." *The Gallup Poll: Public Opinion 1972–1977.* Wilmington, DE:
Scholarly Resources, Inc., 1978, pp. 241–42.

This poll by the Gallup Organization was conducted between January 15
and February 15, 1974, with an undisclosed number of Republican county
chairmen. In the poll, the chairmen were asked their perception of which national
issues would be most important in the 1974 congressional elections. Only 2 percent
of the respondents named environmental, ecology, or land use concerns. (Multiple
responses were received from some respondents.) High cost of living was identified
as the most important issue for the election.

196. Gallup, George H. "October 15, 1976: Issue Important to Voters." *The
Gallup Poll: Public Opinion 1972–1977.* Wilmington, DE: Scholarly
Resources, Inc., 1978.

This Gallup Organization poll was performed during late September 1976
with an undisclosed number of Americans. The respondents were asked to rate the
importance of 20 issues (between one and five) in determining how they would vote
in the next election. On the subject of conservation and the environment, 50 percent of the respondents rated the issue as a "four" or "five" in importance, 22 percent rated it as a "three," 17 percent rated it as a "one" or "two," and 11 percent had
no opinion. Of the 20 issues, inflation and government spending were rated as most
important by those surveyed, and abortion and the Nixon pardon were rated as
least important in choosing a candidate to back.

197. Gallup, George H. "September 21: Campaign Debates." *The Gallup Poll:
Public Opinion 1980.* Wilmington, DE: Scholarly Resources, Inc., 1981,
pp. 197–98.

This telephone survey of registered voters was performed September 12
through 16, 1980. The size of the sample is not given. Those responding to the
survey were asked what issues the presidential candidates should debate. Conservation and environmental issues were listed by 3 percent of the respondents.
(Multiple responses were received from some subjects.)

198. Harris, Louis. "Big Shift in Single Issue Voting Expected This Fall." *The
Harris Survey* 20 (March 11, 1982).

This nationwide telephone poll of 1,253 adults was conducted by the Harris
Survey in February 1982. The survey respondents were asked about what effect a
candidate's position on various issues had on the likelihood that they would vote
for the candidate. When asked about controlling air and water pollution, 50 percent of the sample said they could still vote for a candidate who disagreed with
them on this issue. This "could vote for" percentage was higher than for any of the
other issues listed.

199. Anthony, Richard. "Trends in Public Opinion on the Environment." *Environment* 24 (May 1982): 14–20, 33–34.

This article reviews results from several polls conducted in the 1970s and
early 1980s on environmental commitment and concern. Topics addressed by the
polls include the following: importance of environmental issues, economy versus
environmental protection, energy trade-offs, support for environmental regulations, and the political impact of environmental protection issues. A bar chart

presents results from a September 1981 poll on support for environmental legislation conducted by CBS News/*New York Times*. Responses are broken down by region, education, age, and race. Results from a Democrats National Poll conducted in February 1982 are displayed in a table. The poll, sponsored by the Democratic National Committee, Democratic Congressional Campaign Committee, and Democratic Senatorial Campaign Committee, asked voters which party they thought would do a better job of protecting the environment. Results are shown by region, sex, race, age, occupation, voting record, union membership, income level, and party affiliation. For the total sample, 51 percent thought the Democratic party would do a better job, 11 percent chose the Republican party, 29 percent said both parties, and 9 percent thought neither party would do a good job of protecting the environment.

200. Harris, Louis. "Negative Vote May Result in Close Election." *The Harris Survey* 66 (August 6, 1984).

A nationwide sample of 1,264 likely voters were polled by the Harris Survey in July 1984. The respondents were asked their opinion on enforcement of pollution controls and whether a candidate's position on this issue would affect their vote for the candidate. Of those that said they favored pollution enforcement, one-half said they could still vote for a candidate even if his position differed from their own on this issue. Responses to the question from four prior polls are also included.

201. "Poll Says Most Support Environmental Funding." *Boston Globe*, August 29, 1984.

A nationwide sample of 1,451 adults were contacted by telephone in August 1984. The respondents were questioned about their concern for the environment, importance of environmental issues in selecting a presidential candidate, and their willingness to fund environmental programs. Of those surveyed, 70 percent said they were more concerned about the environment than in the past. Nearly two-thirds said they would be willing to pay 10 percent more in taxes and cost of living to pay for environmental improvements. In deciding between presidential candidates, 21 percent said environmental issues were "very important," 51 percent said they were "somewhat important," and 23 percent said they were "not at all important." The poll was conducted by Media General and Associated Press.

202. Yankelovich, Skelly, and White Poll. *American Public Opinion Index: 1983.* Lexington, KY: Opinion Research Service, Inc., 1985.

Polls conducted in June, September and December 1983 by Yankelovich, Skelly and White included questions about environmental issues. The polls contacted over 1,000 Americans by telephone. The June and September polls asked respondents about their concern for environmental pollution and depletion of natural resources such as oil and minerals. In the September and December polls, respondents were also queried about their perception of the importance of environmental issues during the 1984 election.

203. *Newsweek* Poll. *American Public Opinion Index: 1983.* Lexington, KY: Opinion Research Service, Inc., 1985.

Newsweek magazine contacted 760 Americans by telephone and asked them how important they felt the environment was as an issue in the 1984 presidential campaign. The results of the poll were released on June 27, 1983.

204. Americans Talk Security Poll. *American Public Opinion Index: 1988.*
Boston, MA: Opinion Research Service, Inc., 1989.

Americans Talk Security of Winchester, Massachusetts, conducted this poll
in December 1988. A national sample of 1,006 were contacted by telephone and
queried about the importance of environmental issues in choosing a presidential
candidate.

205. Gallup, George Jr. "February 11: Presidential Election." *The Gallup Poll:
Public Opinion 1988.* Wilmington, DE: Scholarly Resources, Inc., 1989,
pp. 13–16.

This telephone poll was conducted by the Gallup Organization in January
1988. Respondents were asked which issues would be most important to them in
deciding which presidential candidate to support in the 1988 election. Only 4 percent of those surveyed thought the environment would be the most important
issue. Of the voters who were concerned about the environment, 18 percent preferred the Republican candidate, 32 percent preferred the Democratic candidate,
and 50 percent indicated they were supporting another candidate or were undecided.

206. Gallup, George Jr. "November 6, 1988: Priorities for the Next President."
The Gallup Poll: Public Opinion 1988. Wilmington, DE: Scholarly
Resources, Inc., 1989, pp. 219–20.

This poll was conducted by the Gallup Organization for Times Mirror during late October 1988. The telephone survey asked respondents about the importance of various issues for the next president. "Proposing laws to increase
protection of the environment," was viewed as a top presidential priority by 64 percent of the sample. Of the nine issues discussed, this percentage was second only
to reduction of the federal deficit. Of those preferring the Republican presidental
ticket, 60 percent said environmental protection should be a top priority, while 70
percent of those preferring the Democratic ticket thought the environment should
be a priority. (Sample size for this poll is not provided.)

207. Gallup, George Jr. "November 21, 1988: Factor Leading to Bush's Vic-
tory." *The Gallup Poll: Public Opinion 1988.* Wilmington, DE: Scholarly
Resources, Inc., 1989, pp. 228–30.

Interview dates for this telephone survey are given as November 9 and 10,
1988. Voters in the November 1988 election were asked what they thought the
number one priority of the new administration should be. Protecting the environment was cited by 6 percent of those who voted for the Republican candidate and
8 percent of those who voted for the Democratic candidate. The number one
priority for both groups of voters was deficit reduction. (Sample size for this poll
is not provided.)

208. Phillips, Frank. "Money, Education Seen as Voter Priorities; Issues of
Abortion, Environment Rank Lower with G.O.P. in Latest Survey."
Boston Globe, March 18, 1990, p. B72.

This article describes a survey of 600 Massachusetts registered Republicans
and Independents conducted by KRC Communication Research. The date and
methodology of the study are not specified. The Republicans were asked their opinion of the importance of various issues in choosing a candidate for governor and

their view of one method of funding purchases of open spaces. Only 2 percent of the respondents rated the environment as a major issue in the gubernatorial election. The issue ranked nine out of ten in importance. Half of the sample opposed the idea of taxing real estate transfers to raise funds for purchasing open space in the state.

209. Lesher, Dave, and Schwartz, Bob. "Candidates Rally Around Environmental Banner." *The Los Angeles Times* (Orange County edition), April 17, 1990, p. Al.

This article describes results of a *Los Angeles Times* Orange County Poll conducted on the importance of the environment as a political issue. In an interview, citizens of Orange County were asked, "When you vote in local or state elections this year, how important is it that the candidate you would support take a strong pro-environment position?" Over half (55 percent) replied "very important," while 38 percent said "somewhat important," and only 7 percent said a candidate's environmental position was "not important." A large majority of the sample said their interest in the environment had increased in the past few years. The article does not include any details on the sample size or methodology used for the study.

210. Gallup, George Jr. "November 6: Democratic Presidential Candidates." *The Gallup Poll: Public Opinion 1991.* Wilmington, DE: Scholarly Resources, Inc., 1992, pp. 224–26.

This Gallup Poll, conducted between October 31 and November 3, 1991, asked respondents to indicate whether environmental issues were important in choosing a presidential candidate. Although 85 percent of the sample said the environment was important in selecting a candidate, only 5 percent said it was the most important issue.

Environmental Priorities

211. Bart, William M. "A Hierarchy Among Attitudes Toward the Environment." *Journal of Environmental Education* 4 (Fall 1972): 10–14.

The purpose of the research described in this article was to develop a hierarchy of attitudes toward the environment using a sample of college students. Data for the study were collected by a 20-item environmental attitude questionnaire administered to 100 graduate students in the College of Education at the University of Minnesota. The questionnaire solicited "yes" and "no" responses to 20 ecological statements. The proportion of "yes" responses was used to rank the 20 items. The statements receiving the highest percentage of positive responses concerned the importance of discussions on conservation, pollution, overpopulation, action against industrial pollution, and control of beach litter. The statements receiving the lowest percentage of "yes" responses were: conversion to nonleaded gasoline, family size restrictions, and prohibition of cigarette manufacture. "Not favoring liquidating predators" was supported by 78 percent of the sample, ranking the issue fourteenth of the 20 items. "Not favoring widespread use of chemical pesticides" received a positive response from 86 percent of the students, ranking the issue twelfth.

212. "National Wildlife's Readers Rank the Top Ten Environmental Issues." *National Wildlife*, April-May 1977, p. 35.

In this article, results of a *National Wildlife* magazine reader survey are presented. More than 25,000 readers completed and returned the survey which was included in the October-November 1976 issue of the magazine. The questionnaire asked the readers to rank ten environmental issues in the order of their importance. Fighting water, air, and chemical pollution took the top three places in the ranking. Saving endangered plants and animals ranked fourth in importance. Encouraging population control ranked fifth overall but received the largest number of first-place voters. Uniting hunters and nonhunters was ranked last and received the fewest first-place votes.

213. Clary, Bruce B.; Roe, Charles E.; and Swearingen, Emilie. "Environmental Priorities of Opinion-Makers." *Environmental Affairs* 6 (1977-78): 33-61.

The research described in this article compared the environmental priorities of representatives of citizen groups, government, private sector business, and professional occupations. Respondents to the North Carolina survey were nominated by staff of the Environmental Studies Council of the University of North Carolina, and these subjects in turn nominated additional subjects. A total sample of 621 respondents completed mail questionnaires which included rating 40 environmental issues and then selecting the 10 most important concerns. The top five issues as ranked by the total sample were: solid waste disposal, industrial water pollution, protection of natural areas, public participation in environmental decisions, and municipal water pollution. The researchers grouped the issues into 12 clusters. For the total sample, the highest priorities were the water quality, water shortage, and energy use clusters. Water quality was ranked first by respondents from all groups (public sector, private sector, professional, and citizen interest groups). Parks and recreation and pollution and hazards were ranked last by the total sample. The article includes a table that presents the rankings of the 12 issue clusters on the basis of group affiliation and metropolitan/nonmetropolitan residence.

214. Utrup, Kathryn Ann. "How Sierra Club Members See Environmental Issues." *Sierra* 64 (March-April 1979): 14-18.

This article describes a study of the environmental attitudes of members of the Sierra Club conducted by Resources for the Future. This research was part of a larger study that included the attitudes of the general public and members of four additional environmental organizations. A 24-page mail questionnaire was sent to 1,000 Sierra Club members and returned by approximately 70 percent of the randomly selected members. The survey included questions about the perceived seriousness and causes of various environmental issues as well as questions about general quality of life, environmental quality, and energy options. A large majority of Sierra Club members perceived environmental problems, the energy situation, and air and water pollution as serious problems. Industry and the carelessness of the public were identified as the two most important causes of environmental problems followed by population growth and governmental failure to protect the environment. The members ranked the following ten issues as being very important to them personally: wilderness preservation, natural areas preservation, air pollution, water pollution, energy sources and conservation, natural habitat for wildlife, toxic wastes, animal protection, human population, and land use planning.

215. University of Maryland Poll. *American Public Opinion Index: 1981.* Tallahassee, FL: Opinion Research Service, Inc., 1982.

   This poll was conducted during 1981 by the Institute for Governmental Service of the University of Maryland. A sample of 404 residents of the Baltimore metropolitan area were contacted by telephone and interviewed about concern for several environmental problems including pollution, solid waste disposal, and hazardous waste disposal.

216. CBS News/*New York Times* Poll. *American Public Opinion Index: 1983.* Lexington, KY: Opinion Research Service, Inc., 1985.

   CBS News and *The New York Times* conducted this poll in April 1983. A sample of 1,489 Americans were contacted by telephone. The respondents were asked their opinion of the nation's most important environmental problem. Respondents were also asked whether they felt environmental protection had to be maintained regardless of cost and whether they perceived hazardous waste as a problem for the country.

217. The Roper Poll. *American Public Opinion Index: 1984.* Lexington, KY: Opinion Research Service, Inc., 1985.

   This Roper Poll included questions about several environmental problems. The Roper Organization interviewed, in person, 2,000 Americans during November 1984. Respondents were asked how they perceived the following environmental problems: strip mining, acid rain, industrial air pollution, water pollution from manufacturing plants, and oil spills from tankers.

218. "Many Americans Think Environmental Quality Is Slipping." *National Wildlife*, February-March 1986, p. 36.

   This article describes results of a reader survey conducted by *National Wildlife* magazine during late 1985. The article does not provide any details on how the survey of 1,500 readers was performed. Respondents to the survey answered questions about their perception of current and future environmental conditions. The readers also ranked the importance of eight environmental problems as follows: water pollution, air pollution, hazardous waste, overpopulation, acid rain, soil erosion, and pollutants in the home.

219. Cullen, Gerald R.; Hungerford, Harold R.; Tomera, Audrey N.; Sivek, Daniel J.; Harrington, Michael; and Squillo, Michael. "A Comparison of Environmental Perceptions and Behaviors of Five Discrete Populations." *Journal of Environmental Education* 17 (Spring 1986): 24–32.

   This research compared the environmental perceptions of five different groups of people: nature elderhostel participants, environmental problems course enrollees, Soil and Water Conservation District directors, Cooperative Wildlife Research Unit members, and environmental education trainees. Each of these groups completed a survey instrument which included demographic data, environmental issue ranking, and environmental issue interest analysis. Responses to the survey indicated a lack of agreement on the importance of different environmental issues among respondents from the five groups. Overpopulation was ranked as the most important issue to mankind by the elderhostel participants, environmental education trainees, and wildlife biologists. Production of food ranked highest among the Soil and Water Conservation directors, and students in the environmental problems course ranked nuclear waste disposal as the most important issue.

220. Higgins, Richard. "Environmental Worries Dominate Vermont Poll." *Boston Globe*, July 3, 1986, p. A53.

This Vermont Poll was conducted by the University of Vermont for the Vermont Department of Forests, Parks and Recreation. The statewide telephone survey interviewed 504 Vermont residents about their perception of the state's environmental quality and environmental regulations. The quality of the state's lakes and ponds, rivers and streams, ground water, air, and deer herds was rated as declining by nearly two-thirds of those sampled. The respondents indicated that they thought only the quality of the scenery and the state parks were improving. Acid rain, toxic wastes, the loss of agricultural land and increased development were identified as the greatest environmental concerns in the state. A majority thought the state's environmental controls should be strengthened.

221. The Roper Poll. *American Public Opinion Index: 1987.* Boston, MA: Opinion Research Service, Inc., 1988.

The Roper Organization personally interviewed 1,997 Americans about their views of air and water pollution, world population, ozone depletion, and chemical waste disposal. Those surveyed were asked whether they thought these issues would pose serious threats for future generations of Americans. Results of this poll were released on January 24, 1987.

222. The Roper Poll. *American Public Opinion Index: 1987.* Boston, MA: Opinion Research Service, Inc., 1988.

In October 1987, the Roper Organization interviewed 1,990 Americans in person and asked them to indicate their perception of the seriousness of nine different environmental problems. The nine problems included in the poll were the following: strip mining, industrial water pollution, tanker oil spills, auto air pollution, industrial air pollution, acid rain, chemical waste disposal, nuclear waste disposal, and nuclear power plant radiation.

223. Hayes, Paul G. "State Scientists Worry About Global Threats." *The Milwaukee Journal*, April 25, 1988, pp. 1A, 3A.

This report is based on results of a poll of Wisconsin scientists conducted by *The Milwaukee Journal*. A written questionnaire was returned by 874, or 54 percent, of the scientists selected from the membership lists of the American Association for the Advancement of Science. The following topics were included in the poll: optimism toward human well being, anticipated progress on current problems during the next 25 years, and the importance of different problems to the well-being of Americans. The scientists ranked air, water, and land protection as the most important issues to the long-term well-being of the American public. Acid rain control was identified as the scientific issue currently receiving the most inadequate commitment from the federal government. (Other results from this survey are presented in another section.)

224. *The American Public's Hopes and Fears for the Decade of the 1990s.* New York: Research and Forecasts, Inc., 1989.

This poll was conducted by Research and Forecasts, Inc., for the Hearst

Corporation of New York. A national telephone survey of 1,001 Americans were asked what environmental problems the respondents feared the most. Air pollution was the greatest concern of 30 percent of those surveyed. Other environmental fears were the following: toxic waste (28 percent), ocean pollution (12 percent), acid rain (10 percent), and the effects of pesticides (6 percent). Over two-thirds of the sample thought that, in the future, new technology would help the environment. A majority said that the greenhouse effect would be a major world problem in the 1990s.

225. "USA Today Snapshot." *USA Today*, March 6, 1989, 1A.

This item is a graphic depicting public concerns for several environmental problems: hazardous waste disposal, industrial air pollution, industrial water pollution, water pollution from cities, and the greenhouse effect. According to the graphic, hazardous waste disposal was viewed as the most serious environmental problem by 18 percent of the public. (The other problems were seen as being the most serious by lower percentages of respondents.) The statistics were apparently derived from more than one survey, but no details are provided. The National Solid Waste Management Association is credited as the source for the data.

226. *Earth Day Environmental Poll.* Denver, CO: Ciruli Associates, April 1989, 14 pp.

Ciruli Associates of Denver, Colorado, conducted this statewide telephone poll just prior to Earth Day in 1989. The special survey interviewed 512 Coloradoans on a variety of environmental issues. Half of the sample described themselves as environmentalists. Although 70 percent said they would be willing to pay higher prices to accomplish environmental protection, only 37 percent said they would be willing to accept higher unemployment. A slim majority felt that the government was spending "too little" on the environment. Over 40 percent of the sample was willing to spend at least $35 in higher prices each month to allow industries to operate in a way that produces less pollution. The respondents were also asked to indicate the seriousness of various environmental problems. Hazardous waste disposal, air pollution, and groundwater contamination were seen as the most serious problems with at least 30 percent of the sample describing each of these issues as "very serious." At least 20 percent of those surveyed described river and lake pollution, solid waste disposal, loss of endangered plants and animals, loss of open spaces, and loss of wilderness as "very serious" problems. Other problems included in the survey were the following: drinking water contamination, soil erosion, loss of wetlands, and overcrowding in state parks.

227. Clymer, Adam. "Polls Show Contrasts in How Public and E.P.A. View Environment." *The New York Times*, May 22, 1989, p. B7.

This article compares results from two public opinion polls on environmental hazards with a ranking of hazards compiled by the staff of the Environmental Protection Agency. The public opinion polls were conducted by the Roper Organization in December 1987 and January 1988. Details of the polls are not given. Ranking of the hazards was done according to the percent of the public that rated the individual hazard as "very serious." For the public ranking, four of the top five hazards were related to toxic chemicals and wastes. Water pollution, air pollution, pesticides, and ozone layer depletion were also rated as "very serious" by approximately half of the public sample. Oil spills, acid rain, wetlands destruction, and the greenhouse effect were rated as "very serious" by only about one in three respondents. The relatively low public ranking of the greenhouse effect as a hazard contrasted with the E.P.A. ranking which identified the greenhouse effect as a "relatively high" risk.

228. Gallup, George Jr. "May 17: Environmental Issues." *The Gallup Poll: Public Opinion 1989.* Wilmington, DE: Scholarly Resources, Inc., 1990, pp. 120–25.

This Gallup Poll was conducted in early May 1989 with an undisclosed sample of Americans. The poll solicited opinions on several environmental problems and on the banning chlorofluorocarbons. Over three-fourths of those surveyed identified themselves as strong environmentalists. Those most likely to label themselves as environmentalists were middle income, college educated residents of western states. Almost 80 percent said they favored a ban on chlorofluorocarbons. Respondents were asked about the degree of their concern for ten specific environmental issues: pollution of lakes and rivers, toxic waste contamination, air pollution, ocean and beach pollution, loss of wildlife habitat, nuclear waste contamination, damage to the ozone layer, loss of tropical rain forests, acid rain, and the greenhouse effect/global warming. The greatest concern was expressed for pollution of rivers and lakes and toxic waste contamination of soil and water. Of the ten problems, the least amount of concern was shown for the loss of tropical rain forests, acid rain, and global warming. A majority of the respondents said they worried a "great deal" or a "fair amount" about all ten of the issues.

229. *ORC Issue Watch: Environmental Concerns Are Resulting in Changes in Consumer Behavior.* Princeton, NJ: Opinion Research Corporation, June 28, 1990, 5 pp.

This report combines results from two surveys conducted by Opinion Research Corporation of Princeton, New Jersey, in March and April 1990 with over 1,000 respondents. The respondents were asked to rate their degree of concern for environmental problems on a scale from one to ten. Concern for the environment was rated as a seven or eight by 42 percent and as a nine or ten by 34 percent of the sample. Another question asked interviewees to describe the seriousness of various environmental problems. Nuclear waste disposal was viewed as "most critical" by 75 percent. Water pollution, disposal of toxic waste, air pollution, and ozone depletion were also seen as "most critical" by over 60 percent of the sample. Those surveyed were also asked to indicate how harmful they thought the operations of various industries were to the environment.

230. *How Concerned Are Consumers Over Factors Affecting the Environment?* New York: Warwick, Baker, and Fiore, May 1990.

In May 1990, Warwick, Baker and Fiore, Inc. of New York interviewed 410 Americans in a telephone poll that measured attitudes toward environmental problems. The respondents answered questions about their perception of the threats posed to the environment by various products and behaviors. In response to a question about the importance of environmental factors in making purchase decisions, 79 percent rated energy efficiency as "very important." Other factors rated "very important" by at least 70 percent of the sample were nonpolluting nature, recyclable, and ozone-safe. Those surveyed were also asked to indicate the degree of their concern for several environmental problems. A high level of concern was documented for water pollution, toxic wastes, hazardous wastes, air pollution, and oil spills. In the report, item responses are broken down by sex, age, education, income, employment, region, presence of children, and religion.

231. Gallup, George Jr. "April 11: Most Important Problem/Environment." *The Gallup Poll: Public Opinion 1990*. Wilmington, DE: Scholarly Resources, Inc., 1991, pp. 38–43.

This Gallup Poll performed between April 5 and 8, 1990, included several questions on environmental issues. Results are compared with responses to the same questions received in a May 1989 poll. Of the eleven environmental issues addressed in the poll, those surveyed indicated they were most concerned with pollution of drinking water, pollution of rivers and lakes, and contamination of soil and water by toxic waste. Generally, the respondents expressed a "fair amount" or a "great deal" of concern about all of the issues. (The other issues included in the survey were the following: air pollution, ocean and beach pollution, loss of wildlife habitat, damage to the ozone layer, nuclear waste contamination of soil and water, loss of tropical rain forests, the greenhouse effect, and acid rain.) The percentage who were concerned a "great deal" was lower for all of the issues than in the previous year's poll. A large majority of those sampled felt the American public, business, and the government were "not worried enough" about the environment. When judging the amount of progress made in environmental problems since 1970, 63 percent said we have made "only some" progress. (The sample size and methodology of this poll are not given.)

232. University of Nebraska, Lincoln Poll. *American Public Opinion Index: 1991*. Tallahassee, FL: 1991.

The Bureau of Sociological Research at the University of Nebraska–Lincoln administered a telephone poll to 1,924 residents of Nebraska. Respondents to the poll were asked about the degree of their concern for air pollution, drinking water quality, contamination of soil and water from nuclear waste, loss of wildlife habitat, and loss of tropical rain forests. A majority (59 percent) said they were concerned a "great" or a "fair deal" about loss of wildlife habitat, while fewer (48 percent) were concerned the same degree about loss of the rain forests. The interview also asked the respondents what outdoor trail activity they would do more of if they had the time and resources.

233. Carolina Poll. *American Public Opinion Index: 1991*. Tallahassee, FL: 1991.

In the fall of 1991, the Institute for Research in Social Sciences at the University of North Carolina at Chapel Hill contacted 610 North Carolina residents by telephone. Those responding were asked to indicate their degree of personal concern for several environmental problems including acid rain, air pollution, toxic waste, loss of wildlife habitat, and loss of tropical rain forests. The interview also asked whether economic growth or environmental protection should be given priority.

234. *Iowans and the Environment: An Opinion Survey*. Des Moines, IA: Iowa Natural Heritage Foundation, 1991, 79 pp.

Central Surveys, Inc., of Shenandoah, Iowa, conducted this study for the Iowa Natural Heritage Foundation in March 1991. The researchers contacted 1,000 Iowa residents by telephone and asked them about their perceptions of various environmental problems. Those responding to the survey were asked who they felt should be responsible for protecting and cleaning up the environment as well as how much additional money they would be willing to spend each year to protect the environment. Another question asked about reasons for recycling and support for expanding the existing beverage deposit program to other recyclable materials. When asked to rate the seriousness of over 15 different environmental problems, 90 percent rated pollution of lakes and streams and solid waste management as "serious" or "very serious." Other problems rated as "serious" or "very serious" by at least 80 percent of the sample were soil erosion, drinking water contamination, water pollution from chemicals, and hazardous or toxic waste. (Some of the other problems included in this section were the following: greenhouse effect, industrial air pollution, auto air pollution, loss of forests and trees, lack of parks and recreation, water pollution from underground storage tanks, loss of wetlands, loss of wildlife habitat, and loss of prairies.) Another section of the survey requested the respondents to rate the influence of different factors on their attitude toward the environment. The sample indicated that two factors, "concern for future generations" and "information and education," had the greatest influence on their environmental attitudes. (Some of the other influences were the following: "stricter laws and regulations," "peer pressure," "monetary incentives," "product labeling," "religious influence," and "personal convenience.") In response to one question about attitudes toward hunters, 33 percent said the term "hunter" brought to mind unfavorable impressions.

235. *Environmental Opinion Study.* Washington, DC: Environmental Opinion Study, Inc., June 1991, 51 pp.

The Environmental Opinion Study was based on a national telephone poll of 804 adults conducted during 1991. Americans contacted by the survey were asked their perception of government regulations, the ability of technology to solve environmental problems, and the seriousness of various environmental problems. Only 4 percent of the sample identified themselves as "anti-environmentalist," while 60 percent called themselves "environmentalists" and another 30 percent said they were leaning in that direction. When asked what approach would be most successful in solving environmental problems, 54 percent said the actions of individuals would be most effective. Only 23 percent thought technology could solve the problems, and 22 percent thought increased federal spending was the answer. Hazardous and toxic waste, oil spills, and air pollution were rated as the most serious environmental problems with over 80 percent of the sample rating these three issues as "extremely" or "very serious." Solid waste disposal, ozone depletion, ocean pollution, and destruction of forests were also rated as "extremely" or "very serious" by a large majority of the respondents. (Other issues rated were the following: global warming, threat to endangered species, economic development of wetlands, threats to wildlife, and world population.) In response to a question on development of the Arctic National Wildlife Refuge in Alaska, 36 percent favored, and 55 percent opposed development.

236. Marshall, Kenn. "Annual Survey Lists Development, Growth as Top Environmental Issues." *The* [Harrisburg, Pennsylvania] *Patriot-News,* March 16, 1992.

In this annual poll, *The Patriot-News* asked two dozen environmental leaders to identify the most important environmental issues facing Pennsylvania. (The method and date of the survey are not specified in the article.) The top ten issues as ranked by the environmental leaders were the following: need to control and manage growth and development, need for environmental education, urban air pollution, agricultural and other runoff polluting waterways, quality of drinking water, markets for recycled materials, public land acquisition, industrial hazardous wastes, funding for state parks, and hazardous waste disposal facility sites.

Pollution

237. "Democrats Gain in Gallup Poll." *The New York Times*, August 30, 1970, p. 39.

A sample of 1,501 Americans was surveyed for this Gallup Poll conducted between July 31 and August 2, 1970. One question posed in the survey was, "What do you think is the most important problem facing the country today?" Air pollution and water pollution were named by 10 percent of those surveyed. The article compares this percentage to results from a similar poll in June 1970 when only 2 percent of the sample cited pollution concerns.

238. Simon, Rita James. "Public Attitudes Toward Population and Pollution." *Public Opinion Quarterly* 35 (Spring 1971): 93–99.

This survey was performed by the Survey Research Laboratory at the University of Illinois with 170 residents of Illinois. The laboratory contacted residents by telephone and requested their opinions of world population and air and water pollution. When asked to name the most important problem in the United States at the time, 23 percent named population, pollution, or other environmental problems as being first or second in importance. Approximately two-thirds thought the United States and world populations were growing too fast, but only 29 percent said they were worried about the increase. Over 90 percent saw air and water pollution as problems, yet 50 percent disapproved of the president's announcement that he would make pollution the nation's most important domestic issue.

239. "Poll Finds Drugs No. 3 Issue in U.S." *The New York Times*, June 17, 1971, p. 29.

Results of a June 1971 Gallup Poll are presented in this newspaper article. The polling organization interviewed 1,522 adults in more than 300 American communities and asked them to identify the country's most important problem. The results are compared to responses to a similar question posed in a March 1971 poll. Pollution and ecology concerns were named as the country's biggest problem by 4 percent of the respondents in June versus 7 percent of the respondents in March. Vietnam was identified as the number one problem in both polls. Multiple responses were received from some individuals.

240. Chandler, Robert. Public Opinion: *Changing Attitudes on Contemporary Political and Social Issues.* New York: R. R. Bowker Company, 1972, pp. 184–94.

This book chapter describes a test of public attitudes and knowledge of the environment produced by CBS News. The test was administered by telephone to 900 people 16 years and older on April 28–29, 1970, approximately one week after the first Earth Day. All but three of the questions were factual in nature and designed to test the respondents' knowledge of ecology and ecological problems. The three attitude questions related to pollution as a problem facing the country, progress versus ecological conservation, and the elimination of income tax deductions for children to discourage population growth. Pollution was seen as the most important problem in America by 20 percent of the sample. Conservation was supported over progress by 56 percent. Only 29 percent felt that income tax deductions for children should be eliminated.

241. Erskine, Hazel. "The Polls: Pollution and Its Costs." *Public Opinion Quarterly* 36 (Spring 1972): 120–35.

This review article features survey items and results from several early polls on pollution. Topics for the polls include concern over pollution, perception of amount of government spending on pollution, and willingness to spend money to solve the problem. Excerpts are reprinted from the following polls: the California Poll (three polls during 1969–70), Gallup Poll for the National Wildlife Federation (February 1969), Gallup Poll (October 1970), Gallup Poll for *Newsweek* magazine (October 1969), Harris (several polls between 1965 and 1971), Harris for the National Wildlife Federation (July 1969), Minnesota Poll (1965, 1967, 1969–71), Opinion Research Corporation (eight polls between 1965 and 1971), Roper (October 1971), and Roper for *Fortune* magazine (1940). All of the polls involved national samples except for the Minnesota and California Polls. Sample sizes are not given, but results are broken down by size of community and geographic region for several of the polls. (Results of the Gallup Poll for *Newsweek* magazine are presented elsewhere.)

242. Erskine, Hazel. "The Polls: Pollution and Industry." *Public Opinion Quarterly* 36 (Summer 1972): 263–80.

In this article, the author offers results from several early polls conducted on the public's perception of the causes of environmental pollution. The exact wording of the interview items and the break down of responses are presented. Topics covered by the polls include perceptions of antipollution efforts and support for different approaches to prevent further pollution. The article reprints excerpts from the following polls: the California Poll (March 1969), Gallup Poll for the National Wildlife Federation (February 1969), General Electric (May 1970, September 1971), Harris (six polls between 1966 and 1971), Iowa Poll (January 1971), Minnesota Poll (January 1967, August 1970), University of Michigan, Survey Research Center (November–December 1970, January 1971), and Opinion Research Corporation (five polls between 1965 and 1971). All of the polls surveyed national samples except the Iowa, California, and Minnesota Polls. The General Electric poll of September 1971 featured a student sample. Sample sizes are not provided, but results are broken down for some poll items by geographic region and size of community. (Results of the Harris July 1967 poll are presented elsewhere.)

243. Doran, Rodney L.; Guerin, Robert O.; and Sarnowski, Alfred A., Jr. "Assessing Students' Awareness of Environmental Problems." *Journal of Environmental Education* 5 (Summer 1974): 14–18.

In this article, the authors describe the development of an instrument to measure the environmental perceptions, beliefs, attitudes, and values of students. The problems chosen for the study were the following: air pollution, water pollution, noise pollution, land pollution, and a miscellaneous category. In order to test the instrument, junior high students were asked to view slides of local environmental scenes and respond to questions about the existence of the featured environmental problems in their communities. The article describes development of the instrument but does not present specific results of its testing. Included in the article are reviews of other surveys concerning environmental attitudes of school age children.

244. "Population Curb Is Backed in Poll." *The New York Times*, December 1, 1974, p. A47.

This article presents results from a study entitled, "State of the Nation— 1974," sponsored by Potomac Associates of Washington, D.C. The Gallup Organization performed the survey in April 1974 with a sample of 1,865 Americans. The survey respondents were asked their perceptions of population and economic growth and whether limits would eventually need to be set to prevent shortages. Additional questions concerning progress on controlling air and water pollution and the amount of government spending on pollution were also included. Nearly two-thirds (64 percent) of the sample believed world growth would have to be contained, while 54 percent felt growth in their local area should also be regulated. Although the survey showed support for increased spending for air and water pollution, approval for such spending was lower than in a similar survey conducted two years before.

245. *The Harris Survey Yearbook of Public Opinion 1972: A Compendium of Current American Attitudes*. New York: Louis Harris and Associates, Inc., 1976, p. 131.

A nationwide poll was conducted in May 1972 in which the respondents were asked to name two or three of the biggest problems facing Americans that they would like to see the next president address. Pollution concerns were cited by 13 percent of the respondents. Multiple responses were received from some respondents. (The sample size and methodology for this survey are not given.)

246. *The Harris Survey Yearbook of Public Opinion 1973: A Compendium of Current American Attitudes*. New York: Louis Harris and Associates, Inc., 1976, p. 205.

This annual collection of the Harris Survey includes a nationwide poll on the nation's most important problems conducted in September 1973. (The sample size and methodology are not specified.) When the respondents were asked to name two or three of the biggest national problems that they would like to see something done about, 11 percent of the subjects identified pollution and ecology concerns. Multiple responses were received from some respondents.

247. Althoff, Phillip and Grieg, William H. "Environmental Pollution Control: Two Views from the General Population." *Environment and Behavior* 9 (September 1977): 441–56.

The purpose of this study was to examine public opinion in one state toward environmental pollution and pollution control. Funding for the research was provided by the Student Originated Studies Program of the U.S. National Science Foundation. A sample of 471 residents of Kansas completed a mail questionnaire. The survey instrument questioned the respondents about their environmental concern for the current state of environmental pollution, trust in government and industry to solve pollution problems, support for certain pollution control policies, and personal commitment to solving pollution problems. Analysis of the surveys documented the following: high concern for environmental pollution, low trust in government and industry to solve pollution problems, low dedication to environmental protection, and moderate personal commitment to solving environmental problems such as pollution. When the data were analyzed by various demographic variables, two opinion groups were identified on the basis of social class and geographic residence.

248. Gallup, George H. "August 6, 1972: Most Important Problem." *The Gallup Poll: Public Opinion 1972–1977*. Wilmington, DE: Scholarly Resources, Inc., 1978, p. 48.

The interview dates for this Gallup Poll were July 14 through 17, 1972. (The sample size and methodology for the survey are not provided.) When asked to identify the most important problem facing the nation at the time, concerns for pollution and the environment were named by 5 percent of the sample. The greatest percent of responses related to the Vietnam War. Multiple responses were received from some respondents.

249. Gallup, George H. "January 15, 1973: Community Problems." *The Gallup Poll: Public Opinion 1972–1977*. Wilmington, DE: Scholarly Resources, Inc., 1978, pp. 85–86.

In this Gallup Poll, respondents were asked their perception of the worst problem in their community. The survey was conducted in December 1972 with an undisclosed number of subjects. Only 3 percent of all respondents and 4 percent of residents of large cities identified pollution as their community's worst problem. Crime was perceived as the biggest problem by both the general sample and the large city subsample.

250. Gallup, George H. "March 11, 1973: Most Important Problem." *The Gallup Poll: Public Opinion 1972–1977*. Wilmington, DE: Scholarly Resources, Inc., 1978, pp. 101–2.

This compendium of polls performed by the Gallup Organization includes a poll conducted in February 1973 on the most important national problems. The sample size and methodology of the survey are not noted. When asked to identify the two most important problems facing the country at that time, 14 percent of the sample named pollution concerns. (Multiple responses were received from some respondents.) The greatest number of responses concerned the high cost of living. Responses are broken down for respondents under 30 years of age, college educated respondents, and nonwhites. The percent of responses related to pollution were slightly higher for younger and college educated respondents.

251. Gallup, George H. "February 5, 1976: Spending Priorities." *The Gallup Poll: Public Opinion 1972–1977*. Wilmington, DE: Scholarly Resources, Inc., 1978, p. 656.

This poll was conducted by the Gallup Organization during June 1975. An unspecified number of Americans were asked to choose three issues that they thought should be given highest priority if additional federal funds became available. Pollution and conservation issues were named by 4 percent of the respondents. (Multiple responses were received from some respondents.)

252. Gallup, George H. "April 10, 1977: Most Important Problem." *The Gallup Poll: Public Opinion 1972–1977*. Wilmington, DE: Scholarly Resources, Inc., 1978, p. 1040.

In this Gallup Organization poll, respondents were asked to identify the most important problem facing the country at the time. Only 4 percent of the respondents identified pollution and general environmental concerns. (Multiple responses were received from some of the subjects.) The poll was conducted between March 18 and 21, 1977, with an undisclosed sample of Americans.

253. Anderson, Richard W. and Lipsey, Mark W. "Energy Conservation and Attitudes Toward Technology." *Public Opinion Quarterly* 42 (Spring 1978): 17–30.

In the spring of 1974, the Psychology Department of Claremont Graduate School administered a 92-item questionnaire by mail to households in Claremont, California. The purpose of the questionnaire was to measure attitudes toward technology and reactions to the energy shortage of the early 1970s. In addition to the 155 Claremont residents, 100 undergraduate students at Claremont College completed the survey. One question asked of both groups was whether they thought science and technology would eventually solve most problems including pollution. Among the community respondents, 29 percent thought technology would solve most problems, 63 percent thought some problems would be solved, and 8 percent thought technology would solve few problems. The student sample was slightly more pessimistic with 17 percent viewing technology as being able to solve only a few problems. Funding for the study was supplied by the Council of Graduate Students at Claremont Graduate School.

254. "Pollution Is No. 1 Issue . . ." *National Wildlife*, June-July 1978, p. 32.

More than 40,000 *National Wildlife* readers returned a mail-in survey included in the February-March 1978 issue of the magazine. The survey included questions on the most important environmental issue, alternative energy sources, and the performance of the government on environmental issues. Fighting pollution was ranked by the readers as the most important national environmental issue. Over three-fourths of the respondents said they thought pollution could be cleaned up without a decrease in jobs or the standard of living. Developing an energy program was ranked second and received the most first-place votes. Of the eight issues addressed, a simpler life-style was ranked least important by the readers.

255. Mitchell, Robert Cameron. "Silent Spring/Solid Majorities." *Public Opinion* 2 (August-September 1979): 16–20, 55.

This article is a review of the results from several public opinion polls conducted during the middle to late 1970s on American concern for the environment. Topics for the polls described in the article include the following: pollution as a national problem, amount of government spending on the environment, environment-economy tradeoffs, and support for the environmental movement. Among the findings mentioned in the article are results from the following polls: Opinion Research Corporation (1975, 1977), Resources for the Future (1978), Cambridge Reports (February 1978), and National Opinion Research Center, General Social Surveys (1973–78).

256. "Student Attitudes." *The Chronicle of Higher Education*, January 28, 1980, p. 5.

This annual survey of U.S. college and university freshmen was conducted by the American Council on Education and the University of California at Los Angeles. In response to the statement, "Government is not controlling pollution," 84 percent of the female and 77 percent of the male students agreed. The survey also included a question about the importance of personal involvement in environmental cleanup.

257. "Pollution Controls Favored Over Jobs in Poll." *The New York Times*, October 19, 1980, section 11, p. 1.

In this *New York Times*/CBS News Poll, New Jersey registered voters were surveyed about their attitude toward environmental protection versus jobs. When asked, "Would you favor stricter governmental control of industrial pollution, even if it might mean fewer jobs?" 57 percent of likely voters responded "yes."

258. "Fact-File: Freshmen Characteristics and Attitudes." *The Chronicle of Higher Education*, February 9, 1981, p. 8.

This annual survey of college and university freshmen was conducted by the American Council on Education and the University of California at Los Angeles. Nearly 80 percent of the 187,000 freshmen surveyed said the U.S. government was not doing enough to control pollution. The results are broken down by attendance at two-year colleges, four-year colleges, universities, and predominantly black colleges. Students were also asked about the importance of personally participating in environmental issues.

259. Harris, Louis. "Substantial Majorities Indicate Support for Clean Air and Clean Water Acts." *The Harris Survey* 47 (June 11, 1981).

A nationwide sample of 1,250 adults were surveyed by telephone in May 1981. Respondents were asked their opinion of air and water standards and the Clean Air and Clean Water Acts. The survey found 40 percent of those polled thought air pollution standards did not go far enough to protect people's health, and 48 percent thought water pollution standards were not strict enough. Some responses are broken down by demographic variables.

260. *Baton Rouge State Times* Poll. *American Public Opinion Index: 1981.* Tallahassee, FL: Opinion Research Service, Inc., 1982.

This telephone poll was conducted by the *Baton Rouge State Times* with 1,031 residents of the Baton Rouge area. The poll included a question asking the respondents to rate the Louisiana state government's performance in controlling pollution in the state.

261. The Roper Poll. *American Public Opinion Index: 1981.* Tallahassee, FL: Opinion Research Service, Inc., 1982.

This Roper Poll was conducted in January 1981 by the Roper Organization. A national sample of 2,000 adults were polled by telephone. Respondents were asked to identify the problems of most concern to them personally. The sample was also asked about support for relaxing pollution controls and environmental regulations.

262. Tarrance Poll. *American Public Opinion Index: 1981.* Tallahassee, FL: Opinion Research Service, Inc., 1982.

Lance V. Tarrance and Associates of Houston, Texas, performed this survey in May 1981. A sample of 400 residents of the Houston area were polled by telephone. Included in the poll were questions about the respondent's perception of the most important problem facing the Houston area, the importance of the pollution problem, and the most serious type of pollution. The poll also asked those surveyed to indicate their preference for environmental protection or energy development.

263. American Jewish Committee Poll. *American Public Opinion Index: 1981.* Tallahassee, FL: Opinion Research Service, Inc., 1982.

This national telephone poll was conducted by the American Jewish Committee. The sample of 1,215 respondents were asked about the importance of reducing air and water pollution.

264. CBS News Poll. *American Public Opinion Index: 1981.* Tallahassee, FL: Opinion Research Service, Inc., 1982.

This CBS News Poll was conducted by telephone in January 1981 with a national sample of 1,512 adults. One question in the survey asked respondents if they thought federal spending to control pollution should be increased or decreased.

265. Gallup, George H. "April 19, 1981: Urban Problems." *The Gallup Poll: Public Opinion 1981.* Wilmington, DE: Scholarly Resources, Inc., 1982, pp. 82–83.

The interview date for this special Gallup Poll was November 12, 1980. The survey was sponsored by the Charles F. Kettering and Charles Stewart Mott Foundation and the National League of Cities. Residents of cities with a population greater than 50,000 were asked, "If you had a choice, would you like to move away from this city?" Those responding "yes" were asked what things about the city made them want to move away. Pollution problems were named by 8 percent of the respondents. Of the ten problems listed, pollution ranked fifth in motivating people to consider moving.

266. "Fact-File: Freshmen Characteristics and Attitudes." *The Chronicle of Higher Education*, February 17, 1982, p. 12.

This annual survey of college and university freshmen was conducted by the American Council on Education and the University of California at Los Angeles. The sample consisted of 192,000 freshmen at U.S. two-year colleges, four-year colleges, universities, and predominantly black colleges. When asked whether they agreed that the government was not controlling pollution, 78 percent strongly or somewhat agreed. Nearly one-fourth thought it was very important that they personally help to clean up the environment. The percentage of those personally committed to the environment was highest at predominantly black colleges.

267. Harris, Louis. "America Is Not Turning to the Right." *The Harris Survey* 63 (August 9, 1982).

The Harris Survey polled 1,250 adults nationwide by telephone during July 1982. Over 50 percent of the respondents said they favored strict enforcement of the Clean Air and Clean Water Acts.

268. "A Call for Tougher, Not Weaker, Antipollution Laws." *Business Week*, January 24, 1983, p. 87.

Louis Harris and Associates, Inc., conducted this national survey in January 1983 for *Business Week* magazine. Those polled were asked about their support for the Clean Air and Clean Water Acts. Other questions related to enforcement of factory pollution standards, power plant emission standards, and restrictions on hazardous waste dumping in waterways. Responses to the poll showed strong support for making the Clean Air and Clean Water standards more strict. Only 19 percent favored allowing power plants to burn coal and high-sulfur oil. Researchers found the strongest support for strengthening pollution standards among the respondents from western states.

269. "Fact-File: Freshmen Characteristics and Attitudes." *The Chronicle of Higher Education*, January 26, 1983, p. 12.

This article describes results from a survey of freshmen at U.S. two- and four-year colleges, universities, and predominantly black colleges. The poll is conducted annually by the American Council on Education and the University of California at Los Angeles. In response to the statement, "The government isn't controlling pollution," 79 percent of the male and female freshmen agreed. The 188,000 students sampled by the survey were also asked about their personal commitment to cleaning up the environment.

270. "Watt's Departure Is Helping Reagan." *Business Week*, December 19, 1983, p. 14.

Louis Harris and Associates, Inc., conducted this poll in November 1983 for *Business Week* magazine. The poll questioned 1,250 Americans about their support for enforcing the Clean Air and Clean Water Acts. Respondents were asked if they supported relaxing regulations against smokestack pollution from power plants, disposal of hazardous wastes, air pollution standards for national parks and wilderness areas, and factory discharge into lakes and rivers. The researchers found support for strengthening the Clean Air (53 percent) and Clean Water (62 percent) Acts. Only 13 percent thought a polluting factory should be allowed to stay open to provide jobs. The sample also opposed relaxing pollution standards for power plant smokestacks (80 percent), auto emissions (74 percent), and hazardous waste disposal (86 percent).

271. The Roper Survey. *American Public Opinion Index: 1982.* Lexington, KY: Opinion Research Service, Inc., 1984.

The Roper Organization interviewed 2,000 Americans in person during May 1982. One question in the poll asked respondents about their concern for air and water pollution from business operations.

272. "Fact-File: Freshmen Characteristics and Attitudes." *The Chronicle of Higher Education*, February 1, 1984, p. 14.

This annual survey is conducted by the American Council on Education and the University of California at Los Angeles. The poll studied the attitudes of 254,000 freshmen at U.S. two- and four-year colleges, universities, and predominantly black colleges. In response to the statement, "The government isn't controlling pollution," 80 percent of the freshmen agreed. Comparable results were received from students at the different types of academic institutions. The survey also included a question concerning personal involvement in environmental cleanup activities.

273. Harris, Louis. "Negative Reaction to Issues Could Determine Election." The *Harris Survey* 60 (July 16, 1984).

A nationwide sample of 1,259 likely voters were polled by the Harris Survey between July 2 and 7, 1984. When asked if they favored or opposed strict enforcement of air and water pollution controls, 85 percent said they favored enforcement.

274. Eagleton Poll. *American Public Opinion Index: 1983.* Lexington, KY: Opinion Research Service, Inc., 1985.

The Eagleton Poll is conducted by the Eagleton Institute of Politics at Rutgers University. A sample of 800 New Jersey residents were contacted by telephone and asked about maintaining antipollution laws versus relaxing the laws to promote job growth in the state.

275. Gallup, George Jr. "November 18: National Referendum." *The Gallup Poll: Public Opinion 1984.* Wilmington, DE: Scholarly Resources, Inc., 1985, pp. 234-50.

The interview dates for this poll conducted by the Gallup Organization were September 28 through October 1, 1984. Respondents were asked if they favored or opposed, "relaxing pollution controls to reduce costs to industry." Nearly two out of three said they opposed relaxing controls. The responses are broken down by sex, race, education, age, income, political party, and geographic region. The strongest opposition to easing pollution standards came from college graduates (82 percent) and residents of western states (73 percent). (Sample size and survey methodology are not specified.)

276. "Fact-File: Freshmen Characteristics and Attitudes." *The Chronicle of Higher Education,* January 16, 1985, p. 16.

This survey of 182,000 college freshmen was conducted by the American Council on Education and the University of California at Los Angeles. (The sample size and methodology of the survey are not described.) In response to the statement, "The government isn't controlling pollution," 78 percent of the students strongly or somewhat agreed. Respondents were also asked whether they thought helping to clean up the environment was an important objective for their personal lives. A breakdown is provided for students attending two-year colleges, four-year colleges, universities, and predominantly black colleges.

277. Yankelovich, Skelly, and White. *American Public Opinion Index: 1985.* Lexington, KY: Opinion Research Service, Inc., 1986.

This poll was conducted in July 1985 with 1,013 Americans. Included in the national telephone poll was a question about concern for environmental pollution.

278. "Fact-File: Freshmen Characteristics and Attitudes." *The Chronicle of Higher Education,* January 15, 1986, p. 36.

This survey of 192,000 freshmen was conducted by the American Council on Education and the University of California at Los Angeles. When asked to respond to the statement, "The government isn't controlling pollution," 78 percent of the freshmen agreed. The respondents were also asked whether they thought it was very important to help clean up the environment. Responses are broken down by attendance at different types of academic institutions.

279. Talmey Associates Poll. *American Public Opinion Index: 1986.* Boston, MA: Opinion Research Service, Inc., 1987.

Talmey Associates of Boulder, Colorado, performed telephone polls of Colorado residents in May and December 1986. Sample sizes for the two polls were 510 and 454 respectively. The April poll included questions on funding the purchase of open spaces and park areas and the most important problem facing the state. Pollution and the environment was ranked by the respondents as the number one problem that the state will have to face in the following two years. In December, poll respondents were again asked to identify the most important state problem as well as whether they supported increasing state spending on environmental clean up. This time, pollution and the environment was ranked second in importance after the economy and jobs. Both polls were sponsored by the *Denver Post* and NewsCenter 4 of Denver.

280. The Bailey Oklahoma Poll. *American Public Opinion Index: 1986.* Boston, MA: Opinion Research Service, Inc., 1987.

The Bailey Oklahoma Poll is performed by Opinion Research/KDB Associates, Inc., of Tulsa, Oklahoma. In October and December 1986, an undisclosed number of Oklahoma residents were interviewed by telephone for a poll which included questions on the environment. Respondents to the October poll were queried about the extent of their concern for air and water pollution and toxic wastes. In the December poll, interviewers requested the respondents to indicate a preference for solving the litter problem by either a law requiring a beverage container deposit or by educating the public about recycling.

281. Blum, Abraham. "Students' Knowledge and Beliefs Concerning Environmental Issues in Four Countries." *Journal of Environmental Education* 18 (Spring 1987): 7–13.

This study compared the environmental knowledge and beliefs of students in four countries: United States, Australia, England, and Israel. Data from five separate surveys of over 42,000 ninth through twelfth grade students were used to measure environmental knowledge and beliefs. The researcher found that the sex and general achievement level of the students were associated with environmental knowledge. The students' rankings of environmental problems differed by country. Students in the United States ranked pollution as the most serious environmental problem, while students in Israel and Australia ranked road accidents as being most serious. English students ranked population density as most serious in one survey and failed to select one specific environmental problem as being most serious in another survey.

282. "Pollution Control Favored, Poll Finds." *Boston Globe,* March 31, 1987, p. B18.

The poll described in this article was performed by the Hospital Trust–University of Rhode Island with 418 Rhode Island residents. The date and method of the poll are not given. When asked if they would be willing to pay higher energy costs if pollution could be reduced, 71 percent agreed.

283. Consumer Research Center Poll. *American Public Opinion Index: 1987.* Boston, MA: Opinion Research Service, Inc., 1988.

This national telephone poll was conducted in April 1987 with a sample of

5,000 Americans. One of the items included in the poll solicited perceptions of the seriousness of the nation's pollution problem.

284. "Fact-File: Attitudes and Characteristics of This Year's Freshmen." *The Chronicle of Higher Education,* January 20, 1988, p. A36.

This article presents results from an annual survey of freshmen at U.S. two- and four-year colleges, universities and predominantly black colleges. The survey was conducted by the American Council on Education and the University of California at Los Angeles with a sample of 210,000 students. In response to the statement, "The government isn't controlling pollution," 81 percent of the students agreed. Only 18 percent, however, said that they thought helping to clean up the environment was an important objective. Responses are broken down by sex of the students and type of academic institution.

285. Rubenstein, Norm. "AIDS in the Workplace." *Electric Perspectives,* Spring 1988, pp. 16–27.

This article includes a brief description of results from a survey of U.S. companies' top management on the biggest problems facing the country. The study was conducted by Allstate Insurance and *Fortune* magazine. Over 2,000 questionnaires were mailed to U.S. companies. Only 623 companies responded; two-thirds of the responses came from top management. Environmental pollution was ranked as the fifth biggest problem after the federal deficit, drug abuse, AIDS, and the country's negative balance of payments.

286. "Fact-File: Attitudes and Characteristics of This Year's Freshmen." *The Chronicle of Higher Education,* January 11, 1989, p. A34.

The American Council on Education and the University of California at Los Angeles conducted this survey of college freshmen. Over 222,000 freshmen at U.S. colleges and universities were contacted in this annual survey. When asked to respond to the statement, "The government isn't controlling pollution," 84 percent agreed. Results are broken down by sex and type of academic institution.

287. Bowman, James S., and Davis, Charles. "Industry and the Environment: Chief Executive Officer Attitudes, 1976 and 1986." *Environmental Management* 13 (March-April 1989): 243–49.

In this research, the attitudes of industry chief executive officers (C.E.O.s) toward environmental pollution were measured and compared with a prior sampling taken ten years earlier. Data were obtained from mail questionnaires sent to C.E.O.s of the 50 largest mining and manufacturing firms in Colorado, Montana, Utah, and Wyoming. A total of 137 executives (68 percent response rate) replied to the initial survey, and 84 (42 percent response rate) replied to the 1986 survey. Results of the study indicated that the executives were more supportive of environmental concerns in 1986 than 1976, although they were less likely to identify pollution as one of the nation's most serious problems. In 1986, they were also more likely to support eliminating or reducing present problems as opposed to preventing or minimizing future problems. A majority of the C.E.O.s thought tax credits should be offered to industry as an incentive to deal with pollution problems, but the percentage in support of this option was lower than in 1976. In 1976, a majority of the C.E.O.s thought pollution control was the primary responsibility of government, and in 1986, the executives thought the primary responsibility rested with industry.

288. Ward, Sam. "USA Today Snapshot." *USA Today,* April 3, 1989, p. 1A.

The poll featured in this graphic was conducted by the Roper Organization. The date, sample, and method of the survey are not given. Respondents were asked whether they felt various environmental problems would become serious problems in the next 25 to 50 years. Both air and water pollution were perceived as future threats by 82 percent of those surveyed, while 65 percent thought the greenhouse effect would become a serious problem.

289. Harris, Louis. "Public Worried About State of Environment Today and in Future." *The Harris Poll* 21 (May 14, 1989).

The Harris Poll surveyed 1,253 adults in a national telephone poll conducted in April 1989. This poll posed several questions about the environment including concern for specific environmental issues and willingness to pay higher taxes to protect the environment. Nearly all (97 percent) of the respondents said the country should be doing more to protect the environment, and 81 percent were willing to pay higher taxes to prevent pollution.

290. Gallagher, Mike. "Wildlife Groups See Rolls Swell." *USA Today,* May 23, 1989, p. 3A.

This Media General/Associated Press telephone poll interviewed 1,084 adults by telephone between May 5 and 13, 1989. Those responding to the survey were asked their opinion of environmental regulations and the efforts of various groups to protect the environment. Antipollution regulations were seen as too weak by 75 percent of the sample. The majority of those surveyed rated the efforts of the government, business, and citizens to keep the environment clean as only "fair" or "poor." Toxic waste disposal and the quality of drinking water were identified as the environmental problems in greatest need of government attention. (Other details of this survey are presented elsewhere.)

291. ABC News/*Washington Post* Poll. *American Public Opinion Index: 1989.* Boston, MA: Opinion Research Service, Inc., 1990.

The ABC News/*Washington Post* Poll was completed in June 1989 with a national sample of 1,546 Americans. Two questions about air pollution were included in the telephone poll. Respondents to the survey were asked if electric companies should be required to cut emissions even if higher electric bills resulted. Another question inquired about support for raising income taxes to clean up the country's air and water.

292. Blue Grass Poll. *American Public Opinion Index: 1989.* Boston, MA: Opinion Research Service, Inc., 1990.

The Blue Grass Poll was conducted by the *Courier-Journal* and the *Louisville Times* of Louisville, Kentucky. A sample of 609 Kentucky residents were contacted by telephone and asked how much state money should be spent to reduce air and water pollution. Results of the poll were released on August 6, 1989.

293. University of Kansas Poll. *American Public Opinion Index: 1989.* Boston, MA: Opinion Research Service, Inc., 1990.

The University of Kansas, Institute for Public Policy and Business Research completed this telephone poll in February 1989. A sample of 465 Kansas residents were asked its opinion of funding for pollution cleanup and prevention programs.

294. "Pollution, Waste Concern Ohioans." *Columbus Dispatch*, June 5, 1990, p. 7C.

The Ohio Poll detailed in this article was conducted by the University of Cincinnati's Institute for Policy Research. Between April 27 and May 4, 1990, 628 Ohio adults were surveyed in this poll sponsored by the *Dayton Daily News*, the *Cincinnati Post* and WKRC-TV. Included in the interview was a question soliciting respondent opinions on the most important problem facing the state of Ohio. Two environmental issues, pollution and solid waste disposal, were named as the most important problems in Ohio by 20 percent of the sample. Only drug and alcohol abuse was of more concern to those polled.

295. "Most People Want Tough Restrictions on Pollution, Poll Says." *The Atlanta Constitution*, June 12, 1990, p. F4.

A national sample of 1,143 adults were surveyed in this poll conducted by Media General and the Associated Press during May 1990. Topics of the poll included environmental problems in need of government action, perception of anti-pollution laws, and support for mandatory recycling and bans on certain products. Toxic waste disposal and drinking water pollution were identified as the environmental problems most in need of urgent government action. A large majority supported mandatory recycling and bans on certain types of packaging, foam containers and disposable diapers. Only approximately one in five respondents said they considered a manufacturer's record on the environment when making purchase decisions. (Other findings from this survey are presented elsewhere.)

296. Scarlett, Harold. "Texans Surprise Pollster." *Houston Post*, October 2, 1990, p. A9.

The Texas Poll presented in this article was performed by Rice University between July 28 and August 12, 1990. (Other aspects of this poll are described elsewhere.) A sample of 1,000 Texans were contacted by telephone and interviewed regarding support for environmental protection measures and preference for environmental protection or economic development. Over two-thirds of those surveyed said they disagreed with the notion that jobs must take priority over protection of the environment. A large majority supported closing down polluting plants and prosecuting pollution regulation violators. In addition, 77 percent said they would oppose a new plant in their area if it would produce significant pollution. New funding to develop parks and recreation areas was supported by three-fourths of the sample.

297. Chivas Regal Report. *American Public Opinion Index: 1990*. Tallahassee, FL: 1991.

This telephone survey was conducted by Research and Forecasts, Inc., of New York. A sample of 251 Americans was asked to indicate the degree of personal concern for environmental pollution.

298. Flint, Anthony. "Freshmen Attitudes in Flux." *Boston Globe*, February 3, 1991, p. A25.

This article reports the results of an annual survey of college freshmen conducted by the University of California at Los Angeles and the American Council on Education. A total of 194,182 students at 382 two- and four-year colleges and universities completed the questionnaires. Included in the survey were questions about federal efforts to control environmental pollution and the importance of personal commitment to environmental protection. A large majority (88 percent) of the students said, "The federal government isn't doing enough to control environmental pollution." This percentage was 10 points higher than the result received in a similar poll conducted in 1981. Becoming involved in programs to clean up the environment was seen as "essential" or "very important" to 34 percent of the freshmen.

299. Anderson, Bob. "Poll Shows Residents Feel Pollution Problem Serious." [Baton Rouge] *Morning Advocate,* January 14, 1992.

During December 1991, Loyola University administered a telephone poll to 900 Louisiana voters for the *Morning Advocate.* Respondents to the poll were asked their perception of the state's pollution problem and the state government's role in protecting the environment. Pollution in Louisiana was rated as "serious" or "extremely serious" by more than 80 percent of the sample. Slightly more than half thought the state government was doing a good job in protecting the environment. Environmental concerns ranked sixth (out of nine problems) in importance.

300. Manning, Anita. "Thinking Green: Adults May Not, but Kids Call Saving Earth 'Their Mission'." *USA Today,* April 22, 1994, p. 1A.

This article notes findings from two polls on commitment to environmental protection. The National Opinion Research Center poll showed 56 percent of adults supporting increased spending on the environment, down from 75 percent in 1990. Louis Harris conducted the second poll with 10,375 schoolchildren who ranked the environment second in a list of concerns and identified pollution as one of the problems they would most like to fix.

WATER POLLUTION

301. Gallup, George H. "May 16, 1973: Water Resources." *The Gallup Poll: Public Opinion 1972–1977.* Wilmington, DE: Scholarly Resources, Inc., 1978, p. 122.

In March 1973, the Gallup Organization polled Americans about their perception of pollution as a threat to the safety of their water supply. (The sample size and methodology are not provided.) Approximately one-third thought pollution was a "great threat" to drinking water, another third thought pollution was "somewhat of a threat," and the remaining third thought there was "no threat" to their drinking water or had no opinion.

302. Harris, Louis. "Pure Water of Concern." *Chicago Tribune,* July 20, 1978, section 3, p. 4.

This newspaper editorial page column details the results of a Harris Survey poll conducted on American attitudes toward different types of environmental pollution. The Harris Survey interviewed 1,567 adult Americans from across the nation. (The date of the poll is not specified in the article.) In the survey, the respondents were asked about the degree of their concern for 13 different forms of pollution. The greatest amount of concern was expressed for factory pollution of lakes and rivers, industrial air pollution, toxic chemical pollution, ocean pollution, and automobile and truck air pollution. Over 50 percent of the sample said they were very concerned about these five types of pollution. Lower percentages were very worried about other forms of pollution such as solid waste disposal, household sewage, and the effect of strip mining on the landscape.

303. "Are Americans Willing to Spend More . . ." *National Wildlife*, April-May 1980, p. 28E.

This survey was based on the responses of 43,000 readers of *National Wildlife* to a mail-in "Action Ballot" inserted in the February-March 1980 issue of the magazine. The survey asked the readers their view of spending for the environment and wildlife, sources of energy, and the most pressing environmental issues. Almost two-thirds of the responding readers wanted spending for environmental protection increased, while 85 percent supported spending more for wildlife programs. "Cleaning up and conserving water" was ranked as the most important national environmental problem.

304. Worsham, James. "U.S. Opposes Diluting Clean-Water Law, Poll Says." *Chicago Tribune*, December 16, 1982, section 1, p. 10.

This Harris Survey was commissioned by the Natural Resources Council of America and funded by the Council, the Rockefeller Brothers Fund, and the American Fishing Tackle Manufacturers Association. The survey was based on telephone interviews completed during November 1982 with two groups of more than 1,200 Americans. (Additional aspects of this study are presented elsewhere.) Nearly three-fourths of those surveyed thought curbing water pollution was one of the most important factors in maintaining the quality of life in America. Of the respondents, 89 percent thought water pollution control efforts would not have to be sacrificed to achieve economic growth. The article notes that this percentage is 25 points higher than the response received to a similar question in a 1975 poll.

305. Harris, Louis. "Americans Want Strict Standards on Water Pollution." *The Harris Survey* 101 (December 16, 1982).

A national telephone poll of 1,250 adults was conducted October 29 through November 1, 1982, by the Harris Survey. The respondents were asked about their opinion of the Clean Water Act and whether water pollution cleanup should be slowed to stimulate the economy. A majority (60 percent) of the sample said they wanted the Clean Water Act made tougher. Only 3 percent supported weakening it. Almost 90 percent of those polled said it was possible to clean up water pollution and have economic growth.

306. *University of Kentucky Fall Poll, 1984.* Lexington, KY: University of Kentucky Survey Research Center, 1984, 18 pp.

This poll was conducted by the University of Kentucky's Survey Research Center for the Kentucky Division of Water. A sample of 441 Kentucky residents were contacted by telephone and asked about water pollution and fines for water pollution violations. Only 5 percent of those surveyed said they would be willing to tolerate increased water pollution in order to increase economic growth. While two-thirds of the sample agreed that the earth's resources are limited, only one-third thought human modifications of the environment cause serious problems.

307. Florida Annual Policy Survey. *American Public Opinion Index: 1984.* Lexington, KY: Opinion Research Service, Inc., 1985.

The Policy Sciences Program at Florida State University conducted this telephone poll with 911 residents of Florida. Those responding to the survey were asked their opinion of the amount of state spending for environmental protection and to identify the most important problem in Florida. Another question asked the sample about their willingness to pay for an annual beach pass to provide money for beach preservation in the state.

308. Gallup, George Jr. "December 1, 1988: Environmental Problems." *The Gallup Poll: Public Opinion 1988*. Wilmington, DE: Scholarly Resources, Inc., 1989, pp. 247–50.

This telephone survey was conducted between September 25 and October 1, 1988, with an undisclosed sample. Those responding to the poll were asked to rate their concern for four specific environmental pollution problems. Pollution of the ocean and beaches and pollution of drinking water were rated as being of "extreme concern" to 66 percent of the sample. Lower percentages of the respondents were extremely concerned about air pollution (50 percent) and garbage and trash disposal (41 percent). Responses are broken down by sex, education, geographic region, age, and political party. The groups which indicated the greatest concern for pollution problems were females, residents of eastern states, and respondents aged 50 years and older.

309. University of Pittsburgh Poll. *American Public Opinion Index: 1988*. Boston, MA: Opinion Research Service, Inc., 1989.

The University of Pittsburgh's Center for Social and Urban Research conducted this special poll on oil spills in June 1988. The sample for the telephone poll consisted of 653 residents of Robinson and North Fayette townships in Pennsylvania where an oil spill had occurred sometime prior to the taking of the poll. Respondents to the survey were asked about their perception of the effect of oil spills and the threat of oil spills to the environment and quality of life in the area.

310. *The Star Ledger*/Eagleton Poll. *American Public Opinion Index: 1989*. Boston, MA: Opinion Research Service, Inc., 1990.

This telephone poll was performed by the Eagleton Institute of Politics at Rutgers University. A sample of 800 New Jersey residents was asked about concern for ocean pollution and support for funding ocean beach cleanup. The results of the poll were released on July 2, 1989.

311. ABC News/*Washington Post* Poll. *American Public Opinion Index: 1989*. Boston, MA: Opinion Research Service, Inc., 1990.

This national telephone poll was conducted by ABC News and the *Washington Post* in August 1989. As part of the survey, an unspecified number of respondents were questioned about their perception of tanker shipping regulations.

312. Miko, Chris John, and Weilant, Edward. *Opinions '90: Extracts from Public Opinion Surveys and Polls Conducted by Business, Government, Professional and News Organizations*. Detroit: Gale Research, Inc., 1991, pp. 221–29.

This reference book of polls from 1990 includes a section on the environment which summarizes results from nine polls. The topics for these polls include the following: disposable diapers, oil drilling, environmentalism, spending on the environment, industry and the environment, pollution, state of the environment, and sacrifices for the environment. One of the polls was conducted by the Public Policy Resources Laboratory of Texas A&M University for Harte-Hanks Communications, Inc. The poll, which asked respondents their opinion of oil tanker regulations and creation of an emergency response fund, was conducted during August 1990 after an oil spill occurred off the Texas coast. Over three-fourths (79 percent) of the 1,021 Texans surveyed favored stricter regulations on oil tankers, even at an increased cost of oil to consumers. (The other polls included in this source are described elsewhere.)

AIR POLLUTION

313. "Survey Finds Public Upset on Pollution." *The New York Times*, July 25, 1967, p. A14.
   This newspaper item describes results of a national Harris Survey. Details on the interview dates, sample size, and sampling methodology are not included. The poll measured perceptions of causes and degree of air pollution and satisfaction with government and industry efforts to limit pollution. Subjects were asked about their willingness to accept a degree of pollution for a stable economy and willingness to pay increased taxes to control pollution. By a two-to-one margin, the respondents felt industry and the government were doing a poor job of curbing air pollution. Those surveyed were nearly evenly divided on whether they would be willing to pay an additional $15 in taxes per year for pollution control.

314. Swan, James A. "Response to Air Pollution: A Study of Attitudes and Coping Strategies of High School Youths." *Environment and Behavior* 2 (September 1970): 127–52.
   This paper is based on the author's doctoral dissertation on high school students' concern and response to air pollution. The first phase of the research measured concern for air pollution, knowledge of air pollution, and visual awareness of air pollution. The sample for this phase of the study was 173 male senior class students attending a high school in Detroit, Michigan. The second phase involved 56 of the students who had been identified during phase one as being highly concerned about air pollution. These students participated in a game situation where their response to a specific air pollution problem was measured. Results from the study showed that concern for air pollution was not related to either knowledge of air pollution or response to the problem in the gaming situation. When asked to rank spending for various domestic programs, air pollution control was ranked third of twelve programs by the students.

315. "New Type of Gallup Poll Finds Most Favor Total Pullout in '71." *The New York Times*, November 3, 1970, p. 39.
   In this article, a new sampling method for Gallup Polls is described. The Gallup Organization distributed written questionnaires to households in representative counties in four geographic regions of the country. The four counties were New London, Connecticut; Shelby, Tennessee; Montgomery, Illinois; and San Luis Obispo, California. Responses were returned by 1,400, or more than 70 percent, of the families selected for the survey. Another sample survey was taken to confirm the findings of the four counties poll. One question included in the survey asked for opinions on requiring antipollution devices on automobiles. The proposal was supported by 79 percent of the households. The polls were performed in October 1970.

316. Murch, Arvin W. "Public Concern for Environmental Pollution." *Public Opinion Quarterly* 35 (Spring 1971): 100–8.

Duke University performed this survey by administering a mail survey to 205 residents of Durham, North Carolina. The residents were asked about their awareness of environmental problems, their perception of responsibility for the problems, and their opinion of possible solutions. Although at the time, air pollution in Durham exceeded the national average, only 13 percent thought it was a serious problem in the area. Nearly three-fourths of the respondents, however, thought pollution nationally was a serious problem.

317. "What America Really Thinks About Pollution Cleanup." *National Wildlife*, April-May 1972, p. 18–19.

The Gallup Organization performed the nationwide survey described in this article for the National Wildlife Federation. The sample size and details of the survey's methodology are not given. Respondents to the poll answered questions about their willingness to spend more and to live a simpler life-style to protect the environment. Over half of those surveyed said they were "deeply concerned" about the environment and its problems, and nearly three-fourths were willing to spend at least an additional $10 each year to protect their natural surroundings. When asked how they would choose to handle pollution, nearly half were willing to live more simply and buy a less powerful car that caused less pollution. To reduce pollution from power plants, 40 percent were willing to reduce their use of electricity. Differences in results based on socioeconomic and demographic variables are discussed.

318. Eastman, Clyde; Randall, Alan; and Hoffer, Peggy L. "How Much to Abate Pollution?" *Public Opinion Quarterly* 38 (Winter 1974-75): 574–84.

The research described in this article was conducted by the staff of New Mexico State University with funding from the New Mexico Agricultural Experiment Station. The purpose of the study was to measure the willingness of environmental users to pay for pollution abatement. Indian reservation residents (N = 71), nonreservation residents (N = 526), and tourists and recreationists (N = 150) in the Four Corners region of New Mexico comprised the sample for the study. Bidding games were devised to explore how much money the residents and recreationists were willing to pay for pollution abatement as well as how much money the subjects were willing to accept as pollution compensation. The researchers devised separate games to measure response to different payment options including increased electric bills, increased sales taxes, an additional nonspecific monthly payment, and increased user fees.

319. *The Harris Survey Yearbook of Public Opinion 1971: A Compendium of Current American Attitudes.* New York: Louis Harris and Associates, Inc., 1975, pp. 257–62.

This annual collection of Harris Survey results includes a nationwide poll conducted in June 1971 that contained several items related to the environment. (The sample size and methodology are not given.) The subjects were asked about their perception of the amount of local air and water pollution, the connection between pollution and jobs, and willingness to pay increased taxes for pollution control. The respondents rated average citizens as doing the least to help control air pollution. Almost two-thirds of the sample thought some pollution was unavoidable if industry was to provide jobs. Over half said they would be willing to pay $15 more in taxes to finance pollution control.

320. "California Acts on Auto Emission." *The New York Times*, March 23, 1975, p. A60.

This newspaper item includes results from the California Poll conducted in February 1975 by the Mervin Field organization. Questions about auto emissions and gas mileage were asked of 1,011 Californians. When asked to choose between high gas mileage and clean exhaust emissions, 75 percent of respondents chose the clean emissions. The same percentage of respondents said they felt the auto industry could provide both better gas mileage and clean exhausts.

321. Public Opinion on Environmental Issues: *Results of a National Public Opinion Survey*. Council on Environmental Quality, 1980, 49 pp.

This publication describes findings from a national public opinion survey conducted by Resources for the Future for the Council on Environmental Quality. This council is composed of agencies of the U.S. Department of Agriculture, U.S. Department of Energy, and the Environmental Protection Agency. The sample design and field work for the study were performed by the Roper Organization and Cantril Research, Inc. Between January and April 1980, a sample of 1,576 Americans were interviewed on the following topics: attitudes toward growth and energy, concern for environmental problems, opinion of the environmental movement, knowledge of environmental issues, and attitudes toward environmental and economic trade-offs. In this document, results from the Resources for the Future study are compared with results from prior surveys on these issues. Concern for one environmental problem, air pollution, appeared to decline during the 1970s. Only 23 percent of respondents to the 1980 poll said they were concerned "a great deal" about reducing air pollution. In a June 1972 poll by Potomac Associates, 60 percent of the respondents indicated they had a great deal of concern for the problem. (Additional results from this survey are presented in other entries.)

322. Harris, Louis. "Clean Air Act Amendments Are Meeting with Public Resistance." *The Harris Survey* 83 (October 15, 1981).

This Harris Survey polled 1,249 adults by telephone from September 19 to 24, 1981. Respondents to the survey were asked about their perception of the strictness of the Clean Air Act and whether any changes should be made in the act. The sample were also asked whether pollution standards affecting public health should be eased if the costs of enforcement are too high. Almost two-thirds of the adults surveyed said they opposed relaxing standards. Responses are broken down by demographic variables.

323. "Americans Found to Oppose Any Relaxing of Clean Air Act." *The New York Times*, December 13, 1981, section 1, p. 78.

The research noted in this brief newspaper item was conducted by the Opinion Research Corporation for the U.S. Chamber of Commerce. Details on the sample and survey methodology are not included. The national survey found no support among the public for lowering air quality standards or weakening the Clean Air Act.

324. "Clean Air Tops Illinois Survey." *Chicago Tribune*, February 18, 1982, section 1, p. 16.

The survey described in this newspaper item was sponsored by the Chicago Lung Association. A total of 1,400 voters in northern Illinois and the Chicago area were surveyed. Respondents were questioned about their opinion of the Clean Air Act, air standards versus economic growth, and their willingness to pay for air pollution control. Nearly three of every four voters were willing to pay more for air pollution control. A smaller percentage (59 percent) said clean air standards should not be weakened to provide for economic growth.

325. Eagleton Poll. *American Public Opinion Index: 1984.* Lexington, KY: Opinion Research Service, Inc., 1985.

A sample of 804 New Jersey residents were polled by the Eagleton Institute of Politics at Rutgers University about pollution and chemical wastes in New Jersey. The survey included questions about perceptions of pollution and chemical wastes as serious problems in New Jersey and current clean air standards. In addition, respondents were asked whether they would support efforts to reduce air pollution if increased taxes were a result.

326. Yankelovich, Skelly, and White Poll. *American Public Opinion Index: 1984.* Lexington, KY: Opinion Research Service, Inc., 1985.

During 1984, five national telephone polls performed by Yankelovich, Skelly, and White asked respondents to identify the most important problem facing the country. The results of these polls were released on February 2, August 9, September 13, October 25, and December 12. The February 2 poll also asked about the respondents concern for air pollution. Sample size for the polls was 1,021.

327. Seiler, Michael. "3 of 4 in State Would Pay to Help Clean Up Smog." *The Los Angeles Times*, December 17, 1986, section 2, pp. 1, 3.

The poll presented in this article was conducted by the University of Southern California's Institute of Politics for the governing board of the South Coast Air Quality Management District. Between November 8 and 17, 1986, 500 California residents were interviewed by telephone about their attitude toward various air pollution control measures and funding alternatives for controlling pollution. Over two-thirds of the respondents rated the government's performance in controlling air pollution as "fair" or "poor." Almost three-fourths of the sample approved of increases in gasoline taxes and new car prices to help pay to clean up the air.

328. 1986 Florida Annual Policy Survey. *American Public Opinion Index: 1986.* Boston, MA: Opinion Research Service, Inc., 1987.

This telephone survey was conducted by the Policy Services Program at Florida State University. A sample of 929 Florida residents were asked about willingness to contribute to a fund to clean up the air in Florida. Another question requested an opinion on the amount of spending for environmental protection.

329. Rahmatian, Morteza. "Component Value Analysis: Air Quality in the Grand Canyon National Park." *Journal of Environmental Management* 24 (1987): 217–23.

This paper describes research designed to measure the preservation value of the Grand Canyon to the public. In the study, a sample of park users and nonusers from the Denver, Colorado, area were asked to place a dollar value on the preservation of the park by estimating the maximum amount they would be willing to pay in higher electric utility bills to preserve the air quality of the park. Interviews were conducted with 75 Denver residents during the fall of 1981. Each of the residents was shown a series of photographs depicting five different levels of visibility at one point on the south rim of the Grand Canyon. The article compares the amount subjects were willing to pay with different demographic variables: education, age, household size, income, and amount of monthly electric bill.

330. Stammer, Larry B. "43% Feel Business Should Foot Bill for Clean Air, Poll Finds." *The Los Angeles Times*, November 7, 1989, pp. B3–4.

The telephone poll reported on in this article was conducted by the Wirthlin Group for Hitachi Limited in September 1989. A sample of 400 residents of southern California were asked about air pollution controls and funding for air pollution cleanup. When asked who they thought should be "most responsible" for paying to clean up the air, 43 percent of the sample wanted major industry to pay for the cleanup. Nearly 60 percent said they supported air pollution restrictions even if it meant banning certain businesses from the area. Over half of the sample supported a five cent a gallon gasoline tax increase if the funds were used for transportation improvements. Nearly half of the people indicated they would not abide by regulations banning the use of backyard barbecues, aerosol sprays, and gas-powered mowers.

331. Gallup, George Jr. "October 11: Taxes." *The Gallup Poll: Public Opinion 1989.* Wilmington, DE: Scholarly Resources, Inc., 1990.

The Gallup Organization conducted this poll for Times Mirror during October 1989. An unspecified number of respondents were surveyed. Respondents were asked about their attitude toward the amount of federal spending to control air pollution. Almost 60 percent of the respondents said they wanted to see the amount of spending increased. Of 15 issues discussed in the poll, a greater percentage of the respondents thought spending should be increased on air pollution than all other issues except public education, drugs, the homeless, and health care.

332. ABC News/*Washington Post* Poll. *American Public Opinion Index: 1989.* Boston, MA: Opinion Research Service, Inc., 1990.

The ABC News/*Washington Post* Poll was completed in June 1989 with a national sample of 1,546 Americans. Two questions about air pollution were included in the telephone poll. Respondents to the survey were asked if electric companies should be required to cut emissions even if higher electric bills resulted and if they would support raising income taxes to clean up the country's air and water.

333. J. D. Franz Research Poll. *American Public Opinion Index: 1989.* Boston, MA: Opinion Research Service, Inc., 1990.

This poll was conducted by J. D. Franz Research of Sacramento, California, during February 1989. A sample of 1,106 residents of Sacramento County were interviewed by telephone. Respondents were asked about their perception of air quality in their community. Other questions inquired about life-style changes made and considered to reduce air pollution.

334. Harris, Louis. "Public Mood Has Hardened to Advocate Tougher, Stricter Laws on Air Pollution." *The Harris Poll* 13 (April 1, 1990).

A nationwide telephone survey of 1,254 adults was completed in March 1990 by the Harris Poll. The respondents were asked to rate the seriousness of specific air pollution problems. This article compares results from this poll to polls conducted in June 1982 and April 1986. Those completing the survey were also asked whether the Clean Air Act should be strengthened and whether a polluting factory should be granted an exemption from meeting environmental standards for any reason.

335. Harris, Louis. "Trend on Key Issues Is Moderate, No Longer Conservative." *The Harris Poll* 28 (July 8, 1990).

The Harris Poll was performed by telephone in June 1990 with a national sample of 1,254 adults. When asked how they felt about stricter auto emissions standards, 85 percent indicated they supported the proposal.

336. The California Poll. *American Public Opinion Index: 1991.* Tallahassee, FL: 1991.

The California Poll was performed by the Field Institute during July and December 1991. In July, approximately 2,000 Californians were interviewed by telephone about their support for different proposals to improve air quality by reducing auto emissions. The December poll reached 1,005 California citizens and asked their opinion of the amount of state spending for environmental regulations, parks and recreation facilities, and fish and game programs.

337. O'Neil Associates Poll. *American Public Opinion Index: 1991.* Tallahassee, FL: 1991.

O'Neil Associates, Inc., of Tempe, Arizona, contacted 752 residents of Maricopa County, Arizona, for a poll on air pollution. The March 1991 telephone poll asked those interviewed to indicate their willingness to make different personal life-style changes to improve air quality (fewer automobile trips, combined automobile trips, bus trips, car pooling, bicycle trips, and use of other city transit services).

338. "Clean Air a Concern, but Most Are Loath to Act." [New Jersey] *Record,* March 14, 1991, p. A5.

The Eagleton Institute of Politics conducted this poll for Project: Clean Air with 800 residents of New Jersey. (Interview dates and methodology are not given in the article.) Of those responding to the poll, only 16 percent rated the state's air quality as "poor." Traffic congestion was considered a "very serious" problem by nearly half of the sample, but only 19 percent said they would seriously consider using public transportation or car pools.

ACID RAIN

339. Harris, Louis. "The Power of Acid Rain." *Advertising Age,* February 20, 1984, pp. 20, 22.

This article is based on remarks made by the author to the Coalition of Northeastern Governors Conference on Acid Rain and Hazardous Waste held in December 1983. The remarks include findings from polls conducted in the early 1980s on concern for acid rain and hazardous waste and support for environmental antipollution regulations including the Clean Air and Clean Water Acts. (Specific details on the polls such as sample size, methodology, and survey date are not provided.) In one Harris Survey, over 90 percent of the respondents viewed hazardous waste, pollution of lakes and rivers, acid rain, and drinking water contamination as serious problems. The majority of the respondents thought the costs of cleaning up acid rain should be borne by individuals and businesses which use fuels that contribute to the problem (73 percent), shareowners of electric utilities (72 percent), and electric customers nationally (60 percent). Greater than two-thirds of those surveyed said they would be willing to pay up to $100 more each year in higher electric bills to clean up acid rain and water pollution.

340. "Top Issues? Taxes, Taxes, Taxes." *The Milwaukee Journal*, October 9, 1984, pp. 1, 12.

The poll described in this article was conducted by the *Milwaukee Journal* during September 1984. A sample of 998 Wisconsin residents were surveyed. Respondents were contacted by telephone and asked their perception of the importance of seven issues facing the state. Acid rain was viewed as "very important" by 21 percent, "important" by 36 percent, "somewhat important" by 28 percent, and "not important" by 12 percent. On the issue of Indian hunting and fishing rights, 17 percent thought it was "very important" and 28 percent thought it was an "important" issue. The article notes that while the concern for acid rain was found throughout the state, interest in the issue of Indian hunting and fishing rights was stronger in the northern part of the state.

341. The Roper Poll. *American Public Opinion Index: 1983*. Lexington, KY: Opinion Research Service, Inc., 1985.

In July and October 1983, the Roper Organization surveyed 2,000 Americans by personal interview. Both polls asked respondents about their perception of the seriousness of acid rain as an environmental problem. The October poll also included questions about the perceived seriousness of industrial air pollution, auto emissions, chemical waste contamination, and industrial water pollution.

342. North Star Poll. *American Public Opinion Index: 1984*. Lexington, KY: Opinion Research Service, Inc., 1985.

The North Star Poll is performed by the *St. Paul Dispatch and Pioneer Press*. In January 1984, 900 Minnesota residents were interviewed by telephone about their perception of the causes and extent of acid rain. Opinions were also solicited about different methods of funding acid rain reduction.

343. Kentucky Poll. *American Public Opinion Index: 1984*. Lexington, KY: Opinion Research Service, Inc., 1985.

This Kentucky Poll was performed by the University of Kentucky's Survey Research Center for the Kentucky Energy Cabinet. The telephone survey interviewed 757 Kentucky residents about their concern for acid rain and other environmental problems. A majority of the respondents indicated that they were "somewhat concerned" about acid rain. Greater concern, however, was expressed for other environmental problems including toxic waste disposal, nuclear power plants, protection of endangered species, unsafe drinking water, untreated sewage, and the preservation of farm land. When asked whether they would be willing to pay higher electric bills to reduce acid rain problems, 55 percent of the sample said "yes," while 38 percent said "no."

344. Ohio Poll. *American Public Opinion Index: 1984.* Lexington, KY: Opinion Research Service, Inc., 1985.

This telephone poll was conducted in January and in the spring of 1984 by the Institute for Policy Research at the University of Cincinnati. The sample sizes for the polls were 1,056 (January) and 1,044 (spring). Included in the polls were questions about the seriousness of the acid rain problem and willingness to pay higher electric bills to pay for acid rain cleanup.

345. Harris, Louis. "Acid Rain Clean Up: Who Should Pay?" *The Harris Survey* 27 (April 4, 1985).

A Harris Survey nationwide telephone survey was conducted from March 8 to 11, 1985. The sample of 1,254 adults were asked who should pay for acid rain cleanup. Of utility shareowners, electric customers nationally, and electric customers in coal burning states, the largest number of respondents thought it would be fair to expect the shareowners to pay for the cleanup. The responses are broken down by geographic region of the country.

346. Northeast Research Poll. *American Public Opinion Index: 1986.* Boston, MA: Opinion Research Service, Inc., 1987.

Northeast Research of Orono, Maine, performed this telephone poll in October 1986. A sample of 500 Maine residents were asked several questions about acid rain and the state forests of Maine. The poll asked the subjects about their concern for the effects of air pollution and acid rain on the state's forests and to identify the most important problem involving the forests. Respondents were also requested to rate the importance of various functions of the state's forests. Another question asked the subjects if they supported the state acquiring additional forest land for recreation, even if there would be a cost to the public.

347. The Roper Poll. *American Public Opinion Index: 1986.* Boston, MA: Opinion Research Service, Inc., 1987.

This Roper Poll, which was released on March 8, 1986, interviewed 1,993 Americans in person. The respondents were asked their opinion of the seriousness of the acid rain problem and whether they were personally concerned about toxic wastes in their area. In addition, one question asked for an opinion of the National Park Service and another asked those surveyed to rate the value of tax dollars spent on environmental protection.

348. "Acid Rain, Dirty Air Worry Americans." *National Wildlife*, December 1986-January 1987, p. 30.

Opinion Research Corporation conducted this poll for the National Wildlife Federation. A total of 1,000 Americans were surveyed. Respondents were asked their perception of the causes and seriousness of acid rain as well as their view of the change in air quality over the previous five years. Acid rain was viewed as a "very serious" or "somewhat serious" problem by 75 percent of the people polled.

349. Steel, Brent S., and Soden, Dennis L.. "Acid Rain Policy in Canada and the United States: Attitudes of Citizens, Environmental Activists, and Legislators." *The Social Science Journal* 26 (1989): 27–44.

This article presents an evaluation of the attitudes of citizens, environmental activists, and legislators in Michigan and Ontario toward the environmental problem of acid rain. Mail questionnaires were returned by 476 residents of Michigan and 600 residents of Ontario during the fall of 1985. In addition, 684 and 554 activists from Michigan and Ontario, respectively, and 71 and 63 Michigan and Ontario legislators completed the survey. A proposed moratorium on all acid rain causing activities was supported by a majority of all groups with the exception of the Michigan legislators. The Ontario public, activists, and legislators were more supportive of the moratorium than their American counterparts. The highest level of concern for acid rain was expressed by the environmental activists of each country, the lowest, by the legislators. The article briefly discusses the effect of political variables on the level of concern expressed by the respondents of the survey.

350. The West Virginia Poll. *American Public Opinion Index: 1988.* Boston, MA: Opinion Research Service, Inc., 1989.

The West Virginia Poll is conducted by Ryan-Samples Research of Charleston, West Virginia. In September 1988, a sample of 509 West Virginia residents were interviewed by telephone for a survey that included a few items related to environmental issues. One question requested the respondents to choose between stronger laws to protect the environment against acid rain or less strict laws to help the coal industry in the state. Those surveyed were also asked if they could accept out-of-state garbage being brought into the state if laws to protect the environment were passed. An additional question was posed to determine willingness to separate trash for a recycling program.

351. Harris, Louis. "Public Draws Line on Where New Tax Money Should Be Spent: Help the Needy First." *The Harris Poll* 12 (March 12, 1989).

A nationwide telephone poll survey was conducted in February 1989 by the Harris Poll. The sample of 1,250 adults answered questions about federal spending for various issues. Over two-thirds of those polled said they supported more federal spending on controlling acid rain and toxic waste disposal.

352. J. Walter Thompson Company Poll. *American Public Opinion Index: 1989.* Boston, MA: Opinion Research Service, Inc., 1990.

In February 1989, J. Walter Thompson Company of New York interviewed in person 2,100 adults from across the country. Included in the survey were several questions about government environmental regulations and spending as well as specific environmental problems. The respondents were asked if they supported stricter environmental controls and government spending to clean up acid rain and toxic waste dumps. Other questions solicited opinions on the greenhouse effect and soil and water contamination. Those surveyed were asked if they were willing to sacrifice economic growth for environmental protection and whether they would pay higher electric rates to reduce pollution.

353. Pokorny, Gene. "The Greening of America." *Electric Perspectives* 15 (March-April 1991): 16–25.

This is the first article in a two-part series authored by the chairman of Cambridge Reports/Research International. The article describes research conducted by his public opinion organization for the Edison Electric Institute on American customer opinions on environmental issues. The study, conducted in September 1990, included interviews with 1,250 adult Americans. Included in the article is a review of national surveys conducted on environmental issues since the early

1970s. Topics covered by the studies include several related to the electric power industry: acid rain, global climate effects, and disposal of nuclear wastes.

Greenhouse Effect/Ozone Depletion

354. "Iowans Approve Ban on Aerosols." *Current Opinion* 3 (September 1975): 85.

This monthly publication of the Roper Public Opinion Research Center includes results from the Iowa Poll on banning aerosol spray cans. The poll was conducted in June 1975 for the *Des Moines Register.* Of 600 adults sampled, 51 percent favored a ban until more could be learned about ozone depletion. The proposed ban was opposed by 39 percent.

355. "Connolly: Voters Back 'Greenhouse' Fight." *Boston Globe*, February 12, 1989, p. B32.

A survey of 603 Massachusetts Democrats and Independents was conducted during early 1989 for the Massachusetts secretary of state. (The exact interview date and survey methodology are not given.) Respondents to the survey were asked whether they thought state elected officials should be "devoting their time and resources into finding solutions to the greenhouse problem." Over two-thirds said they approved of efforts to fight the problem.

356. "Majority Very Concerned About Environmental Issues." *Journal of Environmental Health* 52 (September–October 1989): 74.

This article briefly describes results from three surveys dealing with concern for environmental issues and willingness to sacrifice to make improvements in the environment. One study conducted by Opinion Research Corporation revealed that 80 percent of the respondents were very concerned about environmental hazards. In another study released by Cambridge Reports, 55 percent of those sampled said they would pay more for environmentally friendly products. The third study was sponsored by the Roosevelt Center for American Policy Studies. This survey found that 47 percent of the respondents were worried about ozone depletion, while only 15 percent were worried about the threat of communism.

357. *Global Warming and Energy Priorities: A National Perspective.* Washington, DC: Research/Strategy/Management, Inc., November 1989, 22 pp.

Research/Strategy/Management, Inc., conducted this telephone poll for the Union of Concerned Scientists of Cambridge, Massachusetts, in November 1989. The 1,200 Americans who responded to the poll were asked questions about environmental problems and the global warming phenomenon. Of those surveyed, 60 percent indicated they were "extremely" or "somewhat worried" about global warming. Respondents were also asked about their concern for various effects of global warming and the importance of various benefits of using renewable energy resources. When asked to identify the most important environmental problem, 52 percent cited problems related to atmospheric quality, while 22 percent named water quality issues, and 19 percent said they were concerned about solid waste disposal.

358. Sperling, Dan. "Greenhouse Effect Has Some in Dark." *USA Today*, November 21, 1989, p. 1A.

The New York Power Authority conducted this survey of 1,003 adults living in New York state. (Interview dates and the survey methodology are not provided in the article.) Those responding to the survey were asked their perception of the greenhouse effect and global warming. After being informed of the greenhouse phenomenon, 81 percent of those polled said they were concerned about it, and 60 percent said action should be taken immediately to counteract it. The respondents indicated a preference for planting more trees and cutting down fewer ones as possible solutions.

359. *The Atlanta Journal/The Atlanta Constitution. American Public Opinion Index: 1989.* Boston, MA: Opinion Research Service, Inc., 1990.

In April 1989, 1,227 residents of 12 southern states were interviewed by telephone for a survey sponsored by the *Atlanta Journal* and *Atlanta Constitution*. The respondents were asked their perception of the seriousness of the greenhouse effect and their willingness to reduce driving and use of aerosol products to reduce the phenomenon. The respondents' opinion of the performance of business and government in protecting the environment was also solicited. Other questions inquired about attitudes toward environmental protection regardless of cost and willingness to pay increased income taxes to clean up the environment.

360. Florida Poll. *American Public Opinion Index: 1989.* Boston, MA: Opinion Research Service, Inc., 1990.

The Institute for Public Opinion Research at Florida International University performed this telephone poll during 1989. A total of 1,232 Florida residents answered questions about their degree of concern for global warming and attitude toward offshore oil drilling in Florida. Respondents were also asked about their support for regulation of wetlands, recycling, and recyclable product packaging, even if it resulted in increased product costs.

361. *America at the Crossroads: A National Energy Strategy Poll.* Washington, DC: Research/Strategy/Management, Inc., 1990, 23 pp.

The Union of Concerned Scientists and the Alliance to Save Energy sponsored this national telephone poll conducted by Research/Strategy/Management, Inc. A sample of 1,200 adults were asked about expanding offshore drilling and limiting carbon dioxide emissions to combat global warming. Expanding offshore drilling was opposed by 72 percent of the sample, while 79 percent were opposed to developing oil reserves on publicly owned wilderness land. Opinion on increased oil development in the Alaskan wilderness, however, was nearly evenly divided. By a margin of three to one, the subjects preferred decreasing energy demand over increasing supply. When asked if the United States should join other countries and commit to limits on carbon dioxide emissions or wait for further proof of global warming, over two-thirds wanted the United States to commit to limits. Those responding were also asked to indicate the maximum extra amount they would be willing to pay each month for fossil fuels to prevent global warming. Approximately two-thirds of the sample said they would be willing to spend up to $15 more each month.

362. The Global Warming Leadership Forum. *American Public Opinion Index: 1991.* Tallahassee, FL: 1991.

Citizens to Preserve Florida commissioned this telephone poll on global warming which was administered to 503 Florida voters. The interview asked voters whether the United States should commit to limiting carbon dioxide emissions or wait for further scientific confirmation of the problem and whether they supported a national energy policy to lower emissions. Those surveyed were also asked about the importance of global warming as an issue for presidential candidates to address.

363. Gallup, George Jr. "April 20: Environment." *The Gallup Poll: Public Opinion 1991.* Wilmington, DE: Scholarly Resources, Inc., 1992, pp. 86–90.
   This Gallup Poll was completed during April 1991 with an unspecified sample. Included in the survey were questions on concern for specific environmental problems and support for a ban on chlorofluorocarbons. Nationally, 78 percent of those surveyed said they consider themselves to be "environmentalists." Responses to this question are broken down by sex, ethnic background, education, region, age, income, and political ideology. Water pollution and soil and water contamination by toxic waste were the problems of greatest concern to the respondents. (The poll also measured concern for other environmental problems: air pollution, ocean pollution, loss of wildlife habitat, ozone layer depletion, nuclear waste contamination, loss of tropical rain forests, the greenhouse effect, and acid rain.) A majority felt it was necessary to take immediate, drastic action to prevent major environmental effects on life on earth. Almost 80 percent of the sample said they supported a ban on chlorofluorocarbons and other chemicals known to damage the ozone layer.

Toxic Waste

364. Harris, Louis. "Toxic Chemical Dumps: Corrective Action Desired." *ABC News–Harris Survey* 2 (July 7, 1980).
   This nationwide telephone poll of 1,493 likely voters was conducted by ABC News–Harris Survey between June 5 and 9, 1980. The respondents were asked about their perception of the seriousness of toxic waste dumping, responsibility for dumps near residential areas, and alternatives for dealing with toxic waste dumps. Over three-fourths of the sample thought toxic waste dumps were very serious. The sample was split on whether the federal government, local and state government, or individual companies were responsible for situations like Love Canal.

365. "A Recent Poll . . ." *The New York Times*, March 25, 1984, section 11, p. 3.
   The poll presented in this article was conducted by the *[Newark] Star Ledger* and the Eagleton Institute of Politics at Rutgers University. Over 800 New Jersey residents were interviewed between February 2 and 12, 1984, about their perception of the significance of the toxic waste problem. By a three-to-one margin, the respondents said they felt increasing concern for the health hazards posed by toxic wastes. Of five problems listed, toxic waste cleanup was perceived as the most serious, followed by water pollution, air pollution, unemployment, and inflation.

366. Georgia Fall Poll. *American Public Opinion Index: 1983.* Lexington, KY: Opinion Research Service, Inc., 1985.
   The Georgia Fall Poll is conducted by the Survey Research Center at the

University of Georgia. During October 1983, 531 Georgians were contacted by telephone and asked several questions about environmental issues. In response to the statement that strict environmental controls will make U.S. products less competitive, 52 percent of those surveyed agreed, while 33 percent disagreed. When asked about pollution of their drinking water, only one-fourth of the respondents said they were not concerned. The poll also included several questions about the location of hazardous waste sites. A large majority (70 percent) agreed that it would be better to have a hazardous waste site in their own area than have illegal dumping of wastes.

367. Twin Cities Area Survey. *American Public Opinion Index: 1983*. Lexington, KY: Opinion Research Service, Inc., 1985.

The Twin Cities Area Survey is conducted by the Minnesota Center for Social Research in the Department of Sociology at the University of Minnesota. Over 1,000 residents of the Twin Cities were contacted by telephone during 1983 and asked questions about support for environmental improvements in their area and perceptions of hazardous waste facilities. Almost 70 percent of the sample was willing to spend up to $50 in higher taxes or prices to improve environmental quality in the Twin Cities area. Nearly all of the respondents thought that hazardous wastes was an "important" or "very important" issue in Minnesota. Over two-thirds said the state should share part of the cost of building a hazardous waste treatment facility in the state, although a majority of those surveyed also thought that a facility should be funded by a tax on industry.

368. Indiana Poll. *American Public Opinion Index: 1983*. Lexington, KY: Opinion Research Service, Inc., 1985.

The Indiana Poll is performed by the Center for Survey Research at Indiana University. In January 1983, 800 residents of Indiana were interviewed by telephone and asked about their attitudes toward hazardous and toxic wastes and water pollution. For both issues, the respondents were asked if they preferred that efforts to control the problem be increased or decreased and whether they would be willing to pay added taxes to increase control efforts.

369. The Roper Poll. *American Public Opinion Index: 1984*. Lexington, KY: Opinion Research Service, Inc., 1985.

The Roper Poll was performed in February 1984 by interviewing in person 2,000 Americans from across the country. One issue included in the survey was perception of the amount of government regulation on the disposal of toxic wastes.

370. The Iowa Poll. *American Public Opinion Index: 1984*. Lexington, KY: Opinion Research Service, Inc., 1985.

The *Des Moines Register and Tribune* interviewed 1,004 Iowans by telephone and asked about their concern for various forms of environmental pollution and the amount of government spending for hazardous waste cleanup. Results of the poll were released on June 24, 1984.

371. Harris, Louis. "Environmental Pollution Causes Deep Concern." *The Harris Survey* 26 (April 1, 1985).

The Harris Survey interviewed by telephone 1,254 adults nationwide in March 1985. Respondents were asked to rate the seriousness of six environmental problems: hazardous waste disposal, factory pollution of lakes and rivers, contaminated drinking water, pollution from nuclear power plants, acid rain, and air pollution from coal-burning power plants. Disposal of hazardous wastes was seen as the most serious problem with 74 percent of the sample rating it as "very serious." Results from this survey are compared with responses to a February 1981 survey.

372. Harris, Louis. "Environmental Issues Could Become a Factor in Congressional Races." *The Harris Survey* 32 (May 19, 1986).
    This entry describes a nationwide telephone survey of 1,254 adults performed by the Harris Survey in early April 1986. Those responding to the survey were asked their opinion of the seriousness of various environmental problems, as well as who should pay for acid rain cleanup and injuries received from landfill wastes. The survey also asked about voting for candidates if the candidate's position on the environment differed from their own. In response to the question of whether Congress should establish a Superfund hazardous waste program, 67 percent said they favored appropriation of money for such a program.

373. *Capstone Poll 86.* University of Alabama, Institute for Social Science Research and School of Communication, December 8, 1986, 4 pp.
    The Capstone Poll is administered by the Institute for Social Science Research and School of Communication at the University of Alabama. This particular poll was conducted by telephone during November 1986 with 499 residents of Alabama. Respondents to the survey were asked to indicate their degree of concern for chemical wastes in the state and their perception of the threat to human health from toxic wastes. Over three-fourths of the sample said they were either "very concerned" or "somewhat concerned" about chemical wastes, and 58 percent thought toxic wastes posed a health threat. Exactly half of the residents supported a ban on burial of hazardous wastes in their state. Asked to "choose between maintaining strict antipollution laws to protect the public's health or relaxing those laws to create more jobs," 68 percent wanted strict laws maintained.

374. The California Poll. *American Public Opinion Index: 1986.* Boston, MA: Opinion Research Service, Inc., 1987.
    The Field Institute performed the California Poll in August 1986 with a sample of 1,028 Californians. Questions in the poll requested the respondents to indicate the extent of their concern for toxic wastes and for protecting the state's environment.

375. Eagleton Poll. *American Public Opinion Index: 1986.* Boston, MA: Opinion Research Service, Inc., 1987.
    The Eagleton Institute of Politics at Rutgers University interviewed 800 residents of New Jersey by telephone in November 1986. Topics for the survey included the following: extent of water pollution problem in New Jersey, seriousness of toxic waste problem in New Jersey, and immediacy of toxic waste cleanup. Respondents were also asked whether they were willing to accept a toxic waste treatment facility in their own community.

376. *The Los Angeles Times* Poll. *American Public Opinion Index: 1986.* Boston, MA: Opinion Research Service, Inc., 1987.

This poll surveyed 1,895 Californians by telephone about the amount of state spending for toxic waste disposal. Results of the poll were released on February 4, 1986.

377. Morell, Jonathan A. "Community and Individual Reaction to Environmental Hazards: Developing a Measurement Technology." *Environmental Management* 11 (January 1987): 69–76.

The research described in this article was conducted by the staff of the Oak Ridge National Laboratory with funding from the National Institute of Health, Biomedical Research Support Grant. In the study, residents of an unnamed community in New Jersey were surveyed about their reactions toward living near an Environmental Protection Agency Superfund toxic waste site. A sample of 132 individuals returned mail questionnaires (response rate of 40 percent) which solicited concerns about the toxic site, opinions of responsibility for the site, and sources of information on the site. The respondents were also asked to complete a satisfaction with life scale. Analysis of the data revealed that the respondents were most concerned about the effect of the waste site on water and air quality and children's health. The residents held the site's owners and manufacturers most responsible for the pollution and thought they should be the ones to pay to clean up the site.

378. Protess, David L.; Cook, Fay Lomax; Curtin, Thomas R.; Gordon, Margaret T.; Leff, Donna R.; McCombs, Maxwell E.; and Miller, Peter. "The Impact of Investigative Reporting on Public Opinion and Policymaking: Targeting Toxic Waste." *Public Opinion Quarterly* 51 (Summer 1987): 166–85.

This article is the fourth installment in a series of studies exploring the effect of news media investigative reporting on the attitudes of the general public and policymakers. In this version, attitudes toward toxic waste were measured before and after the airing of an investigative report on the toxic waste disposal practices of a major Chicago hospital. The study was conducted in May 1984 by the Center for Urban Affairs and Policy Research at Northwestern University. Pre- and post-tests were administered by telephone to residents of the Chicago area. A total of 395 residents completed the pre-test and 235 completed the pre- and post-tests. After analyzing the post-tests, the researchers found no significant differences in the general public's perception of the importance of toxic waste or their degree of concern for the disposal of toxic waste. The research did indicate, however, that the news program changed the attitudes of the policymakers toward toxic waste.

379. Eagleton Poll. *American Public Opinion Index: 1987*. Boston, MA: Opinion Research Service, Inc., 1988.

In August 1987, the Eagleton Institute of Politics at Rutgers University interviewed 800 New Jersey residents by telephone. The poll inquired about support for a mandatory recycling program and asked several questions about toxic waste disposal. Respondents were asked the extent of their personal concern for the toxic waste problem and whether they supported various options for reducing the amount of toxic waste. Those surveyed were also asked how they would react to a toxic waste disposal facility in their community and under what conditions they would accept such a facility.

380. Gilbert, Dennis A. *Compendium of American Public Opinion.* New York: Facts on File Publication, 1988, pp. 121–36.

This reference book contains a chapter on public opinion toward the environment. The results of several polls conducted between 1972 and 1986 are presented. Topics covered in the featured polls are the following: environmental problems, environmental protection, costs, nuclear power, hazardous wastes, and acid rain. A West Virginia Poll, conducted in 1983, found 73 percent of the state residents would "relax the clean air standards and other environmental laws in the community in order to help the economy create new jobs." In another poll conducted by the Eagleton Institute in 1985, 83 percent of New Jersey residents said toxic waste was a "serious" problem, while 59 percent thought water pollution was a "very serious" problem. The University of Minnesota polled residents in July 1985 and found that 90 percent were concerned about the processing and disposing of hazardous waste in the state. Also in 1985, a North Carolina Citizens Survey conducted by North Carolina State University revealed that 71 percent would be "very concerned" if a hazardous waste facility was to be located in their county.

381. *Issues in South Carolina.* Columbia, SC: Metromark Market Research, Inc., December 1988, 8 pp.

In this telephone poll, South Carolina residents were interviewed about their attitudes toward wetland development and the disposal of hazardous wastes. A sample of 520 adults was surveyed by Metromark Market Research, Inc., of Columbia, South Carolina, during December 1988. Over half of the respondents said they supported restricting building in wetland areas, and 62 percent indicated support for a law limiting beach construction to reduce erosion. A large majority of the sample wanted to limit the amount of hazardous wastes brought into the state and buried.

382. Bass, Ellen S.; Calderon, Rebecca L.; and Khan, Mary Ellen. "Household Hazardous Waste: A Review of Public Attitudes and Disposal Problems." *Journal of Environmental Health* 52 (May–June 1990): 358–61.

The authors of this article review results from research conducted on public attitudes toward household hazardous waste. Results from studies conducted in Massachusetts; Madison, Wisconsin; and San Diego, California, are described. In two of the studies, curbside pickup was the preferred option for disposal of hazardous waste followed by a community collection site. The Connecticut Academy of Science and Engineering provided funding for this research.

383. *The Star Ledger*/Eagleton Poll. *American Public Opinion Index: 1990.* Tallahassee, FL: 1991.

A telephone interview was administered to 800 residents of New Jersey in April 1990 by the Eagleton Institute of Politics at Rutgers University. Respondents were asked their opinion of state spending on toxic waste cleanup and state and local spending on environmental programs.

384. Arizona Poll. *American Public Opinion Index: 1990.* Tallahassee, FL: 1991.

The Arizona Poll was performed by the *Arizona Republic* during August 1990 with 805 Arizonans. Included in the telephone poll were questions asking respondents about their attitude toward a hazardous waste facility proposed for an area southwest of Phoenix. Those surveyed were asked if they supported a ban on the importation of hazardous waste and whether they thought incineration and landfill burial were safe methods of disposing of hazardous wastes.

385. Scudder, Karen, and Blehm, Kenneth D. "Household Hazardous Waste: Assessing Public Attitudes and Awareness." *Journal of Environmental Health* 53 (May-June 1991): 18–20.

The Department of Environmental Health at Colorado State University conducted this study for the Larimer County Hazardous Waste Committee. A mail questionnaire was used to measure public knowledge of, and attitudes toward, household hazardous waste in Larimer County, Colorado. From a total of 900 mailed surveys, 472 were returned. Results of the survey showed the residents had limited knowledge about what household products could be hazardous. Only 22 percent were able to name four or more hazardous products commonly found in the home. When asked for their opinion of various disposal options, the residents preferred drop off at a community hazardous waste collection site.

Solid Waste

386. Kentucky Poll. *American Public Opinion Index: 1983.* Lexington, KY: Opinion Research Service, Inc., 1985.

This special survey on solid waste disposal was performed by the Survey Research Center of the University of Kentucky. The telephone poll interviewed 680 Kentucky residents during 1983. Respondents to the survey were asked their perception of the seriousness of the solid waste disposal problem and their opinion of recycling waste materials and alternatives to recycling. Those sampled were also asked whether they supported recycling facilities even if they were more costly than landfills.

387. Hardy, Thomas, and Schmeltzer, John. "Du Page Voters Split Over Trash Disposal." *Chicago Tribune*, September 26, 1988, section 2D, p. 1.

The *Chicago Tribune* sponsored this poll conducted by Market Shares Corporation of Mt. Prospect, Illinois. On September 18 and 19, 1988, 400 Du Page County voters were contacted by telephone and asked to indicate a preference for disposing of the county's garbage by either incineration or shipping the waste outside of the county. Of the voters surveyed, 45 percent chose incineration, 40 percent supported shipping it elsewhere, and 15 percent indicated no preference.

388. *Greater Cincinnati Survey.* Cincinnati, OH: University of Cincinnati, Institute for Policy Research, Fall 1989.

This telephone poll was conducted by the Institute for Policy Research of the University of Cincinnati during the fall of 1989. The survey questioned 1,687 residents of Hamilton County, Ohio, about their perception of the solid waste disposal problem. Also included in the interview were questions about support for recycling and willingness to pay special fees to dispose of nonrecyclable items.

389. Freeman, Laurie. "Diaper Image Damaged." *Advertising Age*, June 11, 1990, pp. 1, 57.

Advertising Age sponsored a national telephone survey conducted by the Gallup Organization on June 6, 1990. A total of 1,029 adult Americans were interviewed. Respondents were asked about their support for banning disposable diapers versus a special tax on the purchase of disposable diapers. A tax on disposable diapers was favored by 52 percent of the respondents, while 43 percent favored a ban on the diapers. Greater support for both a tax and the ban was expressed by residents of the western states.

390. "Most Americans Support Pollution Counteroffensive." *Houston Post,* June 12, 1990, p. A10.

This newspaper article reports on a national poll conducted by Media General and the Associated Press. The survey date, method, and sample size are not given in the article. Topics for the poll included importance of environmental problems, support for environmental protection measures and funding options. A large majority of the sample said pollution threatens the quality of their lives. The poll documented support for mandatory recycling and banning disposable diapers, cancer-causing pesticides, and certain types of consumer product packaging. An oil shipping fee to fund spill prevention was supported by 80 percent of the respondents, and 61 percent favored a ban on old forest timbercutting.

391. Hambrick, Graydon. "Landfills Concern Leaders; Survey Finds Top Local Problems with Environment." *Columbus Dispatch*, August 9, 1990, p. 3D.

For this poll, the Ohio Environmental Council of Columbus, Ohio, surveyed 400 leaders in business, agriculture, local government, and environmental concerns from a seven county area in central Ohio. The response rate for the questionnaire was 45 percent. Respondents to the survey were asked to choose the most serious problem from a list of 40 issues. Of the 40 issues, the shortage of landfills was ranked as most important by 65 percent of the leaders. "A lack of integrated solid waste management that incorporates waste reduction, reuse, and recycling" was ranked second by the total sample and first by the environmental leaders. More than two-thirds of the sample said the government was not effective in protecting the environment in central Ohio. Other environmental issues of concern to those polled were acid rain, the greenhouse effect, loss of topsoil, groundwater contamination, and pollution of waterways by urban-area runoff.

392. National Solid Waste Management Association. *American Public Opinion Index: 1990.* Tallahassee, FL: 1991.

The National Waste Management Association sponsored a national telephone poll that surveyed 1,250 members of the general public and 500 national opinion leaders. Respondents answered questions about the causes and solutions to the solid waste disposal problem. One item asked those surveyed if they would support a new waste-to-energy plant in their community.

393. How Solid Waste Issues are Affecting Consumer Behavior. *American Public Opinion Index: 1990.* Tallahassee, FL: 1991.

The Research Department of the Food Marketing Institute of Washington, D.C., performed this national telephone survey with a sample of 750 Americans. Those responding to the interview were asked their view of the best solution to the garbage problem among recycling, reducing waste, incineration, and landfills. Additional questions covered responsibility for solving the waste disposal problem and the role of consumers, manufacturers, and government in solving the problem.

394. Terrell, Gaynell. "Little Consensus on Garbage, Survey Finds." *The Houston Post*, August 3, 1992, p. A11.

The poll presented in this article was conducted by the American Society of Mechanical Engineers. Although the population and sample size are not specified, the sample apparently included engineers as well as members of the general public. The study compared the perceptions of these groups on the most serious environmental problems and the acceptability of alternative solid waste disposal methods. Solid waste was identified as the nation's greatest environmental problem by engineers, while the public rated waste disposal fourth after air pollution, hazardous waste, and water pollution. The engineers favored incineration and landfills for disposing of garbage.

CONTAINER DEPOSITS/TAXES

395. *The Harris Survey Yearbook of Public Opinion 1971: A Compendium of Current American Attitudes.* New York: Louis Harris and Associates, Inc., 1975, p. 263.

This annual collection of the Harris Survey includes a nationwide poll on the subject of deposits on beverage containers conducted in March 1971. (The sample size and methodology are not noted.) By a two-to-one margin, the respondents said returnable bottles and cans were not "too much trouble to bother with."

396. "Iowans Favor Ban on Disposable Containers." *Current Opinion* 4 (March 1976): 31.

This monthly publication of the Roper Public Opinion Research Center includes results from the Iowa Poll conducted in 1975 for the *Des Moines Register and Tribune*. The poll included a question about support for banning the sale of nonreturnable beer and soft drink containers in Iowa. Of the 602 adults sampled, 70 percent supported a ban, 20 percent opposed the proposed ban, and 10 percent had no opinion.

397. University of Louisville Poll. *American Public Opinion Index: 1981.* Tallahassee, FL: Opinion Research Service, Inc., 1982.

This telephone survey was conducted by the University of Louisville in August 1981 with a sample of 455 residents of the Louisville metropolitan area. The respondents were questioned about their support for a law requiring deposits on cans and bottles.

398. Delaware State College Poll. *American Public Opinion Index: 1981.* Tallahassee, FL: Opinion Research Service, Inc., 1982.

A total of 751 Delaware residents was polled by telephone in March 1981. Those responding were asked their opinion of a mandatory five cent deposit on beverage containers. They were also asked to identify the most important problem facing the state of Delaware.

399. Connecticut Poll. *American Public Opinion Index: 1981.* Tallahassee, FL: Opinion Research Service, Inc., 1982.

The Connecticut Poll is conducted by the University of Connecticut's Roper Center. In telephone polls conducted in March and December 1981 respondents were asked whether they supported a bottle bill requiring deposits on beverage containers. The 500 Connecticut residents that made up the sample were also asked how they thought the bottle bill was affecting the amount of litter in the state.

400. Hollander, Cohen Associates Poll. *American Public Opinion Index: 1982.* Lexington, KY: Opinion Research Service, Inc., 1984.

Hollander, Cohen Associates of Baltimore, Maryland, contacted 800 Maryland residents by telephone during January 1982. The respondents were asked if they supported mandatory deposits on beverage bottles and cans.

401. The Roper Survey. *American Public Opinion Index: 1982.* Lexington, KY: Opinion Research Service, Inc., 1984.

This poll by the Roper Organization was conducted in July 1982 with 2,000 Americans. The respondents were asked in person whether they supported banning the sale of beverages in disposable containers.

402. Connecticut Poll. *American Public Opinion Index: 1982.* Lexington, KY: Opinion Research Service, Inc., 1984.

The Connecticut Poll was conducted by the Roper Center at the University of Connecticut. Opinion on a national bottle bill was asked of 500 Connecticut residents contacted by phone in January 1982. Respondents were also asked about their opinion of the success of Connecticut's bottle bill.

403. Gannett, Gordon Black Poll. *American Public Opinion Index: 1982.* Lexington, KY: Opinion Research Service, Inc., 1984.

In this poll, 1,000 New York residents were polled by telephone about their support for a mandatory deposit on bottles and cans. The survey was conducted in June 1982 by Gordon Black Associates of Rochester, New York.

404. The Delaware Survey. *American Public Opinion Index: 1983.* Lexington, KY: Opinion Research Service, Inc., 1985.

The Department of History and Political Science at Delaware State College conducted the Delaware Survey. A total sample of 800 Delaware residents were interviewed in the telephone poll. Questions included in the survey addressed support for a mandatory deposit on beer and soda bottles and support for expanding a beverage container law to include aluminum cans.

405. North Star Poll. *American Public Opinion Index: 1984.* Lexington, KY: Opinion Research Service, Inc., 1985.

The *St. Paul Dispatch and Pioneer Press* conducted the North Star Poll in March 1984 with a sample of 900 residents of Minnesota. Included in the survey was a question designed to measure support for a five cent deposit on bottles and cans.

406. Eagleton Poll. *American Public Opinion Index: 1985.* Lexington, KY: Opinion Research Service, Inc., 1986.

The Eagleton Institute of Politics at Rutgers University performed this telephone poll in May 1985. A total of 1,000 residents of New Jersey made up the sample. Respondents were asked whether they thought reducing litter and recycling or protecting the glass industry was more important. The respondents were also asked if they preferred to reduce litter by a deposit on bottles or a tax on litter generating businesses.

407. Zia Poll. *American Public Opinion Index: 1985.* Lexington, KY: Opinion Research Service, Inc., 1986.

The Zia Poll is performed by Zia Research Associates of Albuquerque, New Mexico. In January 1985, 404 New Mexico residents were contacted by telephone and asked if they supported a mandatory refundable deposit on beverage containers.

408. Texas Poll. *American Public Opinion Index: 1987.* Boston, MA: Opinion Research Service, Inc., 1988.

The Texas Poll is performed by the Public Policy Resources Laboratory at Texas A&M University. In the winter of 1987, 1,004 Texans were contacted by telephone and asked if they supported a proposal to add five cents to the cost of all soda and beer containers.

409. Northstar Poll. *American Public Opinion Index: 1988.* Boston, MA: Opinion Research Service, Inc., 1989.

The *St. Paul Press and Dispatch* conducted the Northstar Poll by contacting 764 Minnesota residents by telephone. Included in the poll was a question asking respondents their view of a proposed beverage container deposit of up to forty cents. Results of the poll were released on February 8, 1988.

410. The Iowa Poll. *American Public Opinion Index: 1989.* Boston, MA: Opinion Research Service, Inc., 1990.

The Iowa Poll was conducted by the *Des Moines Register and Tribune* with 806 Iowa residents. Included in the survey was one question asking the respondents if they favored a one cent tax on beverage containers to fund Iowa environmental programs. Results of the telephone poll were released by the newspaper on March 16, 1989.

411. Florida Annual Policy Survey. *American Public Opinion Index: 1989.* Boston, MA: Opinion Research Service, Inc., 1990.

For this poll, the Policy Services Program at Florida State University interviewed 1,084 Florida residents by telephone. The respondents were asked to answer a question about their support for a refundable deposit on all glass and aluminum beverage containers. The survey was conducted in January 1989.

412. Kentucky Poll. *American Public Opinion Index: 1991.* Tallahassee, FL: 1991.

Two telephone polls were conducted by the Survey Research Center of the University of Kentucky in May and November 1991. The May poll contacted 646 Kentucky residents and asked their opinion of legislation requiring a five to ten cent refundable deposit on cans and bottles. Respondents were also asked their position on a proposal to increase taxes by two dollars per month to finance a county recycling program. In November, 650 residents were asked their opinion on ground water contamination and seriousness of various threats to water quality.

RECYCLING

413. Steininger, Marion, and Voegtlin, Kathleen. "Attitudinal Bases of Recycling." The *Journal of Social Psychology* 100 (1976): 155–56.

This brief item summarizes results of a survey of 28 recyclers and 28 nonrecyclers conducted in 1974 at a shopping center with a recycling station. The subjects answered a 31-item questionnaire which included items on dogmatism, political ideology, and environmental attitudes. While no significant differences were found between the two groups on ideology or dogmatism, the recyclers and nonrecyclers did differ on environmental attitudes. In response to the statement, "Solving the problems of pollution is even more important than solving the problems of poverty," 46 percent of the recyclers but only 4 percent of the nonrecyclers agreed.

414. Day, Richard. "Is Chicago Ready for Recycling?" *Chicago Tribune,* April 2, 1988, section 1, p. 11.

The survey described in this newspaper article was conducted by Richard Day Research of Evanston, Illinois, for WLS-TV in Chicago. A total of 500 Chicago residents were surveyed. Respondents were asked about their perception of the importance of recycling and their support for a mandatory recycling program. These opinions were measured both before and after the respondents were read a list of arguments for and against recycling. Results of the survey showed the Chicagoans supported a mandatory recycling program by a four-to-one margin. Recycling was not seen as important as other problems facing the city such as crime and the education system. Economic benefits and a solution to the solid waste disposal problem were the most persuasive arguments for mandatory recycling.

415. Crawford, Jan. "Survey Finds Recycling Support." *Chicago Tribune,* July 5, 1988, section 20, p. 8.

Gloria Craven and Associates of Springfield, Illinois, performed this poll for the Solid Waste Planning Committee of Du Page County, Illinois. The population for the survey included local government officials and citizens involved in solid waste disposal planning. Of 1,800 questionnaires mailed, only 631, or 35 percent, were returned. The questionnaire solicited opinions on mandatory recycling for households, businesses, and institutions and the importance of various effects of waste disposal. Nearly three-fourths of those returning the surveys supported mandatory recycling for households, and 87 percent supported mandatory recycling for businesses and institutions. Impact on health was identified as the most important consideration in waste disposal planning, followed by effect on environment, availability, resource conservation, and cost.

416. "USA Snapshots: Interest in Recycled Packaging." *USA Today,* June 7, 1989, p. 1A.

This item consists of a graph showing results of a Gallup Poll on consumer interest in buying products in recycled packaging. The majority of women (55 percent) and men (52 percent) queried by the poll said they were "very interested" in buying products that had been packaged in recycled material. The date and sample size of the survey are not given.

417. "9 of 10 Ohioans Support Recycling, Poll Finds." *Columbus Dispatch,* June 13, 1989, p. 2B.

The Ohio Poll described in this article was conducted in April 1989 by the University of Cincinnati's Institute for Policy Research. This statewide poll of 820 adults was sponsored by the *Cincinnati Post*, *Dayton Daily News*, Cincinnati TV station WKRC, and the University of Cincinnati. Topics for the poll included support for mandatory recycling and perception of solid waste disposal. The survey found 90 percent of Ohioans in favor of mandatory recycling of bottles, cans, and newspapers. A majority of those polled said solid waste disposal was a "very serious" or "somewhat serious" problem.

418. "The Consumer's Opinion." *Packaging* 4 (August 1989): 50–54.

Packaging magazine conducted the nationwide consumer mail survey presented in this article. (The sample size and return rate are not disclosed.) The questionnaire included items on recycling and bottle deposits, funding for recycling programs, willingness to pay for recycled packaging, and preferences for incineration or landfills. Those sampled said that manufacturers of packaging material should be responsible for funding new recycling programs. A majority said they would be willing to pay at least five cents more for a product in an easily recycled package. More than three-fourths of the sample said they would be willing to sort packaging for curbside collection. In addition, more than half of the consumers living in areas with no beverage container deposit law indicated that, given a chance, they would vote in favor of a "bottle bill." Support for new incinerators was nearly twice as high as for new landfills as a means of handling increased solid waste disposal demands.

419. Hume, Scott, and Strnad, Patricia. "Consumers Go Green." *Advertising Age*, September 25, 1989, pp. 3, 92.

The Gallup Organization performed the national poll presented in this article for *Advertising Age* magazine. In August 1989, Gallup interviewed 1,000 adults by telephone and asked them about their concern for the environmental effects of consumer packaging and their willingness to pay more for responsible packaging. On a scale of one to five, the respondents rated their concern for environmental damage from consumer products and packaging as 4.14. The survey also found 97 percent of the sample willing to give up some convenience and 88 percent willing to pay more for environmentally safe products and packaging.

420. Liles-Morris, Shelley. "Top Concerns: Health, Environment." *USA Today*, November 7, 1989, p. 1B.

The nationwide survey reported in this article was conducted by Lempert Media Information Services. The sample is given as 500 consumers, but the interview date and survey method are not mentioned. Of those responding to the survey, 87 percent indicated they wanted more recyclable products.

421. Northeast Research Poll. *American Public Opinion Index: 1989*. Boston, MA: Opinion Research Service, Inc., 1990.

The Northeast Poll was conducted by Northeast Research of Orono, Maine, in January 1989. A sample of 614 Maine residents was interviewed by telephone about support for voluntary sorting of garbage for recycling and other proposed measures to reduce waste.

422. Penn and Schoen Poll. *American Public Opinion Index: 1989*. Boston, MA: Opinion Research Service, Inc., 1990.

Penn and Schoen Associates, Inc. of Washington, D.C., completed this national telephone poll of 1,000 Americans. Respondents to the poll were asked questions about product packaging including their support for recyclable or biodegradable packaging and their willingness to pay more for this type of packaging. The poll also inquired about the importance of environmental concern in product selection. Results of the poll were published on July 20, 1989.

423. Wisconsin Department of Natural Resources. *American Public Opinion Index: 1990.* Tallahassee, FL: 1991.

This telephone poll on recycling was performed during 1990 with 414 residents of the state of Wisconsin. Those surveyed were asked their opinion of a state law that would regulate the recycling of household waste. Respondents were also questioned about their view of the importance of protecting the environment, saving landfill space, preserving the environment, and saving natural resources as reasons for recycling.

424. University of South Carolina Poll. *American Public Opinion Index: 1990.* Tallahassee, FL: 1991.

The Survey Research Laboratory, Institute of Public Affairs at the University of South Carolina conducted this poll during 1990. A sample of 334 residents of four South Carolina counties (Fairfield, Lexington, Richland, and Newberry) were contacted by telephone and asked about support for mandatory recycling and reasons for not participating in recycling.

425. Maritz AmeriPoll. *American Public Opinion Index: 1990.* Tallahassee, FL: 1991.

This telephone poll was performed by Maritz Marketing Research, Inc., of Fenton, Missouri. Results of the poll of 1,000 Americans were released on June 7, 1990. Topics for the poll included reasons for not recycling and willingness to participate in voluntary recycling programs.

426. *Chicago Sun-Times* Poll. *American Public Opinion Index: 1990.* Tallahassee, FL: 1991.

In September 1990, 800 residents of Cook County, Illinois, were interviewed by telephone about recycling. Those responding to the poll were asked if they supported mandatory residential recycling in their community and whether they would be willing to participate in a voluntary recycling program.

427. University of Nevada Poll. *American Public Opinion Index: 1991.* Tallahassee, FL: 1991.

The University of Nevada's Center of Applied Research, College of Human and Communication Sciences conducted this telephone poll during 1991. A total of 1,178 citizens of Nevada were surveyed. Respondents were asked their opinion of the amount of tax money allocated to state parks and recreation areas. Respondents were also asked whether they would be willing to voluntarily sort recyclable trash for curbside pickup. Other questions concerned support for mandatory recycling by state offices and colleges, mandatory household separation of garbage, and mandatory use of recycled paper by newspapers.

428. The Wisconsin Survey. *American Public Opinion Index: 1991.* Tallahassee, FL: 1991.

The Wisconsin Survey of April 1991 was conducted by St. Norbert College Survey Center. A sample of 452 Wisconsin citizens completed a telephone interview on global warming and recycling. Those responding to the survey were asked if they were willing to pay higher prices for recyclable packaging and whether they supported a statewide mandatory recycling program and a ban on nonrecyclable product packaging. Respondents were also asked to indicate their degree of concern for the greenhouse effect.

429. The West Virginia Poll. Charleston, WV: Ryan-McGinn-Samples Research, 1991.

Ryan-McGinn-Samples Research of Charleston, West Virginia, performed this survey for the *Charleston Daily Mail*, WSAZ Television 3, and the Associated Press. During May 1991, 501 citizens of West Virginia were contacted by telephone and questioned about their willingness to separate garbage for recycling and their willingness to pay additional taxes to fund sorting and recycling of household garbage. The respondents were also asked about their approval of a proposed out-of-state garbage landfill. Another question asked about increased state regulation of the timber industry which was supported by 55 percent of the sample. This report provides a breakdown of responses by age, sex, and education.

430. Parrish, Michael. "Poll Finds Wide Support for Recycling." *The Los Angeles Times*, February 13, 1991, p. D2.

This article describes a survey of Californians living in six urban counties conducted by Interviewing Services of America for the Du Pont Company. (The sample size, methodology, and interview dates are not disclosed.) Of the residents surveyed, 45 percent said they were willing to pay more in taxes for curbside recycling. Respondents from lower income households were more supportive of the tax increase than respondents from middle income households.

431. Curtin, Mike. "Voters Balk at $15 Fee But Will Separate Trash." *Columbus* [Ohio] *Dispatch*, June 18, 1991, p. 1A.

A mail survey, administered by the *Columbus Dispatch*, was returned by 1,466 registered voters residing in Columbus, Ohio. The survey was conducted in June 1991 to determine voter support for a citywide mandatory recycling program. By a two-to-one margin, the voters surveyed said they supported mandatory curbside recycling. Only three out of ten respondents, however, were willing to pay $15 per month more for an "environmental services fee."

432. Vining, Joanne; Linn, Nancy; and Burdge, Rabel J. "Why People Recycle? A Comparison of Recycling Motivations in Four Communities." *Environmental Management* 16 (November-December 1992): 785–97.

The research detailed in this article was funded by the Illinois Office of Solid Waste Research. In this study, the attitudes of residents of four Illinois communities (Kankakee, Bloomington, Rockford, and Champaign) toward recycling were measured. A total of 841 residents of the four communities completed questionnaires distributed by college interviewers. The questionnaire solicited perceptions of the importance of 22 reasons for recycling and not recycling. Responses from the subjects were used to identify five recycling motivational factors: altruism, personal inconvenience, social influences, economic incentives, and household storage. Altruism was rated as the most important of the factors by respondents from all four areas. Although the four communities differed significantly on the importance of the five motivational factors, attempts to explain the differences were not successful.

Environmental Protection versus Energy Production

433. "Poll on Energy Problems Finds Skepticism Bars Broad Support for Carter Program." *The New York Times*, September 1, 1977, pp. A1, D12.

This *New York Times*/CBS News telephone poll was performed with a national sample of 1,463 adults. The poll questioned respondents about their attitude toward the U.S. energy crisis and their preference for protecting the environment or producing energy. Respondents indicated they supported increased strip mining and relaxing air pollution laws to produce and use more coal. Yet when asked to choose between producing energy and protecting the environment, a majority of those polled picked the environment.

434. Fusso, Thomas E. "The Polls: The Energy Crisis in Perspective." *Public Opinion Quarterly* 42 (Spring 1978): 127–36.

In this article, the author presents results from several polls conducted on the public's perception of the energy shortage of the mid–1970s. The exact wording of the interview items and the break down of responses are included. Topics covered by the polls include concern over the energy crisis, effect of the crisis on personal driving habits, and perceptions of possible solutions to the crisis. The article reprints excerpts from the following polls: the California Poll (March 1974), the Gallup Poll (several polls during 1974, 1975, 1977), the Harris Survey (1973–77), the Minnesota Poll (1973–75), and the Texas Poll (1973–74). The California, Minnesota, and Texas Polls surveyed state samples. All of the polls consisted of personal interviews with the respondents. In the September 1977 Harris Survey, 80 percent of the sample favored increased strip mining of coal as long as environmental protection was considered.

435. Hummel, Carl F.; Levitt, Lynn; and Loomis, Ross J. "Perceptions of the Energy Crisis: Who Is Blamed and How Do Citizens React to Environment-Lifestyle Trade-Offs?" *Environment and Behavior* 10 (March 1978): 37–88.

Colorado State University Experiment Station supported the research described in this article. The goal of the study was to develop a profile of individuals who support action on environmental problems even during a period of energy or other resource shortage. For the purposes of the study, two samples totaling 238 adult residents of Fort Collins, Colorado, were surveyed by mail. One sampling occurred in late summer 1973 during a period of acute energy shortage and another sampling was completed in November 1973 during a chronic energy shortage period. The respondents were questioned about their environmental and energy related behavior, who they blamed for the energy crisis, their willingness to support various proposals to alleviate the shortage, and their opinion of air pollution versus energy production trade-off options. The study also examined relationships between attitudes and behaviors regarding energy and the environment and several demographic variables (age, sex, political party, political ideology, occupation, education, and owning an automobile).

436. Harris, Louis. "Oil Search Favored." *Chicago Tribune*, July 27, 1978, section 3, p. 4.

This newspaper editorial page column details the results of a Harris Survey poll conducted on American attitudes toward offshore drilling. The exact date of the poll is not given. Harris Survey interviewed 1,567 adults nationwide and asked their perceptions of the risks and benefits of offshore oil and natural gas exploration. A large majority supported increasing oil and gas drilling off the Atlantic (78 percent) and Pacific and Gulf Coasts (76 percent). More than half of those polled agreed that the "need for offshore gas and oil outweighs the environmental risks that may be involved in producing them." A majority of the respondents also agreed that offshore exploration would result in economic benefits such as new jobs (82 percent), increased state revenues for coastal states (77 percent), and new industry (69 percent). In response to questioning about how officials should consider offshore drilling proposals, 36 percent said priority should be given to economic considerations. Environmental concerns were the top priority of 28 percent, and 25 percent thought both could be given equal emphasis.

437. "Opinion Roundup: Environmental Protection: An Idea That Has Come and Stayed." *Public Opinion* 2 (August-September 1979): 21–23.

This article uses graphics to present results from several polls on attitudes toward energy and environmental issues. The polls and their topics include the following: Roper Organization (December 1978) on seriousness of air and water pollution and ozone depletion; Resources for the Future (July 1978) on progress in pollution reduction; ABC News/Louis Harris and Associates (October 1978) on government action to fight pollution; Roper Organization (1973–78), Gallup Organization (1979), and Resources for the Future (July 1978) on environmental versus energy tradeoffs; and ABC News/Louis Harris and Associates (October 1978) and Roper Organization (October–November 1978) on environmental versus inflation tradeoffs. On the question of relaxing pollution standards to increase fuel efficiency, between 33 percent and 55 percent of the respondents to the Roper and Gallup Polls supported relaxing regulations. Over 40 percent of the respondents to the Roper Organization's 1974–78 polls favored eliminating pollution control devices to conserve supplies of energy.

438. Harris, Louis. "Pollution Foes and Energy." *Chicago Tribune*, September 10, 1979, section 4, p. 3.

This ABC News/Harris Survey polled 1,508 adult Americans about their perceptions of environmentalism and environmentalists, the reasonableness of their demands, and their effect on the economy. By 57 percent to 27 percent, those surveyed said they thought the demands of environmentalists were "making it more difficult to produce adequate energy for the country." The article points out differences between the views of young people and those of older Americans. Nearly 60 percent of the sample said they favored industrial growth in their communities, but only 48 percent of young people supported increased industry.

439. "Opinion Roundup: Conservatives Less Likely to Preserve." *Public Opinion* 4 (February-March 1981): 28.

This item consists of a graph depicting results from a Roper Poll conducted on protection of the environment versus development of energy resources. The survey was performed September 27 through October 4, 1980, with an undisclosed sample. Results are shown by pie chart for the nation as a whole and for political liberals and conservatives.

440. "Poll Finds Strong Support for Environmental Code." *The New York Times*, October 4, 1981, p. A30.

The poll described in this article was conducted by *The New York Times* and CBS News from September 22 through 27, 1981. A sample of 1,479 Americans was questioned about the importance of environmental protection, energy production versus environmental protection, and trust in the president to make proper environmental decisions. By a two-to-one margin, those polled said they wanted to keep present environmental laws even at the cost of economic growth. On the subject of air pollution, 61 percent indicated they favored keeping present laws even if some factories had to be closed. The survey showed less support for environmental protection when energy production was at stake. A majority of those polled approved of increased gas and oil drilling off the California coast, but the respondents were evenly divided on whether drilling should be allowed in federal wilderness areas.

441. The Roper Poll. *American Public Opinion Index: 1981.* Tallahassee, FL: Opinion Research Service, Inc., 1982.

This Roper Poll was conducted by telephone with a national sample of 2,000 adults in March 1981. Included in the survey was one item asking respondents whether they supported increased offshore oil exploration. (Results of this poll are presented elsewhere.)

442. CBS News Poll. *American Public Opinion Index: 1981.* Tallahassee, FL: Opinion Research Service, Inc., 1982.

CBS News performed this national telephone survey in September 1981 with a sample of 1,479 Americans. The poll included questions about oil and natural gas drilling off the Atlantic and California coasts and oil and gas drilling in federal wilderness areas. Respondents were also asked about environmental protection versus economic growth.

443. Sindlinger Poll. *American Public Opinion Index: 1981.* Tallahassee, FL: Opinion Research Service, Inc., 1982.

This national telephone poll was performed in October 1981 with a sample of 1,200 Americans. The survey included several questions about the exploration and development of publicly owned lands. Issues covered in the poll included the following: exploration for rare minerals, exploration for oil, gas, and mineral reserves, selling western federal land to buy recreation lands near eastern U.S. population centers, and selling federal lands to private individuals and state and local governments. Respondents were also asked if they thought states should be allowed to deny access to offshore oil and gas reserves. On the subjects of parks, those surveyed were asked if they favored the purchase of land for urban parks and whether emphasis should be placed on restoring national parks versus acquiring more land.

444. The California Poll. *American Public Opinion Index: 1981.* Tallahassee, FL: Opinion Research Service, Inc., 1982.

The California Poll of October 1981 was conducted by the Field Institute with 1,012 California residents. The respondents were asked if they thought it was possible to have oil drilling off the coast and to provide environmental safeguards at the same time. Those surveyed were also questioned about their support for relaxing pollution controls on coal burning power plants and restrictions on oil and gas drilling in government forest reserves and parklands.

445. NBC News Poll. *American Public Opinion Index: 1981.* Tallahassee, FL: Opinion Research Service, Inc., 1982.

NBC News conducted polls in May and October 1981 that included questions about the development of federal lands. The national telephone polls contacted 1,599 Americans in May and 1,598 Americans in October 1981. In the May poll, respondents were asked whether they thought the federal government should allow more or less drilling and mining on federally owned lands in the west. More mining was supported by 44 percent of the sample, while 13 percent wanted the amount of mining cut back, and 29 percent thought the current level should be continued. Respondents to the May poll were also asked about new offshore oil drilling, which 70 percent said they supported. In October, the survey asked whether protecting the environment or keeping prices down was of more importance. Protecting the environment was chosen by 52 percent, with 37 percent choosing keeping prices down, and 11 percent indicating no preference. Both the May and October polls included a question which asked the respondents to choose between wilderness preservation and mineral resource development. The responses reversed between the two polls. In May, 47 percent favored the development of energy resources, and in October, 48 percent favored wilderness preservation.

446. "Environmental Concern Mounts . . ." *The Wall Street Journal*, November 26, 1982, p. A1.

This is a very brief news item that mentions results of a Roper poll on environmental protection and energy exploration. Details on the interview date, population, method, and sample size are not provided. The percentage of those polled who were willing to place environmental concerns ahead of energy development increased by 10 points during the previous year to 46 percent.

447. Langenau, Edward E.; Peyton, R. Ben; Wickham, Julie M.; Caveney, Edward W.; and Johnston, David W. "Attitudes Toward Oil and Gas Development Among Forest Recreationists." *Journal of Leisure Research* 16 (1984): 161–77.

The research described in this article was conducted by the authors with financial support from Shell Oil Company, the Michigan Department of Natural Resources, and the Federal Aid in Wildlife Restoration, Pittman Robertson Project, U.S. Fish and Wildlife Service. A survey of forest recreationists was performed to determine their attitudes toward oil and gas development in the Pigeon River Country State Forest, Michigan. (This area had been the site of a long-term controversy over backcountry natural resource exploration.) From March 1981 through February 1982, mail questionnaires were sent to visitors of the forest area. Of the 931 respondents, 32 percent approved and 60 percent disapproved of oil and gas development in the area. Over three-fourths of the sample agreed that "some areas should be preserved despite the loss of economic benefits."

448. Griffee, Carol. "'Drain, Fill and Build' Attitude Toward Wetlands Called Thing of Past." *Arkansas Gazette*, April 22, 1984.

In this newspaper article, results are presented from a nationwide telephone survey of 1,000 Americans conducted in late 1983. The survey, conducted by Opinion Research Corporation, found 55 percent of its sample supported wetlands protection even if the marshes contain energy resources that could be extracted.

449. The California Poll. *American Public Opinion Index: 1984.* Lexington, KY: Opinion Research Service, Inc., 1985.

In February 1984, the Field Institute contacted 1,511 Californians by telephone and asked whether they supported increased offshore drilling for oil and gas. Those responding to the survey were also asked about their opinion of water and air pollution as problems of concern to Californians.

450. Field, Mervin. "Environmental Issues Rated High." *San Francisco Chronicle*, February 27, 1985.

The California Poll was a statewide telephone poll conducted by the Field Institute. Over 1,000 California voters were interviewed between October 8 and 12, 1984. Included in the survey were questions about environmental problems, environmental protection versus economic growth, environmental restrictions on energy related industries, and energy exploration and development. More than 80 percent of the sample rated five environmental issues as highly important: quality of drinking water, cleanup of toxic waste sites, disposal of toxic waste, providing sewage treatment facilities, and reducing industrial water pollution. Only two issues, limiting timber cutting and reducing unnecessary noise, were seen as highly important by less than 50 percent of the respondents. By a two-to-one margin, the respondents thought it was possible to achieve both environmental protection and economic growth. A majority opposed relaxing environmental controls to allow increased energy development including nuclear power plants and oil and gas drilling in government parklands, in forest preserves, and along the California coast.

451. Yankelovich, Skelly, and White. *American Public Opinion Index: 1985.* Lexington, KY: Opinion Research Service, Inc., 1986.

This national telephone poll was conducted in September 1985 with a sample of 1,014 Americans. In the survey, the respondents were asked whether they supported banning offshore oil drilling even if higher gas prices resulted. The poll also included questions about the strength and enforcement of environmental laws.

452. The Roper Poll. *American Public Opinion Index: 1985.* Lexington, KY: Opinion Research Service, Inc., 1986.

In August 1985, 1,996 Americans were interviewed in person by the Roper Organization. As part of the survey, the respondents were asked if they supported offshore leases for oil and natural gas exploration.

453. Cambridge Reports, Quarterly Opinion Review. *American Public Opinion Index: 1985.* Lexington, KY: Opinion Research Service, Inc., 1986.

Cambridge Reports, Inc., of Cambridge, Massachusetts, performed surveys in February, May, and November 1985 which included questions about environmental protection and energy development. Each of the national surveys personally interviewed over 1,400 people. In all three polls, respondents were asked their opinion of environmental protection versus economic growth. The February poll asked whether priority should be given to protecting the environment or ensuring the development of adequate sources of energy. One question included in the May poll asked respondents to indicate a preference for development or preservation of public wilderness lands. Another question asked those surveyed whether they generally supported energy exploration in public wilderness areas. In addition, the same question was asked for specific types of energy exploration including mining, oil and natural gas drilling, underground mining, and surface coal mining.

454. Gillroy, John M., and Shapiro, Robert Y. "The Polls: Environmental Protection." *Public Opinion Quarterly* 50 (Summer 1986): 270–79.

This review article includes results from several polls conducted during the 1970s and early 1980s on public perceptions of environmental protection. The profiled polls addressed the following topics: spending for environmental protection, government regulation of the environment, energy production versus environmental protection, economic growth versus environmental protection, and willingness to pay for environmental protection. The article reprints the actual questions and results from the following polls: Cambridge Reports (1976–85), NBC News (June 1978, December 1978, September 1979, October 1981), *New York Times*/CBS News (July 1977, July 1979, September 1981, September 1982, April 1983, January 1986), National Opinion Research Corporation (1973–1985), Roper (1971–1983), Survey Research Center, University of Michigan (January, April, June, September, November 1980), Trendex Inc. for General Electric (1965–82), and Yankelovich, Skelly and White (1977, 1979, 1980). The Roper polls of February 1977, March 1979, March 1980, and March 1981 included questions on offshore exploration for oil and strip mining for coal. A slim majority of the respondents to these polls supported more strip mining, while a strong majority approved of increased offshore drilling. All of the surveys were conducted with national samples of at least 1,000 adults.

455. Cambridge Reports. *American Public Opinion Index: 1987.* Boston, MA: Opinion Research Service, Inc., 1988.

Cambridge Reports is compiled by Cambridge Reports Inc. of Cambridge, Massachusetts. This particular poll interviewed 1,450 Americans in person during May 1987. Those completing the interview were asked about federal regulations on oil companies for offshore oil and gas drilling and tolerance of oil spills in order to have offshore drilling. The poll also asked the respondents their perception of the amount of publicly owned wilderness in the United States and whether wilderness preservation or development of energy resources should be a priority. Those surveyed were asked whether they felt the environment was threatened from the following energy development operations: offshore drilling, oil refineries, the development of oil and gas reserves in wilderness areas, and nuclear power plants.

456. *The Los Angeles Times* Poll. *American Public Opinion Index: 1987.* Boston, MA: Opinion Research Service, Inc., 1988.

The Los Angeles Times conducted this telephone poll with 2,055 residents of Los Angeles County, California. Results of the poll were released on June 17, 1987. Included in the poll were questions about offshore drilling and the biggest problem facing the Los Angeles area. When asked if they supported Mayor Tom Bradley's decision to permit drilling off the coast of Los Angeles, 39 percent of those surveyed said they opposed the decision, 19 percent supported the decision, and 34 percent were unaware of the issue.

457. Smith, Kathleen, and Loveland, David. "Natural Resources: Energy Concerns in the 1990s." *Environment* 30 (October 1988): 2–3, 45.

This article reports on the findings of a survey of energy concerns sponsored by the League of Women Voters Education Fund. Polling for the study was conducted by the Gallup Organization with members of the general public and energy opinion leaders. Gallup polled 1,013 Americans by telephone during December 1987 and 271 consumer advocates and energy industry representatives by mail survey in March 1988. Results of the surveys showed that 96 percent of the public interest leaders and 53 percent of the public would not relax environmental controls to produce more energy, while 52 percent of energy industry leaders would relax controls. On the question of opening the Arctic National Wildlife Refuge to energy development, 92 percent of the public interest leaders opposed development in the refuge, and 83 percent of industry leaders strongly favored development. Both the public and the public interest leaders thought future energy needs should be addressed through conservation and renewable energy sources. The industry leaders, however, favored production over conservation.

458. Media General/Associated Press Poll. *American Public Opinion Index: 1989.* Boston, MA: Opinion Research Service, Inc., 1990.

This Media General/Associated Press telephone poll of May 1989 addressed a variety of issues related to the environment. (Other aspects of the poll are described elsewhere.) The national survey queried 1,084 Americans about their preferences for government action to combat deforestation, pollution of drinking water, air pollution, ocean pollution, the greenhouse effect, acid rain, and toxic wastes. When asked if the government should allow increased offshore oil drilling and oil drilling in the Arctic National Wildlife Refuge, 60 percent of the national sample said "no." Larger percentages of respondents in Florida and California were willing to allow the increased drilling. Only 2 percent of those surveyed saw U.S. pollution laws as "too tough," while 75 percent thought pollution laws were "too weak." A large majority supported mandatory recycling and a majority supported bans on aerosol products, charcoal lighter fluid, non-radial tires, and pollution controls on power plants to reduce pollution and atmospheric problems. Toxic waste disposal and drinking water pollution were seen as the environmental problems most in need of urgent government action.

459. The California Poll. *American Public Opinion Index: 1989.* Boston, MA: Opinion Research Service, Inc., 1990.

The Field Institute of San Francisco, California, completed this telephone poll during July 1989. A sample of 994 Californians were asked if oil companies should be allowed to drill new oil and gas wells off the California coast. Nearly three-fourths of the respondents indicated they did not want expanded offshore drilling. The poll report compares these results with responses received to earlier polls conducted from 1977 through 1981 and in 1984. The percent of the sample disapproving of offshore drilling increased between 1984 and 1989.

460. The University of North Carolina Poll. *American Public Opinion Index: 1989.* Boston, MA: Opinion Research Service, Inc., 1990.

The University of North Carolina Poll was conducted by the university's Institute for Social Research in North Carolina. During the fall of 1989, 634 residents of North Carolina were interviewed by telephone and asked their opinion of gas and oil drilling off the coast of North Carolina.

461. Cambridge Reports. *American Public Opinion Index: 1989.* Boston, MA: Opinion Research Service, Inc., 1990.

Cambridge Reports of Cambridge, Massachusetts, personally interviewed 1,500 Americans for a national poll during 1989. Subjects for the poll included attitudes toward development of the Arctic National Wildlife Refuge and offshore drilling for oil and gas exploration. The survey respondents were also asked their perception of the seriousness of the greenhouse effect and whether they supported shutting down coal-burning electric plants to resolve the problem.

462. Drummond, Tammerlin. "New Drilling Opposed Off O[range] C[ounty] Shores." *The Los Angeles Times* (Orange County edition), April 15, 1990, p. A32.

A *Times* Orange County Poll was conducted by Mark Baldassare and Associates two months after a major oil spill at Huntington Beach. The respondents to the poll were asked their opinion of bans on offshore drilling in their own area and elsewhere in the United States. While two-thirds of the county residents said they supported a complete ban on drilling off the Orange County coast, only 38 percent opposed increased oil exploration and production in other areas of the country. The survey method, interview dates, and sample size for the poll are not given in the article.

463. National Survey on the Iraqi Crisis. *American Public Opinion Index: 1990.* Tallahassee, FL: 1991.

Penn and Schoen Associates, Inc. of Washington, D.C., conducted this national telephone poll for Texaco, Inc. The energy poll, which was released in August 1990, interviewed 667 members of the general public and 251 informed members of the public. In response to one question on exploration of energy reserves, 51 percent said they favored allowing increased exploration in wildlife preserves in Alaska.

Forests and Forest Management

464. Quinney, Dean N. "Small Private Forest Landownership in the United States: Individual and Social Perception." *Natural Resources Journal* 3 (January 1964): 379–93.

This article discusses research conducted by the Lake States Forest Experiment Station into small forest owner objectives for forest landownership. The study, performed in 1959 and 1960 in the Upper Peninsula of Michigan, sampled 3 percent of the owners of rural lands between 5 and 5,000 acres in size. The survey revealed that the primary objectives of forest land ownership included: investment and for sale (28 percent), recreation (27 percent), farm use (19 percent), residence (19 percent), and timber values and use (6 percent).

465. Bultena, Gordon L., and Hendee, John C. "Foresters' View of Interest Group Positions on Forest Policy." *Journal of Forestry* 70 (1972): 337–42.

In the research described in this article, foresters were asked their perceptions of interest group positions on timber cutting and trail biking on forest trails. A sample of 118 foresters at five national forests (Mt. Baker, Wenatehee, Snoqualmie, Gifford Pinchot, and Mt. Hood) in the Pacific Northwest completed questionnaires in 1967. The foresters were asked what position they thought 16 different types of interest groups would take on the two issues. The interest groups included the following: trail bike clubs, hunters' organizations, sport fishermen organizations, ski area operators, skiers' associations, conservation organizations, outfitters, and hiking and mountain climbing clubs. Government officials and business groups were also included. On timber cutting, the foresters perceived recreation groups as being opposed to increased timber cuts. And on the issue of trail biking, the foresters felt trail bikers and hunters would support the activity, while hikers and mountain climbers would be opposed, and skiers would be neutral. The researchers apparently made no attempt to measure the actual views of the different interest groups.

466. Cook, Walter L. "An Evaluation of the Aesthetic Quality of Forest Trees." *Journal of Leisure Research* 4 (Fall 1972): 293–302.

The author of this article surveyed visitors to three recreational areas about their preference for different types of mature forest trees. The participants were asked to choose among 12 pairs of trees representing three classes of timber quality. They were also asked to indicate the physical characteristics most responsible for their choice. During the summer of 1970, a total of 390 interviews were conducted in Allegheny National Forest (N = 123), Adirondack Forest Preserve (N = 147), and Robert Treman State Park (N = 120). In most cases, the tree preference indicated a positive relationship between the quality of the timber and the perceived aesthetics of the tree. Preferences were most often based on balanced appearance, attractiveness of the background, straightness of the trunk, and the presence of many branches.

467. Plumb, James W. "Public Attitudes and Knowledge of Forestry." *Journal of Forestry* 71 (April 1973): 217–19.

The Gallup Organization conducted this poll of over 1,500 Americans for the American Forest Institute of the Forest Industries Council during May 1972. Included in the survey were questions on concern for forests and timberlands, attitude toward clear-cutting, attitude toward government control of forestlands, and opinion of type of lands that should be used as a source of lumber and paper. Nearly two-thirds of the respondents thought too little attention was being given to forest conservation, and 44 percent said they worried about using up forests and timberlands. Over three-fourths of the sample thought clear-cutting was a bad practice, and 47 percent wanted tougher government laws and regulations for forests. When asked which federal areas should be used as a source of lumber and paper, 43 percent chose wilderness areas, 32 percent national forests, 10 percent national parks, and 23 percent said no federal forests should be used to provide wood products. The article also mentions a second survey sponsored by the Forest Industries Council designed to evaluate public awareness of forestry terms.

468. Willhite, Robert G.; Bowlees, Donald R.; and Tarbet, Donald. "An Approach for Resolution of Attitude Differences Over Forest Management." *Environment and Behavior* 5 (September 1973): 351–66.

In this article, the authors describe research designed to compare attitudes toward forest management among different groups. The sample included representatives of the following groups: senior forestry students (N = 53), forestry graduate students (N = 8), forest service managers (N = 28), forestry professors (N = 12), beginning forestry students (N = 47), natural science students (N = 18), psychology students (N = 28), general education students (N = 28), and Sierra Club members (N = 38). A questionnaire of 115 statements about forests and forest management was administered to the different groups at California State University, Humboldt and in the community of Arcata, California. The research identified three factors as representing areas of greatest attitude differences: timber industry practices and motives, emotional and social values of forests, and clear-cutting and forest dynamics. The senior and graduate forestry students expressed attitudes most supportive of forestry management practices, while the nonforestry students and Sierra Club members were most critical of forest management. These latter groups also gave the highest ratings to the emotional and social value of forests. The greatest variation in responses was observed for the items related to the practice of clear-cutting. The item receiving the highest overall mean rating (indicating agreement) was, "Natural forests are places where I can feel my connectedness with nature." The lowest overall mean rating (indicating disagreement) was, "The forest is a renewable resource."

469. Willhite, Robert G., and Wise, William R.. "Measurement of Reaction to Forest Practices." *Journal of Forestry* 72 (September 1974): 567–71.

The purpose of this study was to measure the attitudes of forestry students, nonforestry students and forestry professors toward forestry practices. Students and faculty at California State University, Humboldt, comprised the sample for the study. The survey instrument was designed to gauge reaction to statements about forest management practices and visual reaction to selected forest scenes. Factor analysis was used to interpret the reactions. The analysis resulted in the identification of five factors: timber management and utilization; natural forest appearance; clear-cutting, vistas with cover; intermediate regeneration; and clear-cutting, close view with bare earth. The attitudes of the forestry and nonforestry students differed significantly. Forestry students expressed strong approval of the timer industry and its practices, while nonforestry students expressed disapproval of clear-cutting and other timber cutting practices.

470. Metro, Laura J.; Dwyer, John F.; and Dreschler, Erwin S. *Forest Experiences of Fifth Grade Chicago Public School Students.* U.S. Department of Agriculture, Forest Service, 1981, 6 pp.

A total of 269 public school children from the Chicago area made up the sample for this survey. Respondents were asked about their perceptions of the forest and their previous forest experiences. The students were asked why they like visiting the forest, what they learned in a forest, and what they feared about the forest. The largest number of students said they liked visiting the forest because "it's fun." They felt they learned the most about animals and outdoor skills. Approximately 40 percent of the children thought animals in the forest posed a danger to them. Responses are given by race and sex of the children.

471. Becker, Robert H. "Opinions About Clear-Cutting and Recognition of Clear-Cuts by Forest Recreation Visitors." *Environmental Management* 17 (1983): 171–77.

The research presented in this paper was designed to relate opinions of forest recreation visitors toward clear-cutting forestry practices with knowledge and awareness of clear-cutting. A total of 882 visitors to the Savage River State Forest, Maryland, were surveyed at field locations in the forest during the summer of 1974 and the fall and winter of 1974-75. Visitors were classified by whether they were aware they had been through a clear-cut and the time of year of their visit. The summer visitors demonstrated a positive, significant relationship between recognition of a clear-cut and opinions about clear-cutting. These relationships were not documented with the fall and winter visitors. There was no relationship between recognition of a clear-cut area and enjoyment of the forest for either group. The practice of clear-cutting was perceived as a "proper forest management practice" by the majority of both groups of visitors.

472. Cortner, Hanna J.; Zwolinski, Malcolm J.; Carpenter, Edwin H.; and Taylor, Jonathan G. "Public Support for Fire-Management Policies." *Journal of Forestry* 82 (June 1984): 359–61.

The study described in this article was performed by faculty and staff of the University of Arizona. Funding was provided by the Eisenhower Consortium Project, U.S. Forest Service. The study surveyed 1,200 adult residents of Tucson, Arizona, about their attitudes toward forest resources, forest fires, and fire management practices. The questionnaire was administered by telephone during a two-week period in February and March 1981. A majority of the respondents indicated they approved of fire management practices, and 80 percent strongly supported the use of "prescribed fires."

473. Taylor, Jonathan G., and Daniel, Terry C.. "Prescribed Fire: Public Education and Perception." *Journal of Forestry* 82 (June 1984): 361–65.

This research was conducted by staff of the University of Arizona and funded by a grant from the Eisenhower Consortium, U.S. Forest Service. A sample of 193 civic and church organization members were asked to rate slides of forest scenes for scenic quality and acceptability for recreation before and after reviewing informational brochures. The slides depicted varying degrees of fire effects. The subjects' knowledge of forest fire and its effect were also measured. Although exposure to the brochure increased knowledge, it did not affect the ratings of scenic quality or recreational acceptability. The slides showing light fire effects were rated highest for scenic quality, whereas slides depicting severe fire damage were rated lowest. The effect of fire on recreational acceptability differed by recreation preference. Campers were the most sensitive to fire effects and were the only group to prefer unburned areas to areas of light burns.

474. Gardner, Philip D.; Cortner, Hanna J.; and Widaman, Keith F. "Forest-User Attitudes Toward Alternative Fire Management Policies." *Environmental Management* 9 (July 1985): 303–12.

The purpose of this study was to measure and compare the attitudes of different groups of forest users toward fire management policies. Data for the study were obtained from 1,646 members of the following groups: Soil Conservation Society of America, Federation of Fly Fishermen, Audubon Society, Society of

American Foresters, Photographic Society of America, Sierra Club, hunting organizations, off-road vehicle users, and the National Forest Products Association. Each subject completed a questionnaire containing items on fire knowledge, attitudes toward prescribed burning as a management tool, and attitudes toward other fire management policies. Some of the questionnaires were distributed by mail, while others were administered by interviewers at organizational meetings. Responses to the questionnaire revealed differences among the groups but demonstrated general support for prescribed fire and flexible fire suppression policies. Partial funding for the study was provided by the Pacific Southwest Forest and Range Experiment Station, U.S. Forest Service.

475. Taylor, Jonathan G.; Cortner, Hanna J.; Gardner, Philip D.; Daniel, Terry C.; Zwolinski, Malcolm J.; and Carpenter, Edwin H. "Recreation and Fire Management: Public Concerns, Attitudes, and Perceptions." *Leisure Sciences* 8 (1986): 167–87.

The preparation of this paper was funded by the Eisenhower Consortium, the Rocky Mountain Forest and Range Experiment Station, and the Pacific Southwest Forest and Range Experiment Station, U.S. Forest Service. In this article, the authors describe and compare results of three previously reported studies into attitudes toward fire management policies. One of the studies sampled the general public of Tucson, Arizona, another sampled members of citizens' groups in Tucson, and the third used a national sample of forest users. Respondents in two of the studies were asked to rate seven forest uses. The highest ratings were given to forests as a source of food for wildlife and forests as a place for outdoor recreation. Hunting was rated among the lowest of possible forest uses. The forest fire impacts that were of most concern to the subjects were "trees lost," "wild animal death," and "animal food lost." Among different types of recreation users, campers were the most sensitive to severe fire effects. Hikers, backpackers, and participants in nature study were virtually unaffected by light fire damage.

476. McCool, Stephen F., and Stankey, George H. *Visitor Attitudes Toward Wilderness Fire Management Policy: 1971–84.* U.S. Department of Agriculture, Forest Service, January 1986, 7 pp.

This report compares the findings of two mail surveys of wilderness visitor attitudes toward fire management policies conducted by the U.S. Forest Service. The studies surveyed 183 and 275 visitors to the Selway-Bitterroot Wilderness in 1971 and 1984, respectively. The respondents to the 1984 survey were more knowledgeable about natural fire effects and more supportive of fire management than the visitors responding to the 1971 survey.

477. McCool, Stephen F.; Benson, Robert E.; and Ashor, Joseph L. "How the Public Perceives the Visual Effects of Timber Harvesting: An Evaluation of Interest Group Preferences." *Environmental Management* 10 (May 1986): 385–91.

This article describes a study performed to measure preferences for landscape scenes depicting effects of timber harvesting. To test for viewer preference for various levels of harvesting, slides of timber sale areas in Montana and northern Idaho were shown to members of 18 public interest and professional groups at their organizational meetings during the fall and winter of 1982-83. The groups surveyed included motorcycle riders, landscape architects, horse riders, members of conservation organizations, loggers, foresters, and students in recreation and timber management classes. A total of 413 group members rated the scenic quality of 125 slides showing five levels of natural landscape modification by timber harvesting. The results indicated the groups had similar preferences for the scenic quality of the different landscape scenes.

478. Stiegler, Jonathan H. "Public Perception of the Urban Forest." *Proceedings of the Fourth Urban Forestry Conference*, 1989, pp. 40–45.

This report relates details of a study of residents' attitudes toward the concept of an urban forest. The research was conducted by the Department of Forestry and Environmental Services in Robbinsdale, Minnesota. A questionnaire was administered to 58 sixth-grade students and 49 members of a local senior citizen club in Robbinsdale. Analysis of the survey demonstrated that the concept of an urban forest was poorly recognized by both the student and senior citizen groups.

479. Durbin, Kathie. "Poll Respondents Go Opposite Ways on 'Owls vs. Jobs'." *The Oregonian*, June 22, 1989, p. B6.

A poll conducted by *The Oregonian* in 1989 asked state residents their opinion of a proposed ban on logging old-growth forests and whether, in their view, the timber industry could survive such a ban. (Details of the poll's sample size, exact date, and methodology are not provided.) According to the article, the respondents were evenly divided over whether a ban on old-growth logging on public lands would seriously damage the timber industry. Reaction was also evenly divided to the statement, "Forest jobs must be protected, even if it means loss of spotted owl habitat." Over 60 percent of those interviewed agreed that "Too much protection is being given to the spotted owl and its habitat."

480. "Poll Respondents Favor Logging Limits." *The Oregonian*, April 24, 1990, p. B4.

During April 1990, 403 residents of Washington state were surveyed about their attitudes toward logging issues in the northwest. The poll was conducted by Elway Research for the *Seattle Times*. Interviewers told the poll's respondents that banning old-growth logging in western Washington could result in the loss of thousands of jobs in the local communities. Despite the threat to jobs, 52 percent said they would support a logging ban to protect spotted owl habitat. When asked what they personally consider most important in deciding logging issues, 64 percent cited wildlife habitat or the status of the forest, while only 30 percent named jobs or the local economy in logging communities. (Other results of this poll are presented elsewhere.)

481. "Forest Service Gets Mixed Marks in Poll." *The Oregonian*, May 24, 1990, p. E19.

A&A Research of Kalispell, Montana, conducted this survey for the U.S. Forest Service Region 1 which includes areas in Idaho, Montana, and the Dakotas. The telephone poll queried 900 residents of the four states plus residents of Spokane, Washington, who use the forest service area in Idaho. Overall, about half of the respondents gave the forest service a "good" rating with residents of the Dakotas being the most satisfied and residents of western Montana being the least satisfied with the government agency. Wilderness preservation was the greatest forest related concern of the sample with logging issues ranking second in importance.

482. Manfredo, Michael J.; Fishbein, Martin; Haas, Glenn E.; and Watson, Alan E. "Attitudes Toward Prescribed Fire Policies." *Journal of Forestry* 88 (July 1990): 19-23.

This study attempted to measure public attitudes toward "prescribed" or "controlled burn" fire policy following the Yellowstone forest fires in the summer of 1988. The researchers surveyed residents of the states affected by the fires as well as residents of the other 48 states. In March and April 1989, 391 Montana and Wyoming residents and a national sample of 522 Americans were contacted by telephone regarding their attitude toward "prescribed burn" fire policy, their support of the policy, and their beliefs about the outcome of such a policy. Subjects were also asked several factual questions to measure their knowledge of the effects of forest fires. The Montana and Wyoming residents expressed slight support (55 percent) for a "controlled burn" policy, while the national sample was evenly divided on the issue. The regional sample was more knowledgeable about forest fires than the national sample, and those with a positive attitude toward "prescribed burns" were more knowledgeable than those with a negative attitude toward the practice. The research was funded by the U.S. Department of Agriculture, Forest Service, the University of Illinois Department of Forestry, and the University of Illinois Research Board.

483. Bliss, John C., and Martin, A. Jeff. "How Tree Farmers View Management Incentives." *Journal of Forestry* 88 (August 1990): 23-29, 42.

The purpose of this study, funded by the Kickapoo Valley (WI) Reforestation Fund, was to identify factors that motivate nonindustrial private forest owners to manage their forest land. The sample chosen for the study was not random or representative but rather forest land owners who had demonstrated they managed their forest according to professional forestry standards. In order to be included in the study, owners had to meet three criteria that indicated their active involvement in forest management on their land. Personal interviews, written surveys, and Wisconsin Department of Natural Resources records were all used to compile case summaries on 16 forest owners. The case summaries focused on the landowners' attitudes toward timber harvesting and internal and external motivations that affected their forestry management. All of the forest owners felt timber production was a "somewhat" or "very important" reason for owning forest land. A high percentage indicated they used their land for recreation, scenic enjoyment and wildlife habitat. Of various external incentives for managing their land, technical assistance from professional foresters seemed to be the most effective.

484. Eastern Montana College. *American Public Opinion Index: 1991.* Tallahassee, FL: 1991.

In this telephone poll, Eastern Montana College interviewed 410 Montana residents during the winter of 1991. Respondents were queried about their perception of timber management in the national forests of Montana.

485. Yozwiak, Steve. "Protecting Nature, Not Timber Industry, Favored in State Poll." *The Arizona Republic*, April 17, 1992, p. B6.

The Social Research Laboratory of Northern Arizona University conducted a random telephone poll of Arizona residents on March 30 and April 4, 1992. This article reports on the findings of that poll which was completed by 629 residents of five northern Arizona counties. Respondents were questioned about their perception of the importance of protecting timber jobs and maintaining private corporate profits from the use of public lands as well as the importance of environmental protection versus economic growth. The results showed that, when asked to choose, twice as many of the respondents would protect the environment as support economic growth.

486. "Survey Shows Support Strong for Endangered Species Act." *Wildlife Advocate: News from Defenders of Wildlife* 1 (Spring 1993): 8.

Defenders of Wildlife sponsored this poll which was released prior to a forest conference held in Portland, Oregon, on logging issues. Pollster Celinda Lake of the Washington, D.C., firm of Greenberg-Lake surveyed a national sample of 1,000 registered voters. The poll found 73 percent support the Endangered Species Act, up from 66 percent in 1992. Approximately two-thirds of the sample agreed that timber industry jobs in the northwest "will eventually be lost anyway unless the environment is treated so that it can sustain the economy." (Although not given in this article, a UP newswire report of April 1, 1993, on the survey reported differences in responses for voters in the Pacific West and for the nation as a whole. According to the newswire item, the Endangered Species Act was supported by 73 percent of those surveyed nationally and 66 percent of the western voters in the Defenders poll.)

Wilderness

487. Hendee, John C., and Harris, Robert W. "Foresters' Perception of Wilderness User Attitudes and Preferences." *Journal of Forestry* 68 (December 1970): 759–62.

Data from another study by the lead author were used in this research to compare the attitudes of wilderness users toward wilderness management with wilderness managers' perceptions of those attitudes. In the prior aspect of the study, surveys were administered to 1,350 registered visitors to Eagle Cap, Three Sisters, and Glacier Peak Wildernesses in the Pacific Northwest. A similar questionnaire was given to 56 Forest Service recreation managers from Washington and Oregon. The managers underestimated the users' support for behavior control and overestimated the users' support for recreational development in wilderness areas. The managers also tended to view the recreationists as more opinionated and purist in their wilderness attitudes than demonstrated by the user survey. Results of the survey are described in general terms in the article; no specific questions or responses are presented.

488. Young, Robert A., and Crandall, Rick. "Wilderness Knowledge and Values of the Illinois Public." *Journal of Forestry* 77 (December 1979): 768–76.

The research presented in this article was conducted by the Survey Research Laboratory at the University of Illinois with funds from the Illinois Agricultural Experiment Station. The purpose of the study was to compare the knowledge and attitudes of the general public and wilderness users toward the wilderness concept. A telephone survey of Illinois adult residents was performed in May 1977. In addition, a mail survey similar to the telephone questionnaire was sent to users of the Boundary Water Canoe Area in Minnesota. The total sample consisted of 482 members of the general public and 220 wilderness users. Both groups indicated approval of the wilderness concept with the wilderness users expressing much stronger support. Both groups also approved of the current uses of wilderness with the exception of hunting. A large majority of the general public (78 percent) and wilderness users (75 percent) said hunting should not be allowed in wilderness areas. On the other hand, a majority of those sampled indicated they approved of cattle grazing in wilderness areas.

489. "Environment 'Main Concern' in Exploring Public Lands." *Chicago Tribune*, December 2, 1981, section 2, p. 7.

The Heritage Foundation sponsored this poll which was conducted by Sindlinger and Company. A total of 2,289 Americans were interviewed for the poll between October 15 and November 11, 1981. Topics for the poll included support for economic development in wilderness areas and areas with endangered species habitat. A large majority (84 percent) of those polled said they would approve of energy exploration on federal wilderness land if it was done in an environmentally sensitive manner. Respondents were less favorable toward economic development in areas that contain habitat critical to endangered species. The opinion was nearly evenly divided over a question of whether habitat for an endangered species should be protected even at the expense of all economic development.

490. "Poll Finds Majority Oppose Weaker Environmental Laws." *The New York Times*, November 14, 1982, section 1, p. 74.

This newspaper article details results from a survey conducted by Research and Forecasts, Inc., for the Continental Group. Other results from the survey are described elsewhere. The surveyors interviewed 1,300 members of the general public, 263 business executives, and 343 environmentalists. Approximately half of the sample of business executives and two-thirds of the public indicated they believed that certain areas of the country should be left completely undeveloped. The article notes that the number of environmentalists that favor wilderness areas was not available.

491. ABC News Poll. *American Public Opinion Index: 1983*. Lexington, KY: Opinion Research Service, Inc., 1985.

A nationwide telephone poll of 1,516 Americans was conducted by ABC News. Results of the poll were released on April 12, 1983. The poll respondents were asked whether they thought environmental protection was worth the cost and whether environmental regulations on factories and energy producing industries should be relaxed. The survey also asked whether environmental attempts to stop commercial development in federal parks and wilderness areas had gone too far or not far enough. Perceptions of acid rain, toxic waste disposal, and lake and river pollution as problems were also measured.

492. Florida State University Poll. *American Public Opinion Index: 1985*. Lexington, KY: Opinion Research Service, Inc., 1986.

The Florida State University Poll is an annual survey conducted by the Policy Sciences Program at Florida State University. In this poll, 983 Florida residents were contacted by telephone and asked whether they supported prohibiting development in fragile natural areas of the state.

493. Croke, Kevin; Fabian, Robert; and Brenniman, Gary. "Estimating the Value of Natural Open Space Preservation in an Urban Area." *Environmental Management* 23 (1986): 317–24.

This paper details research designed to estimate the value of urban open space to the public. A telephone survey was conducted with 350 households in Lake County, Illinois. The respondents were asked questions about their use of nature and forest preserves and the reasons for valuing preserves. Of those who indicated they visited preserves, the majority said they did so to enjoy the area's scenic beauty. By two to one, the subjects indicated they wanted nature preserves maintained to "know the areas are being preserved" rather than to make personal use of the areas. Respondents were also asked of their willingness to pay to prevent 50 percent and 100 percent conversion of the nature preserve to commercial development and 50 percent conversion to forest preserve. The study's subjects were willing to pay more than twice as much for preservation as for conversion, and over half of them were unwilling to pay anything to prevent conversion of the nature preserve to a forest preserve.

494. Talmey Associates Poll. *American Public Opinion Index: 1986.* Boston, MA: Opinion Research Service, Inc., 1987.

Talmey Associates of Boulder, Colorado, performed telephone polls of Colorado residents in June 1986 with 509 state residents and again in July 1986 with 506 Coloradoans. The June poll included an item on protection of national forest land, and the July poll included items on acid rain and protection of forest land even at an economic cost. In June, 68 percent of the sample said the federal government "should designate more national forest land as wilderness areas to protect it from mining and logging." In the July poll, however, only 46 percent agreed that "The federal government should designate more national forest land as wilderness areas even if it costs some jobs and an increase in the price of lumber and other raw materials." At the same time, 60 percent supported taking action against acid rain including closing down polluting factories. Both polls were sponsored by the *Denver Post* and NewsCenter 4 of Denver.

495. *Survey of Public Attitudes on Open Space in Iowa.* Des Moines, IA: Crowley Market Research Co., January 1988, 8 pp.

This special survey on open spaces was conducted during January 1988 with 400 Iowa residents. Contacted by telephone, the subjects were asked their opinion of different types of open spaces and different funding options for open spaces. Nearly 80 percent of the sample said they preferred public to private ownership for open spaces, and 75 percent said privately owned open spaces should be under the state's protection. Over three-fourths of those surveyed supported acquiring more open spaces in Iowa, and 82 percent thought open spaces were important to the quality of life in Iowa. Priorities for protecting open spaces were ranked as follows: for people to enjoy, for future generations, and to protect wildlife.

496. *Denver Post* Poll. *American Public Opinion Index: 1989.* Boston, MA: Opinion Research Service, Inc., 1990.

Talmey Drake Research and Strategy, Inc. of Boulder, Colorado, conducted this poll in December 1989. A sample of 506 Colorado residents were contacted by telephone for the survey which included a question on designating more national forest land as wilderness areas. When asked if the federal government should designate more wilderness land even at the expense of jobs and higher prices for raw materials, 54 percent of those surveyed agreed while 34 percent disagreed. A slightly lower percentage of the sample indicated they also agreed with the idea of Colorado increasing the purchase of open spaces and park and recreation areas.

497. University of New Hampshire Poll. *American Public Opinion Index: 1991.* Tallahassee, FL: 1991.

The Institute for Policy and Social Science Research at the University of New Hampshire performed this poll by contacting 508 New Hampshire residents by telephone. Respondents to the June 1991 poll were asked their opinion of developing the state's forest lands. A large majority of those sampled said they felt it was "very important" to keep large areas of the state's forest lands in timber production and protected from other development. Nearly all of the respondents supported requiring portions of forest land to be protected from development when a large area is being developed. The sample also approved of the state and federal government purchasing more natural areas to protect them from development.

498. *The Communications Plan for the Gallatin National Forest.* Kalispell, MT: A&A Research, 1991, 43 pp.

A&A Research of Kalispell, Montana, surveyed 203 residents of the Gallatin National Forest service area during 1991. The telephone interviews attempted to measure public attitudes toward various forest issues, particularly support for development of forest resources versus preservation of wilderness values. Some of the subjects covered during the interviews included the following: most important issues facing the Gallatin National Forest, support for timber harvesting in roadless areas, perception of the primary function of the Forest Service, identification with pro- versus anti-development views, support for additional recreational areas, and preference for timber management versus wilderness management. While the "multiple use" concept was supported by 86 percent of the residents, only 24 percent wanted more timber harvested in the National Forest. The primary function of the Forest Service was perceived as natural resource development by 35 percent, outdoor recreation by 21 percent, fish and wildlife management by 18 percent, and timber management by 11 percent. Only 15 percent favored opening more areas of the National Forest to motorized recreation, yet 67 percent supported developing more recreation areas. Almost two-thirds of the sample said they thought the forest should be managed more for wilderness values.

499. Rudzitis, Gundaris, and Johansen, Harley E. "How Important Is Wilderness? Results from a United States Survey." *Environmental Management* 15 (March-April 1991): 227–33.

This article reports on a survey of the importance of wilderness to 2,670 residents of U.S. wilderness counties. Mail questionnaires were sent to residents of 11 wilderness counties in ten states (Arizona, California, Colorado, Georgia, Idaho, Montana, Missouri, New Mexico, Oregon, and Wyoming). The respondents were asked their reactions to five statements about the importance of wilderness as a reason for moving to their area, energy development in wilderness areas, the importance of wilderness areas to a county, and support for additional wilderness areas and access to wilderness areas. Of the total sample, 53 percent said wilderness was an important reason for their move to the area, and 81 percent thought wilderness areas were important to their county. Nearly two-thirds of the sample opposed mineral and energy development in wilderness areas. The research was funded by the National Science Foundation.

500. Echelberger, Herbert E.; Luloff, Albert E.; and Schmidt, Frederick E. *Northern Forest Lands: Resident Attitudes and Resource Use.* U.S. Department of Agriculture, Forest Service, August 1991, 26 pp.

In this research, residents of five New England counties were surveyed about their attitudes toward community environmental problems, local and regional land use planning, and public acquisition of forest lands. The study, sponsored by the U.S. Forest Service, interviewed 175 residents of New Hampshire and 271 residents of Vermont. Disposing of solid waste was rated as the most serious community problem by residents of both states. Public land acquisition for the purpose of wilderness protection was supported by 85 percent of the total sample. Smaller percentages of the sample supported public land acquisition for wildlife habitat (82 percent), recreational opportunities (80 percent), and assuring a timber supply (72 percent). Responses are given for the total sample and by community population size.

Nature and Natural Resources

501. Burton, Ian, and Kates, Robert W. "The Perception of Natural Hazards in Resource Management." *Natural Resources Journal* 3 (January 1964): 412–41.

Included in this article is a brief description of a study of cultural influences on human views of nature. The researchers interviewed 106 respondents from five New Mexico cultural groups: Spanish Americans, Texans, Mormons, Zuni Indians, and Rimrock Navaho Indians. Responses were used to develop a man-nature classification composed of three basic viewpoints: "man subject to nature," "man with nature," and "man over nature." The Spanish American respondents exhibited a "man subject to nature" attitude, while the most common view among the Texans was "man over nature." A "man with nature" attitude was expressed by the majority of the Mormon and Zuni and Navaho Indian subjects.

502. Stronck, David R. "Attitudes on the Population Explosion." *The Science Teacher* 38 (November 1971): 34–37.

This article describes a study which attempted to measure and compare the attitudes of biology teachers and future teachers toward human population growth and natural resources. A sample of 34 biology teachers and 34 college juniors and seniors in secondary education programs from the Austin, Texas, area were asked questions about teaching controversial topics, the condition of the United States in the year 2000, and human population. The future teachers were more optimistic about conditions in the United States in the year 2000. A majority of the students felt America will have solved most problems with population growth and pollution, and technology will have provided new sources and uses of resources. The teachers were more likely to believe that by 2000 the decline of natural resources will present urgent problems. Approximately 90 percent of both groups felt human population should be leveled off well before it approaches the full use of natural resources. Half of the students and 73 percent of the teachers agreed that "Science as it is now taught does not promote respect for nature."

503. Stamm, Keith R., and Bowes, John E. "Environmental Attitudes and Reaction." *Journal of Environmental Education* 3 (Spring 1972): 56–60.

This research measured environmental attitudes as part of a study conducted to explore support for a proposed flood control project. A sample of 174
community leaders and residents of Grafton and Park River, North Dakota, were
interviewed for the study. Responses to survey items on the use of chemical sprays,
feeding and harvesting of deer, water control and use, farming, planting vegetation
and improving wildlife habitat were used to determine attitudes toward resource
scarcity and functional substitutes for scarcity management.

504. Buttel, Frederick H., and Flinn, William L. "The Structure of Support
for the Environmental Movement, 1968–1970." *Rural Sociology* 39 (Spring
1974): 56–69.

This research used data from three statewide surveys to track support for
environmental issues over a three-year period of time. Data for the study were provided by surveys conducted by the Wisconsin Survey Research Lab during the
summers of 1968–70. In each year's survey, approximately 600 respondents were
asked about their concern for air and water pollution and preservation of natural
resources. The percentage of Wisconsin respondents identifying water and air
pollution as one of the two most important problems in the state more than doubled
between 1968 and 1970. The percent identifying preservation of natural resources
as a major problem remained basically unchanged. Examination of several demographic variables (place of residence, education, political ideology, income, and occupation) revealed that support for environmental issues moved downward during
the period to the lower-middle class.

505. Gallup, George H. "October 31, 1973: Attitudes of Youth." *The Gallup
Poll: Public Opinion 1972–1977.* Wilmington, DE: Scholarly Resources,
Inc., 1978, p. 198–204.

This Gallup Poll was conducted in spring 1973 with 1,534 young adults aged
18 to 24 years. When asked to respond to the statement, "Human wisdom will prevent pollution and complete depletion of nature," 58 percent agreed, 41 percent
disagreed, and 1 percent had no opinion.

506. "Opinion Roundup." *Public Opinion* 2 (January-February 1979): 25.

In this article, results from a Roper Poll conducted in March 1978 are
presented. Respondents to the poll were asked about a number of conditions that
might happen in the United States in the coming years. For each condition, the respondents were asked to indicate whether they thought the condition was likely to
happen and whether they perceived the condition as a serious threat. Increasing
population was thought likely to happen by 50 percent of those surveyed, and 21
percent of the sample saw it as a serious threat. The sample was also asked about
the likelihood and seriousness of a rapid depletion of natural resources. Over half
(58 percent) thought loss of natural resources was likely to happen, and 44 percent
thought the possibility posed a serious threat to society. Both of these percentages
were the highest received to any of the 13 conditions included in the survey.

507. Pierce, John C. "Water Resources Preservation: Personal Values and
Public Support." *Environment and Behavior* 11 (June 1979): 147–61.

Partial funding for this study was provided by the Washington State University

Graduate School and U.S. Department of Interior. This study was designed to measure the relationship between personal values and support for water resource preservation. The sample consisted of 687 heads of households in Washington state during late 1974. A questionnaire completed by the respondents measured personal values and ranked priorities for water resource use. The priority of seven water resource uses, as ranked by the subjects, were the following: agriculture, domestic, energy, industry, preservation, transportation, and recreation. The ranking of preservation was significantly correlated with the ranking of several of the personal values. One value, "a world of beauty," was an important factor in support for preservation among the different types of water resource users.

508. Honnold, Julie A., and Nelson, Lynn D. "Support for Resource Conservation: A Prediction Model." *Social Problems* 27 (December 1979): 220–34.

In this research, the authors tested a theoretical model developed to explain support for natural resource conservation. The model was composed of the following variables: socioeconomic status, mobility aspiration, need identification, perceived problem immediacy, assessment of problem solubility, and perceived efficacy. Preliminary testing of the model was conducted in 1976 with 485 undergraduate sociology and anthropology students at a large, mid–Atlantic state university. Analysis of the student surveys revealed that the model was capable of explaining 25 percent of the variance in support for resource conservation. The article includes a copy of the actual survey instrument.

509. The Roper Poll. *American Public Opinion Index: 1981.* Tallahassee, FL: Opinion Research Service, Inc., 1982.

The December 1981 Roper Poll included questions on environmental spending and concern for the future supply of various natural resources. The national poll interviewed 2,000 Americans by telephone.

510. Albrecht, Don; Bultena, Gordon; Hoiberg, Eric; and Nowak, Peter. "The New Environmental Paradigm Scale." *Journal of Environmental Education* 13 (Spring 1982): 39–43.

In this paper, the authors describe the application of an instrument developed to measure how people feel about nature. As opposed to prior instruments which measured concern for specific environmental problems, the 12 items of this tool were designed to explore attitudes toward the general concepts of the balance of nature, limits to human growth, and man over nature. The sample chosen for this study consisted of 348 Iowa farmers and 407 residents of metropolitan areas in Iowa. The mean scores for this sample are compared with scores from a prior sampling of environmental organization members and the general population in the state of Washington. Reliability and validity testing of the scale are described and the actual scale items are presented.

511. Rejeski, David W. "Children Look at Nature: Environmental Perception and Education." *Journal of Environmental Education* 13 (Summer 1982): 27–40.

The goal of the research presented in this article was to evaluate how children perceive nature. A total of 385 children from grades one, four, and eight in six public schools were chosen as subjects for the study. Each student was presented with a piece of paper with "Nature is" printed at the top and asked to respond to the statement in any manner they chose. Many of the children offered graphic interpretations of their ideas about nature and some of these drawings are included in the article. The author used interpretations of the student responses to describe dominant characteristics of the nature perceptions of the first-, fourth-, and eighth-grade students.

512. Bloomgarden, Kathy. "Managing the Environment: The Public's View." *Public Opinion* 6 (February-March 1983): 47–51.

This article presents results from a study performed for the Continental Group by Research and Forecasts, Inc. (Other findings from the study are described elsewhere.) The sample for the survey included 1,300 members of the general public, 263 industry executives, and 343 environmentalists. The article contrasts the opinions of the different groups on a variety of issues including priorities for national goals and trade-off choices between development and economic growth and environmental protection. One of the greatest range of opinions occurred for a question on land use versus maintenance of natural areas. Nearly all (95 percent) of the environmentalists chose keeping a natural state, while two-thirds (65 percent) of the general public and less than half (47 percent) of the large corporate executives chose a natural state over use of the land. Protecting nature was ranked as the number one national goal of environmentalists. The general public sample ranked protecting nature sixth on a list of 12 goals, and executives of small and large corporations ranked the issue eighth. Fighting crime was ranked first by the general public and large corporate executives.

513. Kentucky Poll. *American Public Opinion Index: 1985*. Lexington, KY: Opinion Research Service, Inc., 1986.

This special survey on the environment was conducted by the Survey Research Center of the University of Kentucky for the Kentucky Cabinet for Natural Resources and Environmental Protection. A sample of 680 Kentucky residents were contacted by telephone in June 1985. The survey included several questions about the relationship between man and nature, as well as questions about spending for environmental programs and parks and recreation and support for protecting environmentally sensitive areas. When asked whether they thought the planet was approaching its population limit, 58 percent agreed and 36 percent disagreed. An even greater percentage (72 percent) agreed that the earth has limited room and resources, and 61 percent thought there are limits to human growth and development. Nearly two-thirds of the sample described the balance of nature as delicate. The respondents were also asked to indicate how seriously they viewed seven specific environmental problems: toxic waste, industrial water pollution, drinking water contamination, air pollution, acid rain, open dumps, and hazardous waste sites. Of these seven problems, industrial water pollution and toxic wastes were perceived as the most serious. In response to questions about funding environmental cleanup, 63 percent supported a tax increase to improve water quality, and 49 percent were willing to pay higher taxes to clean up abandoned hazardous waste sites. Almost two-thirds of the respondents wanted to force factories to stop all potentially harmful air emissions despite the cost.

514. The Houston Area Survey. *American Public Opinion Index: 1987*. Boston, MA: Opinion Research Service, Inc., 1988.

The Department of Sociology at Rice University conducted this telephone poll with 645 residents of Harris County, Texas. The poll respondents were asked their view of the amount of spending allocated to protecting the environment and whether they thought there was a limit to the earth's space and resources.

515. The Roper Poll. *American Public Opinion Index: 1987.* Boston, MA: Opinion Research Service, Inc., 1988.

In January 1987, the Roper Organization interviewed in person 1,997 Americans from across the country. Those responding to the poll were queried about their opinion of the amount of money spent on the environment, as well as who they thought was to blame for toxic waste contamination of soil and water. The poll also solicited perceptions of the supply of various natural resources in the next 25 to 50 years.

516. Planned Parenthood Poll. *American Public Opinion Index: 1988.* Boston, MA: Opinion Research Service, Inc., 1989.

The Planned Parenthood Federation of America sponsored this poll to solicit opinions on the world's population. A national sample of 1,250 Americans were contacted by telephone. Respondents were asked their opinion of the United States' involvement in the world population problem. Respondents were also asked their perception of the environmental effects of expanding populations in poor countries.

517. Georgia State University Poll. *American Public Opinion Index: 1988.* Boston, MA: Opinion Research Service, Inc., 1989.

The Center for Public and Urban Research at Georgia State University conducted this special environmental poll in June 1988. A sample of 805 residents of Dade County, Florida, were interviewed by telephone. Respondents to the survey were asked several questions about the relationship between man and nature and the effect of growth and development on the environment. A majority of the subjects thought technology would be able to solve shortages of natural resources, yet 70 percent agreed that limits exist for the earth's population. When asked to choose between environmental protection and economic growth, 13 percent chose growth, 43 percent chose the environment, and 42 percent thought both could be accomplished. While 55 percent said there are no limits to U.S. growth, 61 percent agreed a simpler life was better for people.

518. McLaughlin, Jeff. "Poll: Environment High Among Cape Concerns." *Boston Globe,* February 23, 1991, p. B25.

Residents of Cape Cod, Massachusetts, were surveyed in this study conducted by Clark University's Graduate School of Geography for the Cape Cod Commission. A total of 2,437 out of 4,000 residents returned questionnaires mailed to their homes. Environmental and quality of life concerns were two of the issues included in the surveys. Nearly three-fourths of those responding said they view themselves as environmentalists. Approximately one-fourth agreed with the statement, "We have already gone too far in using natural resources and the balance of nature should be restored. The future use of resources should never harm any part of nature." A large majority (86 percent) said they supported increased town spending to purchase open space for water supply protection.

519. Fortner, Rosanne W., and Mayer, Victor J. "Repeated Measures of Student's Marine and Great Lakes Awareness." *Journal of Environmental Education* 23 (Fall 1991): 30–35.

In 1979, the Ohio Sea Grant Program tested the knowledge and attitudes of Ohio fifth- and ninth-grade students about the ocean and the Great Lakes. The assessment was duplicated in 1983 and 1987. The survey instrument for the study consisted of an attitude assessment, a knowledge assessment, and one question asking about media sources of information about the ocean and Great Lakes. A total of 4,787 fifth graders and 4,105 ninth graders completed the three editions of the survey. Response rates for the 1987 study were very low, 28 percent for fifth grade and 35 percent for ninth grade. Analysis of the three studies showed that attitudes toward the ocean were consistently higher than attitudes toward Lake Erie for both fifth and ninth graders. Attitudes of students in both grades toward the ocean declined between 1979 and 1987.

520. Bass, Frank. "Eagle Soars—Fears Do, Too." The *Houston Post*, March 3, 1992.

The annual Houston Area Survey is conducted by Rice University's Department of Sociology and Telesurveys of Texas for the *Houston Post*. In February 1992, 647 Houston area residents completed the surveyed which included questions related to spending on the environment and attitudes toward natural resources. The percentage of Houston residents who felt too little is spent on the environment was 60 percent, down seven points from a similar survey conducted in 1982. The notion that we are approaching the limits of the earth's resources was supported by 63 percent of the residents surveyed. A majority of the sample did not believe the media had exaggerated environmental problems.

521. "Activist Group Says Poll Shows Majority Backs Population Curbs." The *Houston Post*, March 8, 1992, p. A19.

This article reports on a nationwide telephone poll of 501 Americans conducted for the Population Crisis Committee during November 1991. The survey found that 85 percent of those asked believed the world's environmental problems would worsen unless population growth is slowed.

2

ATTITUDES TOWARD
PARKS AND
RECREATION AREAS

Preferred Outdoor Landscapes

522. Klukas, Richard W., and Duncan, Donald P. "Vegetational Preferences Among Itasca Park Visitors." *Journal of Forestry* 65 (1967): 18–21.

The purpose of this study was to explore vegetation preferences and the importance of vegetative cover to visitors of a Minnesota state park. During July and early September 1965, 600 visitors to Itasca State Park were interviewed at seven tourist attractions and tourist facilities in the park. In addition to the interviews, observations of visitors' reactions to vegetation were made at four locations containing stands of red pine, spruce-fir, aspen, and northern hardwood trees. Interviews revealed that forest vegetation was the major attraction of the park to nearly 40 percent of the visitors. Red pine was the preferred type of vegetation.

523. Calvin, James F.; Dearinger, John A.; and Curtin, Mary Ellen. "An Attempt at Assessing Preferences for Natural Landscapes." *Environment and Behavior* 4 (December 1972): 447–70.

The research discussed in this article was conducted by the authors and sponsored by the Office of Water Resources Research, U.S. Department of Interior and the University of Kentucky, Water Resources Institute. The goal of the study was to determine what criteria are used by people to assess different natural landscapes. A slide presentation was used to show a set of 15 slides to a class of 139 psychology students at the University of Kentucky. The students had three minutes in which to rate each landscape slide on 21 different scales. A factor analysis procedure was used to identify the dimensions that the students used to make their subject assessments of the quality of the landscapes. Two major dimensions were suggested by the results: natural scenic beauty and natural force. These two factors accounted for 85 percent of the variation in preferences among the scenes. Included in the article are reproductions of the 15 landscape scenes and the scales used to rate the scenes.

524. Carls, E. Glenn. "The Effects of People and Man-Induced Conditions on Preferences for Outdoor Recreation Landscapes." *Journal of Leisure Research* 6 (Spring 1974): 113–24.

In this article, the author describes his attempt to measure preferences for different outdoor recreation landscapes. The sample for the study included 290 adults using nine Illinois recreation areas and 75 residents of the Chicago, Peoria, and St. Louis metropolitan areas. Landscape preferences were obtained by requesting that the subjects rank 100 color landscape photographs. The sampling and interviews were conducted by the University of Illinois Survey Research Laboratory. The analysis of the interviews indicated that choice of outdoor recreation landscapes is affected by numbers of people present and level of development.

525. Lane, C. L.; Byrd, W. P.; and Brantley, Herbert. "Evaluation of Recreational Sites." *Journal of Leisure Research* 7 (1975): 296–300.

The authors of this article asked students at Clemson University to view on slide, and in person, selected sites in Clemson University Forest, South Carolina. The five groups of students were members of two recreation and three forestry classes. The slides and actual sites were viewed within three weeks to minimize natural changes to the landscape. A significant difference was found between preferences for a site when viewed on slides and when viewed in person. In most cases, the students gave a higher preference for the site when viewed on slide than when viewed directly.

526. Daniel, Terry C.; Anderson, Linda M.; Schroeder, Herbert W.; and Wheeler, Lawrence, III. "Mapping the Scenic Beauty of Forest Landscapes." *Leisure Sciences* 1 (1977): 35–52.

This paper describes a process used by the authors to map areas of scenic beauty in a forest landscape. The method included showing a series of 25 color slides of scenes from the Woods Canyon Experimental Watershed in the Coconino National Forest to groups of college student volunteers. Each student observer was asked to rate the scenic beauty of the area represented by the slide. The observer ratings were entered into a computer program which produced a scenic beauty map for the area. Financial support for the study was received from the Rocky Mountain Forest and Range Experiment Station, U.S. Forest Service.

527. Schroeder, Herbert W. "Preferred Features of Urban Parks and Forests." *Journal of Arboriculture* 8 (December 1982): 317–22.

In this study, observers were asked to view photographs of urban forest sites in the Chicago, Illinois, area and identify favorable and unfavorable features. The sample for the study included visitors and volunteers at a Chicago nature study center and students at two Chicago universities. A total of 96 individuals observed and evaluated 36 photographs depicting scenes of city parks, suburban forest preserves, and other urban forests. The types of features most often mentioned as desirable for urban forest recreation sites were vegetation and water resources. Least desirable features were man-made characteristics, vegetation problems, and poor maintenance. The article describes differences in preferred features between observers who had lived in urban areas most of their lives and those who had lived in suburban or rural areas.

528. Lyons, Elizabeth. "Demographic Correlates of Landscape Preferences." *Environment and Behavior* 15 (July 1983): 487–511.

This article describes research designed to investigate the relationship between a number of demographic variables (age, gender, residence, and socioeconomic status) and landscape preference. The subjects for the study consisted of 283 individuals of both sexes ranging in age from 8 to 67 and residing in or near a major city in the northeast. In a second part of the study, 36 university students from two different geographic areas were sampled. All respondents were asked to complete questionnaires and to rate slide images representing five different vegetation areas: tropical rain forest, temperate deciduous forest, Northern coniferous forest, Savannah, and desert. Age, gender, and residence were found to be related to preference for different landscapes. Children exhibited the highest landscape preferences and the elderly, the lowest. The highest preferences were for the landscape most familiar to the subjects.

529. Nasar, Jack L. "Physical Correlates of Perceived Quality in Lakeshore Development." *Leisure Sciences* 9 (1987): 259–79.

This research was performed with partial funding provided by a grant from the Ohio Sea Grant Office. In this study, subjects were asked to identify preferences for shorelines by viewing photographs depicting 63 different scenes from the Lake Erie (Ohio) shoreline. The sample for the study consisted of 60 residents of Columbus, Ohio. Interviews were conducted in person with 30 of the residents in their homes and with 30 students at Ohio State University. Shoreline preferences were grouped by demographic variables such as age, sex, income, and marital status, but few differences were found between groups. Analysis of the interviews indicated that preferences for shoreline scenes increased with the level of vegetation, varied elements, and upkeep. Preferences decreased with increased levels of industry, streets, and land/water barriers.

Choice of Recreation Site

530. Lucas, Robert C. "Wilderness Perception and Use: The Experience of the Boundary Waters Canoe Area." *Natural Resources Journal* 3 (January 1964): 393–411.

The research discussed in this article was conducted by the Lake States Forest Experiment Station. Visitors to the Boundary Waters Canoe Area in Minnesota were surveyed to compare the wilderness perceptions of different types of recreationists. A sample of 278 visitors to the canoe area in 1960 were interviewed. Included in the total sample were canoeists (motorized and nonmotorized), day-use visitors, car campers, boat campers, resort guests, and private cabin users. The six types of recreationists differed significantly in the frequency of citing wilderness attributes as the reason for their choice of recreation area. The canoeists most often mentioned wilderness criteria for choosing a site, while boat campers cited "fishing" most often, and resort guests and cabin users gave "scenery" as the most common reason for their choice of site.

531. Shafer, Elwood L., Jr., and Burke, Hubert D. "Preferences for Outdoor Recreation Facilities in Four State Parks." *Journal of Forestry* 63 (July 1965): 512–18.

This study, conducted by the Northeastern Forest Experiment Station, surveyed camper and noncamper preferences for different types of outdoor recreation facilities including swimming areas, fireplaces, camping facilities, and campsite spacings. Personal interviews were conducted with 1,600 day-use and camping visitors to four state parks in northeastern Pennsylvania (Hickory Run, Promised Land, Ricketts Glen, and Tobyhanna). Each selected visitor was asked to view photographs of different types of facilities and indicate their preferences after considering the cost of each option. The preferences of the campers differed significantly from those of the noncampers. For swimming areas, the campers preferred a beach with trees, and for a picnic area, they preferred an area with scattered trees. The campers also chose metal fireplaces over those made of stone and a camping area to pitch a tent over a cabin or shelter. Campsite spacings of 50 to 100 feet were preferred over spacings closer together (10 to 15 feet) and further apart (250 to 400 feet). The article includes photographs of the different facility options.

532. Hecock, Richard D. "Recreation Behavior Patterns as Related to Site Characteristics of Beaches." *Journal of Leisure Research* 2 (Fall 1970): 237–50.

This research was an attempt to understand attendance patterns at outdoor recreation sites at Cape Cod beaches. During the 1964 tourist season, 90 interviews were conducted at 10 beach sites. The sites were chosen on the basis of accessibility, facilities, and physical characteristics and were considered to be representative of different beach conditions at the Cape. The researcher classified groups of beach visitors by the presence of small children, the presence of teenagers, prior experience on Cape Cod, occupation of the head of the group, and length of stay in the area. Although attendance at beach sites with facilities far exceeded attendance at sites without facilities, no one group was more strongly attracted to sites with facilities than the others. Teenagers more frequently visited areas with food facilities and crowds. Higher income groups tended to visit sites considered to have above average scenic qualities.

533. Taylor, Charles E., and Knudson, Douglas M. "Area Preferences of Midwestern Campers." *Journal of Leisure Research* 5 (Spring 1973): 39–48.

State park campers in eight Midwestern states were interviewed to determine reasons for preferences and choices of camping areas. During 1970, 480 campers at 16 state parks in Michigan, Minnesota, Wisconsin, Indiana, Iowa, Ohio, Missouri, and Kentucky were interviewed. When asked the main reason for choosing their preferred area, 31 percent named "close to home." "Scenery" was cited as the reason for their choice by 25 percent, and 21 percent named "facilities." The interview respondents were also asked to give reasons why they did not visit their preferred area. "Distance," "cost," and "no information" were the most common responses.

534. Murphy, Peter E. "The Role of Attitude in the Choice Decisions of Recreational Boaters." *Journal of Leisure Research* 7 (1975): 216–24.

This research examined the role of attitude in a recreationist's selection of an outdoor recreation site. It was believed that the number of visits to selected lake sites would be a function of socioeconomic variables, time, attitude toward the sites, and experience with competing sites. Boaters at Buckeye and Delaware Lakes in Ohio were interviewed in person. A total of 174 completed interviews were accepted for analysis. A stepwise regression analysis was used to determine the contribution of each variable in explaining the variations in the number of visits to the sites. The analysis revealed that five variables, two of them attitudinal, were related to the frequency of visits. Those two variables were the "friendliness rating" of the competing site and the "nice rating" of the chosen site. Separate regression analyses were done for upper, middle, and lower social class boaters. The different variables studied accounted for 50 percent of the variance in the upper class visits, 53 percent of the variance in middle class visits, and 65 percent of the variance in low class visits.

535. Knopp, Timothy B.; Ballman, Gary; and Merriam, Lawrence C., Jr. "Toward a More Direct Measure of River User Preference." *Journal of Leisure Research* 11 (1979): 317–26.

In this article, the authors describe their attempt to identify preferences of river users for different environmental characteristics. Between April and August 1977, a written questionnaire was distributed to 313 river users at the Kettle River in Minnesota. Cluster analysis technique was used to organize 39 environmental items into sets or clusters. The analysis identified the following clusters: noise and development tolerant, activity setting, nature and solitude, nature with comfort and security, and manipulation and regulation. Of the individual 39 items, the subjects responded most positively to "water clean enough for swimming," "natural vegetation, landscapes," and "variety of small wildlife." The most negative responses were received to the items "commercial development," "litter," and "residential development." Support for the research was received from Hatch Act and McIntire-Stennis Cooperative Forestry Research funds.

536. Kaminarides, John S., and Crawford, Jerry L. "Attitudes and Characteristics of Outdoor Recreationists Visiting Sites Near and Far from Interstate Highways." *Arkansas Business and Economic Review* 12 (Winter 1979): 21–26.

The study described in this article was conducted by the Department of Economics at Arkansas State University from the summer of 1977 through the fall of 1978. Questionnaires were distributed at readily accessible recreation sites and remote recreation sites in the state of Arkansas. Recreation areas included in the sampling were national parks, national forests, Corps of Engineers projects, wildlife refuges and Game and Fish Commission areas. The article gives the number of questionnaires distributed as 1,750, although the number completed and the response rate are not specified. The purpose of the research was to compare attitudes of visitors at readily accessible and remote recreation sites toward the importance of access and the area itself in choosing a recreation site. On the question of ease of access to recreation sites, 18 percent preferred direct access, 42 percent wanted convenient access, 13 percent desired remote access, and 28 percent said they desired no access. The survey showed that the site itself was of more importance than the type of access. Access to interstates was of more importance to recreationists at sites near interstates than recreationists at remote sites.

537. Shaw, William W., and King, David A. "Wildlife Management and Non-hunting Wildlife Enthusiasts." *Transactions of the Forty-fifth North American Wildlife and Natural Resources Conference* 45 (1980): 219–25.

Two research studies are presented in this article, one of which is described elsewhere in this volume. Both studies were conducted by the University of Arizona, School of Renewable Natural Resources. The researchers interviewed 1,200 recreationists using Cave Creek Canyon in the Chiricahua Mountains of southeastern Arizona to determine the significance of wildlife resources to visitors of a natural area. Wildlife oriented recreation was the primary activity of 18 percent of the visitors, and the appeal of wildlife resources was the most important characteristic of the area to over 20 percent of the visitors.

538. Schreyer, Rich, and Beauliew, Jean T. "Attribute Preferences for Wildland Recreation Settings." *Journal of Leisure Research* 18 (1986): 231–47.

Support for this research was provided from a grant from the Intermountain Forest and Range Experiment Station of the U.S. Forest Service. In this study, the authors attempted to explain differences in selection of a recreation setting. A questionnaire was administered to 324 visitors to unnamed wilderness areas in the west and 400 members of the Utah Wilderness Association. The survey respondents were asked to choose a site for a hypothetical three-day wilderness trip and to explain the reason for the choice. Responses were received from 264 of the subjects. It was expected that the choice of recreation setting would be related to previous experience at a site and commitment to a specific recreational activity. The results of the research, however, failed to confirm this relationship.

539. "Survey Finds 'Outdoor' U.S. That Wants Nature Areas Kept." *The New York Times*, April 25, 1986, p. A18.

This article reports the results of a telephone survey of 2,000 Americans conducted by Market Opinion Research for the President's Commission on Americans Outdoors. Funding was provided by the National Geographic Society. Topics for the survey included preservation of natural areas, motivations for outdoor recreation, and criteria for choosing an outdoor recreation site. A large majority of the respondents were strongly supportive of the government preserving natural areas and were willing to pay taxes dedicated to that purpose. The most common motivations for outdoor recreation were for escape, physical fitness, social activities, and excitement-seeking competitiveness. Natural beauty and lack of crowding were the two most important criteria for visiting a natural area.

540. Christensen, Harriet H.; Williams, Pamela J.; and Clark, Roger N. *Values and Choices in Outdoor Recreation by Male and Female Campers in Dispersed Recreation Areas.* U.S. Department of Agriculture, Forest Service, 1987, 20 pp.

This research compared differences between men and women in their attitudes, preferences, and perceptions of camping activities. Data for the study were collected by questionnaire from 898 campers in three national forests (Mt. Baker-Snoqualmie and Wenatchee National Forests, Washington, and Mt. Hood National Forest, Oregon) during the summer and fall of 1976. Preferences for different forest recreation areas were similar for both men and women. Dispersed, roaded recreation areas were their first choice followed by minimally developed campgrounds and roadless or wilderness areas. The male respondents were more likely to perceive certain recreational conditions as problems: theft of equipment, vandalism, noise from motorbikes, and lack of maps. Timber clear-cutting and closing roads for hunting were more likely to be supported by men than women. Women were more likely to favor construction of more roads.

541. Shelby, Bo; Vaske, Jerry; and Harris, Rick. "User Standards for Eco-logical Impacts at Wilderness Campsites." *Journal of Leisure Research* 20 (1988): 245-56.

   The research described in this article was supported by the Intermountain Research Station of the U.S. Forest Service. Campers were surveyed to determine acceptance of varying levels of ecological impacts at wilderness campsites. The two ecological impacts selected for study were size of fire ring and area of bare ground. Data were collected from 450 campers using five recreation areas in Mt. Jefferson Wilderness, Oregon. The responses of the subjects were measured after viewing a site, viewing a photograph of a site, or reading a written description of a site. Find-ings from the study included the following: 1.) The wilderness users had opinions about ecological impacts. 2.) Acceptability of bare ground and fire rings differed by location of recreation area. 3.) In some cases, low to moderate impact was more acceptable than no impact. 4.) A fairly high degree of agreement existed among campers.

542. Martin, Steven R.; McCool, Stephen F.; and Lucas, Robert C. "Wilder-ness Campsite Impacts: Do Managers and Visitors See Them the Same?" *Environmental Management* 13 (September-October 1989): 623-29.

   The purpose of this research was to compare the reactions of wilderness managers and campers to the campsite impacts of fire rings, tree damage, and bare ground. Slides produced from color illustrations depicting different levels of the impacts at 14 campsites were shown to 186 members of Montana wilderness user groups and 106 wilderness managers with the U.S. Forest Service and U.S. Bureau of Land Management. The acceptability of the campsites differed between the visitor and manager groups. Fire damage and fire rings were more objectionable to visitors, while managers were more sensitive to the amount of bare ground. Generally, the visitors were more likely than the managers to rate a campsite as unacceptable.

543. Brunson, Mark and Shelby, Bo. "A Hierarchy of Campsite Attributes in Dispersed Recreational Settings." *Leisure Sciences* 12 (1990): 197-209.

   In this article, the authors present details of a study designed to determine the most important characteristics of a campsite to a group of whitewater boaters. The sample for the study consisted of 576 individuals who purchased boating passes in 1985 for a 100-mile stretch of the Deschutes River in Oregon. Of these boaters, 343 identified as overnight river users completed a survey asking them to rate a series of campsite attributes. The attributes were categorized into three groups: necessity (flat ground, shade, place to tie up boat), experience (out of sight and sound of others, good fishing nearby, screened), and amenity (good ground cover, free from cattle grazing, away from railroad tracks). Analysis of the data revealed that the necessity attributes were the most important in evaluating a camp-ing site. The article includes a review of the findings of prior research on campsite attributes. Funding for the study was provided by the Forest Research Laboratory and the Water Resources Research Institute at Oregon State University.

544. University of Illinois Poll. *American Public Opinion Index: 1989.* Boston, MA: Opinion Research Service, Inc., 1990.

   The Survey Research Laboratory of the University of Illinois interviewed 1,000 residents of Illinois about the importance of outdoor recreation. Those responding to the November 1989 telephone poll were asked their motivations for visiting state parks and the importance of various criteria in the decision to visit a particular park.

545. Iowa Department of Natural Resources Poll. *American Public Opinion Index: 1989.* Boston, MA: Opinion Research Service, Inc., 1990.

This telephone poll was conducted in 1989 for the Iowa Department of Natural Resources. The survey contacted 500 residents and questioned them about their satisfaction with Iowa trails and the characteristics of trails that enhance user enjoyment. The respondents identified the following characteristics of trails as being most important to them: "going through a variety of landscapes," "presence of water resources," "trail separate from roadways," and "access to outdoor recreation facilities."

546. Wayne State University Poll. *American Public Opinion Index: 1989.* Boston, MA: Opinion Research Service, Inc., 1990.

Wayne State University's Center for Urban Studies administered this telephone poll during November 1989 to residents of five Michigan Counties. The sample of 2,025 adults was questioned about the importance of various criteria in choosing an outdoor recreation site.

547. Vining, Joanne, and Fishwick, Lesley. "An Exploratory Study of Outdoor Recreation Site Choices." *Journal of Leisure Research* 13 (1991): 114–32.

The North Central Forest Experiment Station of the U.S. Forest Service provided support for this research which studied the process for choosing outdoor recreation sites. The subjects were five female and five male graduate students from the University of Illinois recruited for the study through an advertisement. Each student was asked to choose between paired recreation sites for a total of 45 pairs or 90 sites. Decisions were based on standardized brochures containing a photograph, a page of written text, and a map of the natural area. The students were asked to talk aloud about their choices and all the comments were tape-recorded. The recordings were used to analyze the decision process. Some of the factors involved in the site decision included: site features, site activities, site atmosphere, personal experiences and memories, personal values, and the history of the area.

548. Ewert, Alan, and Pfister, Robert. "Cross-Cultural Land Ethics: Motivations, Appealing Attributes and Problems." *Transactions of the Fifty-sixth North American Wildlife and Natural Resources Conference* 56 (1991): 146–51.

Visitors to a riparian corridor along the San Gabriel River in the Angeles National Forest of southern California were surveyed regarding reasons for visiting that particular recreation site. The research was performed in the summer of 1989 with 473 participants. Both Spanish and English questionnaires were used to measure respondents motivation for visiting the site, most appealing aspect of the visit, and perceived problems at the site. The researchers attempted to determine the effect of place of birth on recreational values by classifying the subjects by cultural heritage and place of birth: U.S.-born Anglos, U.S.-born Hispanics, Mexican-born Hispanics, and Central American–born Hispanics. Generally, the closer to the United States the place of birth, the more similar the responses to U.S.-born Anglo visitors. The most appealing aspect of the visit among all respondents was the opportunity to be with family. Problems encountered at the site that were considered of most concern to U.S.-born visitors were graffiti, vandalism, and water pollution. The most serious problems to foreign born visitors were too few parking places, people breaking the law, and the drinking of alcohol.

549. Shelby, Bo, and Shindler, Bruce. "Interest Group Standards for Ecological Impacts at Wilderness Campsites." *Leisure Sciences* 14 (1992): 17–27.

This study measured the acceptability of different levels of ecological impacts at wilderness campsites. The sample for the study consisted of groups of hunters (N = 33), backcountry horse riders (N = 40), Explorer Scouts (N = 30), hikers (N = 77), Sierra Club members (N = 55), and Forest Service managers (N = 91). Subjects were shown two series of color slides of campsites and asked to complete a questionnaire about acceptability of the sites. One series of slides depicted varying areas of bare ground and the other series showed different sizes of fire rings. Results showed a significant difference in the acceptability of the different sites among the interest groups. For both ground cover and fire ring size, the managers and the Sierra Club members were the least accepting of sites with heavy and severe impact. The hunters, horse riders, and scouts were most accepting of heavy and severe bare ground impact. In fact, for these groups, sites with severe bare ground impact were more acceptable than sites showing only heavy bare ground. Hunters and horse riders were most accepting of fire ring size, while scouts and hikers were less accepting of larger fire rings than these groups but more accepting than the managers and Sierra Club members.

Facilities and Services

550. Fowler, Ronald L., and Bury, Richard L. "Visitor Evaluation of a Developed Outdoor Recreation Area on a National Wildlife Refuge." *Transactions of the Thirty-eighth North American Wildlife and Natural Resources Conference* 38 (1973): 213–19.

This research was funded by the U.S. Bureau of Sport Fisheries and Wildlife, Division of Wildlife Refuges. During the summer of 1971, visitors to the Okefenokee National Wildlife Refuge in southeast Georgia were given mail-back questionnaires at the refuge exit point. Responses were received from 350 groups of visitors. The questionnaire included items regarding visitor satisfaction and response to facilities at the refuge and the identification of activities and benefits associated with a visit to a national wildlife refuge. The more favorable responses to the refuge experience were from those living within 100 miles of the site. The response to variables related to commercialism ("purchasing souvenirs," "talking with tourists") indicated that respondents were unsure whether these opportunities were appropriate at a refuge. The response to variables related to a nature/outdoor benefit ("enjoying nature," "looking at scenery") indicated that the respondents saw these opportunities as important parts of their experience at the refuge.

551. Twight, Ben W., and Catton, William R., Jr. "The Politics of Images: Forest Managers vs. Recreation Publics." *Natural Resources Journal* 15 (April 1975): 297–306.

The purpose of this study was to compare the perceptions of managers and users of an arboretum administered by the College of Forest Resources of the University of Washington. The managers' perceptions of the arboretum were inferred to be as a scientific, educational, and horticultural facility. To measure the perceptions of the arboretum users, 1,812 questionnaires were mailed to registered owners of cars observed visiting the arboretum. In addition, questionnaires were sent to 708 visitors to three local city parks and six area state parks. Less than 40 percent response was received from each of the public samples. Results of the survey analysis revealed that arboretum users viewed the resource different than the managers. The users indicated they valued the arboretum for its pleasant landscape, restful surroundings, and privacy. Although horticultural services were deemed important, when forced to choose between a variety of plants and flowers and either a pleasant landscape or a restful atmosphere, majorities of the sample chose the nonhorticultural attributes. Responses from the city and state park visitors showed weaker scores than the arboretum visitors on a naturalness attitude.

552. Wohlwill, Joachim, and Heft, Harry. "A Comparative Study of User Attitudes Towards Development and Facilities in Two Contrasting Natural Recreation Areas." *Journal of Leisure Research* 9 (1977): 264–80.

In this article, the researchers describe a study funded by the Pennsylvania Office of Environmental Quality and the Center for Environmental Policy at Pennsylvania State University. The purpose of the research was to confirm that users of highly developed recreation areas are more favorable toward development and the presence of facilities. Two separate studies were conducted with campers at Hickory Run State Park in the Poconos and at Leonard Harrison and Colton Point State Parks in the Pine Creek area. The researchers interviewed 110 campers from the Poconos and Pine Creek area during 1972 and another 45 Pine Creek campers during the summer of 1973. A second study surveyed by mail a group of 111 forest site leasees in the two areas. Results from both studies found more favorable attitudes toward development among those using the more highly developed areas.

553. Kaminarides, John S., and Crawford, Jerry L. "An Evaluation of Outdoor Recreationists Attitudes Toward Economic Development in Recreation Areas." *Arkansas Business and Economic Review* 13 (Spring 1980): 12–19.

The Department of Economics of Arkansas State University conducted the research reported on in this article. (Other aspects of this study are described elsewhere.) From the summer of 1977 through the fall of 1978, 1,750 questionnaires were distributed to recreationists at remote and accessible recreation sites throughout the state of Arkansas. The number of completed questionnaires and the response rate are not given in the article. The purpose of the survey was to explore the attitudes of those participating in outdoor recreation in Arkansas toward economic development in recreation areas. Nearly 60 percent of those surveyed disagreed with the need for more traveler services for recreation areas. Those participating in hiking, backpacking and camping were more likely to disagree with the need for traveler services than those participating in picnicking and sightseeing.

554. Bultena, Gordon; Albrecht, Don; and Womble, Peter. "Freedom Versus Control: A Study of Backpackers' Preferences for Wilderness Management." *Leisure Sciences* 4 (1981): 297–310.

The purpose of this research was to measure the attitudes of backpackers toward use limitations at Mt. McKinley National Park in Alaska. A total sample of 2,829 holders of backcountry permits for the park in 1978 completed a pre- and post-trip questionnaire about their wilderness trips. Questions included in the survey were designed to measure perceptions of rationing and other management policies in effect for the Mt. McKinley backcountry. Nearly three-fourths of the backpackers indicated that pursuit of solitude was a "very important" aspect of an enjoyable wilderness trip. Rationing, by means of permits issued on a first-come, first-served basis, was supported by 82 percent of the sample. Backpackers who valued solitude were also those most supportive of the policy of rationing. On the issue of developing the backcountry, 33 percent of the sample was rated as "strongly opposed," 51 percent as "moderately opposed," and 16 percent were identified as "favorable toward backcountry development." The research was sponsored by the Cooperative Parks Study Unit, National Park Service, College of Forest Resources, University of Washington, Seattle, with partial funding from the Iowa Agriculture and Home Economics Experiment Station.

555. West, Patrick C. "Perceived Crowding and Attitudes Toward Limiting Use in Backcountry Recreation Areas." *Leisure Sciences* 4 (1981): 419–25.

The research described in this article was funded by the North Central Forest Experiment Station, U.S. Forest Service. The purpose of the study was to examine the relationship between perceived crowding in backcountry areas and preference for the number of campsites. The site of the study was the Sylvania Recreation Area in Michigan's Upper Peninsula. During July and August 1978, 321 backcountry campers using three sites in the recreation area were interviewed as they returned from their backcountry trips. To measure perceived crowding, the interviewers asked, "Would you say the backcountry was: very overcrowded, somewhat overcrowded, not crowded, or don't know?" Respondents were then asked if they thought the number of campsites should be increased, kept the same, or decreased. Although the researchers found a significant relationship between perceived crowding and preference for the number of campsites, the relationship was not strong. While 22 percent of the sample felt crowded, the majority of those preferred the number of campsites be kept the same. Campers with high education who felt crowded were more likely to want to see the number of campsites decreased.

556. Airola, Teuvo M., and Wilson, David. "Recreation Benefits of Residual Open Space: A Case Study of Four Communities in Northeastern New Jersey." *Environmental Management* 6 (November 1982): 471–84.

This research surveyed residents of four communities in northeastern New Jersey regarding their attitudes toward parks and open spaces in their areas. Questionnaires were distributed to 1,100 residents of West New York, Fort Lee–Edgewater, and two communities in Jersey City. The response rates from the four areas were low, ranging from 9 percent to 18 percent. Parks and open spaces were rated higher in importance than shopping facilities and facilities for teens and the elderly but lower in importance than police and fire protection, sanitation, and transportation. Although demand for different recreational characteristics of city parks varied by community, residents of three of the four communities rated "natural areas" as the most important park feature. Residents of two of the communities rated passive open-space characteristics of parks such as wildlife and trails and hiking paths high. For residents of the other two communities, active characteristics such as playgrounds and tennis and basketball courts rated high. Funding for this study was received from the New Jersey Agricultural Experiment Station and from a grant from the Consortium for Environmental Forestry Studies sponsored by the U.S. Forest Service, Northeast Forest Experiment Station.

557. Tannery, Thomas Allan. "Public Opinion and Interest Group Positions on Open-Space Issues in Albuquerque, New Mexico, U.S.A.: Implications for Resource Management." *Environmental Management* 11 (July 1987): 369–73.

This study compared the preferences for use of open space between city residents and open-space experts in Albuquerque, New Mexico. Data for the research were collected during a telephone survey conducted during May 1986 with 492 citizens and 35 open-space experts. The survey elicited opinions on various uses of open space: recreational trails, citywide trails, wildlife preserves, outdoor education site, outdoor amphitheater, rafting facilities, off-road vehicles, and overnight camping. Preferences for the open-space uses differed between the two groups. The experts ranked the top three uses of open-space: recreational trails, citywide trails, and wildlife preserves, while the citizens chose wildlife preserves, outdoor education site, and rafting facilities.

558. Van Cleave, Rebecca L.; Franz, Cynthia P. G.; Franz, David L.; and Van Cleave, Kent. *Attitudes, Perceptions, and Characteristics of Summer Visitors to the Great Smoky Mountain Region.* U.S. Department of Agriculture, Forest Service, Southeast Recreation Research Conference, 1990, pp. 141–61.

This symposium paper discusses a cooperative research effort of the Uplands Field Research Laboratory, the University of Tennessee, and the Gatlinburg Chamber of Commerce. The purpose of the research was to describe and compare summer visitors to the Great Smoky Mountains National Park and summer visitors to Gatlinburg, Tennessee. A written questionnaire was used to collect data between June and August 1989. Of the 412 completed surveys, 282 were collected in Gatlinburg and 130 were collected in the national park. Although some overlap between the two groups probably existed, the attitudes and expectation of the tourist-oriented and the nature-oriented visitors differed significantly.

559. *Social Impacts of Possible Development at Brushy Creek State Recreation Area, State of Iowa.* University of Northern Iowa, Fall 1990, 45 pp.

Households within 30 air miles of the Brushy Creek State Recreation Area in Iowa were contacted for this poll on outdoor recreation. A total of 415 respondents completed the June 1990 survey conducted for the Iowa Department of Natural Resources. Nearly all of those surveyed agreed that protecting natural areas in their area of the state was important. Respondents were also asked if they support developing new outdoor recreation facilities in their area.

Management Policies

560. Catton, William R., and Hendee, John C. "Wilderness Users: . . . What Do They Think?" *American Forests* 74 (September 1968): 28–31, 60–61.

This article presents an interview with researchers who conducted a survey of visitors to three western wilderness areas during the summer of 1965. Over 1,400 visitors to Glacier Peak, Three Sisters, and Eagle Cap Wilderness areas in Washington and Oregon returned the mail questionnaire. Although the article does not discuss specific survey items or responses, general trends are described. In one section of the survey, the recreationists were asked to respond to 53 statements related to the following areas: administration, nature interpretation, motorized equipment, helicopters, trails, signs, campsite facilities, rationing and charging for use, and restriction of resource management practices. A majority of the wilderness users rejected motorized trail bikes but accepted the use of helicopters for certain management purposes. They felt trails should be developed and maintained based on use and signs should be for direction only and placed at trail junctions. Most users did not support restrictions on recreation use in wilderness areas, but over 40 percent favored a moderate charge for use.

561. King, John Morgan, Jr. *A Comparison of Attitudes Toward Public Camping in State and Federal Outdoor Recreation Areas.* Doctoral dissertation, Indiana University, January 1970.

This doctoral dissertation studied attitudes toward camping practices, policies, and beliefs in state and federal outdoor recreation areas. The research compared the attitudes of camping club members with those of federal and state administrators and private campground owners. Data for the research were collected by questionnaire from 210 representatives of seven different population groups during the spring and summer of 1965. Each respondent was asked to respond to 137 statements concerning campground operations. Decisive agreement or disagreement responses to 62 of the statements were used to formulate 26 recommendations for planning, developing, and operating outdoor recreation areas.

562. McCurdy, Dwight R. "Recreationists' Attitudes Toward User Fees: Management Implications." *Journal of Forestry* 68 (October 1970): 645–46.

In this study, recreationists at the Crab Orchard National Wildlife Refuge in southern Illinois were surveyed in 1966 and again in 1969 regarding their support for federal recreation area user fees. Data for the study were collected from 840 groups of visitors to the refuge in 1966 and 283 in 1969. The recreationists visiting the refuge were participating in a variety of activities including swimming, hunting, and fishing. In 1966, 61 percent of the users favored recreation fees, and in 1969, the percent in support of fees had increased to 69 percent.

563. Fazio, James R., and Gilbert, Douglas L. "Mandatory Wilderness Permits: Some Indications of Success." *Journal of Forestry* 72 (December 1972): 753–56.

This article describes results of a research study conducted for a doctoral dissertation on mandatory permits for backcountry use. The study was conducted at Rocky Mountain National Park during the summer of 1973. A pre- and post-visit questionnaire was administered to 1,020 backcountry visitors. In the pre-visit survey, 69 percent of those surveyed supported a mandatory backcountry permit system. In the post-visit survey, support for the program increased to 86 percent. Approval for the permit system was only slightly lower among those who were unsuccessful in applying for a backcountry permit.

564. Harrison, Gordon S. "The People and the Park: Reactions to a System of Public Transportation in Mt. McKinley National Park, Alaska." *Journal of Leisure Research* 7 (1975): 6–15.

The research described in this item was conducted for the National Park Service by the Institute of Social, Economic, and Government Research of the University of Alaska. In 1972, the National Park Service restricted private automobile traffic in Mt. McKinley National Park and instituted a system of free bus service. At the same time, a policy was established that required advanced reservations for five of the park's campgrounds. This study was designed to measure the response of park visitors and Alaska residents to the new policies. A survey of 1,094 park visitors conducted during the summer of 1972 found 84 percent of the visitors approved of the new transportation policy, and 70 percent of the visitors with campground reservations approved of the new reservation requirement. The Alaska resident study was conducted during the winter of 1973 with 590 residents of Fairbanks and Anchorage. Only about half of the residents, who were aware of the new policy, approved of it.

565. Kantola, William Wayne. *Opinions and Preferences of Visitors Toward Alternatives for Limiting Use in the Backcountry of Sequoia and Kings Canyon National Parks.* Master of Science thesis, University of Oregon, December 1976, 45 pp.

The purpose of this thesis was to determine the opinions and preferences of backcountry visitors to two national parks toward limiting backcountry recreation. Data were obtained from a sample of 1,248 overnight backcountry visitors to Sequoia and Kings Canyon National Parks during the summer of 1976. A majority of the respondents supported several alternatives for limiting use: zone control, trailhead control, wilderness permits, and a reservation and permit system. The respondents preferred a system where half of the permits would be issued based on reservations and half on a first come–first serve basis. Support was also expressed for limiting group size and requiring minimum impact. Only two alternatives were opposed by a majority of the respondents: charging for backcountry use and raffling wilderness permits.

566. Echelberger, Herbert E., and Moeller, George H. *Use and Users of the Cranberry Backcountry in West Virginia: Insights for Eastern Backcountry Management.* U.S. Department of Agriculture, Forest Service, 1977, 8 pp.

In this study, 413 visitors to the Cranberry Backcountry of the Monongahela National Forest were surveyed on their attitudes toward backcountry management practices. The research was conducted by the U.S. Forest Service between April and December 1972. Data were gathered by mail questionnaire sent to visitors registered at the backcountry entrance point. Respondents to the survey identified the following as the most liked characteristics of the backcountry: "solitude and natural scenic beauty," and "fishing and hunting." Least liked characteristics were the following: "overcrowding" and "logging." When asked about adding certain facilities to the area, the subjects supported the addition of interpretative signs, picnic tables, shelters along the river, and parking areas at entrance points. The respondents were also asked their opinions of the effect of 12 proposed changes in management policies on the quality of their backcountry experience. A majority of the sample indicated the quality of their experience would be reduced by the following changes: allowing motorized vehicles in the backcountry, allowing deep mining, providing vehicle access closer to the river, allowing vehicle access only during deer season, allowing snowmobiling, and allowing bear hunting. The only proposed changes that were supported by a majority of the sample were requiring all visitors to register and having a ranger regularly patrol the backcountry.

567. Towler, William L. "Hiker Perception of Wilderness: A Study of the Social Carrying Capacity of Grand Canyon." *Arizona Review* 26 (August-September 1977): 1–10.

The purpose of this study was to measure acceptance of a system restricting the use of hiking trails in Grand Canyon National Park among users of those trails. Motivations for taking a backcountry hiking trip and attitudes toward the use of airplanes, helicopters, and motorboats in the Canyon were also explored. A questionnaire was developed and mailed to holders of backcountry wilderness permits for the park. A small number of surveys were also completed by hikers in the field along wilderness trails. A total of 252 questionnaires were completed and returned by both methods. Among motivations for hiking the park's trails, the beauty and scenery of the area were mentioned most often. The hikers' responses supported the park's policy of setting limits for individual trails and indicated that the use of airplanes, helicopters, and motorboats in the Canyon detracted from the wilderness experience.

568. Stankey, George H. "Use Rationing in Two Southern California Wildernesses." *Journal of Forestry* 77 (June 1979): 347–49.

The research discussed in this journal article was conducted by the author for the U.S. Forest Service. Mail questionnaires were sent to randomly selected successful and unsuccessful 1973 wilderness permittees for the San Gorgonio and San Jacinto wilderness areas in southern California. Completed questionnaires were received from 435 of the 537 potential participants. The survey instrument included questions on the respondent's attitude toward rationing as a solution to overuse of wilderness areas and reasons for and against rationing. Nearly one-half of the respondents thought the wilderness areas had become overused, and 60 percent thought use had exceeded capacity prior to initiation of rationing. Both types of permit applicants, successful and unsuccessful, supported a rationing system. Those opposed to rationing most often cited excessive regulation as the reason for their opposition.

569. Kiely-Brocato, Kathleen. "An Assessment of Visitor Attitudes Toward Resource Use and Management." *Journal of Environmental Education* 11 (Summer 1980): 29–36.

One objective of this study was to measure attitudes toward resource use and management among visitors to Shenandoah National Park, Virginia. A questionnaire composed of 44 belief statements about park resource management policy was administered by mail to park visitors during the summer of 1978. The article includes the 44 survey items and the mean attitude scores of the visitors sampled. Some of the items receiving the most favorable reactions included: "bear-proofing trash cans," "prohibiting off-road vehicles," "identifying and protecting rare animal habitat," and "requiring a permit for camping." The lowest mean attitude scores were received for "not keeping people away from rare animals," "not limiting wilderness access," and "not stocking streams in the park with fish." The research described in this article was funded by the U.S. Department of Interior, Mid-Atlantic Regional Office and Shenandoah National Park and the McIntire-Stennis Program.

570. Lucas, Robert C. *Use Patterns and Visitor Characteristics, Attitudes, and Preferences in Nine Wilderness and Other Roadless Areas.* U. S. Department of Agriculture, Forest Service, July 1980, 89 pp.

   This research compared attitudes and preferences of visitors to nine wilderness areas (Desolation Wilderness, CA; Jewel Basin Hiking Area, MT; Mission Mts. Wilderness, MT; Spanish Peaks Primitive Area, MT; Cabinet Mts. Wilderness, MT; Selway-Bitterroot Wilderness, ID; Bob Marshall Wilderness, MT; Scapegoat Wilderness, MT; and Great Bear Wilderness, MT). Between 1970 and 1972, mail questionnaires were completed by 2,777 visitors to the nine areas. The study examined attitudes toward the following wilderness issues: wilderness satisfaction, solitude, rationing and use control, facilities and structures, regulations, management policies, and acceptable visitor behavior. The study found general support for several wilderness facilities and management policies: rationing access, party size limits, no-horse areas, low standard trails, bridges over large, dangerous streams, fire rings, and fish stocking. Natural fire policies and prohibiting wood fires where firewood is scarce were generally opposed by the sample. The report includes a copy of the actual survey instrument.

571. Heywood, John L. "Off-Road Vehicles and Public Opinion in the California Desert." *Leisure Sciences* 4 (1981): 373–87.

   The public opinion studies described in this article were funded by the U.S. Bureau of Land Management. Results of four public opinion polls on the attitudes of Californians toward use of off-road vehicles in the desert are presented. The four polls were conducted by the Field Research Corporation in 1975 and 1977, the Gallup Organization in 1977, and SRI International in 1978. The Field Research polls were statewide, while the Gallup Poll used a national sample, and the SRI study surveyed residents of the California desert. In the 1975 poll by the Field Research Corporation, 1,124 California residents answered questions about participation in desert activities and the most important issues related to the desert. The sample identified the following as the most important issues: protection of desert wildlife and ecology, protection of historical areas, and limiting all kinds of development. Least important issues to the respondents were the following: increasing motels and restaurants, increasing off-road vehicle use areas, and increasing organized recreation areas. In the 1977 and 1978 statewide polls, over one-fourth of those sampled objected to motorcycle riding and dunebuggy activities. Slightly lower percentages objected to hunting, target shooting, and off-road driving. The author notes that the number of people who objected to off-road vehicle activities was larger than the number who participated or were interested in the activities. In all of the surveys, strong support was expressed for protection of the desert scenery, wildlife, ecology, and historical areas. All groups except desert residents indicated slight to moderate opposition to providing areas for off-road vehicle use. Mining was opposed by the overall sample in each survey, while energy development in the desert received slight to moderate support. The article includes tables summarizing results from the surveys on preferred activities, objectionable activities, and preferences for types of land use.

572. Knudson, Douglas M., and Curry, Elizabeth B. "Campers' Perceptions of Site Deterioration and Crowding." *Journal of Forestry* 79 (February 1981): 92–94.

This journal article describes research performed by the staff of the Department of Forestry and Natural Resources at Purdue University. Funding for the research was provided by the Indiana Department of Natural Resources and the Indiana Agricultural Experiment Station. Visitors to three campgrounds in two Indiana state parks were interviewed about the environmental conditions at their camping sites and alternative site management practices. Questionnaires were administered to 405 campers during 40 evenings from July through October. The interviews revealed that the campers were unaware of environmental damage at their campsite and were only slightly dissatisfied with crowded conditions. The majority of the campers surveyed supported closing campsite areas to allow for groundcover revegetation.

573. Noe, F. P.; Wellman, J. D.; and Buhyoff, Greg. "Perception of Conflict Between Off-Road Vehicle and Non Off-Road Vehicle Users in a Leisure Setting." *Journal of Environmental Systems* 11 (1981–82): 223–33.

This research sampled 597 off-road and non off-road vehicle users of Cape Hatteras National Seashore about their attitudes toward off-road vehicle use. The survey methodology consisted of an on-site interview and mail-back questionnaire. Analysis of the 58 items included in the questionnaire revealed different perspectives on the use of off-road vehicles among users and nonusers. The off-road users supported continued use of the seashore with few restrictions. The pedestrian visitors associated negative consequences with off-road vehicle use and supported greater restriction of both off-road vehicle and other uses of the seashore.

574. *1982–83 Nationwide Recreation Survey.* U.S. Department of Interior, National Park Service, April 1986, 95 pp.

This National Recreation Survey was sponsored by the U.S. National Park Service, Forest Service, Bureau of Land Management, and the Administration on Aging of the Department of Health and Human Services. Topics for the survey included the following: importance of outdoor recreation, reasons for favorite outdoor activity, constraints on participation in outdoor recreation, and opinion on national park fees and methods of rationing use. The survey instrument was developed by the University of Maryland's Survey Research Center, while the actual interviewing was conducted by the U.S. Bureau of the Census. A national sample of 5,757 Americans completed the interviews in their homes during September 1982 and January, April, and June 1983. "Not enough time" and "not enough money" were the most frequently cited reasons for not engaging in favorite outdoor activities. The most popular reasons for enjoying a favorite outdoor activity were to "enjoy nature and outdoors" and to "get exercise and keep in shape." When asked how much they would be willing to pay for entrance to a national park, over half of the respondents said they would pay up to $7.50 per visit. Of four options for rationing national nark access, the majority indicated they preferred "letting people reserve park visits ahead of time with reservations taken on a first come–first serve basis." This government publication contains numerous tables and graphics presenting the various findings of the study.

575. "OSU Survey Shows Support for Wilderness Restrictions to Reduce Use." *The Oregonian,* August 31, 1989, p. D4.

This newspaper article briefly describes research conducted by Bo Shelby and Mark Brunson of Oregon State University. The scientists surveyed users of the Alpine Lakes Wilderness area of the Washington Cascades about their approval of entry permits and use limitations during the summer. A majority of the respondents supported the use restrictions and some respondents supported expanding limitations to a wider area.

576. Yozwiak, Steve. "Arizonans 'Protective' of Canyon." *The Arizona Republic*, March 12, 1993, p. B6.

Results from a Northern Arizona University poll on the attitudes of Arizonans toward the Grand Canyon are presented in this article. The poll was conducted by the Social Research Laboratory at the university. A total of 402 Arizona residents were interviewed for the survey between February 22 and 27, 1993. The poll asked respondents about their support for a variety of measures that have been proposed to protect the canyon's natural resources. The highest level of support (79 percent) was found for willingness to pay higher entrance fees, followed by limiting the number of vehicles in the Grand Canyon National Park (78 percent). Nearly three-fourths of those polled said protecting the canyon's resources was more important than protecting the economic benefits of tourism. A majority favored banning uranium mining in the park (65 percent) and banning sightseeing planes and helicopters over certain areas of the canyon (64 percent). More than half of the respondents were also willing to pay higher electric bills to ease air pollution over the canyon and higher utility bills to stabilize water releases from the Glen Canyon Dam.

577. Libit, Howard. "Compromise by Feinstein on Desert Measure Possible: Opposition by Rep. Jerry Lewis Softens Senator's Stand on Proposed East Mojave National Park." *Los Angeles Times*, April 28, 1993, p. A21.

This newspaper article describes debate on a proposal to preserve seven million acres of California desert by creating numerous wilderness areas and upgrading two national monuments and one national scenic area to national parks. The controversial aspect of the bill surrounds the designation of the East Mojave as a national park which would end hunting in the area. Mentioned in the article are findings from a California Field Institute poll on this issue. The release date of the poll is given as April 27, 1993. The poll surveyed 1,052 California residents, including a subsample of adults residing in desert counties, during February 1993. According to the article, 75 percent of Californians favored creating a national park in the East Mojave area. Additionally, 68 percent of desert county residents supported the measure even though hunting would be banned in the proposed park.

Park Funding

578. Florida State Survey. *American Public Opinion Index: 1982.* Lexington, KY: Opinion Research Service, Inc., 1984.

In October 1982, the Policy Sciences Program at Florida State University interviewed Florida residents by telephone about their opinion of spending for environmental protection and funding for state parks. Of the sample of 1,005 adults, 57 percent supported increased spending on the environment, while 37 percent thought current funding levels were adequate. Respondents were also asked if they would be willing to pay for a beach pass to fund beach preservation.

579. University of Louisville Poll. *American Public Opinion Index: 1982.* Lexington, KY: Opinion Research Service, Inc., 1984.

The Urban Studies Center at the University of Louisville performed a telephone poll with 526 residents of Jefferson County, Kentucky, in March 1982. Included in the survey was a question about the amount of government spending on parks and recreation.

580. The California Poll. *American Public Opinion Index: 1983.* Lexington, KY: Opinion Research Service, Inc., 1985.

The Field Institute conducted the California Poll in March 1983. A sample of 1,505 California residents were contacted by telephone. Respondents were asked their opinion of funding for environmental regulations and parks and recreational facilities. Respondents were also asked their perception of air quality in California.

581. Georgia State University Poll. *American Public Opinion Index: 1984.* Lexington, KY: Opinion Research Service, Inc., 1985.

In November 1984, the Center for Public and Urban Research at Georgia State University administered a telephone poll with 800 residents of Gwinnett County, Georgia. Those responding to the survey were asked their preference for types of parks and their willingness to pay higher taxes to improve park facilities. The poll also inquired about the subjects' preference for fixing up existing parks versus buying new parkland.

582. Twin Cities Area Survey. *American Public Opinion Index: 1984.* Lexington, KY: Opinion Research Service, Inc., 1985.

The Twin Cities Area Survey is performed by the Minnesota Center for Social Research at the University of Minnesota. This telephone poll asked 1,064 adults residing in St. Paul and Minneapolis what they thought was the most important issue facing Minnesotans. Those responding to the poll were also questioned about spending on parks and open spaces in Minnesota.

583. Valerius, Laura, and Perdue, Richard R. *A Comparison of User and Nonuser Preferences for Funding Parks and Recreation Services.* U.S. Department of Agriculture, Forest Service, Southern Recreation Research Conference, 1987, pp. 67–75.

In this study, residents of Lincoln, Nebraska, were surveyed about preferences for funding park and recreation services. During 1983, a questionnaire was hand delivered to selected Lincoln households. Completed questionnaires were retrieved from 573 of 587 adults selected for the study. The subjects were questioned about their preference for funding recreation services by reducing services, increasing taxes, or increasing user fees. By a two-to-one margin, the respondents indicated they preferred increasing user fees over reducing services. By more than a three-to-one margin, they said they preferred increasing user fees to raising taxes. Those surveyed also put a higher priority on increasing recreation programs and improving existing parks than developing new parks. Responses were similar for both users and nonusers of recreation services.

584. The California Poll. *American Public Opinion Index: 1987.* Boston, MA: Opinion Research Service, Inc., 1988.

This telephone poll was conducted by the Field Institute in January 1987.

The survey asked a sample of 1,019 Californians if they would support bond proposals of varying amounts to purchase coastal lands and wildlife habitat and to add to the state's park and recreation areas. Those interviewed were asked their opinion of the importance of maintaining and adding to the state's park and recreation areas and of maintaining coastal areas and wildlife and natural areas.

585. Indiana Poll. *American Public Opinion Index: 1988.* Boston, MA: Opinion Research Service, Inc., 1989.

    The Indiana University Center for Survey Research conducted this special survey on parks and recreation. During the summer of 1988, 1,208 residents of Marion County, Indiana, were contacted by telephone and asked their opinion of the importance of spending tax dollars on parks and recreation services. Those responding to the survey were also questioned about the need for more natural, undeveloped areas in the county and whether they thought street trees were an important aspect of their city.

586. The California Poll. *American Public Opinion Index: 1988.* Boston, MA: Opinion Research Service, Inc., 1989.

    The Field Institute conducted the California Poll in February 1988 with 1,011 residents of California. When reached by telephone, the respondents were asked their view of the importance of maintaining and enlarging state parks and recreation areas and of preserving wildlife and natural areas. Those surveyed were also asked if they would support a $776 million bond issue to acquire land for coastal and wildlife protection and to maintain and add to the state parks and recreation areas.

587. Shukovsky, Paul. "Park Funds Adequate, Floridians Say." *Miami Herald,* October 31, 1989, p. 1B.

    This newspaper article reports on aspects of a Florida poll designed to measure attitudes toward park spending. The Florida Poll was conducted during August and September 1989 by Florida International University. A total of 1,232 randomly selected Florida adults were interviewed by telephone. Respondents were asked their opinion of the amount of money the state allocates to parks. Of those surveyed, 65 percent thought spending should be kept at the current level, 8 percent thought spending should be cut, and almost one-fourth thought park spending should be increased. Of those who supported increased spending, 61 percent said they would be willing to pay higher taxes, and the remainder wanted to see spending decreased for other programs to pay for parks. The article offered a breakdown of responses by political ideology and income level.

588. University of Maryland Poll. *American Public Opinion Index: 1989.* Boston, MA: Opinion Research Service, Inc., 1990.

    This telephone poll was conducted by the Survey Research Center at the University of Maryland. A sample of 652 residents of Montgomery County, Maryland, were surveyed. Respondents were asked their perception of county government spending for parks and recreation.

589. Dallas Issue Survey. *American Public Opinion Index: 1989.* Boston, MA: Opinion Research Service, Inc., 1990.

    Residents of Dallas, Texas, were polled by the *Dallas Morning News* during

February 1989. The 500 adults who answered the telephone poll were asked if they would be willing to pay more taxes to improve park and recreation facilities in their area.

590. Arizona Poll. *American Public Opinion Index: 1990.* Tallahassee, FL: 1991.

The *Arizona Republic* conducted this poll in September 1990 with 601 registered Arizona voters. Included in the survey was one question asking the respondent's position on a proposed measure to provide $10 million in state funds each year for trails, natural areas, historic preservation, and protection of endangered species habitat.

591. University of Baltimore Poll. *American Public Opinion Index: 1991.* Tallahassee, FL: 1991.

Telephone polls on the environment were conducted by the William Donald Schaefer Center for Public Policy at the University of Baltimore during 1991. In April 1991, 4,300 residents of Baltimore completed a quality of life survey that included questions on the amount of spending for parks and recreation and willingness to pay increased taxes to finance a special cleanup fund. The importance of a clean environment and parks and open spaces to the quality of life in a community were also measured. The April survey also asked respondents their opinion of the amount of spending for recycling and solid waste management. Other questions concerned approval for various proposals to restrict land use and development in order to protect the state's environment. The December poll, which surveyed 844 registered Maryland voters, asked those interviewed their opinion of allowing private business to manage the state parks and the collection of recyclable materials. This poll also asked about the amount of spending for environmental protection and willingness to fund a special cleanup fund.

592. *Citibank MasterCard and Visa Report on Our National Parks: Preserving a Priceless Heritage.* New York: Research and Forecasts, Inc., 1991, 40 pp.

This report was prepared by Research and Forecasts, Inc. for Citibank MasterCard and Visa. A sample of 1,006 Americans responded to the national telephone poll on perceptions of our national parks. The respondents answered questions about reasons for visiting national parks, perception of major issues facing the parks, willingness to pay additional taxes for park maintenance, and support for commercialism and energy development in national parks. "Seeing nature" was given as the most common reason for visiting a national park, and "preserving nature" was identified as the most important issue facing the National Park Service. The national park system was perceived as fulfilling environmental needs, followed by recreational, landmark, and governmental needs. Nearly half of the sample strongly agreed with the idea that the public should increase financial support for the parks to avoid increased commercialism. Only 18 percent strongly supported oil and gas exploration in national parks. When asked if they would be willing to pay an additional $5 federal tax per year to maintain national parks, 70 percent of the respondents said they would pay the increase.

593. Powers, Scott. "Survey: People Protective of Parks." *Columbus* [Ohio] *Dispatch*, November 2, 1991, p. 4D.

The Columbus City Council Parks and Recreation Committee sponsored the research discussed in this newspaper article. The purpose of the study was to explore the public's involvement in parks decisions and opinion of park funding and the need for additional parkland. Written questionnaires were mailed to 1,000 members of local civic associations, church groups, and other organizations. The response rate was slightly less than 50 percent. Of those surveyed, 58 percent thought the city was not spending enough money for parks and recreation. The survey also showed strong support for more greenbelts (90 percent) and parklands in outlying areas (71 percent). Opinion was nearly split, however, on the need for additional parkland in the downtown area.

594. Crompton, John L., and Lue, Chi Chuan. "Patterns of Equity Preference Among Californians for Allocating Park and Recreation Resources." *Leisure Sciences* 14 (1992): 227–46.

The research described in this article was developed by the authors and administered by a private contractor for the California Department of Parks and Recreation. This study was performed to explore patterns of preference for allocating park and recreation resources among a sample of California residents. A sample of 2,142 residents was initially contacted by telephone, and 1,807 agreed to complete a written questionnaire. Of the mailed questionnaires, 971, or 54 percent, were completed and returned. The survey asked respondents to choose among eight different options for how the state parks and recreation department should spend its funds. The spending priorities receiving the strongest agreement were areas where facilities receive the most use, areas where user fees cover a large share of the operating expenses, and areas which have the fewest facilities. The least support was expressed for spending funds in the areas where the cost of the facilities is the lowest and in areas that pay the most taxes. The article discusses the effect of nine socioeconomic variables on the responses.

595. Hall, Trish. "Have Backyards Supplanted Parks? Survey Says No." *The New York Times*, August 26, 1992, p. C1,6.

Researchers at Pennsylvania State University interviewed a random sample of American households by telephone with a follow-up questionnaire to determine attitudes toward city parks. A sample of 1,305 Americans were interviewed in early 1992 for the study sponsored by the National Recreation and Park Association with funding from the National Recreation Foundation. The article reports on the survey's findings concerning use of local parks and attitudes toward the benefits of parks and municipal spending for parks and recreation facilities. Although few specific statistics are given, the article does note that 75 percent of the respondents thought they got their money's worth from government spending on local parks, and many supported spending more on parks.

3

ATTITUDES TOWARD OUTDOOR RECREATION

Outdoor Recreation in General

596. Hendee, John C.; Gale, Richard P.; and Catton, William R., Jr. "A Typology of Outdoor Recreation Activity Preferences." *Journal of Environmental Education* 3 (Fall 1971): 28–34.

In conducting this research, the authors used results from a prior questionnaire to develop a typology of preferred outdoor recreation activities. The sample included 2,401 recreationists at campgrounds and backcountry areas in two national parks (Mt. Rainier and Olympic) and six national forests (Mt. Baker, Snoqualmie, Wenatchee, Goat Rocks and Glacier Peak Wildernesses, and North Cascades Primitive Area). Mail-back questionnaires were used to collect the recreationists' top six choices of 26 outdoor activities. Analysis of the first and second choices provided the basis for developing five outdoor activity types. Those types and the corresponding activities are as follows: appreciative-symbolic (57 percent), seeing natural scenery, hiking, mountain climbing, photography; extractive-symbolic (21 percent), hunting, fishing; passive-free play (17 percent), relaxing, sightseeing from a car, doing camp chores, boating or canoeing; sociable-learning (3 percent), nature study, socializing; and active-expressive (3 percent), swimming, motorcycle riding, water skiing.

597. Cicchetti, Charles Joseph. "A Review of the Empirical Analyses That Have Been Based Upon the National Recreation Survey." *Journal of Leisure Research* 4 (Spring 1972): 90–107.

This review article presents some of the findings from the 1960 and 1965 National Recreation Surveys. The surveys were sponsored by the Outdoor Recreation Resources Review Commission and conducted by the Bureau of the Census. In 1960–61, 4,000 respondents were interviewed for four quarterly surveys. During 1965, over 7,000 respondents were interviewed for a single survey. The interviews included questions related to participation and frequency of participation in various outdoor recreation activities. Respondents were also asked the reasons for restricting participation in their favorite activity and not participating in other desirable activities. In 1960 and 1965, the three most common reasons for not participating as often as one would like in an activity were "lack of time due to work," "lack of equipment," and "lack of time due to family obligations." The most common reasons for not participating at all in a desirable activity were "lack of time due to work," "lack of ability," and "lack of equipment."

598. Knopp, Timothy B. "Environmental Determinants of Recreation Behavior." *Journal of Leisure Research* 4 (Spring 1972): 129–38.

This research was conducted by the author with funding provided by the Hatch Act. The purpose of the study was to explore differences in outdoor recreation motivations between urban and rural residents and to test whether recreation preferences are related to home and work environmental factors. The subjects for the research were urban, rural farm, and rural nonfarm male residents of Winona City, Minnesota. The total number of interviews for all three groups was 126. Analysis of the results demonstrated a significant difference in the importance of exercise and solitude in outdoor recreation among the three different groups of males. Several work and home characteristics were significantly related to the importance of solitude and privacy as motivations for participating in outdoor recreational activities.

599. Driver, B. L., and Knopf, R. C. "Temporary Escape: One Product of Sport Fisheries Management." *Fisheries* 1 (March-April 1976): 21, 24–29.

In this article, the authors summarize the results of prior research into the satisfactions gained from fishing and other forms of outdoor recreation. (One of the reviewed studies is described in Knopf et al. 1973) In a study conducted by one of the authors in 1972, an experience preference scale was administered to 12 different types of Michigan recreationists including fishermen, campers, canoeists, and trail bike riders. To "experience nature" was rated highest by warm water lake fishermen, campers, and canoeists, while "exploration" was the preferred experience of the trail bikers. In another study, bank fishermen and picnickers at Belle Isle Park near the city of Detroit were asked about their recreation preferences. The highest ranked reasons for participating in their outdoor activity were "find it relaxing," "can take it easy," and "get away from hustle and bustle." Another national survey of 1,300 households conducted in the early 1970s found "relieving tension" to be the most important reason for engaging in hunting and fishing.

600. Rossman, Betty B., and Ulehla, Z. Joseph. "Psychological Reward Values Associated with Wilderness Use: A Functional-Reinforcement Approach." *Environment and Behavior* 9 (March 1977): 41–66.

In this article, the authors describe their research designed to explore the rewards of wilderness use and whether those rewards can be obtained in nonwilderness environments. The main phase of the study involved administering a questionnaire to 94 undergraduate college students. The questionnaire was composed of four sections: importance of 30 wilderness rewards, likelihood of obtaining these rewards in different environments, amount of leisure time spent in different environments, and reasons for enjoying wilderness. Ratings of the 30 wilderness rewards were used to identify five wilderness experience factors: emotional or spiritual experience, challenge and adventure, esthetic enjoyment of natural settings, escape from urban stress, and reaction against social activities. The respondents indicated some of the rewards could only be obtained in natural environments such as wilderness and improved mountain country and not in outdoor urban recreation areas. The respondents also indicated that if money and distance were not obstacles, they would increase the amount of leisure time spent in both wilderness and improved mountain country. The amount of time the students said they would spend in outdoor urban recreation areas did not change when money and distance were removed as obstacles to recreation.

601. Noe, F. P. "Identifying Attitudinal Predictors Among Youth Toward National Parks." *Journal of Leisure Research* 10 (1978): 203–13.

This research explored attitudes toward national parks among youths. The sample for the study consisted of 600 students in grades nine through twelve at 21 schools in the suburban area surrounding Atlanta, Georgia. One hour interviews were conducted with the predominantly white, middle class students in their homes. The survey analysis identified two factors, playfulness and solitariness, as being related to the youths' park attitudes. A model made up of a number of independent variables was most effective in explaining variance for the solitude factor. The model was unsuccessful in explaining the playfulness factor.

602. Peine, John D. "The 1977 National Outdoor Recreation Survey." *Transactions of the Forty-third North American Wildlife and Natural Resources Conference* 43 (1978): 108–16.

The research reported on in this article was conducted by the Heritage Conservation and Recreation Service in 1977. Two samples, one of the general population and one of recreationists on federal lands, were surveyed. The general population sample of 4,029 people were interviewed by telephone, and the federal land users, a total of 11,039 people, were interviewed in person. Subjects were questioned about the importance of outdoor recreation, the importance of individual activities, satisfaction with outdoor recreation experiences, deterrents to outdoor participation, and preferences for federal spending on outdoor recreation. Outdoor recreation was considered very important to 57 percent of the general sample and 80 percent of the federal lands sample. Only four percent of the federal land users were dissatisfied with their experience. The two most commonly cited deterrents to outdoor recreation for both samples were "lack of time" and "areas too crowded."

603. Hendee, John C. "Social Benefits of Fish and Wildlife Conservation." *Proceedings of the Western Association of State Fish and Game Commissioners* 58 (1978): 234–54.

This conference paper addresses sociological research into human benefits derived from outdoor recreation. The paper includes a figure listing 55 studies conducted from the late 1950s through the mid–1970s on wildlife related recreation (primarily hunting and fishing). Included in the listing are the specific human satisfactions documented by the individual studies. The most common satisfactions reported in the studies were nature appreciation, esthetic enjoyment, escapism, relaxation, and general enjoyment.

604. Godbey, Geoffrey. "Theory of the Leisure Mass." *Public Opinion* 2 (August-September 1979): 47–48.

This article describes the results of a study on outdoor recreation conducted by the Opinion Research Corporation for the Heritage Conservation and Recreation Service of the U.S. Department of Interior. A sample of 4,000 Americans aged 12 and older answered questions about the importance of outdoor recreation and reasons for not participating more in outdoor recreation. Outdoor recreation was described as "very" important by 57 percent and "somewhat" important by 29 percent of the Americans surveyed. "Lack of time," "over-crowding," and "lack of money" were given as reasons for limited participation in outdoor activities.

605. Gramann, James H., and Burdge, Rabel J. "The Effect of Recreation Goals on Conflict Perception: The Case of Water Skiers and Fishermen." *Journal of Leisure Research* 13 (1981): 15–27.

The purpose of this study was to test the theory that conflict will result if the behavior of one group of outdoor recreationists interferes with the goal attainment of another group of outdoor recreationists. For this particular study, visitors to Lake Shelbyville, Illinois, were surveyed during the summer of 1978. The visitors were asked to complete and return an eight-page questionnaire about their visit. Approximately 1,500 of the 2,003 initially contacted eventually returned the survey. The survey was designed to determine preferences for five recreation components: achievement, risk-taking, social contact, relationship with nature, and exercise. Analysis of the survey provided only modest support for the conflict theory. Fishermen who were motivated by tension release, escape, and nature enjoyment, however, were more likely to characterize speed boating as "reckless."

606. Wellman, J. D.; Dawson, M. S.; and Roggenbuck, J. W. "Park Managers' Predictions to the Motivations of Visitors to Two National Park Service Areas." *Journal of Leisure Research* 14 (1982): 1–15.

The research described in this article was conducted by the authors with the financial assistance of the U.S. National Park Service and the U.S. Forest Service Rocky Mountain Forest and Range Experiment Station. The goal of the study was to evaluate the ability of national park managers to predict the motivations of specific groups of park visitors. Backcountry pedestrian and off-road vehicle visitors to Cape Hatteras National Seashore and Shenandoah National Park were given mail-back questionnaires during the summer and fall of 1978. A total of 240 off-road vehicle users and 209 pedestrian visitors returned the questionnaires along with 41 management personnel. A similar survey was used with 110 visitors and 36 managers at Shenandoah National Park. Analysis of the survey showed that the predictions of the Shenandoah managers were generally accurate, while the Cape Hatteras manager predictions were wrong for a majority of the motivation scales. The managers tended to underestimate the rating visitors gave to different recreation motivations. In particular, the managers underestimated the importance of "enjoying scenery," "family togetherness," and "meeting new people."

607. Vaske, Jerry J.; Donnelly, Maureen P.; Heberlein, Thomas A.; and Shelby, Bo. "Differences in Reported Satisfaction Ratings by Consumptive and Nonconsumptive Recreationists." *Journal of Leisure Research* 14 (1982): 195–206.

In this study, the authors compared reported satisfaction levels between consumptive and nonconsumptive outdoor recreationists from 12 previously conducted studies. All of the studies included the question, "Overall, how would you rate your day/trip?" Consumptive users in these studies included various types of hunters and fishermen, while the nonconsumptive users were hikers, campers, day visitors, and different types of river users. The consumptive users, even those who were successful, reported significantly lower satisfaction ratings than the nonconsumptive users. The article presents information about the location, population, year, sample size, response rate, and method of study for the 12 studies.

608. Manning, Robert E. *Studies in Outdoor Recreation: A Review and Synthesis of the Social Science Literature in Outdoor Recreation.* Corvallis, OR: Oregon State University Press, 1985.

As the title states, this book is a summary of the findings of research studies on the social aspects of outdoor recreation. Hundreds of studies conducted between the early 1960s and the early 1980s are reviewed and analyzed. Some of the aspects of outdoor recreation included in the book are the following: user attitudes and preferences, perceptions of environmental impacts, visitor versus manager perceptions, satisfaction, and motivations for recreation. The reference list for the book contains approximately 500 entries.

609. Lucas, Robert C. *Visitor Characteristics, Attitudes, and Use Patterns in the Bob Marshall Wilderness Complex, 1970–82.* U.S. Department of Agriculture, Forest Service, June 1985, 32 pp.

Outdoor recreation visitors to one wilderness area were surveyed on their attitudes toward wilderness recreation and wilderness management policies in 1970 and again in 1982. Mail questionnaires were sent to visitors registering at lightly used trailheads in the Bob Marshall Wilderness during the summer and fall of the two years. Completed surveys were received from 502 visitors in 1970 (91 percent response rate) and 785 visitors in 1982 (82 percent response rate). The questionnaires measured attitudes toward the following wilderness issues: satisfaction, solitude, rationing and use control, regulations, other management policies, trails, other facilities, and acceptable visitor behavior. The following are the most important aspects of wilderness, as ranked by the 1970 visitors: "to fish," "scenic beauty," and "to hunt." In 1982, the top three appeals of wilderness use were the following: "scenic beauty," "to relax," and "to escape civilization." (The 1970 survey results are reported as part of another research project that compared visitor attitudes at nine wilderness areas.)

610. McClaskie, Stephen L. Napier, Ted L., and Christensen, James E. "Factors Influencing Outdoor Recreation Participation: A State Study." *Journal of Leisure Research* 18 (1986): 190–205.

The goal of this study was to develop models to be used in predicting participation in outdoor recreation activities. For the purpose of the study, outdoor activities were grouped into four categories: hunting, fishing, boating, and an "extensive" category which included hiking, bicycling, picnicking, swimming, and beach activities. Randomly selected Ohio license plate owners were sent mail questionnaires, and 2,341 returned usable surveys which were included in the analysis. Results of the study showed that early life experiences with traditional outdoor recreation activities were among the best predictors of participation in all four categories of outdoor recreation. The Ohio Agricultural Research and Development Center at Ohio State University and the Ohio Department of Natural Resources funded the research.

611. "Protect Wild Lands." *American Forests* 92 (July 1986): 49–50.

This brief item presents results from a nationwide survey conducted by Market Opinion Research of Detroit with funding from the National Geographic Society. Of the 2,000 Americans surveyed, 97 percent "strongly agreed" or "agreed" that the government should preserve natural areas for future generations to use for recreation. (Details on the date and methodology of the survey are not provided in the article.) The survey's findings were presented to the President's Commission on Americans Outdoors.

612. "Poll: Outdoor Recreation, Activism Are High Priorities." *USA Today*, March 28, 1991, p. 7C.

The Recreation Roundtable, whose members represent Disney, Coleman, Brunswick, L. L. Bean, and REI, commissioned the poll described in this article. Peter Hart Research Associates of Washington, D.C., conducted the telephone survey between February 28 and March 5, 1991. The 798 adults who completed the survey represented a cross-section sampling of the continental United States. Those surveyed were asked the importance of outdoor recreation to their lives, perception of local environmental cleanup efforts, and willingness to participate in community cleanup projects. Over three-fourths of the sample said outdoor recreation opportunities were "very" or "fairly important" to their lives. When asked about willingness to become personally involved in environmental cleanup, 43 percent indicated they would be interested "a great deal" or "quite a bit" in spending one day in a community cleanup project.

613. "Return to Outdoor Activities a Priority for Many in '90s." *USA Today*, October 31, 1991, p. 9C.

The study mentioned in this newspaper article was conducted by Yankelovich, Clancy and Shulman for *Outside* magazine. (The sample size, population, and methodology are not specified.) The survey questioned respondents about their attitude toward and participation in outdoor recreation and vacations. Of those polled, 73 percent said vacations are becoming a more important aspect of their lives. The respondents also indicated a desire to participate in more active forms of outdoor recreation in future vacations.

Fishing

MOTIVATIONS AND SATISFACTION

614. Moeller, George H., and Engelken, John H. "What Fishermen Look for in a Fishing Experience." *Journal of Wildlife Management* 36 (1972): 1253–57.

The research presented in this article was conducted by the U.S. Department of Agriculture, Forest Service and the State University College of Environmental Science and Forestry, Syracuse, New York. In the summer of 1969 and 1970, 100 licensed fishermen at the Heiberg Memorial Forest Fishing Ponds in New York were interviewed regarding the importance of different factors in their enjoyment of a typical day of fishing. Of the eight factors included, "water quality," "natural beauty," and "privacy while fishing" received the highest rankings by the fishermen. "Size and number of fish caught," "weather conditions," and "ease of access" were rated of moderate importance. The quality of facilities received the lowest overall ranking of the factors.

615. Knopf, Richard C.; Driver, B. L.; and Bassett, John R. "Motivations for Fishing." *Transactions of the Thirty-eighth North American Wildlife and Natural Resources Conference* 38 (1973): 191–204.

   In this conference paper, the authors describe and compare results from three studies on why fishermen fish and what possible conflicts arise between fishermen and canoeists. Study one included 50 canoeists and 25 trout fishermen on Au Sable River in Michigan and 30 fishermen on suburban lakes in the Detroit area. Study two sampled 100 recreationists including bank fishermen in Belle Isle Park, Michigan. Study three surveyed 834 canoeists and 593 trout fishermen on the Au Sable River. In study one, the researchers found the fishermen were motivated by four needs: "temporary escape," "achievement," "exploration," and "experiencing natural settings." The results from study one also showed that the motivational needs of fishermen and other recreationists differ, with canoeists expressing a much greater need for human interaction. They also found that motivations varied between different types of fishermen. Fishermen who had a low need for interaction and a high need to experience nature were more likely to perceive conflicts with canoeists.

616. Kennedy, James A., and Brown, Perry J. "Attitudes and Behavior of Fishermen in Utah's Uinta Primitive Area." *Fisheries* 1 (November-December 1976): 15–17, 30–31.

   Motivations of fishermen using a wilderness area are explored in this article. On-site interviews and follow-up mail questionnaires were administered to fishermen using the Uinta Primitive Area in Utah during the summer and fall of 1972. A total of 131 fishermen completed interviews and 100 completed both interviews and the mail-back questionnaire. The most important reason given for visiting the wilderness area was to "get away, escape." "Fishing" was cited as the most important reason for visiting the area by only 8 percent, and was the second most important reason for only 14 percent of the interviewees. In response to the question, "How important is fishing to your wilderness experience?" 28 percent rated it "very important," 57 percent "fairly important," and 15 percent said fishing was "not at all important" to their experience.

617. Manfredo, Michael J.; Brown, Perry J.; and Haas, Glenn E. "Fishermen Values in Wilderness." *Proceedings of the Western Association of State Game and Fish Commissioners* 58 (1978): 276–97.

   The purpose of this study was to explore the fishing values of fishermen using three wilderness areas in Colorado and to compare the wilderness values of fishermen and nonfishermen in the three areas. Funding for the research was received from the U.S. Forest Service, Rocky Mountain Forest and Range Experiment Station and the McIntire-Stennis Forestry Research program. The subjects for the study included 796 fishing and nonfishing recreationists at the Eagles Nest, Rawah, and Weminuche Wilderness areas. Data were collected by use of both personal interviews and mail questionnaires. Included in the surveys were questions on psychological outcomes desired from wilderness recreation and the importance of natural resource features. Results of the study indicated similar wilderness values among recreationists at all three areas and between fishermen and nonfishermen. The most common motivations for wilderness use were the following: "experiencing nature," "change of pace," and "physical fitness." "Water related resources," "forests and meadows," and "rugged terrain" were the most important natural resource features.

618. Weithman, A. Stephen. and Anderson, Richard O. "An Analysis of Memorable Fishing Trips by Missouri Anglers." *Fisheries* 3 (January-February 1978): 19–20.

   This paper presents findings from a doctoral dissertation conducted by one of the authors on factors influencing the quality of fishing. To collect data on the issue, a telephone survey was conducted with 200 licensed Missouri fishermen. Each respondent was asked to describe their most memorable fishing trip. The most frequently mentioned factors among those describing a trip were the following: species of fish, type of water, location, number of fish caught, size of fish caught, and companions.

619. Howard, Ilo C. "Opinions, Preferences, Satisfactions, and Importance of Women Anglers in Massachusetts." *Fisheries* 4 (November-December 1979): 32–34.

   This article describes a 1977 study of females holding Massachusetts fishing licenses. Of the 1,500 mail questionnaires sent, only 285 were included in the data analysis. The survey included questions about attitudes toward fishing, motivations for fishing, and problems encountered during fishing as well as questions designed to provide demographic data. A majority of the female anglers responding to the survey believed that fish were beautiful and that surroundings are an important factor when fishing. The most common reasons given for fishing were "relaxation" and "communing with nature." Funding for the survey was provided by the Massachusetts Division of Fisheries and Wildlife and the Fenwick Corporation, California.

620. Hicks, Charles E.; Belusz, Lawrence C.; Witter, Daniel J.; and Haverland, Pamela S. "Application of Angler Attitudes and Motives to Management Strategies at Missouri's Trout Parks." *Fisheries* 8 (September-October 1983): 2–7.

   The purpose of this study was to explore the attitudes of fishermen at Missouri's four trout parks toward selected fisheries management alternatives. Although approximately 16,000 fishermen were contacted during the two years of the study (1979–80), completed questionnaires were returned by fewer than 20 percent of the total sample. Respondents to the 1979 survey were asked to rate the importance of 16 reasons for fishing at a Missouri trout park. The reasons rated "very important" by a majority of the fishermen were: "relaxation," "enjoy nature," "catch at least one trout," "escape daily routine," and "escape work pressure." On one question concerning ways to improve fishing, limiting anglers and reducing limits were both rejected by over 80 percent of the fishermen. Establishing catch-and-release zones was the most popular option, yet only 46 percent of the fishermen supported this alternative. This research was conducted by the Missouri Department of Conservation.

621. Driver, B. L.; Phillips, Clynn; Bergersen, Eric P.; and Harris, Charles C. "Using Angler Preference Data in Defining Types of Sport Fisheries to

Manage." *Transactions of the Forty-ninth North American Wildlife and Natural Resources Conference* 49 (1984): 82–90.

This article describes two studies performed to determine angler preferences for different types of fisheries. Mail questionnaires were used to survey fishermen in Wyoming in 1975 and in Colorado in 1982. Responses were received from approximately 840 Wyoming fishermen (42 percent response rate) and approximately 460 Colorado fishermen (53 percent response rate). The initial results from the Wyoming fishermen were used to identify six distinct classes of fishermen: general outdoors, yield, social, general recreation, trophy, solitude, and wild.

622. Graefe, Alan R. and Fedler, Anthony J. "Situational and Subjective Determinants of Satisfaction in Marine Recreational Fishing." *Leisure Sciences* 8 (1986): 275–95.

Funding for this study was received from the University of Delaware Sea Grant Marine Advisory Program, the University of Maryland Sea Grant Marine Advisory Program, and the University of Maryland Computer Science Center. In this study, the researchers used data from two previous studies to explore components of fishing satisfaction. One study surveyed by mail approximately 600 Delaware fishermen using charter services during the summer of 1982. The second study sampled 326 participants in charter boat fishing on the Chesapeake Bay during the summer of 1983. The study found that three situational variables (number of fish caught personally, number of fish caught by group, and quality of captain and crew) were significantly related to fishing satisfaction for both samples. Subjective evaluations of the trip, however, were more strongly associated with fishing satisfaction than the situational variables. When both types of variables were combined, 50 percent of the variance in satisfaction was explained.

623. Baur, Richard J., and Rogers, Richard A. "1983 Illinois Sport Fishing Survey." *Fisheries* 11 (January-February 1986): 32.

This one-page item is the abstract from a 1983 sport fishing survey conducted by the Illinois Department of Conservation. Questionnaires were returned by 3,120 fishermen at the end of an April through September period and 3,321 fishermen at the end of a second period from October through March. The response rates for the two periods were 43 percent and 46 percent, respectively. In the questionnaire, fishermen were asked about their participation in fishing and their motivation and preferences for fishing. In the 1983 survey, as well as in previous surveys in 1977 and 1980, the primary reasons for fishing were the following: "to enjoy the outdoors," "for the thrill of catching fish," "for peace and solitude," and "for food."

624. Fedler, Anthony J., and Ditton, Robert B. "A Framework for Understanding the Consumptive Orientation of Recreational Fishermen." *Environmental Management* 10 (March 1986): 221–27.

The research described in this article attempted to determine how the importance of catching fish varied among fishermen. Financial support for the study was received from the Texas A&M University Sea Grant College Programs, Texas Agricultural Experiment Station, and the University of Maryland Computer Science Center. A sample of 765 Texas saltwater fishermen completed a mail questionnaire on the importance of three fish-related variables (keeping fish, number of fish caught, and trophy/challenge aspect of fishing) and reasons for going fishing.

The questionnaire responses were used to identify three types of fishermen by their consumptive orientation (low, mid, and high). Each of the three groups was unique in the importance placed on other fish-related variables. Fishermen in the low consumptive group rated the importance of fishing for "relaxation," "escaping the daily routine," and "interacting with nature" higher than did the fishermen in the high consumptive group.

625. Helfrich, Louis A., Chipman, Brian D., and Kauffman, John W. "Profiles of Shenandoah River Anglers Fishing Under Three Black Bass Length Limit Regulations." *Proceedings of the Annual Conference of the Southeast Association of Fish and Wildlife Agencies* 41 (1987): 178–86.

The purpose of this study was to compare the motivations, perceptions, and preferences of black-bass fishermen using three areas with different bass length regulations. Between September 1984 and August 1985, fishermen using three different sections of the Shenandoah River in Virginia were contacted in the field and later sent mail questionnaires. Responses were received from 280 fishermen for a response rate of 83 percent. When asked to rank their top three motivations for fishing, all three groups of fishermen gave similar responses. "Enjoying the outdoors," "fishing for sport," and "fishing for escape" were the top three choices. The three groups also expressed similar perceptions of a quality fishing experience but differed on their preferences for fisheries management regulations.

626. Falk, James M., Graefe, Alan R., and Ditton, Robert B. "Patterns of Participation and Motivation Among Saltwater Tournament Anglers." *Fisheries* 14 (July-August 1989): 10–17.

This article reviews the results of 20 studies conducted between 1974 and 1987 on the fishing motivations of saltwater tournament anglers. Results from the 20 studies are summarized in tables for the following: number of anglers, percent of male anglers, percent of local participants, number of previous years of participation, percent of first-time participants, number of days fished, perceived skill, percent belonging to fishing clubs, portion of vacation spent fishing, and motivations for going fishing. For fishing motivation, results from studies of tournament fishermen are compared with the results from general fishermen. While "sport/challenge" was the highest ranked motivation in seven of ten studies of tournament fishermen, "relaxation" was the number one motivation identified by general fishermen in seven of twelve studies.

FISHERIES MANAGEMENT

627. King, Thomas R.; Thompson, Raymond R.; and Buntz, Jon C. "Comparison of Attitudes of Average Fishermen and Fishing Club Members." *Proceedings of the Annual Conference of the Southeast Association of Fish and Wildlife Agencies* 32 (1978): 657–65.

A telephone survey was conducted by the Communication Research Center of Florida State University for the Florida Game and Fresh Water Fish Commission. The survey was conducted between January 10 and February 15, 1977, with a random sampling of Florida fishing license holders and members of Florida fishing clubs. The sample size was 1,132 for fishing license holders and 128 for members of fishing clubs. The respondents were questioned about their fishing behaviors and preferences and their opinions about the Florida Game and Fresh Water Fish Commission. Responses from average fishermen and fishing club members differed on a majority of the questions.

628. Schoolmaster, F. Andrew, and Frazier, John W. "An Analysis of Angler Preferences for Fishery Management Strategies." *Leisure Sciences* 7 (1985): 321–42.

Funding for this research was provided by grants from North Texas State University, Montana Department of Fish, Wildlife and Parks, and the U.S. Bureau of Land Management. The purpose of the research was to determine what factors contribute to the preferences of fishermen for different fishery management strategies. A questionnaire was sent to private and commercial float anglers who had registered while using the Madison River, Montana, during the summer of 1980. Of the 450 anglers selected for inclusion in the study, 347 completed and returned the survey. At least 20 percent of the anglers identified the following factors as moderate or serious problems: number of fish, size of fish, and number of commercial fishermen. When asked about various management plans, less than one-third of the respondents supported any single option. The strongest support was received for a fish stocking program (32 percent) and for limiting commercially guided float fishing (31 percent). For this group of fishermen, experience was the most important factor in determining support for the various management options.

629. Hardin, Scott; Rayburn, J. D., II; and Posnansky, Gary. "Attitudes, Practices, and Preferences of Licensed Fresh Water Anglers in Florida." *Proceedings of the Annual Conference of the Southeast Association of Fish and Wildlife Agencies* 41 (1987): 168–77.

This Florida angler survey was conducted for the Florida Game and Fresh Water Fish Commission by the Communication Research Center of Florida State University. Funding was provided by the Federal Aid in Fish Restoration Project. A sample of 602 licensed Florida fresh water fishermen completed a telephone survey of attitudes toward fishing and fishing management in Florida. The telephone interviews were conducted with fishermen who had completed and returned postcards indicating their willingness to participate in the study. (Only 47 percent and 32 percent of two selected samples of license holders returned the cards.) Responses to the telephone surveys indicated the fishermen favored a reduced "bag" limit, trophy bass management, and increased emphasis on largemouth bass as a sport fish. When questioned about the prior ten years, over half of the fishermen said fishing had declined in quality in Florida, and pollution was most often given as the reason for the decline. "Fun and relaxation" were given as their primary reasons for fishing by 80 percent of the respondents.

630. Watt, Bill. "Survey of 1985 Urban Anglers." *Proceedings of the Western Association of Fish and Wildlife Agencies* 67 (1987): 194–206.

This conference paper describes results from a 1985 survey of fishermen participating in Arizona's Urban Fishing Program. During February 1985, a mail questionnaire was sent to 10 percent of all holders of the state's urban fishing license. Responses were received from 240, or 23.5 percent, of the selected sample. The survey questioned the anglers about the level of their participation in urban fishing, their satisfaction with the Urban Fishing Program, and their opinion of a proposed reduction in the daily "bag" limit.

631. University of Louisville. *American Public Opinion Index: 1991.* Tallahassee, FL: 1991.

The Urban Research Institute, College of Urban and Public Affairs at the University of Louisville administered this telephone poll during 1991. A sample of 1,225 Kentucky fishermen were asked various questions about fishing including reasons for frequency of fishing, reasons why children do not fish, and reasons for not fishing more often. The respondents were also asked to identify factors that determine the quality and success of a fishing trip. Other questions requested opinions on several fishing regulations: number of fishermen, fishing seasons, mandatory catch and release, number of fish kept, size of fish kept, number of fishing rods used, and outboard motor size.

Hunting

MOTIVATIONS/SATISFACTION

632. Peterle, Tony J. "Characteristics of Some Ohio Hunters." *Journal of Wildlife Management* 31 (April 1967): 375–89.

This article describes research conducted by the author and sponsored by the Ohio Cooperative Wildlife Research Unit and the U.S. Bureau of Sport Fisheries and Wildlife. A mail questionnaire was administered in September 1960 to 4,144 licensed Ohio hunters. The questionnaire included items designed to identify respondent knowledge about hunting, satisfaction gained from hunting, and pleasure gained from nongame aspects of hunting. Additional items were included to identify respondent attitudes toward wildlife management, specifically willingness to pay increased fees and the perceived role of scientific research. Attitude findings were correlated with number of days spent hunting and number of game killed. The research reported numerous correlations between respondent demographics and attitudes toward hunting and wildlife management.

633. Greene, Jeffrey C. "Characteristics of Some Michigan Shooting Preserve Users." *Journal of Wildlife Management* 34 (1970): 813–17.

The Fisheries and Wildlife Department of Michigan State University conducted this study of shooting preserve users in October 1969. A mail questionnaire was sent to 10 percent of the users of Michigan shooting preserves during the 1968-69 hunting season. Responses were received from 241 hunters who answered questions about their reasons for using shooting preserves and their satisfaction with the experience. The majority (67 percent) indicated they "always" found the experience at shooting preserves enjoyable and worthwhile. Michigan shooting preserves were thought to be an "excellent" or "good" place to hunt by 84 percent of the respondents. The most popular reasons for using preserves were "abundant game birds — assured of shooting" and "lack of game birds during open season." The majority who had negative perceptions of shooting preserves said they were "not like natural hunting."

634. Potter, Dale R., Hendee, John C., and Clark, Roger N. "Hunting Satisfaction: Game, Guns, or Nature?" *Transactions of the Thirty-eighth North American Wildlife and Natural Resources Conference* 38 (1973): 220–29.

This research was conducted by the U.S. Department of Agriculture, Forest

Service with additional funding from the Wildlife Management Institute and the American Petroleum Institute. Washington state residents with hunting licenses for 1970 were surveyed in order to study factors related to hunting satisfaction. Sample size for the survey was 5,540 with a response rate of 85 percent. Respondents to the mail questionnaire were asked to indicate the extent each of 73 elements added to or detracted from their personal satisfaction with hunting. Of 11 dimensions of hunting satisfaction identified by the research, nature, escapism, and companionship appeared most important to the hunters. Certain dimensions were more important to different types of hunters, while seven of the dimensions were important to all hunters.

635. More, Thomas A. "Attitudes of Massachusetts Hunters." *Transactions of the Thirty-eighth North American Wildlife and Natural Resources Conference* 38 (1973): 230–34.

The author of this article conducted research into the attitudes of hunters in the state of Massachusetts in the fall 1969. A sample of 325 hunters responded to his mail survey of randomly selected licensed hunters. In the questionnaire, the hunters were asked to indicate their agreement with 52 statements concerning reasons for hunting. The research identified seven independent factors or categories of motivations for hunting: display, aesthetics, affiliation, pioneering, killing, exploration, and challenge. The reasons for hunting that received the strongest agreement were the following: "being out in the fields and forests," "tranquility of nature," "relaxation and relief of tensions," "watching nongame wildlife," and "tracking and stalking game."

636. Stankey, George H.; Lucas, Robert C.; and Ream, Robert R. "Relationships Between Hunting Success and Satisfaction." *Transactions of the Thirty-eighth North American Wildlife and Natural Resources Conference* 38 (1973): 235–42.

Resources for the Future sponsored this research which attempted to determine the relationship between hunters' definitions of "quality big game hunting" and success in hunting. The study consisted of a mail questionnaire distributed to hunters using the Sapphire Mountains in Montana during the 1971 hunting season. Responses were received from 418 hunters. Over two-thirds of the hunters described quality big game hunting as killing an animal or seeing game or game signs. Similar responses were given by successful and unsuccessful hunters. Of those hunters who felt the quality of hunting was declining in the area, the unsuccessful hunters attributed the decline to dwindling game populations, while the successful hunters were more likely to cite other reasons such as excessive road development and increased number of hunters.

637. Schole, Bernhard J.; Glover, Fred A.; Sjogren, Douglas D.; and Decker, Eugene. "Colorado Hunter Behavior, Attitudes, and Philosophies." *Transactions of the Thirty-eighth North American Wildlife and Natural Resources Conference* 38 (1973): 242–47.

In this conference paper, the authors describe research on hunter attitudes and behavior conducted with 400 Colorado licensed hunters in 1971. The research was conducted by the Colorado Cooperative Wildlife Research Unit, Colorado State University, and the Human Factor Research Laboratory. Funding was provided by Colorado State University, Colorado Division of Wildlife, the Wildlife

Management Institute, and the U.S. Bureau of Sport Fisheries and Wildlife. Methodology for the survey consisted of one hour personal interviews with randomly selected hunting license holders. Subjects were questioned regarding the following items: who introduced license holder to hunting, age introduced to hunting, factors that initiated interest in hunting, factors that confirmed interest in hunting, most and least satisfying hunting experiences, and reasons for participating in hunting. "Love of outdoors," "influence of people," and "proximity to hunting areas" were the three most common factors responsible for stimulating interest in hunting. Participation in big game hunting that resulted in a trophy was the most satisfying hunting experience. "Love of outdoors" was the most frequently mentioned reason for hunting.

638. Kennedy, James J. "Some Effects of Urbanization on Big and Small Game Management." *Transactions of the Thirty-eighth North American Wildlife and Natural Resources Conference* 38 (1973): 248–55.

The purpose of this research was to determine the effect of success rates on satisfaction with hunting. The Maryland Department of Forest and Parks and Game and Inland Fish and Virginia Polytechnic Institute sponsored the study. (Additional aspects of the study are reported elsewhere in this volume.) The sample consisted of 373 deer hunters using the Pocomoke State Forest in Maryland during the 1969 deer hunting season. Responses to the mail questionnaire indicated that despite a low success rate, 62 percent of the hunters had an "excellent" or "good" hunting experience that season. "Suspense and the challenge of the hunt" was ranked as the most satisfying aspect of hunting. "Getting out-of-doors," "companionship," "escape," and actually "killing a deer" were ranked second through fifth in importance. When asked whether they would be disappointed if they were unable to kill a deer during the next season, 78 percent said they would be "slightly" or "not disappointed at all."

639. Thomas, Jack Ward; Pack, James C.; Healy, William M.; Gill, John D.; and Sanderson, H. Reed. "Territoriality Among Hunters—the Policy Implications." *Transactions of the Thirty-eighth North American Wildlife and Natural Resources Conference* 38 (1973): 274–80.

This study was conducted by the U.S. Department of Agriculture, Forest Service, Northeastern Forest Experiment Station, Monongahela National Forest, and the West Virginia Department of Natural Resources with funding from the Pittman Robertson Project. Personal interviews were conducted with hunters exiting the Middle Mountain hunting area in West Virginia during the 1968–70 small game hunting seasons. The sample was subdivided into 747 nonreturning (one season only) hunters and 340 home-range (using one area more than once) hunters. All hunters were asked why they chose their particular site for hunting and if they intended to return to that area. The most important reason for choosing a particular site differed between the two groups of hunters. Home-range hunters said "good hunting—more game" was most important, while nonreturning hunters said "advice from others" was the reason they chose the site. For hunters that did not intend to return to the area, "not enough game" was most often cited as the reason.

640. Bjornn, T. C., and Williams, R. M. "Idaho Hunters, Their Attitudes and Preferences." *Proceedings of the Western Association of State Game and Fish Commissioners* 54 (1974): 129–43.

This study of the attitudes of Idaho hunters was funded by the Idaho Fish and Game Department, the University of Idaho, and the U.S. Fish and Wildlife Service. Data for the study were obtained by a mail questionnaire returned by over 4,400 resident and 1,800 nonresident holders of Idaho hunting licenses for the 1971 hunting season. Topics for the survey included the following: reasons for hunting, sources of wildlife management information, preferred type of hunting, satisfaction with hunting, and opinion of several wildlife management practices (limitations on nonresident hunting, state versus federal land, supplemental winter feeding of game animals, hunting of game farm pheasants, need for roads for big game hunting, big game seasons, and quantity vs. quality hunting). The reasons for hunting differed for resident and nonresident hunters. Resident hunters cited "meat" as their most important hunting motivation, while nonresident hunters said they hunted for "relaxation" or "the challenge of the hunt." "Hunting for trophy" was the prime motivation of only 1.5 percent of the Idaho residents and 16.4 percent of the nonresidents. Supplemental winter feeding of deer and elk was supported by 49 percent of the resident and 56 percent of the nonresident hunters.

641. Kennedy, James J. "Attitudes and Behaviors of Deer Hunters in a Maryland Forest." *Journal of Wildlife Management* 38 (1974): 1–8.
      The author of this article conducted research supported by the Maryland Department of Forest and Parks and the Maryland Department of Game and Inland Fish into the attitudes and behaviors of Maryland deer hunters. The research consisted of a pretested questionnaire and final mail questionnaire distributed after the 1969 deer season. The sample included 373 hunters contacted in November and December 1969 in the Pocomoke State Forest in Maryland. The questionnaire measured attitudes toward hunter density, unsafe hunting behaviors, deer hunting rewards, and the importance of killing a deer to hunting satisfaction. The majority (67 percent) of hunters responding to the survey indicated they were "seldom" or "never" bothered by other hunters during deer season. Relationships were noted, however, between the number of other hunters seen and the sense of being bothered, and between being bothered and a sense of one's safety being threatened. The "suspense and challenge of seeking deer" was ranked as the top direct reward of deer hunting. "Getting outdoors" was ranked as the top indirect reward. In response to questioning about possible disappointment with not killing a deer next season, 78 percent replied they would be "very much" or "a little disappointed," while 22 percent said they "would not be disappointed."

642. Kennedy, James J. "Motivations and Rewards of Hunting in a Group versus Alone." *Wildlife Society Bulletin* 2 (1974): 3–7.
      The author of this article conducted this research which was sponsored by the Maryland Department of Forest and Parks and Game and Inland Fish and the Virginia Polytechnic Institute in March 1970. (Other aspects of the study are presented in an additional reference by the same author.) The research included both personal interviews with small samples of student hunters, rural hunters, and urban hunters and a mail questionnaire sent to a large sample (340) of urban hunters. All subjects had experience hunting in the Pocomoke State Park in Maryland. The instrument featured questions about the advantages and disadvantages of hunting in a group and the comparison of the enjoyment from hunting with companions to that of actually killing a deer. The wildlife students were least positive about hunting with a group, expressing concerns for personal safety and success in hunting as a result of hunting with others. The urban hunters were the

most positive about hunting with others. Nearly three-fourths of the respondents indicated they would choose hunting with companions even if their chance of success was only one-fifth what it might be hunting in a different area alone.

643. Shaw, William W. *Sociological and Psychological Determinants of Attitudes Toward Hunting.* Doctoral dissertation, University of Michigan, 1974, 92 pp.

In this doctoral dissertation, the author describes the results of a mail questionnaire that surveyed attitudes of different groups toward hunting. The sample included members of three groups: consumptive wildlife users (Michigan deer hunters), conservation organization members (Michigan Audubon Society members), and humanitarian, anti-hunting organization members (Michigan Fund for Animals members). The survey instrument was designed to measure 13 variables hypothesized as being predictive of hunting attitudes and attitudes toward hunting. No one variable predicted hunting attitudes. The research found that three predictors (urbanization in early life, education level, and experience with bloodshed) when combined accounted for 45 percent of the variance in attitudes.

644. Copp, John D. "Why Hunters Like to Hunt." *Psychology Today* 9 (December 1975): 60, 62, 67.

This magazine article discusses the author's observations of hunters. Included is a brief description of a written questionnaire and personal interviews administered to duck and goose hunters at Delevan National Wildlife Refuge in California. The sample size for the interviews was 100, but the number completing the written questionnaire was not given. The date of the research was also not reported. Questionnaire items covered hunting experience, distance travelled to hunt, and reasons for choosing a particular site to hunt. The interview consisted of asking hunters, "Why do you hunt?" Most respondents cited more than one reason. The most common reasons related to the desire to escape from the routine, frustration, and pressure of their work and everyday lives. No respondents gave the desire to kill or the desire to obtain food as their primary reason for hunting.

645. Minser, William G. "Hunter and Landowner Attitudes Concerning State-Leased and Fee Dove Hunting in Tennessee." *Proceedings of the Annual Conference of the Southeast Association of Fish and Wildlife Agencies* 30 (1976): 400–3.

In the fall of 1975, the author surveyed dove hunters at 58 hunting areas in Tennessee about their attitudes toward fee dove hunting, their willingness to pay for dove hunting, and their willingness to travel to hunt dove. The hunting areas were divided into three different types: privately owned land open for hunting for a fee, state-owned land open to the public for a fee, and privately owned areas leased to the state where the public is admitted to hunt without charge. Written questionnaires were given to hunters as they left the field after hunting. Completed questionnaires were returned by 532 hunters. Following dove season, the researcher also sent mail questionnaires to landowners participating in the state-leased dove hunting program. The hunters in the three different areas identified the same factors as influencing the quality of a hunt. Respondents related the quality of the hunt to the number of doves seen, the number of hours hunted, the number of shells fired, the number of doves killed, and the space interval between hunters. Of the 61 landowners who completed the mail survey, 46 percent had no complaints.

Litter, too many hunters, objections from neighbors, hunters in unauthorized areas, and parking problems were the most frequently voiced landowner complaints.

646. Smith, Robert I., and Roberts, Roy J. "The Waterfowl Hunter's Perception of the Waterfowl Resource." *Transactions of the Forty-first North American Wildlife and Natural Resources Conference* 41 (1976): 188–93.

In this conference paper, the authors describe a survey of waterfowl hunters sponsored by the U.S. Fish and Wildlife Service. The sample was selected from Federal Duck Stamp purchasers for the 1973-74 hunting season. Mail questionnaires were sent to 6,000 stamp purchasers; 3,600 were returned. The purpose of the survey was to select questions for use in a subsequent larger survey of waterfowl hunters. The following topics were addressed in the questionnaire: importance of waterfowl hunting to the lives of the subjects, sources of satisfaction in waterfowl hunting, ability to identify waterfowl, importance of wildlife management practices, and perceived seriousness of various hunting etiquette and legal violations. Less than half of the sample (40 percent) expressed a strong commitment to waterfowl hunting. "Mastery of hunting skills" was the most frequently mentioned source of pleasure from waterfowl hunting. Certain etiquette infractions were seen as more serious than legal violations. "Protecting nesting grounds" was felt to be the most important activity of waterfowl management.

647. Frazier, Kenneth D. "Characteristics and Attitudes of West Central Texas Hunters, 1971–72." *Proceedings of the Annual Conference of the Southeast Association of Fish and Wildlife Agencies* 30 (1976): 408–13.

This study surveyed licensed hunters in Taylor County, Texas, about perceived benefits and satisfactions from hunting. The survey was conducted by telephone with 201 hunters from September through November 1972. Of 217 responses to the question of why the subjects hunted, 182 were nonconsumptive reasons. "Outdoor recreation" was cited as the motivation for hunting by 82 percent of the subjects with 15 percent giving "food" as the chief motivation. All other motivations received less than 5 percent of the responses.

648. Ratti, John T., and Workman, Gar W. "Hunter Characteristics and Attitudes Relating to Utah Shooting Preserves." *Wildlife Society Bulletin* 4 (Spring 1976): 21–25.

The research described in this article was conducted by the authors and sponsored by the National Rifle Association of America, Utah State University's Ecology Center, Department of Wildlife Science, the Utah Cooperative Wildlife Research Unit, and the Utah Division of Wildlife Resources. Groups of hunters using and not using shooting preserves were surveyed concerning their attitudes toward preserves. The total sample of 545 preserve hunters and 665 nonpreserve hunters responded to mail questionnaires distributed during the 1971-72 hunting season. The questionnaire response rates for both types of hunters were less than 50 percent. Items on the questionnaire dealt with knowledge about preserve operations, reasons for using or not using shooting preserves, and satisfaction with hunting on preserves for those who made use of them. The findings indicated that shooting preserve hunters were more likely to have been raised in an urban area and have higher incomes and more education. Those who used shooting preserves said they did so because they felt preserves were less crowded, had longer hunting seasons, and offered higher hunting success rates than public lands. Those who did not use shooting preserves expressed a negative attitude toward hunting on preserves.

649. Miller, Ronald R.; Prato, Anthony A.; and Young, Robert A. "Congestion, Success and the Value of the Colorado Deer Hunting Experience." *Transactions of the Forty-second North American Wildlife and Natural Resources Conference* 42 (1977): 129–36.

This conference proceeding reports on one aspect of a study of deer hunting satisfaction. (Other findings from the study are presented elsewhere.) Resources for the Future funded this study of Colorado deer hunting license holders. Mail questionnaires were distributed to an unspecified number of hunters. Subjects were asked about their willingness to pay for their deer hunting experience and comparisons were made among willingness to pay, residency status, hunter density, and hunter success. Nonresident hunters were willing to pay significantly more for their deer hunting experience than residents. Willingness to pay increased with hunter success and decreased with hunter density. Willingness to pay also varied by the eight hunter types described in the other report on the research.

650. Peterle, Tony J. "Changes in Responses from Identical Ohio Hunters Interviewed in 1960-61 and 1973-74." *Transactions of the Forty-second North American Wildlife and Natural Resources Conference* 42 (1977): 156–68.

The purpose of this research was to compare results of two surveys conducted 14 years apart on the attitudes toward hunting held by a group of Ohio hunters. The author mailed questionnaires to a cohort of the Ohio hunters who responded to the original survey in 1960–61. Only 591, or 14 percent of the original sample, responded to the second survey. The questionnaire included the following topics: attitudes toward different hunting methods, hunting philosophy, wildlife management practices, conservation principles, and gun control. A number of statistically significant differences were found between responses to the two surveys. In the later survey, the respondents expressed less interest in hunting and indicated they received less satisfaction from hunting and greater enjoyment from experiencing nature while hunting. Fewer respondents were supportive of wildlife management practices. The items which received the most different responses between the two surveys were on the issue of stocking game and the practice of hunting until game is killed. The research did not attempt to measure the percent of the original hunters who had quit hunting and why.

651. Wright, Vernon L.; Bubolz, Thomas A.; Wywialowski, Alice; and Dahlgren, Robert B. "Characteristics of Individuals Involved in Different Types of Hunting." *Transactions of the Forty-second North American Wildlife and Natural Resources Conference* 42 (1977): 207–15.

The research presented in this article attempted to classify hunters by the type of animals hunted and determine possible relationships between hunter type and motivation for hunting. The Iowa Cooperative Wildlife Research Unit conducted the research which was sponsored by the U.S. Fish and Wildlife Service, Iowa State Conservation Commission, Iowa State University, and the Wildlife Management Institute. Data were collected by mail questionnaire from two separate samples during the summer of 1976. One sample consisted of randomly selected members of the general Iowa public, and the other sample was made up of 1,225 licensed Iowa hunters. (Results of the general public surveys are detailed elsewhere in this volume.) Hunters were grouped into six classifications: quail, rabbit-squirrel, waterfowl, furbearer, avid generalist, and casual generalist. Responses to many of the statements about value derived from hunting were significantly related to the type of hunter. The following were the most common reasons (multiple answers) given by former hunters for no longer hunting: "work around home takes too much time" (29 percent), "job or business takes too much time" (25 percent), "physical disability" (25 percent), and "developed guilt feelings about killing animals" (19 percent).

652. Brown, Perry J.; Hautaluoma, Jacob E.; and McPhail, S. Morton. "Colorado Deer Hunting Experience." *Transactions of the Forty-second North American Wildlife and Natural Resources Conference* 42 (1977): 216–25.
     The staff of Colorado State University performed the research described in this article. Mail questionnaires were administered to Colorado deer hunting license holders who were separated into subsamples on the basis of their license type. This article reports on results from 1,971 hunters with all types of licenses and 694 in-state rifle license holders. Researchers used the cluster analysis technique to produce nine dimensions of hunting satisfaction from responses to the 73-item questionnaire. Different types of hunters were identified by four dimensions of hunting satisfaction: "easy hunt," "harvest," "out-group contact," and "nature." A profile of eight different hunter types resulted. Of the four dimensions, "nature" was most positively rated by the total sample of hunters. The "nature" and "harvest" dimensions added to hunting satisfaction for all eight hunter types. "Out-group contact" and "easy hunt" dimensions varied among hunter types. Respondents were also asked for their reactions to 10 management practices of the state Division of Wildlife. There were significant differences among the hunter types to three of the management items.

653. Gilbert, Alphonse H. "Influence of Hunter Attitudes and Characteristics on Wildlife Management." *Transactions of the Forty-second North American Wildlife and Natural Resources Conference* 42 (1977): 226–35.
     The Vermont Fish and Game Department and the staff of the University of Vermont collaborated on this research conducted in February 1974. Mail questionnaires were sent to resident and nonresident Vermont hunting license holders for the 1973 hunting season. Responses were received from 3,539 hunters for a response rate of 53 percent. Subjects addressed by the questionnaire included the following: reasons for hunting, criteria for a successful hunt, reasons for increasing or decreasing participation in hunting, and management practices for improved hunting. Subjects were asked to rank the importance of 11 factors in explaining why they hunt. A multidimensional factor, "to enjoy the sport" was ranked highest. Next highest were "to get out into the woods" and "to test hunting skills." The criteria for a successful hunt receiving the highest overall rankings were "just getting into the field" and "having the right equipment." The most important reasons for both increasing and decreasing participation in hunting was related to time available for the sport. "Controlling deer-killing dogs" and "enforcing the law" were the management practices seen as most important.

654. McDonough, Maureen H., and Harris, Larry D. "Perception and Use of Wildlife by North Central Florida People." *Proceedings of the Annual*

Conference of the Southeast Association of Fish and Wildlife Agencies 31 (1977): 204–11.

The research presented in this conference paper was conducted in four stages: an initial unstructured interview, a pre-test questionnaire, a final mail questionnaire, and in-depth personal interviews. The sample consisted of residents of 11 north central Florida counties. Only 26 percent, or 559, of the mail questionnaires were returned. Interviews were conducted with an additional 150 individuals, 124 of whom also returned a completed questionnaire. The subjects were questioned about their attitude toward hunting, the importance of various outdoor recreational activities, personal motivations for hunting, and knowledge of wildlife and wildlife management. Slightly more than one-fourth of the nonhunting respondents considered themselves "anti-hunters," and 57 percent of the anti-hunters indicated they had once hunted. Of various outdoor activities, hunting was rated as most important by the respondents. "Enjoying nature" was identified as the most important motivation for hunting followed by "the sport" itself, "peace and quiet," "friendship," "getting away," "skill," and "the bag limit." Hunters were more knowledgeable about wildlife and wildlife management than both nonhunters and anti-hunters.

655. Hautaluoma, Jacob, and Brown, Perry J. "Attributes of the Deer Hunting Experience: A Cluster-Analytic Study." *Journal of Leisure Research* 10 (1978): 271–87.

This research was conducted by the authors using data collected in 1970 for another research project. Deer hunters in the state of Washington completed a mail questionnaire about their deer hunting experience. The sample consisted of a total of 3,924 hunters representing four different types of deer hunters: deer only hunters, deer and other big game hunters, deer and small game hunters, and deer plus big and small game hunters. This research used the cluster analysis technique to identify dimensions of hunting satisfaction for the four types of deer hunters. The dimensions of "nature," "harvest," "equipment," "out-group contact," and "skill" were found to be important determinants of hunting satisfaction for all deer hunters. For these five dimensions, the researchers were able to determine if the dimension was neutral, added, or detracted from the hunting experience of 10 different hunter types. "Nature" and "skill" were the most positively rated attributes of the hunting experience.

656. Beattie, Kirk H. "A Comparison of Hunting Satisfaction of *Virginia Wildlife* and *Colorado Outdoors* Hunter Subscribers." *Proceedings of the Annual Conference of the Southeast Association of Fish and Wildlife Agencies* 32 (1978): 738–44.

This article discusses a survey of the hunting attitudes of subscribers to two state wildlife management publications. The major focus of the reader survey was the importance of different dimensions of hunting satisfaction. Questionnaires were inserted in the March-April 1977 issue of *Colorado Outdoors* and the August 1977 issue of *Virginia Wildlife*. Responses were received from 707 *Colorado Outdoors* and 1,047 *Virginia Wildlife* readers. A response rate cannot be determined, as no indication of total subscribers is given. Three dimensions, "nature," "escapism," and "skill" were ranked most important by both groups of subscribers. Although the mean responses differed significantly for seven of the eleven dimensions, the overall rankings of the two groups were very similar.

657. Burt, Charles J. "White-tailed Deer Hunter Attitudes in East-Central New York." *Wildlife Society Bulletin* 8 (1980): 142–49.

In this article, the researcher describes a study of attitudes among deer hunters in southern Schoharie County, New York. The research was supported by the Power Authority of the State of New York. Hunters were approached during deer hunting season in 1974, 1975, and 1976 and asked to respond to a written questionnaire. A total of 563 hunters completed the survey which included items on past hunting experience, reasons for hunting, and effect of power plant development on deer hunting. "Getting out-of-doors and seeing wildlife" was the reason for hunting most frequently chosen as "very important." Only 10 percent of the hunters felt the power plant projects would greatly reduce hunting in the area.

658. Van Dyke, Fred. "Hunter Attitudes and Exploitation on Crippled Waterfowl." *Wildlife Society Bulletin* 8 (1980): 150–52.

The research reported on in this journal article was a sub-study of the Wisconsin Hunter Performance Survey conducted by the Department of Psychology of the University of Wisconsin. A mail survey was used to question Wisconsin waterfowl hunters who use retrievers about the retrieval of other hunters' crippled waterfowl and its effect on their hunting experience. A total of 57 hunters, or 73 percent of the selected subjects, returned the survey. Slightly more than half (54 percent) of the responding hunters reported retrieving no crippled waterfowl from other hunters that year. For those who did report retrievals, the average number was 7.5 ducks and geese. Nearly three-fourths of the hunters reported that finding cripples was either a positive or a neutral aspect of hunting, while 26 percent considered it a negative aspect of their hunting experience.

659. Decker, Daniel J.; Brown, Tommy L.; and Gutierrez, R. J. "Further Insights into the Multiple-Satisfaction Approach for Hunter Management." *Wildlife Society Bulletin* 8 (1980): 323–31.

The authors of this article studied satisfaction with hunting among deer hunters at the Arnot Teaching and Research Forest southwest of Ithaca, New York. At the conclusion of the 1978 deer season they surveyed hunters about their satisfaction with their hunting experience, components of their satisfaction or dissatisfaction, and reasons for choosing that particular site for hunting. The mail questionnaire was returned by 144 of the 196 hunters who used the forest during that season. The respondents were generally satisfied with that particular hunting experience. Satisfaction was not correlated with amount of hunting experience or days spent hunting in 1978. Satisfaction was affected by whether the hunter was able to kill a deer or not. The two components of hunting that were of most importance to the respondents were "to get outdoors and enjoy nature" and "to see deer or deer signs."

660. Langenau, Edward E.; Moran, Richard J.; Terry, James R.; and Cue, David C. "Relationship Between Deer Kill and Ratings of the Hunt." *Journal of Wildlife Management* 45 (1981): 959–64.

The Michigan Department of Natural Resources conducted this study with funding from the Michigan Federal Aid to Wildlife Restoration Project. Mail questionnaires were distributed to a 5 percent sampling of deer hunters using a forest research area in the lower peninsula of Michigan. The survey was returned by 1,704 hunters for a 81 percent response rate. The purpose of the study was to determine the relationship between the rating of a deer hunt and the number of antlered bucks killed by hunters for the hunting seasons from 1972 through 1979. The number of antlered deer killed as confirmed by wildlife personnel and the number of "good" and "very good" ratings by the hunters were closely related. Several variables were found to be correlated with hunter ratings of the hunt. The strongest correlation was found with the attitude that deer were abundant in the area. Researchers concluded that increasing the deer population would result in an increase in satisfaction with the hunt. A distinction between satisfaction with the hunt and satisfaction with the hunting experience was made.

661. Beattie, Kirk H. "The Influence of Game Laws and Regulations on Hunting Satisfaction." *Wildlife Society Bulletin* 9 (1981): 229–31.

This article describes research conducted by the author and funded by numerous organizations including the National Wildlife Federation, the Wildlife Management Institute, the American Petroleum Institute, the National Rifle Association, the Georgia Division of Fish and Wildlife, the South Carolina Wildlife and Marine Resources Department, the Tennessee Wildlife Resources Agency, and the Virginia Commission of Game and Inland Fisheries. Data for the study were gathered in two phases from two independent samples of Virginia small and big game firearm hunters. In the first phase, the hunters identified different sources of hunting satisfaction. In phase two, 1,245 Virginia hunters were asked to express their perception of the effect of game laws and regulations on the 36 hunting satisfactions identified by the hunters in phase one. (Response rates for both phases of the study were below 50 percent.) The findings indicated that hunters generally felt game laws helped aspects of hunting considered satisfying. The most frequently cited aspect of hunting affected by game laws was the "regulation of game populations." "Promotion of safety" and the "preservation of wildlife" were also given as examples of positive effects of game laws.

662. Heberlein, Thomas A.; Trent, John N.; and Baumgartner, Robert M. "The Influence of Hunter Density on Firearm Deer Hunters' Satisfaction: A Field Experiment." *Transactions of the Forty-seventh North American Wildlife and Natural Resources Conference* 47 (1982): 665–75.

The staff of the Department of Rural Sociology of the University of Wisconsin performed this study of deer hunters using the Sandhill Wildlife Area in central Wisconsin. Field questionnaires were distributed to hunters as they entered one of the hunting areas and collected as the hunters checked out of the areas. Each area was classified as having either high or low hunter density. The 346 hunters who completed the questionnaire were asked about their perceptions of satisfaction, hunting quality, and crowding. The researchers used the results to determine the effect of hunter density on success, perceived crowding, reported interference from other hunters, and satisfaction with the deer hunting experience. Hunters in the high density areas were more likely to rate their experience as "good" or "very good," while hunters in low density areas were more likely to rate their experience as "poor" or "fair." The success rate was higher for the hunters in the high density area. Not surprisingly, increased density resulted in an increase in reported interference from other hunters.

663. Adams, Clark E., and Thomas, John K. "Characteristics and Opinions of Texas Hunters." *Proceedings of the Annual Conference of the Southeast Association of Fish and Wildlife Agencies* 37 (1983): 244–51.

A telephone survey of Texas hunters was conducted by the Department of Rural Sociology at Texas A&M University between February and May 1982. The study was supported by the Texas Parks and Wildlife Department, the Texas Agricultural Experiment Station, and the Caesar Kleberg Research Program. Of 3,473 licensed hunters contacted for the study, 3,081 participated. The survey questioned respondents about their participation in hunting, reasons for hunting, reasons for stopping hunting, wildlife management, and hunting regulations. In response to why they hunt, 70 percent responded "for recreation and sport," 52 percent responded "for food," 32 percent indicated they hunted "to be close to nature," and 30 percent said they hunted "to be with friends." Only 7 percent cited obtaining trophies as their reason for hunting. If the respondent was to quit hunting, 22 percent said it would be because of lease costs, and 18 percent said it would be due to lack of game.

664. Vaske, Jerry J.; Fedler, Anthony J.; and Graefe, Alan R. "Multiple Determinants of Satisfaction from a Specific Waterfowl Hunting Trip." *Leisure Sciences* 8 (1986): 149–66.

Support for this paper was received from the Division of Human and Community Resources, Small Grants Program, Maryland Wildlife Administration and the Computer Science Center at the University of Maryland–College Park. The research presented in this article attempted to determine the factors influencing hunter satisfaction with a specific waterfowl hunting trip. During the autumn of 1982, waterfowl hunters at the Fishing Bay Wildlife Management Area were contacted after their hunt and asked to complete a one-page questionnaire. Samplings were performed on 12 days during the waterfowl hunting season, and 230 hunters completed the survey. Overall satisfaction with their trip was measured with six items, while satisfaction with three specific aspects of the hunt (wildlife, social, and nature/sport) were measured with additional items. The results indicated that these three aspects accounted for 36 percent of the variance in overall satisfaction. Responses to the nature/sport items were the best predictor of overall satisfaction. The authors note that some of the results differed from the findings of previous studies, and they offer possible reasons for the discrepancies.

665. Applegate, James E. "Patterns of Early Desertion Among New Jersey Hunters." *Wildlife Society Bulletin* 17 (1989): 476–81.

The research reported in this article was conducted by the author and supported by the New Jersey Agricultural Experiment Station and McIntire-Stennis Funds. Graduates of New Jersey's mandatory hunter education program were surveyed between 1976 and 1981. Telephone surveys were administered by the Eagleton Institute of Politics at Rutgers University. Sample sizes varied from 581 to 997, with 393 people completing all four of the surveys. Survey items included questions about the respondent's participation in hunting, hunting success, and reasons for not continuing hunting after completion of the course. Only 41 percent of the 393 who answered each survey purchased hunting licenses in all four years of the study. Almost half of the total sample never hunted again after not purchasing a license in one year. The three most common reasons for quitting hunting were the "availability of other preferred recreational options," the "presence of too many other hunters," and the "lack of places to hunt." Less important reasons for quitting hunting related to economics, lack of success, and ethical concerns. Age was the only socioeconomic demographic factor related to hunting desertion. Close proximity to hunting did not affect desertion rates, but desertion was affected by hunting with family members.

666. Austin, Dennis D.; Bunnell, S. Dwight; and Urness, Philip J. "Responses of Deer Hunters to a Checking Station Questionnaire in Utah." *Proceedings of the Western Association of Fish and Wildlife Agencies* 69 (1989): 208–29.

Utah deer hunters were surveyed by use of a mail-back questionnaire distributed at 10 check stations on the opening day of the 1988 deer hunting season. Fewer than 1,500 of the 7,210 surveys were returned, for a response rate of only 20 percent. Included in the survey were questions about hunting opportunities, trade-off preferences between quality and quantity hunting, and number of unretrieved deer for the season. When asked which was more important, the number of hunters seen or the number of hunting days, two-thirds of the hunters chose the number of days. The hunters were evenly split on preferences for killing any size of buck frequently versus killing a larger buck less often. By two to one, the hunters indicated they would rather hunt every year than hunt less often with fewer hunters in the field. The article includes a reproduction of the actual survey as well as all survey results. For the attitude questions, responses are reported separately for resident and nonresident hunters.

667. Decker, Daniel J., and Connelly, Nancy A. "Motivations for Deer Hunting: Implications for Antlerless Deer Harvest as a Management Tool." *Wildlife Society Bulletin* 17 (1989): 455–63.

In this article, the authors discuss the results of their research into attitudes toward deer hunting and the New York deer hunting permit system. The research was funded by the New York Federal Aid in Fish and Wildlife Restoration Project. In April 1988, mail surveys were completed and returned by 733 New York deer hunting permit holders. Hunters responding to the survey were classified by three hunting motivation orientations: appreciative, achievement, and affiliation. Achievement-oriented hunters tended to be younger and had less hunting experience. Affiliated hunters were the oldest and had the most experience. Appreciative-oriented hunters fell in the mid-range for both age and years of hunting experience. Hunters who shot a deer that season were more satisfied with the deer hunting permit system than those who did not.

668. Manfredo, Michael J.; Sneegas, Janiece J.; Driver, Bev; and Bright, Alan. "Hunters with Disabilities: A Survey of Wildlife Agencies and a Case Study of Illinois Deer Hunters." *Wildlife Society Bulletin* 17 (1989): 487–93.

This research was conducted in April 1988 with funding from the U.S. Department of Agriculture Forest Service. Mail questionnaires were sent to participants in the Illinois special permit Handicapped Deer Hunts. The disabled hunters were questioned about their perceptions of desirable attributes of a hunting experience, constraints to hunting participation, and personal values of a hunting experience. Cluster analysis produced five clusters of desired attributes: experiencing nature, hunting strategy, outgroup affiliation, equipment related, and harvest related. The items in the experiencing nature cluster added more to the hunters' experiences than the other attribute clusters. Responses to items concerning personal values of a hunting experience resulted in the identification of 11 value clusters. The most highly rated values were "family togetherness," "independence," "positive self image," and "physical effectiveness."

669. Hultsman, Wendy Z.; Hultsman, John T.; and Black, David R. "Hunting Satisfaction and Reciprocal Exchange: Initial Support from a Lottery-Regulated Hunt." *Leisure Sciences* 11 (1989): 145–50.

This research was designed to determine the effect a lottery regulated hunt in which the hunting day was assigned had on the level of hunting satisfaction. The lottery system affected the chance of success after the first day as less deer were available to be killed on subsequent days. A total of 228 hunters at the Naval Weapons Support Center in Crane, Indiana, were interviewed on the three days assigned to the hunters by the Indiana Department of Natural Resources. The hunters were grouped by the day of their hunt to test the effect of the lower success rate on reported hunting satisfaction. Hunting satisfaction differed by day of the hunt with the hunters on the second of the three days reporting the highest level of satisfaction. Three variables were found to be significant predictors of satisfaction with this group of hunters: "killed a deer," "buddy killed a deer," and "satisfaction with the area."

670. Hammitt, William E.; McDonald, Cary D.; and Noe, Francis P. "Wildlife Management: Managing the Hunt versus the Hunting Experience." *Environmental Management* 13 (July-October 1989): 503–7.

This study of deer hunter satisfaction was funded by the Southeastern Regional Office of the National Park Service and the Agricultural Experiment Station of the University of Tennessee, Knoxville. Deer hunters in the Big South Fork National River and Recreation Area were sent mail questionnaires following contact in the field during the 1984 firearms deer hunting season. A total of 266 hunters returned surveys concerning satisfaction with the hunt and satisfaction with the overall hunting trip experience. Results indicated that the number of deer seen, the number of deer shot at, and the number of deer killed were the best predictors of a good deer hunt. The factors most important to a good deer hunting trip were being outdoors, the number of deer, and the actions of other hunters. (Other aspects of this research are described elsewhere.)

671. Hammitt, William E.; McDonald, Cary D.; and Patterson, Michael E. "Determinants of Multiple Satisfaction for Deer Hunting." *Wildlife Society Bulletin* 18 (1990): 331–37.

The purpose of the study described in this article was to determine the effect of various independent variables on hunters' overall satisfaction with their deer hunting experience. The study was conducted in November 1984 with funding from the U.S. Department of Interior, National Park Service and the Agricultural Experiment Station of the University of Tennessee. Deer hunters at the Big South Fork National River and Recreation Area in Tennessee were surveyed on eight days during deer hunting season. The hunters were contacted at various sites in the recreation area and asked to complete a half-page questionnaire. The 300 respondents were also mailed a longer questionnaire which was completed and returned by 260, or 87 percent, of the hunters. Analysis of the responses demonstrated that the overall satisfaction with the deer hunting experience at the

Big South Fork Recreation Area was moderately high. Of the seven variables studied, five were significant predictors of overall satisfaction: crowding, hunter behavior, natural outdoor experience, wildlife/harvest, and quality of the hunt. A regression model, with the five variables included, accounted for 50 percent of the variance in deer hunting satisfaction.

672. Hazel, Kelly L.; Langenau, Edward E., Jr.; and Levine, Ralph L. "Dimensions of Hunting Satisfaction: Multiple-Satisfaction of Wild Turkey Hunting." *Leisure Sciences* 12 (1990): 383–93.

   The research detailed in this paper was funded through the Federal Aid in Wildlife Restoration, Pittman Robertson Project. This study explored aspects of hunting satisfaction specific to one sample of wild turkey hunters. A total of 483 hunters who received a permit to hunt wild turkey in Michigan during one season completed the mail questionnaire. The survey asked the respondents to rate the importance of 24 different aspects of a wild turkey hunt to their satisfaction with that year's hunt. Results of the survey showed that hunters who were able to kill a turkey were more likely to be satisfied with their hunt. Of the 24 aspects of turkey hunting, those rated most important by the hunters were, "getting away from problems," "observing other wildlife," and "opportunity to appreciate nature." The researchers identified seven aspects of hunting satisfaction for the wild turkey hunter: preparation, search, harvest, nature, out-group social, companionship, and season.

PUBLIC PERCEPTIONS

673. Kimball, Thomas L. "What Do You Think?" *National Wildlife*, October-November 1973, p. 22.

   In this article, results of a 1973 National Wildlife Federation survey are described and compared with a similar survey conducted for the organization in 1966. The survey was based on a sampling of the organization's 620,000 members. (The sample size and survey method are not described in the article.) When asked their response to the statement, "Hunting is acceptable as a sport when biologists declare a surplus of game, birds, and animals," 79 percent of the respondents agreed. This percentage was down eight points from 1966 when the same question was asked. By at least a three-to-one margin, the readers supported more wilderness areas and increased government purchases of land for recreational and conservation purposes. Responses to these two questions were unchanged since 1966. The 1973 questionnaire also included items on the damming of rivers, draining swamps and lagoons, and overpopulation.

674. Linder, Raymond L.; Wagner, Robert T.; Dimit, Robert M.; and Dahlgren, Robert B. "Attitudes of South Dakota Residents Toward Dove Hunting." *Transactions of the Thirty-ninth North American Wildlife and Natural Resources Conference* 39 (1974): 163–72.

   This study was conducted to determine why the voters of South Dakota approved a ban on mourning dove hunting in a statewide referendum in 1972. The research was sponsored by the South Dakota Cooperative Wildlife Research Unit with funding supplied by the Federal Aid to Wildlife Restoration Project. Subjects for the study were selected from a listing of all South Dakota property tax payers.

Personal interviews were completed with 474 individuals. Topics discussed in the interviews included how the residents would vote if the vote was held again and intensity of the respondents commitment to their position on the issue. If the mourning dove vote was held again, 26 percent indicated they would vote for a hunting season, 61 percent would vote against it, and 13 percent were undecided. Those against mourning dove hunting were more willing to encourage others to vote as they would. Those against mourning dove hunting believed (incorrectly) that the mourning dove is not a game bird in most of the United States and felt the dove should be classified as a songbird. Although the survey did not reveal a general opposition to hunting, those against a hunting season for mourning doves were characterized by a belief that "hunters just like to kill animals."

675. Shaw, Dale L., and Gilbert, D. L. "Attitudes of College Students Toward Hunting." *Transactions of the Thirty-ninth North American Wildlife and Natural Resources Conference* 39 (1974): 157–62.

   The National Rifle Association and Welder Wildlife Foundation funded this research into college students' attitudes toward hunting. In January and February 1973, students at 10 randomly selected U.S. colleges and universities were presented questionnaires in a classroom situation. Questionnaires were completed by 937 students. The survey included questions regarding attitude toward hunting, reasons for opposition to hunting, reasons for quitting (if appropriate), and influences on attitude. Slightly fewer than half of the male students and only 6 percent of the female students indicated they were hunters. Of those who once hunted and had quit, "lack of time" was given as the main reason, followed by "don't want to kill animals" and "no longer interested." The majority of both males (60 percent) and females (73 percent) said they were neither "all for" nor "all against" hunting. But three-fourths of all students indicated some degree of negative attitude toward hunting or hunters. The top five reasons for being anti-hunting were the following: 1.) "sport hunting endangers some species," 2.) "don't believe in trophy hunting," 3.) "don't believe in killing for sport," 4.) "too much meat is wasted," and 5.) "too many hunters are game hogs." Anti-hunting sentiment was strongest among those from urban areas and nonhunters. Anti-hunter sentiment was strongest among those from rural areas and hunters.

676. Peterson, George L. "A Comparison of the Sentiments and Perceptions of Wilderness Managers and Canoeists in the Boundary Waters Canoe Area." *Journal of Leisure Research* 6 (Summer 1974): 194–206.

   Different aspects of this research were funded by Northwestern University, U.S. Forest Service, and the U.S. Public Health Service. In this study, the researcher attempted to compare the attitudes, motivations, and preferences of wilderness managers and summer canoeists for the wilderness experience. The Boundary Waters Canoe Area, Minnesota, was chosen as the site for the study. During the summer of 1970, questionnaires were administered in the field and by mail to a total of 185 canoeists, 127 of whom completed both forms of the survey. In addition, 17 U.S. Forest Service personnel working in the canoe area completed the survey. The greatest disagreement between the two groups was found for approved uses of the Boundary Waters Canoe Area. The managers expressed strong approval for several forms of hunting that were flatly rejected by the canoeists. The two groups agreed, however, on approval of fishing and canoeing and disapproval of mining.

677. Groves, David L., and Matula, George J. "Hunting Popularity: A Case Study in an Organizational Setting." *Proceedings of the Annual Conference of the Southeast Association of Fish and Wildlife Agencies* 29 (1975): 753–58.

Funding for this study was provided by the National Rifle Association and the Wildlife Management Institute in cooperation with the Pennsylvania Cooperative Wildlife Research Unit, Pennsylvania State University, and the Pennsylvania Game Commission. The purpose of the research was to identify similarities and differences between strong opponents and strong supporters of hunting. In order to select individuals for inclusion in the study, officers of pro- and anti-hunting organizations were asked to identify members with strong views on hunting. Personal interviews asked the subjects about their adolescent experiences and attitudes toward different uses of land in nearby recreation areas. Sex, occupation, type of adolescent residence, type of adolescent recreational activities, and occupation of father were the variables found to be significantly related to attitude toward hunting. Those opposed to hunting were more likely to be female, employed, from an urban background with adolescent participation in nonremote activities, and a child of a white collar worker. Hunting supporters tended to be white collar males, from a rural background with adolescent participation in remote activities, and children of blue collar workers. Generally, there were many similarities in attitudes and demographics between the two groups.

678. Applegate, James E. "Attitudes Toward Deer Hunting in New Jersey: A Second Look." *Wildlife Society Bulletin* 3 (1975): 3–6.

This article describes the second in a series of surveys conducted by the author into the attitudes of New Jersey residents toward deer hunting. In this article, results from a 1974 survey were compared with results from a similar study conducted in 1972. Both telephone polls were conducted by the Eagleton Institute for Politics at Rutgers University. A total of 1,190 New Jersey residents over 18 years of age was surveyed. Respondents were questioned about their attitude toward deer hunting in May 1974. Results of the two polls showed that disapproval of deer hunting had increased from 38 percent to 43 percent. The percentage of respondents who approved of hunting was still larger than the percentage disapproving (49 percent versus 43 percent). The change between the two years was statistically significant.

679. Shaw, William W. "A Survey of Hunting Opponents." *Wildlife Society Bulletin* 5 (Spring 1977): 19–24.

This article describes research into opposition to hunting conducted by the author in the spring of 1974. The research was supported by the Michigan Department of Natural Resources, the Wildlife Management Institute, and the American Petroleum Institute. A mail questionnaire was used to survey 179 members of the Fund for Animals residing in the state of Michigan about their attitudes toward hunting and wildlife. A majority of the sample (69 percent) indicated they strongly disapproved of hunting and identified a number of reasons as being important in their decision to oppose hunting. When those that disapproved of hunting were asked, "Have you always felt as you do about hunting?" 72 percent responded "yes." Loss of habitat, and not hunting, was cited as the greatest threat to wildlife populations.

680. "Iowans Oppose Dove Hunting." *Current Opinion* 5 (November 1977): 131.
   Current Opinion is a monthly review of public opinion polls published by the Roper Public Opinion Research Center. In this item, results from the Iowa Poll performed for the *Des Moines Register and Tribune* are presented. Of 605 adult Iowans surveyed, 18 percent favored mourning dove hunting, 65 percent were opposed to the activity, and 17 percent had no opinion.

681. Rohlfing, A. H. "Hunter Conduct and Public Attitudes." *Transactions of the Forty-third North American Wildlife and Natural Resources Conference* 43 (1978): 404–11.
   This conference proceeding describes research funded by the National Shooting Sports Foundation. Men and women who were judged to be neutral on the issue of hunting were interviewed to determine what hunting issues are of concern to people. The research was undertaken in order to develop a media campaign to change public perceptions of hunters and hunting. The group interview sessions were held with 152 men and women in Minneapolis, Rochester (New York), Denver, and Dallas/Fort Worth. Trained moderators were used to solicit and categorize all negative ideas about hunting voiced by the participants. A total of 115 anti-hunting perceptions was identified by the participants. The five least bothersome problems were the following: "hunters are lower class people," "hunters are loners," "hunters are slobs," "hunters are insincere people," and "hunters are rednecks." The five most bothersome problems were the following: "hunters kill other hunters accidentally," "wounded animals die a slow death," "wounded animals die a painful death," "hunters don't have to know anything to buy a rifle," and "leaving a wounded animals to die is sadistic." The researchers concluded that most of the serious problems, as viewed by the participants, were not related to hunting itself but to the behavior of individual hunters.

682. Kellert, Stephen R. "Attitudes and Characteristics of Hunters and Anti-hunters." *Transactions of the Forty-third North American Wildlife and Natural Resources Conference* 43 (1978): 412–23.
   The research described in this article was conducted by the author and funded by the U.S. Fish and Wildlife Service. A sample of 553 randomly selected Americans responded to mail questionnaires distributed between 1973 and 1975. The survey included items covering the following topics: knowledge of animals, hunting participation, approval of hunting, reasons for hunting, attitudes toward animals, and participation in various animal related activities (hunting, trapping, bird watching, zoo visitation, backpacking, pet ownership, animal breeding, rodeo attendance). The occurrence of different animal attitude types was compared with participation in various animal related activities. The highest level of knowledge about animals was among bird watchers, the lowest among anti-hunters and sport hunters. Of the entire sample, 29 percent reported strong disapproval of sport hunting while a similar number (26 percent) indicated strong approval. Of those who once hunted, 20 percent strongly agreed that sport hunting is wrong. Among hunters, 44 percent indicated their primary reason for hunting was to obtain meat. Another 39 percent indicated they hunted primarily for sport, and 18 percent said they hunted for the purpose of being close to nature.

683. "The American Disposition Toward Hunting in 1976." *Wildlife Society Bulletin* 6 (Spring 1978): 33–35.

William W. Shaw, Edwin H. Carpenter, Louise M. Arthur, Russell L. Gum, and Daniel J. Witter conducted the research described in this article. The study was performed with the cooperation of the Economic Research Service of the U.S. Department of Agriculture and the U.S. Department of Interior, Fish and Wildlife Service. Randomly selected residents of the 48 contiguous states and the District of Columbia were interviewed by telephone during May and June of 1976. The national survey was completed by 2,041 Americans. An additional sample of 419 respondents from the intermountain region were included in the regional analysis. The respondents were asked to indicate their approval of sport hunting and the strength of their opinion. Responses were compared by region of the country. In response to the question, "In general, do you tend to approve or disapprove of legal hunting?" 55 percent indicated approval and 45 percent disapproval. Approval of hunting was highest in the south central states and lowest in the middle Atlantic states.

684. LaHart, David E, and Barnes, Lehman W. "The Influence of Knowledge and Animal-Related Activities on Consumptive and Non-Consumptive Resource Orientations." *Proceedings of the Annual Conference of Southeast Association of Fish and Wildlife Agencies* 32 (1978): 783–89.

The authors surveyed animal knowledge and attitude levels of eighth grade students in Broward County, Florida. Support for the study was provided by the National Wildlife Federation. A total of 1,315 students responded to teacher-administered questionnaires designed to measure animal knowledge, attitudes toward animals, and attitudes toward non-consumptive and consumptive animal activities. Non-consumptive animal appreciation was the dominant orientation of the sample. Attitudes toward hunting for sport and hunting for food differed significantly. Of the sample, 69 percent disapproved of hunting for fun, while 62 percent approved of hunting for food. Only 29 percent thought hunting should be against the law. Responses to all questions are broken by knowledge level.

685. Samson, Jack. "Editorial." *Field and Stream*, July 1979, p. 4.

In this editorial, the editor of *Field and Stream* magazine reviews results from a poll of teenage Americans conducted by the Gallup Organization. The poll of 1,115 teenagers included a question on support for a total ban on private hunting. Of the teens surveyed, 57 percent opposed a hunting ban, 34 percent favored it, and 9 percent were undecided. The article reviews some of the differences in hunting activity among teens by sex and economic status. Gallup's interpretation of the poll findings are criticized in the editorial.

686. Mattingly, Marion C. "Kentucky's Hunter Education Student Attitude Survey." *Proceedings of the Annual Conference of the Southeast Association of Fish and Wildlife Agencies* 34 (1980): 639–43.

The Kentucky Department of Fish and Wildlife Resources performed the research discussed in this conference proceeding paper. The purpose of the study was to evaluate student attitudes toward hunting before and after attendance at a hunter education course. Over 6,000 campers at three summer camps completed the 15-question survey. Responses were sorted into four groups by sex and first or second year of camping. The majority of the questions on the survey were ethical in nature and dealt with man's right to kill wild animals for food and sport. Prior to the education class, the majority of all four groups of campers felt hunting for food should be the only type of hunting allowed. After the class, each group indicated they were accepting of other forms of hunting. The percent of responses judged to be negative by the researchers actually increased for two of the questions after the course. Both of these questions dealt with suffering as an integral part of nature.

687. Connecticut Poll. *American Public Opinion Index: 1981.* Tallahassee, FL: Opinion Research Service Inc., 1982.

    The Institute for Social Inquiry of the University of Connecticut conducted telephone interviews on the topics of firearms ownership, participation in hunting, attitude toward hunting, and support for gun control. Five hundred residents of Connecticut were contacted between January 27 and February 1 of 1981. When asked to respond to the statement, "Hunting is a brutal and inhumane sport," 41 percent of the respondents agreed, and 52 percent disagreed. Sex had a strong effect on the response. Half of all female, but only 31 percent of male, respondents saw hunting as brutal.

688. Eagleton Poll. *American Public Opinion Index: 1982.* Louisville, KY: Opinion Research Service, Inc., 1984.

    This survey was performed by the Eagleton Institute of Politics at Rutgers University. A telephone poll was conducted with 1,005 New Jersey residents. The respondents were questioned about their participation in hunting and their approval of deer hunting. Of those sampled, 49 percent approved and 44 percent disapproved of deer hunting. Results are broken down by several demographic variables including occupation, age, race, income, education, sex, and residence. As expected, the residents of rural areas were more accepting of deer hunting than residents of large cities and suburbs.

689. Applegate, James E. "Attitudes Toward Deer Hunting in New Jersey: 1972–1982." *Wildlife Society Bulletin* 12 (1984): 19–21.

    This article reports on the continuation of a 10-year study of attitudes toward deer hunting. The research was performed by the author and supported by the New Jersey Agricultural Experiment Station, the Wildlife Management Institute, and the National Rifle Association. New Jersey residents were interviewed by telephone by the Eagleton Institute for Politics at Rutgers University in May of even-numbered years from 1972 through 1982. Sample sizes ranged from 796 to 1,218. Respondents were questioned about their personal and family participation in hunting and their attitudes toward hunting. The researcher found little overall change in hunting approval/disapproval levels during the 10-year period. Approval of hunting was 54 percent in 1972 versus 49 percent in 1982. The percent of respondents indicating they hunted declined during the period as well as the percent of nonhunters who indicated they had family or friends who hunted. (Other aspects of this research are presented elsewhere.)

690. Eagleton Poll. *American Public Opinion Index: 1987.* Boston, MA: Opinion Research Service Inc., 1988.

    The Eagleton Institute of Politics at Rutgers University conducted a telephone poll of New Jersey residents in May 1987. Respondents were asked about their hunting experience, association with hunters, and attitude toward deer hunting. Of the 788 adults who completed the survey, 54 percent indicated they approved and 39 percent said they disapproved of deer hunting.

691. Ascani, Terri Lea. *Pennsylvania Wildlife and Its Use: A 1988 Public Opinion Survey. Wildlife Conservation Report #9.* Allentown, PA: Wildlife Information Center, September 1989.

In this report, results from a 1988 survey of wildlife attitudes in Pennsylvania
are presented and compared with results from a similar survey performed in 1986.
Both surveys were conducted by the Wildlife Information Center of Allentown.
The 1988 survey questioned 193 urban and rural residents of eastern Pennsylvania
about their attitudes toward hunting in general, urban deer hunting, leghold trapping, the use of furs, raptor and owl protection, the practice of keeping wild birds
as pets, and live pigeon shoots. (The methodology for the study is not specified.)
On the subject of sport hunting of game species, 54 percent of those surveyed indicated they approved of the activity, and 46 percent said they disapproved. When
asked about hunting urban deer when nonlethal methods of management are
available, only 21 percent approved, while 79 percent disapproved.

692. Groller, Ingrid. "Do Animals Have Rights?" *Parents Magazine* 65 (May
1990): 33.

Parents Magazine commissioned the poll presented in this article. (Information regarding date, sample size, and methodology are not provided.) The poll
measured attitudes toward the concept of "animal rights" and specific human uses
of animals including killing animals for fur coats, for leather, for food, for use in
cosmetic testing, for sport, for medical research, and for entertainment. One question regarding protection of endangered species was also included. Hunting for
sport was opposed by 60 percent of the sample, and 33 percent felt it should be
made illegal. A large majority (85 percent) felt killing animals for fur coats was
wrong, and 63 percent thought the practice should be banned. Regarding species
protection, 60 percent said humans should avoid actions that endanger species,
while 30 percent said such actions might be acceptable under some circumstances.

693. Schara, Ron. "Hunting Is Popular in Minnesota, but Criticism Is Growing." *The* [Minneapolis] *Star Tribune,* December 20, 1992, p. 1A.

The Minnesota Poll on hunting was conducted by Project Research for *The
Star Tribune* and WCCO-TV of Minneapolis. The telephone survey polled 1,009
randomly selected Minnesota adults between November 17 and 25, 1992. The
survey, which focused on attitudes toward the concept of animal rights, included
questions on participation in hunting and fishing and approval of hunting in
general, hunting for food, and bow hunting. Almost three-fourths (72 percent) of
the Minnesotans surveyed said they approved of hunting as a natural human activity. A similar percent approved of bow hunting and believed the practice did not
cause unnecessary suffering. A large majority (89 percent) said hunting was acceptable as long as the animal was eaten. Of the six hunting issues measured by the poll,
41 percent of the respondents had no objection to any of the issues. Participation
in hunting and fishing is broken down by sex, age, education, income, and residence.

694. Balzar, John. "Creatures Great and Equal?" *Los Angeles Times,* December 25, 1993, p. A1.

The *Los Angeles Times* conducted this poll during early December 1993 with
1,612 adult Americans. Follow-up interviews were also held with an undisclosed
number of selected respondents. The article presents responses to questions on

animal protection laws, the similarity between humans and animals, the wearing of fur, and the hunting of animals for sport. Nearly half of the respondents felt that "Animals are just like humans in all important ways." Animal protection laws were seen as adequate by 46 percent of the respondents. Half of the sample was opposed to wearing clothing made of animal fur, and 54 percent opposed sport hunting.

Trapping

MOTIVATIONS/SATISFACTION

695. Guynn, David C.; Mason, Carl E.; Dubose, J. Stephen; and Hackett, Edward J. "Trapping Satisfactions of Mississippi Trappers." *Proceedings of the Annual Conference of Southeast Association of Fish and Wildlife Agencies* 34 (1980): 503–7.

This research was conducted by the authors in June 1978. A mail survey was sent to 1,000 trappers licensed in the state of Mississippi and slightly more than half (527) responded. In response to the question "Why do you trap?" 38 percent indicated they trapped primarily for sport, but also for income. For sport only was selected by 24 percent of the respondents. The trappers were also asked to rank seven dimensions of trapping satisfaction including skill, nature, income, exercise, escapism, hunting or fishing privileges, and food. Skill was ranked most important by 43 percent of the respondents. Nature and income were both ranked most important by 19 percent of the sample, and the other four dimensions were all ranked first by less than 10 percent of the trappers.

696. Bailey, Theodore N. "Characteristics, Trapping Techniques, and Views of Trappers on a Wildlife Refuge in Alaska," in *Worldwide Furbearers Conference Proceedings*, edited by Joseph A. Chapman and Duane Pursley. Frostburg, MD: 1981, pp. 1904–18.

This conference paper details the results of a study of persons obtaining permits to trap on the Kenai National Moose Range Wildlife Refuge in Alaska during the 1977–78 trapping seasons. All trappers (a total of 86) using the refuge were contacted at the refuge headquarters by refuge personnel and requested to complete a written questionnaire. Questions were included in the survey about participation in trapping and trapping experiences, reasons for trapping, attitude toward increased regulation, and perceived obstacles to trapping satisfaction. "Experiencing the outdoors" (67 percent) was the most commonly cited reason for trapping. "Supplemental income" (42 percent) and "main income" (8 percent) were given less frequently as trapping motivations. The majority of trappers said they supported additional regulations or closed areas to protect furbearers from over-trapping.

697. Boddicker, Major L. "Profiles of American Trappers and Trapping," in *Worldwide Furbearers Conference Proceedings*, edited by Joseph A. Chapman and Duane Pursley. Frostburg, MD: 1981, pp. 1919–49.

The author of this conference paper conducted a study of trapper attitudes by analyzing responses to a subscriber survey from a trapping periodical. The research was sponsored by the Nebraska Fur Harvesters, the Arkansas Trapper's Association, and the Colorado Trapper's Association. Approximately 800 trappers from the United States and Canada completed and returned a questionnaire printed in the August 1979 issue of *Trapper Magazine* (*Trapper Magazine* at that time had a circulation of 40,000.) From the 800 responses, 100 questionnaires were randomly chosen for analysis. Items in the questionnaire addressed participation in trapping, motivation for trapping, perceptions of humaneness of trapping, response to theoretical outlawing of leghold traps, and attitudes toward trapper education and wildlife management agencies. Responses to the item regarding reasons for trapping included "for the outdoor experience" (63 percent) and "for the challenge and excitement" (26 percent). Only 6 percent indicated they trapped "mainly for the money" and 2 percent said "predator control" was their motivation for trapping. Almost all (96 percent) of the sample felt their trapping methods and devices were not cruel or inhumane.

698. Marshall, A. D. "Characteristics of Georgia Trappers," in *Worldwide Furbearers Conference Proceedings*, edited by Joseph A. Chapman and Duane Pursley. Frostburg, MD: 1981, pp. 2004–8.

The Department of Natural Resources of the Georgia State Game and Fish Division conducted the research described in this conference paper. At the conclusion of the 1976-77 trapping season, all Georgia licensed trappers were sent a mail questionnaire which asked, "Why do you trap?" Responses were received from 793 trappers. "Recreation only" was cited by 27 percent, "supplemental income only" by 24 percent, "control of crop and property damage" by 5 percent, and no response was given by 5 percent. The remaining 39 percent of the respondents said they trapped for more than one of the previous reasons. Only 7 percent of the sample indicated they earned 50 percent or more of their total income from trapping.

699. Samuel, David E., and Bammel, Lei Lane. "Attitudes and Characteristics of Independent Trappers and National Trappers' Association Members in West Virginia," in *Worldwide Furbearers Conference Proceedings*, edited by Joseph A. Chapman and Duane Pursley. Frostburg, MD: 1981, pp. 2021–35.

This research was conducted by the Division of Forestry of West Virginia University in February and March 1979. A mail questionnaire was sent to all state members of the National Trappers' Association and to a random sample of the state's independent trappers. Completed questionnaires were returned by 263 of the NTA members and 113 independent trappers. The total response rate from the two groups combined was 42.6 percent. The respondents were asked to rate degree of agreement with ten possible reasons for their participation in trapping. When responses from the two subsamples were combined, the rank order for the ten reasons was the following: "challenge," "wildlife management," "nature enjoyment," "relaxation," "hobby," "additional income," "companionship," "food or clothing," "primary income," " satisfaction from the kill." The two groups differed significantly on the importance of three items: "primary income," "relaxation," and "companionship."

PUBLIC PERCEPTIONS

700. Goodrich, James W. "Political Assault on Wildlife Management: Is There a Defense?" *Transactions of the Forty-fourth North American Wildlife and Natural Resources Conference* 44 (1979): 326–36.

This article reports the findings of two polls performed before and after a 1977 Ohio election that included a proposed measure to ban trapping in the state. The polling was conducted in September and November 1977 by the Creative Research Service of Cleveland, Ohio, for the Wildlife Legislative Fund of America. The September poll surveyed potential voters, and the poll in November surveyed those who had actually voted in the election. Sample size and methodology were not given in the article. In September, 68 percent of the respondents indicated support for the trapping ban, but in November, 63 percent of the sample said they had voted against the ban. Before the election, 64 percent agreed that trapping was cruel and after the election, 59 percent felt it was not cruel. The article details differences in attitudes toward trapping by age, sex, and residence.

701. Heintzelman, Donald S. *Pennsylvania Wildlife and Its Use: A 1986 Public Opinion Survey.* Wildlife Conservation Report #1. Allentown, PA: Wildlife Information Center, November 1986.

This report relates results from a study of public attitudes toward wildlife in Pennsylvania conducted by the Wildlife Information Center of Allentown. The survey sampled 400 residents of eastern and central Pennsylvania during the summer and autumn of 1986. In addition, results from a separate study of attitudes toward mourning dove hunting conducted in the spring of 1986 are included. (The methodology is not given for either study.) The fall survey included questions on hunting, raptor and owl protection, leghold trapping, and the use of wild animal fur. On the question of leghold trapping, 11 percent of those surveyed approved, while 89 percent were opposed to use of the traps. In the spring survey, 17 percent of the sample approved of dove hunting, and 83 percent were opposed to the practice.

702. Russell, Susan. "Public Attitudes Toward Fur—Definitely Against." *The Skin Trade Primer.* Neptune, NJ: Friends of Animals, 1987.

This booklet contains a brief item on a poll conducted on hunting and raising animals for fur. The survey was conducted in 1983 by Doyle, Dane Bernbach, Inc., and showed 65 percent to 75 percent of the sample disapproving of the practices of hunting and raising animals for their skins or pelts. No other details of the survey are offered.

703. Liss, Cathy. "Trapping and Poisoning," in *Animals and Their Legal Rights.* Washington: Animal Welfare Institute, 1990 (4th ed.), pp. 157–89.

In this book chapter, the author describes research into the attitudes and experience of veterinarians with leghold traps. The research was sponsored and conducted by the Animal Welfare Institute of Washington, D.C., in 1986. Veterinarians in Illinois, Michigan, New York, Texas, North Dakota, Washington, and Louisiana were asked to complete a questionnaire about their approval of steel-jaw leghold traps and their personal experiences with animals caught in the traps. A majority (79 percent) of the 936 veterinarians completing the survey indicated they disapproved of the use of steel-jaw traps.

704. Fogarty, Thomas A. "Animal Rights," *Des Moines Register*, August 12, 1990.

This newspaper article describes the results of the Iowa Poll conducted July 16–25, 1990 by the *Des Moines Register*. In this particular poll, 803 Iowa residents were questioned by telephone interview about the concept of "animal rights." The adult respondents were asked about their approval of various human uses of animals: trapping, hunting, fishing, dog and horse racing, medical experimentation, zoos, circuses, food, and pet ownership. The greatest level of disapproval (50 percent) was for trapping animals for fur. Fewer respondents objected to bird hunting (25 percent), deer hunting (18 percent), and fishing (2 percent). Approval for the different activities varied by sex and age with women and younger adults expressing greater disapproval of the various animal uses.

705. Richards, Rebecca T., and Krannich, Richard S. "The Ideology of the Animal Rights Movement and Activists' Attitude Toward Wildlife." *Transactions of the Fifty-sixth North American Wildlife and Natural Resources Conference* 56 (1991): 363–71.

The research described in this article was conducted in 1990 by the authors and supported by the Utah Division of Wildlife Resources and the Utah State University Office of Research. The researchers sampled 853 animal rights subscribers to the *Animals' Agenda*. A mail questionnaire was developed to compare the attitudes and demographics of the animal rights sample with the general U.S. population. Respondents were questioned about the degree of their concern for specific animal treatments and environmental issues, their view of wildlife habitat protection, and their involvement in other social movements. The findings indicated that the respondents had a greater degree of concern for environmental issues than previous samples of the general population. A majority (72 percent) of the sample indicated they were active in the environmental movement as well as the animal movement. Leghold trapping was viewed by the respondents as the most wrong treatment of animals by humans among the 15 options listed.

706. Yozwiak, Steve. "Ban on Steel-Jawed Traps Favored 3–1 in Arizona Poll," *The Arizona Republic*, February 6, 1992, p. B4.

The Rocky Mountain Poll described in this newspaper article was conducted by the Behavior Research Center of Phoenix, Arizona. A sample of 707 Arizona residents were polled by telephone in January 1992 regarding support for riparian protection and a ban on the use of leghold traps on public lands. Over two-thirds (69 percent) of the adults surveyed said they supported a ban on steel-jaw traps on public lands. Slightly fewer than half (47 percent) expressed support for riparian protection even if grazing of cattle had to be prohibited, while 41 percent disapproved of riparian protection if grazing was banned as a result.

707. *Proposition 200 Voter Survey.* Phoenix, AZ: Behavior Research Center, Inc., July 1992, 12 pp.

The poll described in this report was conducted by the Behavior Research Center of Phoenix, Arizona, and sponsored by Arizonans for Safety and Humanity on Public Lands. Arizona voters were polled in July 1992 about the likelihood they would vote for an initiative on the general election ballot that would ban the use of steel-jaw traps to take wildlife on public lands in Arizona. Telephone interviews were conducted with 575 voters throughout the state. Items in the poll included the following: support for the initiative to ban steel-jaw traps on public lands, reasons for support or opposition, and perceptions of trapping as cruel and inhumane, as a threat to humans and pets, and as a wildlife management tool. Respondents were also questioned about the effect on their position of various endorsements. A majority (74 percent) of the sample indicated they would vote to ban the traps on public lands. The most common reason for supporting a ban was because, "Traps are cruel and inhumane." "Will lead to hunting/fishing ban" and "management tool to control predators" were the reasons most often given for opposing the ban. The majority of the sample agreed with the statements "Traps are cruel and inhumane" (82 percent) and "Traps pose a threat to humans and pets" (78 percent). The sample disagreed that "trapping is an essential wildlife management tool" (65 percent) and a trapping ban "is a first step toward eliminating all hunting and fishing in Arizona" (71 percent).

708. Rebuffoni, Dean. "Protestors Haven't Dissuaded Many on Killing Animals for Fur." *The* [Minneapolis] *Star Tribune*, December 14, 1992.

The Minnesota Poll was conducted November 17 through 25, 1992, by Project Research for the *Star Tribune* and WCCO-TV of Minneapolis. A telephone survey was used to poll 1,109 randomly selected Minnesota adults about their attitudes toward different animal issues. This newspaper item details the aspects of the poll dealing with killing animals for their fur. When asked whether "it is OK to kill an animal only for its fur," 47 percent said it is always OK, 34 percent said it is always wrong, and 45 percent said it is OK in some circumstances. Responses to this question are broken down by sex, age, education, income, and residence. The newspaper account of the poll does not disclose whether the subjects where asked their opinion of wild fur trapping versus fur farming. Women aged 18 to 54 years were the most critical of killing animals only for fur. On the question of whether "plants and animals exist primarily to be used by humans," the response was nearly evenly divided.

Wildlife Observation

709. Witter, Daniel J.; Wilson, James D.; and Maupin, Gordon T. "'Eagle Days' in Missouri: Characteristics and Enjoyment Ratings of Participants." *Wildlife Society Bulletin* 8 (1980): 64–5.

This study was conducted by the Missouri Department of Conservation in cooperation with the U.S. Fish and Wildlife Service. Participants at three "Eagle Day" programs held by the Missouri Department of Conservation were surveyed regarding their response to the program. The "Eagle Days" were held at three separate sites between December 1978 and February 1979. Participants in the program were presented with information about eagles and given the opportunity to travel to areas where they could actually view eagles. The program was evaluated as "very enjoyable" by 64 percent of the respondents and as "one of the most enjoyable wildlife viewing days I've ever had" by an additional 32 percent of the participants responding to the questionnaire. There was no difference between how hunters and nonhunters evaluated the program.

710. Kellert, Stephen R. "Birdwatching in American Society." *Leisure Sciences* 7 (1985): 343–60.

This paper describes results of a study on birdwatching. The data for the study were collected as part of a national survey of American attitudes, knowledge, and behaviors toward wildlife performed for the U.S. Fish and Wildlife Service in the late 1970s. (This study is described in another section.) Personal interviews were conducted with 2,455 residents of the 48 contiguous states and Alaska. The topics for the interview included reasons for participating in birdwatching and the knowledge and attitudes of birdwatchers toward wildlife and a variety of wildlife related issues. Motivations for birdwatching differed between casual and committed participants. While casual birdwatchers most often cited aesthetic reasons for birdwatching, personal fascination with birds was the primary motivation of the committed birdwatchers. The opportunity to identify as many birds as possible was given as the primary reason for birdwatching by only 3 percent of the committed birdwatchers and none of the casual birdwatchers. On the knowledge and attitude scale, the birdwatchers scored high in knowledge and high in the naturalistic, ecologistic, and scientific attitude scales. The groups scored low on the humanistic, moralistic, and utilitarian scales. On alternatives for funding wildlife programs, over three-fourths supported additional sales taxes on fur clothing and off-road vehicles and increased entrance fees at wildlife areas.

711. Applegate, James E., and Clark, Kathleen E. "Satisfaction Levels of Bird-watchers: An Observation on the Consumptive-Nonconsumptive Continuum." *Leisure Sciences* 9 (1987): 129–34.

    The New Jersey Agricultural Experiment Station and McIntire-Stennis Act funds supported the research described in this article. The goals of the study were to measure satisfaction levels of nonconsumptive visitors to a national wildlife refuge and to compare reported satisfaction among birdwatchers with different levels of ability. Visitors to Forsythe National Wildlife Refuge near Atlantic City, New Jersey, were asked to complete a questionnaire after taking a self-guided auto tour of the refuge. A total of 92 visitors who took the tour on two days in June 1984 comprised the subjects for the study. The visitors to the refuge, which is known for its bird diversity, were also asked to take a test of their bird identification and natural history knowledge. Overall, the refuge visitors reported a high degree of satisfaction with their visit. Visitors scoring higher on the bird identification quiz reported lower levels of satisfaction than less knowledgeable birders.

712. Loomis, John B. "Valuing Nonconsumptive Use and Preservation Values of Game and Nongame Wildlife in California: Results of Surveys on Deer, Birds, and Mono Lake." *Proceedings of the Western Association of Fish and Wildlife Agencies* 69 (1989): 51–59.

    In this conference paper, the author reports on a California wildlife viewing survey conducted in the fall of 1987 by the University of California–Davis. The California Department of Fish and Game funded this mail survey of 3,000 randomly selected California households. (A response rate of 44 percent was realized after deleting undeliverable questionnaires.) This survey questioned the California respondents about trips taken with the primary purpose of seeing birds or deer and trips taken for all outdoor recreation purposes when birds or deer were seen. Approximately 10 percent of the sample said they took trips for the purpose of viewing deer, and two-thirds said seeing deer added to the enjoyment of their outdoor recreation trips. The article does not disclose the responses to the same question for viewing birds. Respondents to the survey were also questioned about the maximum amount they would be willing to pay for a trip where viewing birds or deer was one aspect or the primary purpose of the trip. Above the cost of the trips, the respondents were willing to pay an additional $16.25 to view deer during any trip and $22.12 to view deer as the primary purpose of a trip. For birdwatching, the respondents indicated they would be willing to pay an additional $8.21 to view birds as part of any outdoor recreation trip and $15.70 to take a trip for the primary purpose of birdwatching.

Camping/Hiking/Backpacking

713. Etzkorn, K. Peter. "Leisure and Camping: The Social Meaning of a Form of Public Recreation." *Sociology and Social Research* 49 (October 1964): 76–89.

 In this early study on camping, recreationists at a public campground north of Los Angeles were questioned about their camping values and satisfactions. Questionnaires were completed by 64 camping parties (30 percent response rate) using the campground during one week in August 1962. One question asked of the campers was, "What do you like most about camping?" "Getting away from it all" was cited by 22 percent of the sample. Other responses included "outdoor life" (18 percent), "meeting people" (14 percent), "rest and relaxation" (12 percent), "fresh air" (5 percent), "quiet" (4 percent), "informality" (3 percent), "good fellowship" (2 percent), and "no telephones" (2 percent). The researcher grouped the responses into three clusters of camping values: rest and relaxation, meeting people, and outdoor life.

714. Merriam, L. C., Jr., and Ammons, R. B. "Wilderness Users and Management in Three Mountain Areas." *Journal of Forestry* 66 (May 1968): 390–95.

 Funding for this study was received from a Reserve Fund grant of the McIntire-Stennis program. During the summer and early fall of 1964, the authors of this article surveyed visitors to three Montana wilderness areas (Bob Marshall Wilderness, Mission Mountains Primitive Area, and Glacier National Park) about the wilderness concept. A total of 108 wilderness users in these areas were interviewed on the meaning of wilderness, things important for wilderness, where wilderness begins, and possible changes in wilderness management. The characteristics most important to the visitors for wilderness were few people and staying out overnight. Opinion of whether wilderness began at the end of the road or three miles or more beyond the end of the road differed for the users of the three areas. Of seven possible wilderness management changes, only "informational signs" was supported by the majority of the users of all three areas.

715. Bultena, Gordon L., and Klessig, Lowell L. "Satisfaction in Camping: A Conceptualization and Guide to Social Research." *Journal of Leisure Research* 1 (1969): 348–54.

 This article is a review of prior research conducted on camping satisfaction. (Two of the studies are described elsewhere.) In one study of a sample of Indiana campers, 29 percent identified "being in the out-of-doors" as the most important aspect of camping. An additional 14 percent said "change of pace" was most important. Another analysis of campers in the Pacific Northwest showed that spartanism was the strongest factor in the wilderness concept of campers. Crowding was not as great a factor in camping satisfaction as expected, according to a Wisconsin study. Only one-third of the campers named lack of solitude as a problem in an area the researchers considered to be crowded.

716. Shafer, Elwood L., Jr., and Meitz, James. "Aesthetic and Emotional Experiences Rate High with Northeast Wilderness Hikers." *Environment and Behavior* 1 (December 1969): 187–97.

Wilderness hikers in the Adirondack and White Mountains were surveyed in this research to examine the value they placed on different aspects of their wilderness experience. Interviews were conducted during July and August with 76 randomly selected hikers along trails in each of the areas. The hikers were asked to respond to five statements about wilderness values. Of the five values measured, aesthetic experiences were judged by the hikers to be of most importance to them, followed by emotional, physical, educational, and social experiences. The researchers found that aesthetic values were 10 times more important to the hikers than social values.

717. Clark, Roger N.; Hendee, John C.; and Campbell, Frederick L. "Values, Behavior, and Conflict in Modern Camping Culture." *Journal of Leisure Research* 3 (Summer 1971): 143–59.

The authors conducted this research with the cooperation of the U.S. Forest Service and the University of Washington, College of Forest Resources and Institute for Social Research. In the first phase of this study, camper behaviors were observed at campgrounds in a national forest in Washington during the summer of 1968. Questionnaires were distributed to campers in seven campgrounds in Washington during the second phase. The third phase involved mailing questionnaires to recreation managers in Washington national parks, national forests, and state parks. The purpose of the questionnaire was to measure camper attitudes toward camping and campground behaviors and to compare the camper attitudes with manager perceptions. Questionnaires were returned from 2,055 campers (55 percent) and 261 (83 percent) managers. Analysis of the data showed the managers underestimated the importance of environmental motivations such as "getting away from other people," "teaching my children about the out-of-doors," and "getting awareness of unspoiled beauty." There were also differences in the way campers and managers perceived conditions in the campgrounds, with campers generally being much more tolerant of noise, littering, and crowding.

718. Merriam, L. C.; Wald, K. D.; and Ramsey, C. E. "Public and Professional Definitions of the State Park: A Minnesota Case." *Journal of Leisure Research* 4 (Fall 1972): 259–74.

Support for this study was provided by McIntire-Stennis Cooperative for Research Funds. The goal of the research was to compare perceptions of campers and park managers of state parks and the motivations for camping. The camper population for the study consisted of campers at Scenic and St. Croix State Parks and George Washington State Forest, Minnesota. A total of 346 campers were interviewed between June 15 and September 10, 1970. The manager interviews were conducted with six key state park and forestry officials. Both the campers and the administrators rated "seeing the beauties of nature" and "seeing wildlife in its natural habitat" as the most important reasons for camping. The main difference between the two groups was that the campers perceived a state park principally as a recreation area, while managers perceived a park as a natural area for preservation.

719. Hollender, John W. "Motivational Dimensions of the Camping Experience." *Journal of Leisure Research* 9 (1977): 133–41.

This research was conducted by the author to identify motivational factors in a decision to go camping and in the choice of camping sites. Interviews conducted with campers at Unicoi Recreation Experiment Station in Georgia were used to develop an instrument of 42 camping motivation statements. This instrument was administered to 99 campers and 112 college students during the summer and fall of 1973. Factor analysis of the responses identified seven motivational factors: primitive life style, escape from routine responsibilities, security of the campground, entertainment, aesthetic outdoor experience, escape from urban stress, and escape from the familiar. These seven factors accounted for more than 85 percent of the variance in the camper and student survey responses.

720. LaPage, Wilbur F., and Cole, Gerald L. *1978 National Camping Market Survey.* U.S. Department of Agriculture, Forest Service, 1979, 34 pp.

This government publication reports the findings of a 1978 national camping survey conducted by the Opinion Research Corporation of Princeton, New Jersey, for the U.S. Forest Service. The report compares the findings of this survey with two prior camping surveys conducted in 1971 and 1973. Approximately 2,000 Americans were interviewed in person for the study during November and December 1978. Included in the interviews were questions on camping satisfaction, attitudes toward the costs of camping, and opinion of public campground fees. Satisfaction was measured for several aspects of camping: overall trip, campsite availability, hookup availability, recreation facilities, cleanliness and condition of campground, and level of camping fees. The interview instrument and numerous tables of results are provided in the document.

721. Dorfman, Peter W. "Measurement and Meaning of Recreation Satisfaction: A Case Study in Camping." *Environment and Behavior* 11 (December 1979): 483–510.

The purpose of the research presented in this article was to identify factors related to camping satisfaction for three independent samples of campers. One sample consisted of 352 campers using the Gallatin Canyon of Montana during the summer of 1973. These campers were interviewed in person in the field by researchers from Montana State University. Another sample consisted of 201 psychology students at Montana State University who had camped recently, and the final sample consisted of 188 adults who had camped at least once during the previous year. Factor analysis identified the following factors as important to a satisfying camping experience: relaxation, naturalism, social-interpersonal relationships, and absence of negative conditions. The absence of negative conditions such as annoying, inconsiderate campers, crowding, and pollution was extremely important in the level of satisfaction for all three samples of campers.

722. Brown, Perry J., and Haas, Glenn E. "Wilderness Recreation Experiences: The Rawah Case." *Journal of Leisure Research* 12 (1980): 229–41.

This research was performed by the authors with funding from the McIntire-Stennis Forestry Research Program of the U.S. Department of Agriculture. The purpose of the study was to define the wilderness recreation experience of different groups of recreation users. Trail registration cards at Rawah Wilderness, Colorado, were used to mail wilderness visitors a written questionnaire during the winter of

1976. The surveys were returned by 164, or 88 percent, of the selected visitors. Analysis of the surveys clustered responses to the 62 recreation outcome items into eight domains. These eight domains were the following: relationships with nature, escape pressure, achievement, autonomy, reflection on personal values, sharing/recollection, risk taking, and meeting/observing other people. The responding visitors were grouped into five recreationist types based on their scores on these eight outcome domains.

723. Twight, Ben W.; Smith, Kenneth L.; and Wissinger, Gordon H. "Privacy and Camping: Closeness to Self vs. Closeness to Others." *Leisure Sciences* 4 (1981): 427–41.

The purpose of this research was to determine the influence of the need for privacy on car camping and wilderness backpacking. The sample for the study was 339 car campers in the Allegheny National Forest, Pennsylvania, and 465 backpackers in the Shenandoah National Park, Virginia. Mail-back questionnaires were distributed to both groups during the summer of 1976. The questionnaires included items representing five aspects of privacy (as identified by earlier research): intimacy, not neighboring, solitude, anonymity, and seclusion. Analysis of the surveys revealed the campers and backpackers differed significantly on all five of the dimensions, with the backpackers demonstrating a stronger need for four of the five aspects of privacy. The best predictors of backpacker versus camper use were need for intimacy and level of education. The authors concluded that intimacy, the need to be alone with others, was of more importance to wilderness users than solitude, the need to be alone with oneself. The article includes a condensed version of the privacy instrument. Funding for this study was provided by the McIntire-Stennis Act.

724. West, Patrick C. "Effect of User Behavior on the Perception of Crowding in Backcountry Forest Recreation." *Forest Science* 28 (1982): 95–105.

This research was performed to determine the effect of other campers' behavior on the perception of crowding in backcountry forest recreation. A total of 321 canoe campers at the Sylvania Recreation Area in the Ottawa National Forest, Michigan, were interviewed in person and by telephone during July and August 1978. Over 30 percent of the campers said they were bothered by the behavior of others during their trip. The most frequent complaints were noisy, loud behavior and littering and polluting the waterways. Of the sample, 22 percent felt the backcountry was "very" or "somewhat" overcrowded. The research found that the negative behavior of others appeared to have an effect on the campers' perceptions of crowding. The effect of behavior on perceived crowding was contingent on the number of other parties encountered during a trip. Funding for the study was received from the U.S. Forest Service, North Central Forest Experiment Station. (Other aspects of this study are described elsewhere.)

725. Hammitt, William E., and Brown, George F., Jr. "Functions of Privacy in Wilderness Environments." *Leisure Sciences* 6 (1984): 151–66.

The purpose of this study was to identify functions of privacy for wilderness users. The sample consisted of students at Southern Illinois University (N = 56), the University of Illinois (N = 14), and the University of Tennessee (N = 36). All of the subjects had prior backpacking experience and were students in outdoor recreation and natural resource classes at the time of the study. A questionnaire asking the students to rate the importance of 28 functions of wilderness solitude was distributed. Factor analysis was then used to identify five categories of privacy functions: emotional release, personal autonomy, reflective thought, limited communication-personal distance, and limited communications-intimacy. "Emotional release" was rated as the most important of the five functions. Of the 28 total items, the highest rated individual privacy item was "resting the mind from anxiety and mental fatigue."

726. Hammitt, William E., and Hughes, Janet Loy. "Characteristics of Winter Backcountry Use in Great Smoky Mountains National Park." *Environmental Management* 8 (March 1984): 161–66.

In this study, winter backcountry users in Great Smoky Mountains National Park were surveyed about their reasons for choosing the off-season for participating in backcountry camping. Data for the research were collected from over 400 holders of camping permits during January and February of 1979. In the mail-back questionnaire, the backpackers were asked to rate the importance of 18 reasons for winter backpacking in the park. Factor analysis of the responses identified three factors of winter backpacking motivations: experience winter environment, solitude, and skill development/challenge. The highest rated individual reasons for winter backpacking were the following: "to enjoy winter scenery," "to get away from crowds," "to experience the winter environment," and "fewer people than during the summer."

727. Lucas, Robert C. *Proceedings-National Wilderness Research Conference: Current Research.* U.S. Department of Agriculture, Forest Service, July 1986, 553 pp.

This is the first of three volumes of papers from the National Wilderness Research Conference held in Fort Collins, Colorado, in July 1985. In this volume, over 70 papers are presented on the following subjects: wilderness fire research, wilderness air quality research, wilderness soil and vegetation research, wilderness fish and wildlife research, wilderness water research, wilderness use and user characteristics, wilderness visitor attitudes and behavior research, wilderness benefits research, wilderness management concepts and tools research, and a wilderness planning-application example. Several of the papers present research on wilderness user attitudes toward wilderness recreation satisfaction, user attitudes toward crowding, and user preferences for wilderness management policies.

728. Lucas, Robert C. *Proceedings-National Wilderness Research Conference: Issues, State-of-Knowledge, Future Directions.* U.S. Department of Agriculture, Forest Service, June 1987, 369 pp.

This is a collection of papers presented at the National Wilderness Research Conference held during July 1985 in Fort Collins, Colorado. Included are three papers concerning wilderness user attitudes: "Wilderness Use and User Characteristics," Roggenbuck, Joseph, and Lucas, Robert, pp. 204–45; "Attitudes Toward Wilderness and Factors Affecting Visitor Behavior," Stankey, George, and Schreyer, Richard, pp. 246–93; and "Wilderness Benefits," Driver, B. L., Nash, Roderick, and Haas, Glenn, pp. 294–319.

729. Virden, Randy J., and Schreyer, Richard. "Recreation Specialization as an Indicator of Environmental Preference." *Environment and Behavior* 20 (November 1988): 721–39.

In this study, backcountry hikers from three Intermountain West primitive areas were surveyed to determine the relationship between the level of hiking specialization and preference for environmental settings. Hiking specialization had been defined as a reflection of a hiker's level of experience, skill, utilization of equipment, and value orientation. The sample for the study consisted of day hikers and backpackers in the Superstition Wilderness area in Arizona, the Uinta Primitive Area in Utah, and Bridger Wilderness in Wyoming. A total of 619 backcountry hikers from all three areas completed and returned mail questionnaires during the fall and winter of 1982-83. The survey was designed to measure the importance of physical, social, and managerial aspects of a backcountry setting. Over half of the setting attributes were found to be significantly related to hiking specialization. The strongest predictors of hiking specialization among the physical attributes of a setting were: rugged terrain, presence of bears, and availability of firewood (negative correlation). Seeing others on the trail, seeing motorized recreationists, and hearing loud recreationists were the social setting attributes most strongly related (all negatively) to a positive hiking experience. The managerial attributes of a setting which were most strongly associated with hiking experience were: presence of logging, well-maintained trails, domestic livestock on trails, and presence of mining. All of these characteristics were negatively related to hiking specialization.

730. Stewart, William P., and Carpenter, Edwin H. "Solitude at Grand Canyon: An Application of Expectancy Theory." *Journal of Leisure Research* 21 (1989): 4–17.

The National Park Service provided support for this study which attempted to measure the fulfillment of backpackers' need for solitude at Grand Canyon National Park. Data used in the study had been collected previously for a comprehensive Grand Canyon backcountry study. During 1984, mail questionnaires had been sent to a sampling of backcountry trip leaders within two weeks of the completion of their trip. Analysis of 1,975 completed surveys revealed that only one-third of the leaders who indicated solitude was of extreme importance to them were very satisfied with the number of other groups they encountered on their trip. Solitude was more important to repeat hikers than first-time hikers, and solitude was also more important to those who chose a low use area of the canyon.

731. Hammitt, William E., and Madden, Mark A. "Cognitive Dimensions of Wilderness Privacy: A Field Test and Further Explanation." *Leisure Sciences* 11 (1989): 293–301.

The study reported in this article was an attempt to field test a scale developed to measure aspects of privacy to wilderness users. Backpackers on the Appalachian Trail in the Great Smoky Mountains National Park were chosen as the subjects for the research. A total of 184 overnight backpackers completed and returned the questionnaire. Factor analysis of the responses to 20 items resulted in the identification of five wilderness privacy components: natural environment, individual cognitive freedom, social cognitive freedom, intimacy, and individualism. For this sample, natural environment was the most important aspect of wilderness privacy. The individual survey items receiving the highest rating by the respondents were, "tranquility and peacefulness of the remote environment," and "an environment free of man-made noises." This project was funded in part by the Intermountain Research Station, U.S. Forest Service.

Boating and River Recreation

732. Anderson, Dorothy H.; Leatherberry, Earl C.; and Lime, David W. *An Annotated Bibliography on River Recreation.* U.S. Department of Agriculture, Forest Service, 1978, 62 pp.

This annotated bibliography includes over 300 entries on various aspects of river recreation. The entries are organized by the following sections: water resource management and research, role of river resources in outdoor recreation, inventory and classification methods, economic evaluations, investigations of environmental impacts, identification of use and users, management of river resources, and federal wild and scenic river legislation. Several surveys of river recreation user attitudes and preferences are offered in the "identification of use and users" section. An author index is included.

733. Vaske, Jerry J.; Donnelly, Maureen P.; and Heberlein, Thomas A. "Perceptions of Crowding and Resource Quality by Early and More Recent Visitors." *Leisure Sciences* 3 (1980): 367–81.

The research described in this paper surveyed boaters to determine if the environmental conditions during their first boating trip to an area affected their subsequent evaluation of the area. Data for the survey were collected from a mail questionnaire completed by 647 boaters at the Apostle Islands National Lakeshore in Wisconsin. The boaters were divided into three classes: those who made their first trip before the area received national designation, those who made their first trip between 1971 and 1974, and those who made their first trip during 1975, the year of the survey. Although there was no significant difference in the number of other boaters contacted during their trips, the boaters using the area since before the national designation were more likely to feel there were too many boaters in the area. The boaters who had been visiting the area the longest were also more likely to perceive the environment as being damaged from such sources as litter, overuse of campsites, trampling of natural vegetation, and poor water quality.

734. Lime, David W., and Field, Donald R. *Some Recent Products of River Recreation Research.* U.S. Department of Agriculture, Forest Service, 1981, 61 pp.

This publication presents papers from the Second Conference on Scientific Research in the National Parks held in November 1979 in San Francisco, California. Included are four papers dealing with recreation user attitudes and preferences: "Recreational Satisfaction at Buffalo National River," Ditton, Robert B., Graefe, Alan R., and Fedler, Anthony J., pp. 9–17; "User Perceptions of River Recreation Allocation Techniques," Utter, Jack, Gleason, William, and McColl, Stephen F., pp. 27–32; "Displacement of Users Within a River System," Becker, R. H., Niemann, B. J., and Gates, W. A., pp. 33–38; and "Visitor Images of National Parks," Schreyer, Richard, and Roggenbuck, Joseph W., pp. 39–44.

735. Manning, Robert E., and Ciali, Charles P. "Recreation and River Type: Social-Environmental Relationships." *Environmental Management* 5 (March 1981): 109–20.

The purpose of this study was to determine whether river recreation use and reporting of associated problems varied by river type. Generalized geomorphology and cultural setting were two classification factors used to identify six main river segments of four Vermont rivers (Winooski, Mad, White, and Batten Kill). The six river types were the following: primitive torrent, rural pool, village pool, rural meander, village meander, and urban meander. A sample of 866 river users participating in fishing, swimming, and floating activities completed mail-back questionnaires during late spring and summer of 1978. Analysis of the data revealed significant differences in recreational activity and reports of selected problems depending on river type (lack of access, water pollution, lack of parking, litter, overcrowding, and user conflicts).

736. Gramann, James H., and Burdge, Rabel J. "Crowding Perception Determinants at Intensively Developed Outdoor Recreation Sites." *Leisure Sciences* 6 (1984): 167–86.

This research examined the causes of perceptions of crowding at a multiple-use reservoir in central Illinois. Visitors to Lake Shelbyville during the summer of 1978 were mailed a survey following their visit. The final sample consisted of 949 recreationists, the majority having visited the reservoir for fishing, boating, swimming, or water skiing. Perceptions of crowding at the lake were found to be related to age, bringing a boat to the lake, and exposure to adverse boating impacts (reckless boating, boating hazards, inadequate rule enforcement, and vandalism). The most important psychological goals for lake recreation, as identified by this sample, were "having a change from daily routine" and "forgetting about pressures of daily work." The Division of Water Resources of the Illinois Department of Transportation provided support for the research.

737. Heywood, John L. "Experience Preferences of Participants in Different Types of River Recreation Groups." *Journal of Leisure Research* 19 (1987): 1–12.

In this article, the author describes research supported by the Ohio Agricultural Resource and Development Center of Ohio State University. The goal of the study was to explore the relationship between preferences for different outdoor recreation experiences and type of participation group. Data used in the study had been previously collected from recreationists who used 25 U.S. rivers for the 1979 National River Recreation Study conducted by the U.S. Forest Service. The river users were contacted before or after their river trip for registration purposes and later mailed a questionnaire. Responses were received from 5,172 participants. The activity preferences were grouped into four clusters: change, quiet/escape, group adventure, and general adventure. Those people participating in group activities where they did not know most of the other participants tended to prefer adventuresome, socially oriented experiences. Those in small familiar groups preferred experiences oriented toward quiet, escape, and change.

738. Roggenbuck, Joseph W.; Williams, Daniel R.; Bange, Steven P.; and Dean, Denis J. "River Float Trip Encounter Norms: Questioning the Use of the Social Norms Concept." *Journal of Leisure Research* 23 (1991): 133–53.

The National Park Service supported this research which attempted to determine whether river rafters have standards about the acceptable level of crowding during an outing. The site of the research was the New River Gorge National Park, West Virginia. A sample of 616 commercial and private river floaters were contacted before rafting trips and sent follow-up surveys following the trip.

The questionnaire asked the floaters to identify the highest number of other boats that would be acceptable to encounter during different kinds of river trips. Analysis of the surveys showed the presence of other boats made a difference to floaters seeking certain experiences such as wilderness whitewater rafting. Seeing other boats made no difference to over half of the floaters participating in boating for social recreation purposes. In addition to type of experience, the research compared encounter expectations for subgroups based on commercial versus private trip, time of year, day of week, and number of prior trips.

739. Williams, Daniel R.; Roggenbuck, Joseph W.; and Bange, Steve. "The Effect of Norm-Encounter Compatibility on Crowding Perceptions, Experience, and Behavior in River Recreation Settings." *Journal of Leisure Research* 23 (1991): 154-72.

The research presented in this article was part of a larger study of boaters' perceptions of crowding described elsewhere. This portion of the study was designed to determine if expectations about the number of other recreationists and actual encounters affected satisfaction with an outdoor experience. The sample consisted of commercial and private river floaters using the New River Gorge National Park in West Virginia from the summer of 1982 through the spring of 1983. A total of 616 floaters completed surveys before and after their float trips. The study found that floaters who experienced more encounters than they expected were more likely to report not having the trip they expected, seeing too many people, feeling disturbed by the number of other people, and taking action to avoid encounters. This was more likely to occur with river users seeking a scenic trip versus a wilderness trip. Trip satisfaction was not related to compatibility between expected and actual encounters. The National Park Service provided funding for the study.

740. Herrick, Theresa A., and McDonald, Cary D. "Factors Affecting Overall Satisfaction with a River Recreation Experience." *Environmental Management* 16 (March-April 1992): 243-47.

The purpose of this research was to test a multi-dimensional outdoor recreation visitor satisfaction model. Data for the study were collected from a sample of 682 rafters and floaters on the Ocoee River in southeastern Tennessee during the summer of 1988. The river users received mail-back questionnaires following their river experience. Each respondent was asked to what degree five campsite variables (encounters, time waiting, parking, setting attributes, and group behavior) and three independent variables (perceived crowding, use levels, and previous experience) affected the quality of their white-water experience. The setting attribute variable added the most to satisfaction, while time waiting detracted the most. Group behavior was also important to satisfaction. A model made up of six of the original variables (minus use levels and time waiting) accounted for 31 percent of the variance in visitor satisfaction.

Other

741. Rosenthal, Donald H., and Driver, B. L. "Managers' Perceptions of Experiences Sought by Ski-Tourers." *Journal of Forestry* 81 (February 1983): 80-90, 105.

The purpose of this study was to measure the preferences of ski-tourers for different recreational experiences and to measure forest managers' perceptions of these preferences. To that end, the Recreation Experience Scale was administered to 793 randomly selected ski-tourers at selected western national forestlands and 40 U.S. Forest Service employees working in the same areas. The questionnaire included one item from each of the 19 Recreation Experience Scales and was completed by 682 skiers. Analysis of the surveys from the two groups showed close agreement on the majority of the items. The skiers' and the managers' perceptions differed significantly on four types of experiences. The managers underestimated the importance of "experiencing peace and calm," "keeping physically fit," and "enjoying the sounds and smells of nature" to the skiers. They also overestimated the importance that the skiers attributed to "doing something with your family."

742. Mills, Alan S. "Participation Motivations for Outdoor Recreation: A Test of Maslow's Theory." *Journal of Leisure Research* 17 (1985): 184–99.

This article presents research performed by the author with assistance from Hatch Act funds and the California Agricultural Experiment Station, U.S. Department of Interior. The study attempted to determine whether Maslow's theory of motivation could be applied to a group of skiers participating in downhill skiing. The research also explored what motivational needs were activated by skiers of different abilities. A total of 708 downhill skiers at Lake Tahoe resorts during the winter of 1978 comprised the sample for the study. A self-administered survey asked the skiers to rate the importance of different components of a successful day of skiing.

743. Wagner, Eric A., and Hlad, Lawrence G. "Sport as a Reflector of Change: Football, Wilderness Sport and Dominant American Values." *Arena Review* 10 (July 1986): 43–54.

The purpose of this research was to compare wilderness sport enthusiasts with football players and college students on traditional American values. The authors chose participation in orienteering for the study because of the increasing number of recreationists involved in sports associated with the outdoor environment. Orienteering is a competitive navigational sport set in a wilderness forest environment. The sample for the study consisted of 83 football players from a midwestern university, 454 orienteers participating in a national meet, and 219 university students enrolled in a beginning sociology course. A value orientation instrument was used to measure orientation toward activity, man and nature, time, and relationships. On man/nature orientation, more orienteers preferred harmony with nature (82 percent) than did the college students (75 percent) and the football players (67 percent). The orienteers were also more oriented toward the future (time orientation) and the individual (relationship orientation).

4

ATTITUDES TOWARD
WILDLIFE

Wildlife in General

744. Erickson, David L. "Attitudes and Communications About Wildlife."
Journal of Environmental Education 2 (Summer 1971): 17–20.

This article describes a technique used to identify types of attitudes toward
wildlife and wildlife management. A sample of 49 individuals from the Columbus,
Ohio, area were asked to respond to 80 statements about wildlife. The subjects
were classified by their wildlife orientation into four classes: hunter, wildlife
watcher, farmer, and other. Factor analysis of the responses indicated two types
of wildlife attitudes labeled "protectionist" and "reductionist." The protectionist
wanted to preserve wildlife species by providing habitat and protection from hunting. The reductionists viewed wildlife as destructive to crops and livestock and
strongly favored hunting. Both types appeared to be concerned about environmental problems such as water pollution.

745. Kellert, Stephen R. "American Attitudes and Knowledge of Animals."
*Transactions of the Forty-fifth North American Wildlife and Natural
Resources Conference* 45 (1980): 111–23.

The research described in this article was part of a large study of American
attitudes toward domestic and wild animals funded by the U.S. Fish and Wildlife
Service. (Other results of the study are reported on elsewhere in this volume.) The
five phases of the study are also described in detail in government documents produced by the U.S. Department of Interior, Fish and Wildlife Service. The study was
conducted in 1978 and randomly sampled 3,107 members of the general American
public residing in the 48 contiguous states and Alaska. In addition, 433 members
of the National Cattlemen's, American Sheep Producers, and National Trapper's
associations were interviewed. The extensive interview included the following subjects: knowledge of animals, preferences for specific animals, participation in
animal related activities, and attitudes toward specific wildlife issues (endangered
species, predator control, wildlife habitat protection, hunting, species population
control, trapping, harvesting of furbearers and marine mammals, and funding of
wildlife management). The study also tested the author's proposed typology of

195

attitudes toward animals which included 10 attitude types: naturalistic, ecologistic, humanistic, moralistic, scientistic, aesthetic, utilitarian, dominionistic, negativistic, and neutralistic.

Analysis of the surveys demonstrated an extremely limited knowledge of animals among the general population sample. Horses and dogs were chosen by the respondents as the most preferred animals. The majority of the respondents indicated they disapproved of killing furbearers for clothing (57 percent) and the use of steel leghold traps (78 percent), but 60 percent disagreed that wildlife would be better off if populations were not managed by government wildlife agencies. On the issue of hunting, 85 percent approved of hunting for meat, but only 20 percent approved of trophy hunting. While 64 percent approved of hunting for sport if the meat is used, the majority indicated they opposed hunting for sport only. The most commonly occurring attitudes toward animals were the humanistic, negativistic, moralistic, and utilitarian. The research demonstrated numerous correlations between demographic variables and attitude type.

746. Lahart, David E. "The Influence of Knowledge on Young People's Perceptions About Wildlife." *Proceedings of the Annual Conference of the Southeast Association of Fish and Wildlife Agencies* 35 (1981): 661–68.

Partial funding for this research was received from the National Wildlife Federation, the U.S. Fish and Wildlife Service and the Florida Game and Fresh Water Fish Commission. In this study, the researcher measured knowledge of wildlife concepts among 1,300 eighth-grade students in Broward County, Florida. A written questionnaire was used to test the children's wildlife knowledge and to measure their attitudes toward wildlife and involvement in animal activities. Although significant associations were documented between wildlife attitudes and wildlife knowledge and between attitudes and animal activities, the relationships were not strong. Wildlife knowledge in the youths was related to the demographic variables of sex, race, and parental education. The youths involved in nonconsumptive wildlife activities were more knowledgeable, and their knowledge was more closely associated with nonconsumptive activities such as hiking, reading about wildlife, and having pets than with participation in hunting and fishing.

747. Sheriff, Steven L.; Witter, Daniel J.; Kirby, Samuel B.; and Babcock, Kenneth M. "Missouri's Landowners: How They Perceive the Importance of Wildlife." *Transactions of the Forty-sixth North American Wildlife and Natural Resources Conference* 46 (1981): 118–24.

This conference paper describes research conducted in the spring of 1980 with Missouri farm operators and landlords. Mail questionnaires were returned by 277 landlords and 5,264 farm operators. The questionnaire included items related to the following topics: participation in wildlife-related recreation, use of own farmland for wildlife-recreation activities, land restrictions of recreational use by others, extent of wildlife damage to property, and importance of wildlife in farm management decisions. A large majority (83 percent) of the landowners said wildlife considerations were of some importance in the management of their farm, but only 20 percent said wildlife was extremely important in farm operations.

748. Witter, Daniel J.; Tylka, David L.; and Werner, Joseph E. "Values of Urban Wildlife in Missouri." *Transactions of the Forty-sixth North American Wildlife and Natural Resources Conference* 46 (1981): 424–31.

The authors of this conference paper conducted research into the perceived value of wildlife of adult residents of three Missouri cities. The research was funded by the Missouri Department of Conservation. In January 1980, 487 residents of St. Louis, 527 residents of Kansas City, and 506 residents of Springfield completed telephone interviews conducted by the Opinion Research Division of Fleishman-Hillard, Inc., of St. Louis, Missouri. The interviews included items on the following subjects: preference for different types of recreation, participation in nature-oriented activities, wildlife related problems around the home, satisfaction with opportunities for wildlife viewing near home, and interest in and use of local wildlife areas. Wildlife problems had been experienced by 13 percent of the residents. Wildlife near homes was described as "enjoyable" rather than "pests" by 93 percent of the sample.

749. Kelley, Richard G. *Forests, Farms and Wildlife in Vermont: A Study of Landowner Values.* Wildlife Society, Wildlife Management on Public Lands Symposium, May 1981, p. 102–10.

In this symposium paper, the author reports on preliminary results of research conducted into farmer attitudes toward wildlife. A previously developed typology of animal attitudes was used to analyze a questionnaire administered to Vermont farmers during the summer and fall of 1981. Personal and telephone interviews were conducted with 200 landowners, an undisclosed number of which were farmers. The researcher concluded the farmers generally expressed attitudes of the naturalistic and humanistic classifications and also expressed utilitarian attitudes toward certain wildlife species during hunting season.

750. Kellert, Stephen R., and Westervelt, Miriam O. "Historical Trends in American Animal Use and Perception." *Transactions of the Forty-seventh North American Wildlife and Natural Resources Conference* 47 (1982): 649–64.

This conference proceeding details one phase of a five-part study of American attitudes toward wildlife conducted by the authors for the U.S. Fish and Wildlife Service. (Other aspects of this study are described elsewhere.) Unlike the other aspects of the study which surveyed children and adults to determine attitudes, this phase attempted to monitor trends in attitudes toward animals by analyzing the content of newspaper articles. A sample of four newspapers were chosen as representative of urban and rural America: *Los Angeles* [CA] *Times, Hartford* [CT] *Courant, Buffalo* [WY] *Bulletin,* and the *Dawson* [GA] *News.* The researchers reviewed 17 to 18 newspaper issues per year two-to-three year intervals from 1900 to 1976. Trained coders recorded 17 types of information on each article. Each article was also classified by a typology of attitudes toward animals that had been previously developed. The ten attitude types in this typology included the following: aesthetic, dominionistic, ecologistic, humanistic, moralistic, naturalistic, negativistic, neutralistic, scientistic, and utilitarian. The researchers found no increase in the number of animal-related articles during the time period. Although utilitarian was by far the most common attitude portrayed in the articles, its occurrence declined during the century, especially in urban areas. The aesthetic, humanistic, and ecologistic attitudes all increased in urban areas. The moralistic attitude was the least frequently occurring animal-related perspective in the newspaper articles reviewed.

751. Kellert, Stephen R., and Westervelt, Miriam O. *Children's Attitudes, Knowledge and Behaviors Toward Animals.* Washington, DC: U.S. Department of Interior, Fish and Wildlife Service, 1983.

This government document presents the fifth and final phase of a study commissioned by the U.S. Fish and Wildlife Service on American attitudes, knowledge, and behavior toward wildlife and natural habitats. (Other aspects of the study are described elsewhere.) The authors performed this aspect of the study in April 1979. The study's population consisted of school children in grades two, five, eight, and eleven at 22 primary and secondary public schools in Connecticut. Personal interviews were conducted with a total of 267 children at the students' schools. The children were questioned about their attitudes, knowledge, and perception of animals and their involvement in animal related activities. They were also asked to view a film about animals, and their responses to the film were recorded.

The study found the children's knowledge about animals was fairly limited. When compared with adult responses to the same questions, children were more knowledgeable about invertebrates and biological characteristics of animals. Adults showed greater knowledge about animal caused human injuries and domestic animals. Both groups had very low scores on knowledge of endangered species. Humanistic was the most common attitude toward animals among the children included in the survey. Favorite animals of the children were dogs, horses, and cats. The three least favorite kinds of animals were wasps, mosquitoes, and cockroaches. Fewer than one in four students felt that an animal should be killed for its fur. When asked to respond to the statement, "It's okay to hunt animals for fun," 11 percent agreed and 84 percent disagreed.

752. Byford, James L., and Munsey, Sheila. "Attitudes on Wildlife and Knowledge Retained by 4-H Alumni." *Transactions of the Forty-ninth North American Wildlife and Natural Resources Conference* 49 (1984): 410–20.

The Department of Forestry, Wildlife and Fisheries of the University of Tennessee conducted this study with alumni of Tennessee's 4-H Wildlife Conference from 1973 through 1981. The 4-H alumni included men, women, boys, and girls aged 14 to 25 years. Mail questionnaires were sent to 571 alumni of the program, and responses were received from 226 for a 40 percent response rate. The survey included knowledge and attitude questions, many of which were taken from another researcher's previous study of wildlife knowledge and attitudes. Questions from the 4-H Conference's pre-conference exam were also included to study knowledge retention. The purposes of the research were to determine how knowledge changed over time and how knowledge and attitudes of the 4-H alumni differed from a similar age group of the general population sampled in prior research. Scores on the knowledge questions indicated high retention among the conference attendees. The conference alumni scored higher than the general public sample on 26 of 27 knowledge questions. Conference alumni also consistently expressed more positive attitudes toward wildlife and habitat preservation. Evaluated by an established typology of attitudes toward animals, the alumni were less negativistic and utilitarian and more ecologic, naturalistic, and scientistic than the general sample.

753. Peyton, R. Ben, and Langenau, Edward E. "A Comparison of Attitudes Held by BLM Biologists and the General Public Toward Animals." *Wildlife Society Bulletin* 13 (1985): 117–20.

The purpose of this research was to compare the attitudes of Bureau of Land Management (BLM) biologists toward animals with those of the general public using a previously tested typology of animal attitudes. The sample consisted of 63 BLM wildlife biologists participating in inservice training on wildlife values between 1981 and 1984. Results of the survey were compared with results obtained by another survey of the general public. This study documented a different profile of attitudes toward animals among biologists than among the general public sample. Mean scores differed significantly for seven of eight scales of the instrument. Biologists had higher scores on the naturalistic, ecologistic, scientistic, and dominionistic scales than the general public. Lower scores were recorded by the biologists on the moralistic, utilitarian, and negativistic measures. Similar scores were found on the humanistic scale. This research was funded by the Federal Aid in Wildlife Restoration, Pittman-Robertson Project and the Michigan Agriculture Experiment Station, U.S. Forest Service.

754. Kellert, Stephen R. "Attitudes Toward Animals: Age-Related Development Among Children." *Journal of Environmental Education* 16 (Spring 1985): 29–39.

Attitudes toward animals among students in second, fifth, eighth, and eleventh grades were examined in this research study. (Additional aspects of this research are presented in other entries.) A total of 261 Connecticut children was surveyed. The children were administered tests to determine their knowledge and attitudes toward animals and their interactions with animals. As a result of the survey responses, the author was able to identify three stages of development in children's perceptions of animals. The first stage was characterized by an affective, emotional relationship to animals. An increase in factual understanding and knowledge occurred during the second phase, and the third stage involved a shift to ethical and ecological considerations of animals.

755. Westervelt, Miriam O., and Llewellyn, Lynn G. *Youth and Wildlife: The Beliefs and Behaviors of Fifth and Sixth Grade Students Regarding Nondomestic Animals.* U.S. Department of Interior, Fish and Wildlife Service, October 1985, 77 pp.

This government publication describes a national survey of fifth- and sixth-grade student attitudes toward wildlife. In the study sponsored by the U.S. Fish and Wildlife Service, 3,087 students completed questionnaires published in the March 13, 1983, issues of *Weekly Reader Eye* and *Senior Weekly Reader*. The questionnaire measured knowledge of wildlife, preferences for specific species, and popularity of wildlife related activities. Of the different animal attitude types described by another researcher, the students scored highest on the humanistic and moralistic scales. The children's favorite animals were the rabbit, eagle, and robin, while the mouse, skunk, and rat were least liked. On the issue of hunting, 79 percent of the children disapproved of sport hunting, and 42 percent disapproved of hunting for food. The document includes the survey instrument and numerous tables of results. Responses to some questions are broken down by region, sex, and urban versus rural residence. Other results are compared with findings from a prior survey of adult wildlife attitudes.

756. Dick, Ronald E., and Hendee, John C. "Human Responses to Encounters with Wildlife in Urban Parks." *Leisure Sciences* 8 (1986): 63–77.

Support for this research was provided by the National Wildlife Federation, the Wildlife Management Institute, the Pacific Northwest Forest and Range Experiment Station and the Southeastern Forest Experiment Station, U.S. Forest Service. Visitors to seven suburban park areas in Seattle, Washington, and Denver, Colorado, were observed and interviewed to determine human reactions to encounters with wildlife. A total of 3,697 visitors were observed directly and 246 were interviewed at the park sites. Of those interviewed, 71 percent gave "leisure" reasons for visiting the park, while 26 percent gave work-related reasons. Almost all (92 percent) of those who said they had contact with wildlife felt the contact enhanced their visit to the park. The article describes what types of behavioral responses the visitors made to wildlife such as observation, investigation, and direct contact.

757. Adams, Clark E.; Newgard, Laura; and Thomas, John K. "How High School and College Students Feel About Wildlife." *The American Biology Teacher* 48 (May 1986): 263–67.

High school and undergraduate college biology students were surveyed in this study of wildlife attitudes. The survey was administered to 118 biology students at a central Texas high school and 110 undergraduate students in a wildlife and fisheries science class at a Texas university. Each group completed a three-part survey of attitudes toward wildlife, perception of wildlife, and participation in wildlife related activities. The students' responses were grouped into four dimensions of social behavior. Those four dimensions and their observed frequencies in the two samples were as follows: "action" (16 percent high school; 77 percent college), "satisfaction" (26 percent high school; 10 percent college), "frustration" (37 percent high school; 13 percent college), and "apathy" (21 percent high school; 0 percent college). Differences in the occurrence of the dimensions between the two groups were statistically significant and persisted regardless of the particular wildlife species addressed.

758. Adams, Clark E.; Thomas, John K.; Lin, Pei-Chien; and Kirkpatrick, Phyllis. "Perceived Factors Influencing Students' Interest in Wildlife." *Proceedings of the Annual Conference of the Southeast Association of Fish and Wildlife Agencies* 41 (1987): 497–501.

This study explored the influence of various factors on students' interest in wildlife, comparing students in fifth, seventh, ninth, and eleventh grades in Hualien, Taiwan, and Victoria, Texas. During the spring of 1986, 389 Taiwan and 568 Texas students were asked to identify to what degree they believed their interest in wildlife was influenced by television, their parents, teachers, books, a school class, and friends. Analysis of the surveys revealed that the Taiwanese students perceived a greater influence from teachers and school classes, and a lesser influence from parents than the American students. Both groups of students perceived the greatest influence on their wildlife interest as coming from television and books.

759. Siemer, William F.; Peyton, R. Ben; and Witter, Daniel J. "Teachers' Attitudes Toward Animals: Implications for Conservation Education." *Transactions of the Fifty-second North American Wildlife and Natural Resources Conference* 52 (1987): 460–67.

The research presented in this conference paper was conducted by the state of Missouri's Department of Conservation. Missouri teachers receiving Department of Conservation education materials were surveyed by mail to determine their attitudes toward wildlife. The results of the survey were compared with three other samples: Michigan teachers, U.S. Bureau of Land Management biologists, and the general public. The instrument used with all four samples was developed by another researcher for his study of American attitudes toward animals. Slightly fewer than half of the 3,000 teachers receiving the survey responded. The Missouri teacher sample scored high on the instrument's moralistic scale and low on the scientistic, utilitarian, and dominionistic scales. Responses suggested a similar attitude profile to that of the Michigan teachers, but major differences were found between the teacher samples and the biologist and general public samples. Teacher attitudes fell between those of the other two groups. Biologists demonstrated stronger ecologistic and naturalistic attitudes and weaker humanistic and moralistic attitudes. On the issue of hunting, 22 percent of the sample were categorized as hunters, 56 percent as nonhunters, and 22 percent as antihunters.

760. Dolin, Eric Jay. "Black Americans' Attitudes Toward Wildlife." *Journal of Environmental Education* 20 (Fall 1988): 17–21.

This article on the attitudes of black Americans toward wildlife mentions results from two previously conducted studies on the subject. The first study was conducted in 1976 with a sample of black students and adults in Denver, Colorado. Although the respondents indicated an "interest and concern for wildlife and natural resource conservation," the researcher concluded the subjects were dissatisfied with their knowledge and understanding of wildlife and exhibited only a passing interest in the subject. In the second study, researchers examined a subsample of black Americans from an extensive national survey of attitudes toward wildlife (described elsewhere). Generally, the results indicated that black Americans in the study expressed significantly less knowledge and concern for wildlife than the white Americans in the study.

761. Leuschner, William A.; Ritchie, Viola P.; and Stauffer, Dean F. "Opinions on Wildlife: Responses of Resource Managers and Wildlife Users in the Southeastern United States." *Wildlife Society Bulletin* 17 (1989): 24–29.

This study was conducted by the Departments of Forestry and Fisheries and Wildlife Sciences at Virginia Polytechnic Institute and State University. The researchers sent mail questionnaires to five different groups (professional foresters, professional wildlife managers, bird watchers, environmentalists, and hunters) to compare the views of resource managers and their clientele on the importance of wildlife and wildlife management. Subjects were chosen randomly from lists of hunting license holders and membership lists of various professional and special interest organizations. A total of 461 individuals responded for an overall response rate of 77 percent. When asked to rank the three most important reasons why wildlife is important, the largest percentage of all groups said because "wildlife is part of the ecological balance." Managers and nonconsumptive respondents felt outdoor trips were enhanced by seeing different wildlife species and species they had never seen before. Hunters preferred to see wildlife family groups. Users preferred habitat management, and resource managers preferred hunting and timber harvesting to manage wildlife.

762. Schreyer, Richard; Krannich, Richard S.; and Cundy, Donald T. "Public Support for Wildlife Resources and Programs in Utah." *Wildlife Society Bulletin* 17 (1989): 532–38.

Utah State University staff conducted this research with funding support from the Utah Agricultural Experiment Station and Utah State University. In September 1986, 900 Utah residents randomly selected from telephone listings were interviewed by telephone. The sample was divided into three subsamples: hunters, nonconsumptive users, and nonparticipant wildlife users. Topics for the interview included the following: general interest in wildlife, perception of quality of wildlife resources, attitude toward specific wildlife management issues, trade-offs between wildlife and other resource uses, and alternative funding sources for wildlife programs. The findings revealed that the hunter subgroup expressed the greatest interest in wildlife and the greatest support for improving wildlife habitat. All three groups showed generally positive attitudes toward wildlife values. The respondents were more willing to restrict housing development and road construction if they jeopardized wildlife than cattle grazing, energy development, or dam construction. A variety of alternative fund raising sources for wildlife programs was supported by the respondents.

763. Race, Therese M.; Decker, Eugene; and Taylor, Jonathan. "A Statewide Evaluation of Project WILD's Effect on Student Knowledge and Attitude Toward Wildlife." *Transactions of the Fifty-fifth North American Wildlife and Natural Resources Conference* 55 (1990): 363–71.

The researchers involved in this study represented the Department of Fisheries and Wildlife Biology at Colorado State University and the U.S. Fish and Wildlife Service. In the spring of 1989, sixth- and seventh-grade students were asked to complete written questionnaires designed to study knowledge and attitudes toward wildlife. Results from students participating in project WILD were compared with those from students not involved in the program. (Project WILD is a supplemental environmental education program provided to teachers that focuses on wildlife.) The sample included 680 students from 26 classrooms representing each school district in Colorado. No significant differences in student knowledge or attitudes were found on the basis of participation in project WILD. The researchers commented that the results of their study may not be valid because many of the students in the control group received exposure to other environmental programs affecting their knowledge and attitudes. Urban students scored higher than rural students on both knowledge and attitude toward wildlife. Male students scored higher on knowledge, while females scored higher on attitude. There was no difference between hunters and nonhunters on the knowledge scale, but nonhunters scored higher than hunters on attitude. There were no differences between anglers and nonanglers on knowledge or attitude.

764. Savage, Harlin. "The Knowledge Gap." *Defenders*, Summer 1993, pp. 32–34.

The research described in this article was conducted by Peter D. Hart Research Associates and Yale professor Stephen R. Kellert for Defenders of Wildlife. A nationwide survey questioned Americans about their view of various environmental problems, concern about the impairment of ecological services, sources of information about environmental issues, and the persuasiveness of different arguments for saving biodiversity. Respondents were also asked about support for protecting various species. Details about the methodology and the date of the survey are not provided in the article. The environmental problem of most concern to the respondents was pollution followed by ozone depletion, solid waste, deforestation, nuclear/toxic waste, rainforests, global warming, acid rain, and endangered species. Biodiversity loss and habitat destruction were not mentioned as significant problems by the survey respondents. A large majority of the respondents indicated they were "very concerned" about possible impairment of nature's air and water cleansing capacity as a result of biodiversity loss. Ethical and ecological reasons for saving biodiversity were more persuasive than economic arguments.

Preferred Species

765. Bart, William M. "A Hierarchy Among Attitudes Toward Animals." *Journal of Environmental Education* 3 (Summer 1972): 4–6.

The purpose of this research was to develop a hierarchy of attitudes toward animals based on a sample of college students. A total of 88 male and female students at the University of Minnesota was surveyed. Respondents were asked to indicate whether they "liked" or "disliked" 30 animals. The proportion of "like" responses was used to rank the popularity of the 30 animals. The top five animals as ranked by the students were the following: horse, dog, deer, man, and cardinal. The bottom five animals were the following: shark, spider, snake, rat, and scorpion. Other species were ranked as follows: eagle—eleven, mountain lion—sixteen, bobcat—eighteen, wolf—nineteen, and hawk—twenty-three.

766. Badaracco, Robert J. "Scorpions, Squirrels, or Sunflowers?" *The American Biology Teacher* 35 (December 1973): 528–30, 538.

In this study, the preferences of California school students for 12 aspects of natural history are examined. A total of 328 students in grades one through twelve (except sixth) in Chico, California, public schools were surveyed. The survey consisted of drawings of various natural history subjects. The students were asked to rank 12 picture cards in order of preference for the opportunity to "look at, study, or enjoy" the subject. In order to test for regional differences, the same exercise was repeated with three classes of students in Tucson, Arizona, schools. Overall, the Chico students ranked the natural history subjects in the following order of preference: mammals, birds, fish, Indians, geology, trees, history, flowers, reptiles, harmless invertebrates, amphibians, and biting and stinging invertebrates. The results were similar for the Tucson students. Included in the article are tables detailing preferences by sex, individual grade, and grades one through five and grades seven through twelve.

767. Fazio, James R., and Belli, Lawrence A. "Characteristics of Nonconsumptive Wildlife Users in Idaho." *Transactions of the Forty-second North American Wildlife and Natural Resources Conference* 42 (1977): 117–27.

In this research, Idaho residents were surveyed by mail questionnaire about their participation in wildlife related outdoor activities. The research was conducted by the University of Idaho College of Forestry, Wildlife and Range Sciences and the University of Idaho Forest, Wildlife and Range Experiment Station. The 470 residents who responded to the survey were categorized by the type of wildlife activities they participated in: nonconsumptive only (observing, photographing or painting wildlife), consumptive only (hunting, fishing, trapping), combination, and nonparticipant. For nonconsumptive users, observing birds was the most popular nonconsumptive wildlife activity. For combination users, observing big game was the most popular nonconsumptive activity. Deer, bear, and elk were among the most preferred species for observation for all three wildlife user groups. Bighorn sheep and mountain goats also ranked high for the consumptive and combination groups, while the observation of birds (eagle, songbirds, waterfowl) was popular with nonconsumptive users.

768. Brown, Tommy L.; Dawson, Chad P.; and Miller, Robert L. "Interests and Attitudes of Metropolitan New York Residents About Wildlife." *Transactions of the Forty-fourth North American Wildlife and Natural Resources Conference* 44 (1979): 289–97.

This article presents research sponsored by the New York State Department of Environmental Conservation and conducted by the Department of Natural Resources at Cornell University. Residents of New York City, Buffalo, Rochester, Syracuse, Utica-Rome, and Binghamton were randomly selected from telephone directories to receive a mail survey. Of 6,894 surveys mailed, 3,447, or 50 percent of the sample, responded. The questionnaire included items on the following issues: participation in wildlife-related activities, importance of sighting wildlife to outdoor recreation, preference for individual wildlife species, occurrence of wildlife-related problems, and interest in wildlife-related programs. Observing birds, mammals, and other wildlife was considered at least moderately important to the majority of the respondents. Preferred species to be seen near the home included butterflies, robins, cardinals, and sparrows. Ducks and geese, turtles, pheasants, and chipmunks were preferred species to be seen at nearby parks. Those surveyed wanted to see foxes, raccoons, skunks, and rabbits in the country, while 37 percent of the sample did not want to see pigeons and snakes at all.

769. More, Thomas A. "Wildlife Preferences and Children's Books." *Wildlife Society Bulletin* 7 (1979): 274–78.

The purpose of this research was to analyze animal themes in children's literature and to identify preferred animal species. To this end, the author searched the title index of Children's Books in Print for the year 1972. All titles with names of animals in them were recorded and the recommended age level was noted. Of 40,250 children's books in print in 1972, 13 percent or 5,326 had an animal name in the title. Mammals were the most popular class of animals with 62 percent of the books featuring them. The 10 most common animals in children's book titles were the following: horse, dog, cat, bear, mouse, rabbit, lion, goose, elephant, and pig.

770. Pudelkewicz, Patricia J. "Visual Response to Urban Wildlife Habitat." *Transactions of the Forty-sixth North American Wildlife and Natural Resources Conference* 46 (1981): 381–89.

The author of this paper surveyed residents whose homes bordered open spaces in urban neighborhoods to measure attitudes toward urban wildlife and open spaces. Questionnaires were hand delivered and later picked up or returned by mail by 191 residents, or 81 percent of the residents contacted. The questionnaire included items about urban wildlife and 32 photos of different types of open spaces that the respondents were asked to rate according to their personal preferences. The most preferred category of open space was the woods category, and the least preferred was the tall grass category. A substantial majority of the residents indicated they received much enjoyment from viewing wildlife. When asked which species they would most enjoy seeing near their homes, five species (cardinal, squirrel, cottontail rabbit, goldfinch, and box turtle) were chosen by over 50 percent of the respondents.

771. Yeomans, Jennifer A., and Barclay, John S. "Perceptions of Residential Wildlife Programs." *Transactions of the Forty-sixth North American Wildlife and Natural Resources Conference* 46 (1981): 390–95.

Funding for the research reported in this paper was provided by the National Wildlife Federation and the Oklahoma Cooperative Wildlife Research Unit. In October 1979, participants in the National Wildlife Federation's backyard wildlife program were surveyed about their experiences with the program. The mail questionnaire was returned by 862 participants. Respondents answered questions about personal benefits of attracting wildlife to their yards, what type of wildlife they encouraged, the success of their program, and problems associated with attracting wildlife to residential areas. Among the perceived benefits of attracting wildlife, three were most frequently cited: "enjoyment," "beauty of wildlife," and "the opportunity to help wildlife." Birds and mammals were the two categories of wildlife the participants said they most wanted to attract. Problems associated with residential wildlife included attracting dogs and cats, damaging gardens, lawns or shrubbery, and droppings and seed hulls.

772. "Big Animals with Appeal Get More Affection, Funds." *Boston Globe*, February 20, 1994, p. 12.

This newspaper article describes evidence suggesting that Americans value large, spectacular animals like eagles and bears over more ordinary species like rodents and insects. The article mentions the research conducted by University of Chicago scientist Donald Coursey and presented at the annual meeting of the American Association for the Advancement of Science. Coursey performed a national mail survey which asked 270 respondents about the importance of saving 247 different species listed as endangered or threatened. The following species were identified by the respondents as top priorities for saving from extinction: bald eagle, whooping crane, the green and leatherback sea turtles, southern sea otter, grizzly bear, Arctic peregrine falcon, Hawaiian hawk, Key deer, and the Eastern cougar. The species of least concern to the respondents were the Kretschmarr Cave mold beetle, the Tooth Cave spider, the Tipton kangaroo rat, and several other rats, bats, snails, shrews, beetles, and mussels. Coursey noted that all the 20 lowest ranked species were rodents, snakes, insects, or snails. The researcher also compared the survey rankings to actual federal expenditures on endangered species programs and found an association between the two lists. Endangered species spending is dominated by a few species with the following animals receiving the most spending: Florida panther, California condor, Bachman's warbler, Puerto Rican parrot, Mississippi sandhill crane, Bridled white-eye, White warty-black pearly mussel, and the Hawaiian crow.

Individual Species

BEARS

773. Decker, Daniel J.; Brown, Tommy L.; Hustin, Deborah L.; Clarke, Stephen H.; and O'Pezio, John. "Public Attitudes Toward Black Bears in the Catskills." *New York Fish and Game Journal* 28 (January 1981): 1–20.

This research project was supported by the New York Federal Aid in Fish and Wildlife Restoration Project. The purpose of the study was to explore the attitudes of private landowners, corporate landowners, and camp managers in the Catskill Mountain area toward black bears. A mail questionnaire was used to collect data on experiences with bears, willingness to tolerate bear damage, attitudes toward bear hunting and desired bear populations. Responses were received from 1,549 (72 percent) of the private landowners, 237 (65 percent) of the camp managers, and 305 (52 percent) of the corporate landowners. Opinion regarding bear hunting was split among the camp managers and private landowners, while hunting was supported by a plurality of the corporate landowners in three of the four geographic regions surveyed. A plurality of both resident and absentee landowners wanted to see bears on their property. Respondents in all three groups wanted bear populations maintained with the private landowners favoring an increase in the number of bears. Private landowners were also the most tolerant of bear damage. The research documented a positive relationship between bear experiences and attitudes toward bears for respondents of all three groups. The article contains several tables of the study's findings including reported bear sightings and incidents.

774. Jope, Katherine L., and Shelby, Bo. "Hiker Behavior and the Outcome of Interactions with Grizzly Bears." *Leisure Sciences* 6 (1984): 257–70.
    In this article, the authors mention previously conducted research on attitudes toward grizzly bears. One of the studies, performed with visitors to Great Smoky Mountains National Park, found that most visitors felt all types of animals, including bears, should be allowed to exist in the park. In another study, 65 percent of visitors to Glacier National Park, Montana, expressed positive attitudes toward bears. This study found factors such as past experience, reading outdoor literature, membership in conservation organizations, and knowledge about bears had little effect on attitudes.

775. McCool, Stephen F., and Braithwaite, Amy M. "Beliefs and Behaviors of Backcountry Campers in Montana Toward Grizzly Bears." *Wildlife Society Bulletin* 17 (1989): 514–19.
    The School of Forestry at the University of Montana conducted this research in the fall of 1987. Overnight backcountry campers at Glacier National Park and Jewel Basin Hiking Area in Montana were surveyed on their knowledge and beliefs about bears. Campers were contacted at the beginning or end of their stay and mailed a questionnaire approximately one month after returning from their trip. Responses were received from 186 campers at Jewel Basin and 460 campers in Glacier National Park. Cluster analysis technique was used by the researchers to identify four major belief domains (as described by previous research): negativistic, ecologistic, naturalistic, and moralistic. The ecologistic was the most strongly held type of belief about bears among the campers. Most of the campers said they felt "safe" or "very safe" in the wild.

WOLVES AND OTHER PREDATORS

776. Erickson, David L., and Van Tubergen, G. Norman. "The Wolf Men." *Journal of Environmental Education* 4 (Fall 1972): 26–30.
    In November 1969, "The Wolf Men," a television documentary designed to

stimulate support for preservation of the timber wolf, was shown by 181 affiliated stations of the National Broadcasting Company. This article describes an attempt to analyze letters written in response to that program. A random sampling of 320 letters was drawn from the first 1,600 of a total 6,000 letters received by the U.S. Bureau of Sport Fisheries and Wildlife. Analysis of the letters included selection and ranking of representative statements and distribution of letters by sex and region of the country. The most common comments concerned government action to protect wolves (88 percent), endangered status of wolves (87 percent), and disapproval of bounty payments (65 percent). The analysis suggested a greater concern among females than males and among residents of the West than residents of the South.

777. Johnson, Roger T. "On the Spoor of the 'Big Bad Wolf'." *Journal of Environmental Education* 6 (Winter 1974): 37–39.

The purpose of this study was to determine the prevailing attitude of Minnesotans toward wolves. Data for the study were collected from 1,692 visitors to a wolf display sponsored by the University of Minnesota at the Minnesota State Fair of 1972. The display featured a stuffed wolf and a computer terminal where participants typed in their answers to questions displayed on the computer monitor. Responses were tabulated to six questions concerning danger posed by wolves, value of a wolf population, effect of wolves on deer and moose populations, and preferred method of dealing with wolves. Only 30 percent of the subjects thought wolves were dangerous to people, and 90 percent thought the state's wolf population had some value. Over two-thirds of the sample thought wolves kept deer and moose numbers under control. Only 2.5 percent of the respondents wanted wolves exterminated, while 56.5 percent thought they should be protected, and 41 percent said they should be left alone. Of several variables included in the study (age, sex, urban-rural residence, region of the state), age was most closely related to attitudes toward wolves. Children under 10 years of age were most likely to view wolves negatively.

778. Llewellyn, Lynn G. "Who Speaks for the Timber Wolf?" *Transactions of the Forty-third North American Wildlife and Natural Resources Conference* 43 (1978): 442–52.

This conference paper describes an attempt to use content analysis to assess the public's attitude toward a proposal that would reclassify the eastern timber wolf from endangered to threatened in the state of Minnesota. The analysis was conducted by a researcher with the U.S. Fish and Wildlife Service. From June 9 to August 8, 1977, 1,083 letters were received by the Office of Endangered Species during a public comment period on reclassification of the timber wolf. Over 90 percent of the "out-of-state" commentors were opposed to any change in the wolf's status. Many of these letters minimized livestock losses from wolves and accused hunters and trappers of attempting to exterminate the wolf. Approximately one-third of the letters from Minnesota were analyzed, and of these, 12 percent were from urban residents and 88 percent were written by residents of rural areas. Of the in-state sampling, 23 percent favored retaining the endangered status, 7 percent favored reclassifying the wolf as threatened, and 70 percent favored complete declassification. A significant relationship was noted between attitude toward wolf status and residence. The researcher also analyzed the responses by a previously developed typology of animal attitudes. She found utilitarian to be the dominant attitude of those advocating complete declassification, while ecologistic and moralistic were the most common attitude types of those favoring the endangered status. The author notes that comments received on the proposed change in status cannot be interpreted as representative of the views of the general public.

779. Powell, Constance B., and Powell, Roger A. "The Predator-Prey Concept in Elementary Education." *Wildlife Society Bulletin* 10 (1982): 238–44.

The authors of this journal article conducted research into how elementary school students and teachers react to the predator-prey concept. Personal interviews with 25 kindergarten and first-grade students from the Laboratory Schools of the University of Chicago in Chicago, Illinois, were tape-recorded. The children were questioned about their knowledge and attitudes toward predatory behavior and one particular predator (the weasel). Teachers were surveyed for their knowledge of predator-prey relationships and their attitudes toward including the concept in school curriculum. The researchers also examined the treatment of predator-prey concepts in children's literature. Only two of the 25 students had any knowledge of the weasel. Among the children, nine had positive reactions toward an explanation of predation, six were neutral, and nine expressed negative reactions. Among the teachers, the majority indicated an acceptance of predation as a natural process. Teacher knowledge of the weasel was fairly low. In response to questioning about allowing students to witness an act of predation in the classroom, 62 percent were positive, 19 percent were neutral or uncertain, and 19 percent were negative. Concerning the review of children's books, 79 percent of the predators in the books were represented in a positive manner, 13 percent were pictured only, and 8 percent were treated negatively.

780. Hook, Richard A., and Robinson, William L. "Attitudes of Michigan Citizens Toward Predators," in *Wolves of the World: Perspectives of Behavior, Ecology, and Conservation*, edited by Fred H. Harrington and Paul C. Paquet. Park Ridge, NJ: Noyes Publications, 1982, p. 382–94.

This book chapter details research conducted by the authors and supported by the Michigan Department of Natural Resources, the Huron Mountain Wildlife Foundation, the National Audubon Society, and the National Rifle Association. Michigan residents holding driver's licenses and residing in three counties from the Upper Peninsula and three counties from the Lower Peninsula were sent mail questionnaires. The questionnaire was returned by 1,664 of the 3,382 residents sampled for a response rate of 49 percent. Respondents answered questions about several topics: knowledge of predators, attitude toward predators and predator restoration, fear of predators, perception of the economic impact of predators, participation in consumptive and nonconsumptive outdoor activities, and membership in consumptive and nonconsumptive oriented organizations. Results indicated a generally favorable attitude toward predators with a majority (54 percent) of the respondents indicating support for wolf restoration. A significant positive correlation was noted between fear of wolves and antipredator attitude and a negative correlation between knowledge of predators and antipredator attitude. Hunting activity did not increase antipredator activity, in fact, participation in all outdoor activities (with the exception of trapping) increased favorable attitudes toward predators. The most positive predator attitudes were found among backpackers and members of the National Audubon Society.

781. Kellert, Stephen R. "The Public and the Timber Wolf in Minnesota." *Transactions of the Fifty-first North American Wildlife and Natural Resources Conference* 51 (1986): 193–200.

This article describes research conducted to look into the attitudes of different groups of Minnesota citizens toward the timber wolf. The research was supported by the Mardag and Dodge Foundations, the U.S. Fish and Wildlife Service, the U.S. Forest Service, and Defenders of Wildlife. The sample for the study included 369 members of the general public, 97 livestock producers, 102 hunters, and 53 trappers. A telephone interview was used to determine attitudes, knowledge, behaviors, and perceptions about the timber wolf, as well as participation in animal-related activities. City residents, females, nonwhites, and respondents with less education were found to have low knowledge sources. The highest scores were noted among trappers and respondents with higher income levels. The wolf was ranked low compared to other animals, and the respondents indicated a moderate degree of fear of the animal. A majority of the sample supported protection of the wolf but felt that farmers and livestock producers should have the right to eliminate individual animals that threaten their property. The respondents also indicated a preference for humane methods of controlling the wolves. The responses revealed that most of the sample viewed the wolf as part of the natural environment and appreciated what its presence had to offer to their own outdoor experience.

782. McNaught, David A. "Wolves in Yellowstone? Park Visitors Respond." *Wildlife Society Bulletin* 15 (1987): 518–21.

The research discussed in this article was conducted by the author and supported by the University of Montana and Defenders of Wildlife. In June and July 1985, overnight visitors to Yellowstone National Park were approached and requested to complete a written questionnaire. A total of 331 lodge and 752 campground visitors to the park completed the survey. The survey included questions about fear of wolves and the respondent's attitude toward wolf presence in the park, wolf restoration, and wolf-human conflicts. A large majority (82 percent) of the respondents felt wolves had a place in Yellowstone National Park. Fewer than half felt human safety would be jeopardized if wolves were restored. Almost 60 percent thought wolves should be reintroduced if they did not return on their own. Stronger wolf support was expressed by campers (versus lodgers), males, college graduates, adults under 65 years, and local residents (versus tourists).

783. Tucker, Pat, and Pletscher, Daniel H. "Attitudes of Hunters and Residents Toward Wolves in Northwestern Montana." *Wildlife Society Bulletin* 17 (1989): 509–14.

This article details research conducted by the authors and supported by the University of Montana, the Flathead Audubon Society, Defenders of Wildlife, and the National Wildlife Federation. The 1986 research surveyed hunters from Flathead County, Montana, and part- and full-time residents of North Fork, Montana. Mail questionnaires were completed by 363 hunters and 165 residents. Respondents were questioned on the following topics: attitude toward presence of wolves in the area, concern for human safety, support for outdoor recreation and hunting restrictions to promote wolf recovery, attitude toward hunting and trapping of wolves, and personal source of information on wolves. The majority of residents and hunters approved of the presence of wolves in their area, and responses indicated a low level of personal safety concerns. The majority of the residents (51 percent) and the hunters (57 percent) expressed approval for hunting and trapping wolves for furs or trophies if the number of wolves allowed it. There was limited support for restricting human commercial and recreational activities to promote wolf restoration.

784. Bath, Alistair J., and Buchanan, Thomas. "Attitudes of Interest Groups in Wyoming Toward Wolf Restoration in Yellowstone National Park." *Wildlife Society Bulletin* 17 (1989): 519–25.

   In this article, the authors describe a study of attitudes among different interest groups toward wolf restoration in Yellowstone National Park. Funding for the research was provided by the U.S. National Park Service, the Wyoming Wildlife Federation, and Defenders of Wildlife. The research, conducted in 1987, used a mail survey to measure knowledge and attitudes toward wolves and wolf restoration, the cost of reintroduction, and the effect on livestock and outdoor wildlife opportunities. The population for the study included the Wyoming general public, Wyoming public residing in counties near Yellowstone National Park, members of the Wyoming Stock Growers Association, Defenders of Wildlife, and the Wyoming Wildlife Federation. Sample sizes for the different groups ranged from 80 (livestock growers) to 371 (state residents). The study's results indicated that group membership had an effect on attitudes toward the wolf and support for reintroduction. Predictably, stock growers had the least positive attitude toward wolves and reintroduction, while members of Defenders of Wildlife had the most positive. The statewide public was more accepting of reintroduction and its costs than the neighboring counties residents. The attitude of the Wyoming Wildlife Federation members was similar to that of the general statewide public.

785. Bath, Alistair J. "Public Attitudes in Wyoming, Montana, and Idaho Toward Wolf Restoration in Yellowstone National Park." *Transactions of the Fifty-sixth North American Wildlife and Natural Resources Conference* 56 (1991): 91–95.

   The research presented in this article was an extension of previous research by the author. Attitudes toward wolves and wolf restoration in Yellowstone National Park were compared for residents of Wyoming, Montana, and Idaho. Results from a mail survey of Wyoming residents conducted in 1987 were combined with responses to a similar survey of Idaho and Montana residents administered in 1990. A total of 371 Wyoming residents, 672 Montana residents, and 618 residents of Idaho completed the questionnaire. The survey response rate was 48 percent for the Wyoming sample, 61 percent for the Montana sample, and 57 percent for the Idaho sample. A low level of knowledge about wolves was noted among respondents from all three states. Attitudes toward wolves were generally positive, with the residents of Idaho expressing the most positive view and residents of Montana, the least positive. The majority of the residents of all three states supported wolf restoration with Idaho residents being the most favorable.

786. Kellert, Stephen R. "Public Views of Wolf Restoration in Michigan." *Transactions of the Fifty-sixth Wildlife and Natural Resources Conference* 56 (1991): 152–61.

   The author of this article conducted research into the attitude, knowledge, and behavior of Michigan residents toward wolf restoration in Michigan's upper peninsula. The U.S. Forest Service, the Michigan Department of Natural Resources, the National Park Service, the U.S. Fish and Wildlife Service, the International

Wolf Center, and the Sigurd Olson Institute sponsored the research. Data for the study were gathered from mail questionnaires completed by 292 Michigan citizens during the summer of 1990. Special samples of deer hunters (N = 113), trappers (N = 113), and farmers (N = 121) were also included for a total sample of 639. All groups except the farmers supported restoration of the wolf to Michigan's Upper Peninsula. Strongest support for restoration was found among deer hunters and trappers. A majority of the respondents did not support curtailing human activities or the development of natural resources to accomplish restoration. Nonlethal methods of control were preferred by a majority of the respondents except in cases where individual animals were known to be killing livestock. The most popular reasons given for restoration were the wolf's natural right to exist and for human aesthetic enjoyment. The least popular reasons for supporting restoration were for hunting and trapping of the animal.

DEER

787. Brown, Tommy L.; Decker, Daniel J.; and Dawson, Chad P. "Willingness of New York Farmers to Incur White-tailed Deer Damage." *Wildlife Society Bulletin* 6 (1978): 235–39.

   This article describes one aspect of a study discussed elsewhere. The study attempted to assess farmers' attitudes toward deer, deer damage, and deer population trends. Attitudes expressed were compared with the amount of deer damage the respondents incurred. This report includes results from all farmers surveyed in the study, while the following article focuses on the responses of only those farmers who derived over 75 percent of their income from farming. In this aspect of the research, 68 percent of the farmers reported no damage, 30 percent light or moderate damage, and 2 percent reported substantial or severe damage. When asked how they felt about the damage, only 2 percent indicated they thought the damage was unreasonable. A large majority (79 percent) of the farmers said they enjoyed having the deer in their neighborhood, and 9 percent said they enjoyed their presence but were concerned about crop damage. The same percent (47 percent) wanted to see the deer population increase as wanted the population to remain the same, while 7 percent wanted the number of deer decreased.

788. Brown, Tommy L., and Decker, Daniel J. "Incorporating Farmers' Attitudes into Management of White-tailed Deer in New York." *Journal of Wildlife Management* 43 (1979): 236–39.

   This research was conducted by the Department of Natural Resources at Cornell University with funding from the New York Federal Aid in Wildlife Restoration Project. Full-time farmers residing in 60 towns in the Lake Plains region of New York were mailed questionnaires that asked about their attitudes toward deer and their desire for the deer population to increase, decrease, or remain the same. This article reports on the responses received from those farmers who indicated they derived over 75 percent of their income from farming. The researchers compared responses from 1,030 farmers with the actual deer population levels in the farmers' areas. The article concludes that the majority of towns had lower levels of deer than the farmers indicated was desirable.

789. Decker, Daniel J., and Brown, Tommy L. "Fruit Growers' vs. Other Farmers' Attitudes Toward Deer in New York." *Wildlife Society Bulletin* 10 (1982): 150–55.

This study comparing the attitudes of fruit growers and other farmers toward deer was supported by the New York Federal Aid in Wildlife Restoration Project. A mail questionnaire was returned by 428 full-time farmers from 46 towns in the Hudson Valley of New York. Approximately one-third of the farmers were fruit growers. All of the farmers in the study were questioned about their attitudes toward deer, deer damage and desired deer population trends. The farmers were also asked to describe the extent of deer damage incurred on their farms. Responses to all of these questions differed significantly between the fruit and non-fruit farmers. The fruit growers were more likely to have sustained moderate to severe crop damage and were more than twice as likely to consider the deer damage unreasonable than the nonfruit growers. Over half of the fruit growers were concerned about crop damage from deer, and almost 60 percent wanted to see the number of deer decreased. Fewer than 30 percent of the nonfruit farmers said they would like to see a decrease in the deer population.

790. Tanner, Gary, and Dimmick, Ralph W. "An Assessment of Farmers' Attitudes Toward Deer and Deer Damage in West Tennessee." *Proceedings of the Eastern Wildlife Damage Control Conference* 1 (1983): 195–99.
  The authors of this conference paper used a mail questionnaire to measure farmers' attitudes toward deer and deer damage in three counties in western Tennessee. A sample of 338 farmers in Henry, Montgomery, and Stewart counties returned the surveys (response rate of 35 percent). The survey instrument requested an estimate of deer damage incurred, opinions about deer, and desired future deer population trend. Results were analyzed by income level and the farmers' previous experience with hunters. Farmers in the highest income group were twice as likely to desire a decrease in the deer population and three times as likely to consider deer a nuisance compared to farmers in the lowest income group. Only 15 percent of the total farmer sample perceived deer as a nuisance, while 62 percent said they enjoyed deer, and 13 percent said they enjoyed deer but worried about damage. The farmers were divided on their preference for deer population trends; 35 percent favored an increase, 28 percent favored a decrease, and 37 percent wanted to see the number of deer remain the same. Support for the study was received from McIntire-Stennis funds.

791. Decker, Daniel J., and Gavin, Thomas A. "Public Attitudes Toward a Suburban Deer Herd." *Wildlife Society Bulletin* 15 (1987): 173–80.
  Property owners were surveyed regarding their attitudes toward the presence of deer in their neighborhood, and the results were reported in this journal article. The authors conducted their research with the support of Cornell University's Agricultural Experimental Station. Residential property owners adjacent to the Seatuck National Wildlife Refuge on Long Island, New York, were mailed questionnaires in the spring of 1985. The survey was completed and returned by 406 residents. Topics covered in the survey included the following: involvement in wildlife related recreational activities, observation of deer or evidence of deer on property, deer damage to property, concerns regarding deer presence, attitude toward deer, preference for size of deer population, and attitude toward different economic and noneconomic uses of wildlife. Very few respondents (9 percent) saw deer as a nuisance in their neighborhood. A majority (57 percent) enjoyed the presence of deer, while about half that number (29 percent) preferred a few deer but were concerned about disease and property damage as a result of their

presence. Most of the respondents (72 percent) wanted the deer population in their neighborhood to stay at present numbers or increase. The survey showed strong disapproval of consumptive uses of wildlife such as trapping (76 percent), sport hunting (70 percent), and meat hunting (62 percent).

OTHER

792. Morgan, J. Mark, and Gramann, James H. "Predicting Effectiveness of Wildlife Education Programs: A Study of Students' Attitudes and Knowledge Toward Snakes." *Wildlife Society Bulletin* 17 (1989): 501–9.

The authors tested student knowledge and attitudes toward snakes before and after the students participated in various programs about snakes. The study was conducted from September through November of 1976 with fifth through eighth-grade students visiting the Pocono Environmental Education Center in Dingman's Ferry, Pennsylvania. Students were randomly assigned to one control and seven treatment groups, with each group containing approximately 15 students. The different treatments included mere exposure to snakes, modeling (viewing someone else handle a snake), direct contact with snakes, and an information program on snakes. Providing information on snakes by a slide show improved the students' knowledge but not attitude toward snakes. Attitude was most positively affected by the modeling technique.

793. Glass, Ronald J.; More, Thomas A.; and Stevens, Thomas H. "Public Attitudes, Policies, and Extramarket Values for Reintroduced Wildlife: Examples from New England." *Transactions of the Fifty-fifth North American Wildlife and Natural Resources Conference* 55 (1990): 548–57.

The U.S. Department of Agriculture, Forest Service and the Department of Resource Economics at the University of Massachusetts performed this research in the winter of 1989. Mail questionnaires were returned by 452 of 1,497 randomly selected New England residents. (This resulted in a response rate of only 37.5 percent.) Items on the survey instrument dealt with the following subjects: the importance of the existence of the bald eagle and wild turkey in New England, reasons why the existence is viewed as important, and willingness to make an annual contribution to help maintain eagle and turkey populations. The existence of the bald eagle was seen as very or somewhat important by 89 percent, while 82 percent viewed the existence of the wild turkey as important. Only 30 percent of the sample were willing to make an annual contribution to help maintain the wild turkey, while 48 percent were willing to contribute to protect the bald eagle. The main reason given for unwillingness to contribute was the feeling "money should come from taxes and license fees."

5

ATTITUDES TOWARD WILDLIFE MANAGEMENT

Support for Wildlife Conservation

794. "National Wildlife Readers Speak Out." *National Wildlife*, June-July 1979, p. 16.

A mail-in survey included in the February-March 1979 issue of *National Wildlife* magazine was returned by more than 26,000 readers. The survey asked the readers to rank the importance of nine environmental issues and to answer questions on nuclear waste disposal and federal water projects. Although fighting pollution was ranked first overall among the environmental issues, saving endangered species received the largest number of first-place votes for most pressing problem. Expanding parks and refuges was ranked sixth of the nine problems addressed.

795. Snyder, Arlene P., and George, John L. "Wildlife-related Activities and Attitudes of Pennsylvanians." *Transactions of the Forty-sixth North American Wildlife and Natural Resources Conference* 46 (1981): 455–62.

Funding for the research presented in this paper was supplied by McIntire-Stennis Act funds and the U.S. Forest Service Consortium for Environmental Forestry Studies. From May to July 1979, 261 randomly selected Pennsylvania residents completed a telephone survey designed to measure attitudes toward nature and wildlife and funding for nongame species management. The statement about nature which received the highest level of agreement was, "Forests are important primarily for seeing beauty and wildlife." A large majority (81 percent) felt that "More research efforts should be put into nongame species."

796. *The Los Angeles Times* Poll. *American Public Opinion Index: 1983.* Louisville, KY: Opinion Research Services, Inc., 1985.

The Los Angeles Times conducted this national telephone poll in April 1983. A sample of 1,233 Americans were asked about federal air and water pollution regulations and whether protecting the environment or encouraging economic

215

growth was more important. The respondents were also asked their perception of the adequacy of federal laws for wildlife preservation.

797. Kellert, Stephen R. "Social and Perceptual Factors in Endangered Species Management." *Journal of Wildlife Management* 49 (1985): 528–36.

This article describes one aspect of a broad study of American attitudes toward animals conducted for the U.S. Fish and Wildlife Service by the author. (Other aspects of the study are described elsewhere.) The specifics of the sample selection and methodology of the study are not repeated in this report except for the notation that the sample consisted of 2,455 adults. The respondents to the survey were asked whether they would approve or disapprove of various water uses if doing so would endanger a species of fish and whether they would approve of protection of an individual endangered species even if higher energy costs resulted. Water diversion for human drinking received 87 percent approval, and 83 percent approved of diversion for crop irrigation. Only 39 percent approved of water being dammed for recreational purposes if it would endanger a species of fish. Higher energy costs would be tolerated for protection of a bird species such as the bald eagle (89 percent) and the eastern mountain lion (73 percent). The sample was much less willing to pay more to protect a particular reptile (43 percent) or insect (34 percent) species.

798. Hayes, Paul G. "Scientists in State Worry About Excellence at U.W." *The Milwaukee Journal*, April 24, 1988, p 1A.

The Milwaukee Journal conducted this poll in January 1988 by distributing written questionnaires to Wisconsin members of the American Association for the Advancement of Science. Responses were received from 874, or 54 percent of the scientists contacted. One series of questions asked the scientists their perceptions of the state's commitment to solving several problems. When asked about the commitment to protecting wildlife and wildlife habitat, 28 percent said the commitment was inadequate. (Other results from this survey are presented elsewhere.)

799. Stolzenburg, William. "Americans Stand Behind Endangered Species." *Nature Conservancy* 42 (May-June 1992): 6.

The Nature Conservancy and the National Audubon Society sponsored a nationwide poll conducted by Greenberg-Lake: the Analysis Group, Inc., and the Tarrance Group. The survey was conducted in December 1991 with a sample of 1,000 registered voters. Respondents were questioned about their support for the Endangered Species Act and their perception of the importance of a candidate's stand on protection of endangered species. Voters were also asked to decide whether protection of the environment or jobs should be given the highest priority. The Endangered Species Act was supported by 66 percent of the sample.

800. "Members Rank Wolf, Panther Highest." *Defenders* 67 (September-October 1992): 37.

Defenders of Wildlife sponsored this 1992 survey of their members' attitudes toward wildlife issues. Approximately 450 members returned a mail survey which asked respondents to indicate which species should receive highest priority for preservation efforts. The survey also questioned members about their support for the organization's actions on several issues including working for reform in the management of the national wildlife refuge system, lobbying Congress for the reauthorization of the Endangered Species Act, and seeking legislative enforcement of the United Nations moratorium on high-seas driftnets. The members indicated they wanted high priority given to preservation of the wolf (59 percent), Florida panther (54 percent), grizzly bear (35 percent), polar bear (29 percent), and Louisiana black bear (22 percent).

801. "Random Survey of Arizona Residents Shows High Support for Wildlife, AGFD." *Wildlife Bulletin.* Arizona Game and Fish Department, January 26, 1993, p. 3–4.

This bulletin released findings of a study conducted by Behavior Research Center of Phoenix for the Arizona Game and Fish Department. The study was conducted by telephone during October 1992 with 1,508 Arizona adults. Included in the survey were questions on involvement in wildlife related recreation activities, importance of viewing wildlife, and perceptions of the role and performance of the state Game and Fish Department. Respondents who indicated they participated in outdoor recreation activities were asked to rate the importance of seeing wild animals when taking part in outdoor activities. Approximately three-fourths of the hikers and campers and two-thirds of the picnickers and horseback riders rated seeing wildlife as "very important" or "important." Those surveyed were also asked to indicate which wildlife management issues should receive more emphasis in the future. At least half of the respondents thought the Game and Fish Department should give increased attention to: providing environmental programs to schools, providing information on Arizona wildlife, protecting endangered species, habitat management, and providing information and enforcement of off-road vehicle laws.

802. "Arizonans Favor Protecting Wildlife When Cities and Towns Expand." *Wildlife Bulletin.* Arizona Game and Fish Department, February 9, 1993, p. 2.

Behavior Research Center of Phoenix conducted the research described in this bulletin for the Arizona Game and Fish Department. (Other results of this survey are offered elsewhere.) Telephone interviews were completed with 1,508 Arizona adult residents during October 1992. This article details the responses to questions about protection of native fish and wildlife protection with urban expansion. A large majority of the sample (83 percent) thought that "Cities and towns should plan their growth and expansion into natural areas, so as to minimize disruption of wildlife populations." Over two-thirds of those surveyed also supported restricting the stocking of sport fish if necessary to protect native fish species.

Hunting as Wildlife Management

803. Taylor, Susan E., and Samuel, David E. "Wildlife Knowledge and Attitudes of Public School Teachers." *Proceedings of the Annual Conference of the Southeast Association of Fish and Wildlife Agencies* 29 (1975): 759–65.

The research presented in this conference paper was conducted by the Division of Forestry at West Virginia University with funding from the American Archery Council. The subjects for the study included public school teachers and college seniors with an education major who taught or would be teaching elementary school or secondary school general science or biology classes. Written surveys were administered to 312 students during class time at three West Virginia colleges. The teachers and senior students were questioned about their knowledge of wildlife and wildlife management and their attitudes toward wildlife management issues, particularly hunting. On the issue of hunting, 45 percent expressed approval, 37 percent expressed disapproval, and 17 percent were undecided. Attitude was related to knowledge of wildlife management for a number of items with those supportive of hunting more likely to provide correct answers. Generally, the knowledge level for all respondents was low. In response to the question, "Do you feel that game species or wildlife should be harvested as a crop when excesses exist?" only 27 percent said yes. The largest number (43 percent) felt wildlife should be "harvested" only if they were destroying habitat, and 29 percent said wildlife should not be "harvested" at all. But when asked what the appropriate action should be if a species exceeds the capacity of the habitat, 58 percent thought the excess should be reduced by hunting. A hands-off approach was supported by 26 percent, sterilization by 10 percent, and supplemental feeding by 5 percent. Another item stating that "Man should quit interfering with wildlife and let nature take care of her own," received nearly an equal number of positive and negative responses.

804. Peterle, Tony J., and Scott, Joseph E. "Characteristics of Some Ohio Hunters and Non-Hunters." *Journal of Wildlife Management* 41 (1977): 386–99.

   This journal article details results of a research study into the characteristics and attitudes of hunters and nonhunters. (Other results of this study are reported on elsewhere.) For the nonhunter sample, 946 Ohioans holding valid state driver's licenses were surveyed. The responses of the nonhunters to 20 questions dealing with gun control, hunting, and wildlife management were compared with hunter responses to the same questions. When presented with the statement, "Hunting should be banned in Ohio," 22 percent of the nonhunters agreed. Of the female nonhunters, 80 percent said they did not want their sons to become hunters. The hunters were more likely than the nonhunters to view wildlife as belonging to everyone and not just the individual landowner. A large percentage of both hunters and nonhunters said they supported setting aside more land as wilderness.

805. Dahlgren, Robert B.; Wywialowski, Alice; Bubolz, Thomas A.; and Wright, Vernon L. "Influence of Knowledge of Wildlife Management Principles on Behavior and Attitudes Toward Resource Issues." *Transactions of the Forty-second North American Wildlife and Natural Resources Conference* 42 (1977): 146–55.

   In this study, 1060 Iowa residents completed a mail questionnaire about their knowledge of wildlife issues and their attitudes toward hunting, trapping, land-use regulations, and gun control. The researchers examined relationships among socioeconomic factors, involvement in various organizations, and knowledge and attitude of issues. Significant relationships were noted among many of the socioeconomic variables, wildlife knowledge, and attitudes toward hunting. Males, farmers, former and present hunters, adults 50 years and older, and those with only a grade-school education were the groups with the highest knowledge scores. Only 11 percent of the sample were opposed to hunting, 22 percent were against trapping, and 33 percent were against gun control. The demographic groups most opposed to hunting were females, professionals, those who never hunted, adults 69 and older, four-year college graduates, and those who had childhood residences within a population of 50,000 or more. The research was conducted by the Iowa Cooperative Wildlife Research Unit and sponsored by the U.S. Fish and Wildlife Service, Iowa State Conservation Commission, Iowa State University, and the Wildlife Management Institute.

806. Shaw, William W.; Witter, Daniel J.; King, David A.; and Richards, Merton T. "Nonhunting Wildlife Enthusiasts and Wildlife Management." *Proceedings of the Western Association of State Game and Fish Commissioners* 58 (1978): 255–63.

The University of Arizona, School of Renewable Natural Resources conducted this research in 1977. Visitors to seven birdwatching locations in southeastern Arizona were mailed questionnaires following their return from the sites. The 604 respondents to the survey answered questions about their perceptions of wildlife management and hunting, the importance of wildlife oriented recreation, and the financing of nongame management programs. Although the majority of the respondents agreed that "Hunting is essential to prevent wildlife overpopulation," 54 percent felt that "Nongame animals are being neglected by wildlife management agencies." Almost all of the sample (92 percent) said, "Nonhunters should have an equal say in wildlife management," and 66 percent agreed that "Wildlife management benefits mostly the hunter." Over 50 percent indicated that wildlife appreciation was their favorite form of outdoor recreation. Several methods of financing nongame management programs were supported by a large majority of the respondents.

807. Witter, Daniel J., and Shaw, William W. "Beliefs of Birders, Hunters, and Wildlife Professionals About Wildlife Management." *Transactions of the Forty-fourth North American Wildlife and Natural Resources Conference* 44 (1979): 298–305.

Funding for this study was provided by Mcintire-Stennis Forestry Project, the Wildlife Management Institute, the American Petroleum Institute, and the National Wildlife Federation. In this research, subjects from the American Birding Association, Ducks Unlimited, and the Wildlife Society were surveyed regarding their attitudes toward game and nongame wildlife management. Mail questionnaires were completed and returned by 180 birders, 111 hunters, and 168 wildlife professionals. When asked to rate 27 ways in which wildlife might be valued, all three groups placed relatively low values on consumptive uses and high values on scientific and esthetic values. The three highest ranked values were the same for the birders and the wildlife biologists, but two of the three differed for the hunting sample. On wildlife management issues, the opinions of the three groups differed widely, with the biologists often expressing a view somewhere between that of the other two groups. Similar responses were received to questions about banning hunting, the opportunity for nonconsumptive users to contribute, and the benefits of wildlife management. The three groups differed in their opinions on the benefits of game management to nongame and the representation of nonhunters in wildlife management. Over 90 percent of the birders felt that nonhunters on game commissions would improve wildlife decisions, while only 60 percent of biologists and 15 percent of hunters agreed. On the issue of funding for wildlife management, birders and biologists preferred "use of general tax revenue," while hunters chose "federal or state income tax checkoff."

808. *1981 Annual Report.* Wyoming Game and Fish Department, August 1981, 132 pp.

This report includes results from a 1981 *Wyoming Wildlife* reader survey. (*Wyoming Wildlife* is a general interest publication of the Wyoming Game and Fish Department.) The report cites a survey sample size of 1,935, although the magazine's total circulation is not given. The report also lacks any details about the survey's methodology such as whether the survey was mailed separately or printed in an issue of the magazine. Included in the survey were questions about the reader's attitude toward wildlife, wildlife management, and outdoor recreation. Respondents were also asked about funding and management priorities and preferences for different funding alternatives. Nearly all (99 percent) of the readers who responded to the survey agreed that "Wildlife plays an important role in the enjoyment of my outdoor recreational activities." The majority of the readers supported hunting grizzly bears in some circumstances and disapproved of hunters receiving a lifetime limit of only one moose, bighorn sheep, or mountain goat. Over 60 percent of the respondents thought increased outdoor recreational activities were negatively affecting wildlife. In response to the statement, "Wildlife causes significant economic losses to ranchers and farmers in Wyoming," 27 percent agreed, 52 percent disagreed, and 21 percent indicated they were unsure. Readers thought elk, mule deer, and moose were the most important wildlife species to the state. Small game animals, partridges and nongame animals were identified as being less important to the state. If additional funding was needed to manage wildlife, the majority of the respondents favored using a portion of the state's mineral severance taxes.

809. Armstrong, James B., and Odom, Ron R. "Gifted Students' Attitudes Toward Endangerment: Some Observations." *Proceedings of the Annual Conference of the Southeast Association of Fish and Wildlife Agencies* 36 (1982): 764–69.

In this study, 209 gifted Georgia students were asked to suggest solutions to the problem of wildlife species endangerment. The students, representing grades four and five, seven through nine, and ten through twelve, were participating in the 1982 offering of the annual Future Problem Solving Bowl. Responses to the problem of endangered species were categorized as "realistic" or "unrealistic" and then classified by six types of solutions. The six categories of student solutions and the frequency of the responses were as follows: habitat preservation or acquisition (9 percent), elimination of pollution (4 percent), management of populations (19 percent), public education (70 percent), restriction or elimination of hunting or hunters (14 percent), and other (6 percent). (The response total exceeds 100 percent due to multiple solutions being offered by some students.) A table presented in the article shows responses for the three different grade groupings.

810. Wywialowski, Alice P., and Dahlgren, Robert B. "Beliefs About Wildlife Management Among Iowans with Differing Attitudes Toward Hunting." *Wildlife Society Bulletin* 13 (1985): 328–32.

This study was conducted by the Iowa Cooperative Wildlife Research Unit. Funds for the study were provided by the U.S. Fish and Wildlife Service, the Iowa State Conservation Commission, Iowa State University, and the Wildlife Management Institute. In 1976, 1,060 Iowa residents 18 years old and older completed and returned mail questionnaires that asked about attitudes toward wildlife management priorities and funding and ways of improving sport hunting. Respondents were placed in subgroups on the basis of their acceptance of hunting: pro-hunters (64 percent), anti-hunters (22 percent), and a group neutral on hunting (14 percent). More anti-hunters than pro-hunters or neutral respondents wanted increased funding for wildlife conservation. Anti-hunters were also more willing to contribute money to a special fund for nongame wildlife. All three groups viewed purchasing wildlife habitat as the most important spending priority. Hunters and the neutral group identified predator control efforts as the lowest spending priority, while stocking game animals was chosen as the lowest priority by the anti-hunters. All groups thought sport hunting could be improved by requiring a hunter safety course. The majority of the anti-hunters and the neutral group felt sport hunting could be improved by requiring tests of knowledge and shooting accuracy before granting hunting licenses.

811. Brown, Tommy L., and Decker, Daniel J. "Identifying and Relating Organized Publics to Wildlife Management Issues: A Planning Study." *Transactions of the Forty-seventh North American Wildlife and Natural Resources Conference* 47 (1992): 686–92.

In this conference paper, the authors describe a process used to identify and classify organizations according to their interest in and approach to wildlife management. The research was supported by the New York Federal Aid in Fish and Wildlife Restoration Project. The study was conducted in several phases. In the first phase, staff of the New York Department of Environmental Conservation (DEC) identified 211 organizations involved in wildlife issues in the state. Of the 211 organizations, 40 were identified as key organizations. Selected DEC staff members were asked to describe the organizations' attitudes toward specific wildlife groups and various wildlife management policies. In the final phase of the study, leaders of 38 of the key organizations were interviewed about their organization's attitude toward specific wildlife, their attitude toward wildlife management, their evaluation of state wildlife management, and communications between their organization and the state wildlife agency. The researchers used the data from the interviews to identify five types of wildlife organization attitudes toward wildlife and to classify the different organizations according to type. Although the article does not include classifications for all 38 organizations, each attitude class is described and organizational examples given.

812. "Hunting: A Closer Look." *USA Today*, July 16, 1992, p. 12C.

This newspaper item consists of a graphic representation of results of a nationwide poll on hunting as a method of wildlife management. The poll, which was conducted by ICR Survey Research Group, surveyed 1,003 adults between June 26 and June 30, 1992. Respondents were asked whether they thought hunting should remain legal and whether hunters should be required to pass certification courses. Only 17 percent of those surveyed thought hunting should be made illegal. If hunting were banned, 50 percent of the respondents said the money to manage wildlife should come from increased public lands user fees. Mandatory hunter education courses were strongly favored by three-fourths of those polled.

Wildlife Management Practices

813. Eisele, Timothy T. "Wisconsin Waterfowl Hunter Attitudes and Communications." *Transactions of the Thirty-eighth North American Wildlife and Natural Resources Conference* 38 (1973): 303–9.

The research described in this conference paper was conducted by the Wisconsin Department of Natural Resources. In May 1970, 513 Wisconsin waterfowl hunters were surveyed by mail questionnaire to determine their sources of waterfowl information, knowledge of technical aspects of waterfowl hunting, and attitudes toward hunting regulations. The researcher found that the three most common sources of information on waterfowl and waterfowl hunting were the state Department of Natural Resources, federal publications, and local newspapers. Of 11 knowledge questions, the most common correct score (mode) was 8. Respondents were supportive of species-oriented regulations, and the majority indicated they preferred extra hunting days to an increase in the number of waterfowl they could shoot.

814. Hill, Harry; Purol, David; Hussain, Nemah; Stoll, George; and Dahl, George. "Michigan Deer Hunters' Perceptions and Attitudes Toward Law Enforcement." *Proceedings of the Western Association of State Game and Fish Commissioners* 58 (1978): 50–69.

The research described in this conference paper was funded by the Federal Aid to Wildlife Restoration, Pittman-Robertson Project. In this study, a sample of 4,341 licensed Michigan deer hunters were surveyed by mail about attitudes toward wildlife management law enforcement. The hunters were asked if they had seen a deer illegally killed and their perception of the seriousness of illegal deer killing both during and beyond the established hunting season. Comparisons were made between perceptions of levels of illegal kills and effect on deer populations and effect on hunting enjoyment. Over 40 percent of the hunters said they felt illegal deer killing, both in and out of deer hunting season, had a moderately serious to extremely serious effect on deer populations. The hunting violations seen as most serious to deer populations and hunting enjoyment were "killing doe in a non-doe area" and "nonseason deer kill."

815. Whiteside, Richard W.; Guynn, David C., Jr.; and Jacobson, Harry A. "Characteristics and Opinions of Mississippi Deer Hunters Using Public Areas." *Proceedings of the Annual Conference of the Southeast Association of Fish and Wildlife Agencies* 35 (1981): 167–73.

This conference paper compares the attitudes of deer hunters using two public hunting areas in Mississippi toward hunting and wildlife management practices. Mail questionnaires were completed and returned by 359 deer hunters using the Choctaw Management Area and 365 hunters using the Tallahala Wildlife Management Area. The survey responses of the two groups of hunters were similar. Both groups indicated they approved of daily hunting permits, daily "bag" limits, closing logging roads, food plots, and implementing a trophy program. The practice of hunting with dogs, however, was approved of by the Tallahala hunters and opposed by the Choctaw hunters. The opinions of both groups were split on the issue of antlerless hunting. When asked to rank seven hunting values derived from deer hunting, both groups of hunters placed the values in the following order: "suspense and challenge," "getting outdoors," "hunting success," "solitude," "companionship," "meat," and "exercise."

816. Steffen, David E., and Beckman, Terry E. "Attitudes Toward Mandatory Hunter Education and Hunter Education Backgrounds of Mississippi Sportsmen." *Proceedings of the Annual Conference of the Southeast Association of Fish and Wildlife Agencies* 36 (1982): 786–90.

The purpose of the research described in this conference paper was to explore the attitudes of Mississippi hunters toward mandatory hunter education. Questions on the issue of hunter safety training were included in a mail survey returned by 1,786 Mississippi hunters holding resident hunting licenses for the 1981-82 hunting season. Mandatory hunter safety education training for new hunters was supported by 62 percent of the responding sample. Hunters who had previously completed a training course were more likely to support mandatory training than hunters who had not completed such a course.

817. Petko-Seus, Pamela A.; Hastings, Bruce C.; Hammitt, William E.; and Pelton, Michael R. "Public Attitudes Toward Collars and Ear Markers on Wildlife." *Wildlife Society Bulletin* 13 (1985): 283–86.

This research investigated the responses of national park visitors to markers on deer and black bears. The study was supported by the Great Smoky Mountain Conservation Association, the University of Tennessee Graduate Program of Ecology, and the McIntire-Stennis Program. The "bear" aspect of the study sampled 150 backpackers and 200 campers from June to October 1982 by personal interview. Interviewees were asked about their attitude toward seeing markers on bears, their preference for different types of markers, and their preference for different colors of markers. A large majority of the backpackers and campers were not disturbed by any of the bear markers. Of the different types of markers, most preferred the ear tag. The "deer" survey was conducted by mail questionnaire with 340 park visitors. Although 31 percent of the visitors indicated they were disturbed by collars on deer, the disapproval level dropped following an explanation of the purpose of the collars. After understanding the purpose, 18 percent of the visitors still objected to colored collars on deer and 8 percent objected to brown collars.

818. The West Virginia Poll. *American Public Opinion Index: 1985*. Louisville, KY: Opinion Research Service Inc., 1986.

Ryan-Repass Research, Inc., surveyed West Virginia residents about whether their state should limit the number of deer that hunters may kill during hunting season. The telephone surveys were completed with 503 adults on January 31, 1985. Limiting the number of deer that may be killed was supported by 71 percent of the sample. More women than men favored setting limits.

819. Peyton, Ben. "A Profile of Michigan Bear Hunters and Bear Hunting Issues." *Wildlife Society Bulletin* 17 (1989): 463–70.

The Michigan Department of Natural Resources and Michigan State University conducted the research described in this article with randomly selected holders of Michigan bear hunting licenses. Responses to the mail questionnaire were grouped according to the type of bear hunter: dog, bait, dog and bait, still (neither dog nor bait), and generalist (varied according to circumstances). The bear hunters were questioned about their attitudes toward the status of bear populations, the use of bait and dogs, and various options to manage bear hunting. A slight majority (55 percent) thought the bear population was stable in the area where they hunted, 33 percent thought the population was decreasing, and 12 percent thought the population was increasing. Hunting over bait was seen as unethical by 39 percent of the hunters. Given a stable bear population, 39 percent were satisfied with current bear hunting regulations, while 42 percent wanted some form of change. The hunters who used neither dogs nor bait were the most dissatisfied with the current regulations. Given a declining bear population, 30 percent would limit the number of hunters, 22 percent would ban dogs and bait, 18 percent would ban dogs only, and 16 percent would ban bait only.

820. Hooper, John K., and Fletcher, James E. "Public Perceptions of and Participation in Fish and Wildlife Law Enforcement." *Transactions of the Fifty-fourth North American Wildlife and Natural Resources Conference* 54 (1989): 359–63.

The research presented in this article was conducted by the Survey Research Center at California State University in cooperation with the California Department of Fish and Game. In June 1988, telephone interviews were conducted with 2,525 California residents. The subjects were questioned about the following topics: perception of seriousness of fish and game violations, effectiveness of law enforcement activities in protecting fish and wildlife, personal involvement with observing or reporting violations, effectiveness of different approaches to reducing violations, and willingness to contribute financially to improve law enforcement. A large majority (85 percent) of respondents felt fish and game violations were either "very serious" or "somewhat serious." Consumptive users of wildlife perceived violations to be less serious than other types of users. Heavy fines were seen as the most effective option for reducing violations. The majority of hunters and fishermen (75 percent) and nonconsumptive users (72 percent) indicated they would be willing to pay a $5.00 fee to the California Department of Game and Fish for improved law enforcement services.

821. Talmey Research Poll. *American Public Opinion Index: 1988.* Boston, MA: Opinion Research Service Inc., 1989.

A telephone survey performed by Talmey Research and Strategy, Inc., of Boulder, Colorado, measured the attitude of Colorado residents toward harassment of hunters and fishermen. The survey was conducted in March 1988 with 508 randomly selected adult residents. More than half of the sample (57 percent) said they supported a law that would make it illegal for someone to intentionally interfere with a hunter or fisherman legally practicing his sport.

822. *Hunter/Harvest Survey and Deer Hunter Survey: 1989.* Louisville, KY: Urban Research Institute, University of Louisville, July 1990, 55 pp.

This report combines results from two surveys sponsored by the Kentucky Department of Fish and Wildlife Resources during the spring of 1990. The deer hunter survey was conducted by the Urban Research Institute of the College of Urban and Public Affairs at the University of Louisville. A sample of 855 Kentucky hunters were contacted by telephone and asked various questions about wildlife management practices. When asked whether they supported requiring hunters to purchase special wildlife stamps, 69 percent favored the stamps to fund purchasing land for hunting and wildlife management, and 78 percent supported the stamps to fund improving wildlife habitat. Over two-thirds of the hunters supported mandatory hunter education, and 64 percent thought deer hunters were considerate of landowner rights. A large majority (77 percent) of the hunters said the goal of the deer management program should be to provide as many deer as possible, while only 49 percent thought the goal should be to produce large trophy deer even if fewer deer were available to hunters.

823. *National Shooting Sports Foundation Public Opinion Study.* Wilton, CT: National Shooting Sports Foundation, August 1990.

The National Shooting Sports Foundation public opinion poll was conducted by the Gallup Organization during June 1990. A national sample of 1,000 adults was asked questions about hunting. When asked about a total ban of all types of hunting, 21 percent of the sample supported such a ban, while 77 percent opposed a ban of hunting. The disruption of hunts by animal rights activists was supported by 9 percent and opposed by 90 percent of the sample. Of the 90 percent opposed to activities that disrupt hunts, 72 percent were strongly opposed.

824. "6th Annual Reader Survey." *USA Today*, January 8, 1991, p. 6C.

This annual *USA Today* reader survey included one question on hunter harassment. Of the 12,000 readers who responded, 74 percent indicated they felt hunters had a right to practice their sport without being "harassed" by hunting opponents. The poll was unscientific and only approximately 20 percent of the respondents were females.

825. *Research Survey on Wildlife Preserves and Bear and Cougar Hunting.* Salt Lake City, UT: Insight Research, January 1991.

This research was conducted by Insight Research for the Utah Wilderness Association. A random sample of 607 Utah residents answered questions about wildlife preserves and black bear and cougar hunting practices. Over three-fourths of the respondents indicated they supported establishing state preserves for wildlife. And 87 percent felt that in considering preserve locations, wildlife interests are just as important or more important than the interests of humans who want to hunt or study them. The use of dogs and bait to hunt bears was opposed by 75 percent and 72 percent of the sample, respectively. Despite these findings, less than half of the respondents supported discontinuing bear hunting in Utah. Similar responses were received to questions to cougar hunting.

Predator and Damage Control

826. "51 percent Say Hunting Aids Environment." *The Minneapolis Tribune*, November 29, 1970.

This newspaper article released results of a September 1970 Minnesota Poll conducted by *The Minneapolis Tribune*. A statewide sample of 1,000 adults was interviewed in person. Respondents were asked about their view of hunting and the effect of predator bounties. The poll's respondents were asked, "Does hunting generally help the environment or generally damage it?" Of those interviewed, 51 percent said hunting helps the environment, and 32 percent said it damaged the environment. Responses to the question are also given for those who liked to hunt and those who did not hunt. Among those who did not like to hunt, opinion on the effect of hunting was nearly split. When asked about the effect of bounties on the number of predators, 56 percent felt they substantially reduced the number, while 32 percent felt bounties had little effect on predator numbers.

827. Buys, Christian J. "Predator Control and Rancher Attitudes." *Environment and Behavior*, 7 (March 1975): 81–98.

This article reports on research conducted by the author and sponsored by the New Mexico Institute of Mining and Technology. The author surveyed New Mexico ranchers with permits to graze their livestock on public land about their attitudes toward predator control. The research was performed in March 1973 with a sample of 384 ranchers. The survey response rate was 43 percent. Issues included in the study were the following: rancher attitude toward predator damage to livestock, coyote damage to wildlife, effectiveness of various predator control methods, ecological role of predators, necessity of predator control, and perception of agency predator control programs. Results revealed that ranchers felt predator damage was a major problem and that a large amount of predator control was necessary to maintain their livelihood. Sheep producers indicated poison, aerial gunning and trapping were the most effective coyote control methods. Cattle producers selected trapping, poison, and bounties as the most effective methods. A larger percentage of sheep grazers than cattle grazers saw poisons as necessary predator control devices. Most cattlemen (56 percent) and many sheepmen (49 percent) felt ranchers should be allowed to handle their own predator problems.

828. Hines, Tommy C., and Scheaffer, Richard. "Public Opinion About Alligators in Florida." *Proceedings of the Annual Conference of the Southeast Association of Fish and Wildlife Agencies* 31 (1977): 84–89.

This article details research on the public's perception of alligators funded by the Federal Endangered Species Program. The target population for the study included the general public and hunters with valid Florida hunting licenses. Only 25 percent of the 4,000 questionnaires mailed to the general public sample were returned, while 46 percent of the 3,000 questionnaires sent to hunters were returned. Respondents to the questionnaire answered questions about their perception of the alligator as a dangerous animal, their view of the value of alligators, and their opinions about how alligators should be managed. Approximately one-third of the sample perceived large alligators as a threat to humans only if provoked, and 25 percent felt small alligators were dangerous in urban situations. The majority of respondents thought alligators in urban areas should be relocated by wildlife officers as opposed to destroying them. Both regulated commercial and sport hunting of large alligators in wild areas received moderate support from both hunters and the general public. The general public was more likely to support the option of complete protection and the option of destruction or relocation than the hunters. Respondents were more likely to support hunting of alligators if they reported they frequently observed them as opposed to never seeing them.

829. Arthur, Louise M.; Gum, Russell L.; Carpenter, Edwin H.; and Shaw, William W. "Predator Control: The Public's Viewpoint." *Transactions of the Forty-second North American Wildlife and Natural Resources Conference* 42 (1977): 137–45.

The researchers who conducted the study described in this article represented the U.S. Department of Agriculture, Economic Research Service, the U.S. Fish and Wildlife Service, and the University of Arizona. They administered telephone surveys to 2,041 adult residents of the 48 contiguous states and the District of Columbia during May and June of 1976. Topics covered by the interviews included the following: knowledge and interest in predator control issues, perceived importance of various consumptive and nonconsumptive wildlife uses, attitudes toward different wild and domestic animals, knowledge of coyotes, attitudes toward different predator control measures, concerns for cost effectiveness, specificity, humaneness of different control methods, and attitudes toward predator impact on farmers and ranchers. Approximately one-third of the total respondents were eliminated from the complete study because they were uninformed and disinterested in the issue of predator control. Nonconsumptive wildlife uses were rated as more important by the respondents than consumptive uses. The coyote was rated as the second least liked among the different animals included in the study. Slow poisons and trapping were seen as the least acceptable methods of coyote control and fast poisons and ground shooting as the most acceptable. Humaneness and specificity of the control method were seen as more important variables in choice of control method than cost-effectiveness.

830. Stuby, Richard G.; Carpenter, Edwin H.; and Arthur, Louise M. *Public Attitudes Toward Coyote Control.* U.S. Department of Agriculture, Economics, Statistics, and Cooperative Service, 1979, 11 pp.

This government document presents results of a study also described in a wildlife conference proceeding reviewed elsewhere. The study was funded by the U.S. Fish and Wildlife Service and the University of Arizona. During May and June 1976, 2,041 adults residing in the 48 contiguous states and the District of Columbia were interviewed by telephone about their beliefs, attitudes, and preferences regarding coyote control in the western United States. In addition to the results discussed in the conference paper, this document reports on the respondents' views of nonlethal predator control and the acceptability of different levels of control as losses of livestock increase. Potential nonlethal predator control measures such as guard dogs, repellants, and birth control were rated more acceptable by the respondents than all lethal methods of control. Acceptability of severe control measures increased among the subjects as hypothetical lamb loss levels were increased.

831. Arthur, Louise M. *Measuring Public Attitudes Toward Natural Resource Issues: Coyote Control.* U.S. Department of Agriculture, Economic Research Service, Technical Bulletin No. 1657, 1981, 67 pp.

This government document describes the development of a survey instrument to measure public attitudes toward predator control. (Findings from the study are discussed in other entries.) The study was conducted by the U.S. Department of Agriculture and the University of Arizona during May and June 1976 with a sample of 2,041 Americans. Included in the survey were items designed to measure attitudes toward legal hunting and the perception of animal suffering under different conditions. Legal hunting was approved of by 55 percent of the respondents, while 45 percent said they disapproved. Given a list of six types of animal treatments, respondents indicated they thought trapping with steel-jaw leghold traps resulted in the greatest amount of animal suffering. The respondents were also asked if they thought a farmer should have the right to kill an animal that is killing the farmer's livestock. Nearly three-fourths (73 percent) of the sample said the farmer has the right to kill the individual animal, but only 43 percent said the farmer should have the right to kill other animals to prevent future losses. This document emphasizes the research design of the study and development of the survey instrument. The actual questionnaire with responses to each question is included at the end of the report.

832. Kellert, Stephen R. "Public Perceptions of Predators, Particularly the Wolf and Coyote." *Biological Conservation* 31 (1985): 167–89.

The research discussed in this article was part of an extensive study of American attitudes toward animals conducted by the author and funded by the U.S. Fish and Wildlife Service. (Additional findings from this research are discussed in other entries.) Personal interviews were performed in the autumn of 1978 with 3,107 randomly selected Americans residing in the 48 contiguous states and Alaska. In addition, special mail surveys were administered to trappers, cattle ranchers and sheep producers. Respondents were questioned about their knowledge of predators, their attitude toward predators, and their attitudes toward animals in general. Livestock producers were questioned about their attitude toward various predator control methods.

The general public expressed the following attitude towards coyotes: 38 percent "positive," 37 percent "negative," and 22 percent "ambivalent." The following responses were noted toward wolves: 42 percent "positive," 38 percent "negative," and 18 percent "ambivalent." Positive attitudes toward the wolf among the general public were higher than among cattle ranchers (30 percent) and sheep producers (14 percent) and lower than among trappers (78 percent). Positive attitudes toward the wolf among the public decreased with age and increased with education of the respondent. The survey also asked the public, sheep producers and cattle ranchers to indicate their approval of several methods of controlling livestock losses from predators: "Shooting or trapping as many coyotes as possible," "Poisoning, because it is the least expensive solution even though other animals may be killed," "Hunting only individual coyotes known to have killed livestock," and "Capturing and relocating coyotes away from sheep even though this is very expensive." While shooting and trapping coyotes were favored by 97 percent and 95 percent of sheep producers and cattle ranchers, respectively, only 35 percent of the informed public favored that option. Poisoning was supported by only 8 percent of the public but by 75 percent of sheep producers and 71 percent of cattlemen. More than two-thirds of the public approved of hunting only offending animals. This option was supported by only 43 percent of sheep producers and 52 percent of cattlemen.

833. Delany, Michael F.; Hines, Tommy C.; and Abercrombie, C. L. "Selected Public's Reaction Following Harvest of American Alligators." *Proceedings of the Annual Conference of the Southeast Association of Fish and Wildlife Agencies* 40 (1986): 349–52.

The research described in this article was conducted in October 1982 by the Florida Game and Fresh Water Fish Commission following an experimental alligator "harvest." Questionnaires about the effect of reducing the number of alligators were returned by 353 sport fishermen and area residents of Newnans Lake, Alachua County, Florida. (The questionnaire response rate was 30 percent.) A majority of the survey respondents indicated they enjoyed seeing alligators, yet three-fourths said they approved of the reduction. Only 19 percent said the alligator "harvest" decreased their enjoyment of the outdoors. The article describes differences in responses based on sex and age.

834. Wigley, T. B., and Garner, M. E. "Landowner Perceptions of Beaver Damage and Control in Arkansas." *Proceedings of the Eastern Wildlife Damage Control Conference* 3 (1987): 34–41.

This research was designed to determine Arkansas landowner perceptions of beaver damage and beaver control programs. Data for the study were collected by mail questionnaires from 1,716 rural noncorporate landowners residing in Arkansas in 1985. The 30-item instrument included questions about land use practices, beaver caused damage, methods used to control beaver damage, and perceptions of government control programs. Beaver damage was described as severe by 50 percent and unreasonable by 46 percent of the landowners with beavers present on their land. Beavers were thought of as a nuisance by 64 percent of the landowners with beavers, and 74 percent of them wanted beaver numbers decreased. Only 10 percent said they enjoyed beavers, and another 17 percent said they could enjoy a few beavers but were concerned about damage. Of all landowners responding to the survey, 90 percent thought the government should provide assistance with beaver control. Desired government services differed significantly for respondents with and without beaver. The most popular government services were distribution of information on controlling beaver and instruction on beaver removal.

835. Timm, Robert M., and Schemnitz, Sanford D. "Attitude Change Toward Vertebrate Pest Control." *Proceedings of the Vertebrate Pest Conference* 13 (1988): 26–33.

The purpose of the research described in this conference paper was to compare the attitudes of college students toward wildlife damage control practices before and after attendance in a course on the subject. Students at the University of Nebraska–Lincoln and New Mexico State University–Las Cruces completed a pre- and post-class questionnaire on predator control during the spring semester 1987. In the paper, the authors compare the results of the student surveys with results received from a similar instrument administered to samples of the general public. The student surveys showed that, as a result of the class, the students at both universities became more supportive of lethal predator control practices. The students were more accepting of all forms of lethal control than the public samples. When asked to rank the importance of three considerations in evaluating damage control techniques, the students ranked specificity as most important, while the public thought that humaneness should be the first priority. Apparently the student surveys did not include questions on the acceptability of nonlethal methods of predator control which were included in the survey of public attitudes. The actual survey instrument is presented at the end of the paper.

836. *Survey Among Alaska Residents Regarding Wolf Hunting.* Anchorage, AK: Dittman Research Corporation, October 1992.

Dittman Research Corporation performed this survey for the Alaska Wildlife Alliance and Wolf Haven International. During October 1992, 641 adult Alaska residents were interviewed by telephone regarding wolf hunting practices. The respondents answered questions on wolf population control, hunting in national parks, and the hunting of wolves by trapping and snaring, from snowmobiles, and from aircraft or from the ground after spotting from aircraft. A majority of the respondents rejected the idea that reducing the number of wolves would result in more moose and caribou for hunting. Only 8 percent of the sample wanted to see the number of wolves killed for population control increased, while 43 percent wanted the number decreased, and 28 percent wanted the number killed to remain at the current level. The sample was generally opposed to hunting wolves in national parks and from snowmobiles, and aircraft or from the ground after spotting from aircraft. Opinion on hunting wolves by trapping and snaring was fairly evenly divided. The report notes differences in hunter and non-hunter responses.

Landowner Rights and Obligations

837. Brown, Tommy L. "New York Landowners' Attitudes Toward Recreation Activities." *Transactions of the Thirty-ninth North American Wildlife and Natural Resources Conference* 39 (1974): 173–79.

This conference paper describes research conducted by the Department of Resources at Cornell University and sponsored by the Wildlife Management Institute, the New York State Conservation Council, the New York State Department of Environmental Conservation, and the New York State Cooperative Wildlife Research Unit. In 1972, owners of at least 10 acres of land in 28 towns in rural New York were sent mail questionnaires to determine their attitudes toward hunting and snowmobiling on private land. A total of 1,263 landowners returned completed questionnaires. The survey included items related to the following topics: reasons for posting land, attitudes toward hunting and hunters, perception of ownership and management of wildlife on private land, and attitudes toward snowmobiling and snowmobilers. A large majority of the landowners who said they posted their land did so because of the poor behavior of recreationists. Only two percent felt man has no right to hunt, and 68 percent said hunting is acceptable as long as hunters respect property rights and obey game laws. A large majority (75 percent) of the landowners felt hunters should be required to seek permission to hunt regardless of whether the land is posted. Snowmobilers were perceived as irresponsible, and 54 percent of the landowners did not welcome them on their property.

838. Kitts, James R., and Low, Jessop B. "Utah Landholders' Attitudes Toward Hunting." *Transactions of the Thirty-ninth North American Wildlife and Natural Resources Conference* 39 (1974): 180–85.

The research presented in this article was sponsored by the U.S. Bureau of Sport Fisheries and Wildlife and funded by the National Rifle Association and the Wildlife Management Institute. A mail questionnaire was used to survey farmers and ranchers who controlled land in eight northern and five southern counties in Utah in August of 1971. Slightly more than half of the 2,076 landholders selected for the survey returned usable questionnaires. Landholders were questioned about their attitudes toward hunting, hunting restrictions on their own land, and the effectiveness of the State Division of Wildlife Resources wildlife management and law enforcement programs. Both hunters and nonhunters favored the concept of hunting. Only 4 percent of the sample expressed an unfavorable attitude toward hunting. No correlation was found between attitude toward hunting and tendency to restrict hunter access. Attitude toward hunting was positively correlated with attitude toward wildlife management in the local area.

839. Jackson, Robert M., and Anderson, Raymond K. "Hunter-Landowner Relationships: A Management and Educational Perspective." *Transactions of the Forty-seventh North American Wildlife and Natural Resources Conference* 47 (1982): 693–704.

The research described in this report was conducted by staff of the University of Wisconsin. Wisconsin landowners, deer hunters, wildlife managers, and conservation officers were all interviewed regarding the posting of private land and deer hunting problems. Personal interviews were conducted with 218 landowners, while 409 deer hunters, 51 wildlife managers, and 120 conservation officers completed written questionnaires. Landowners were also asked to keep a log of hunter behavior on their land during the nine-day-long deer season. Participating landowners were contacted three years later and asked to complete a mail survey similar to the original interview. When asked to rank deer-gun hunting problems, hunters and conservation officers chose "poaching" as the most serious hunting problem. Landowners and wildlife managers ranked "failure to seek permission from landowner" as the number one problem, followed by "poaching." Although a majority of landowners indicated they did not post their land or posted with permission, 78 percent of those maintaining a log observed trespassing on their land during deer hunting season.

840. Svoboda, Franklin J. "Minnesota Landowner Attitudes Toward Wildlife Habitat Management." *Transactions of the Forty-ninth North American Wildlife and Natural Resources Conference* 49 (1984): 154–58.

The Minnesota chapter of the Wildlife Society conducted this research with funding provided by the U.S. Fish and Wildlife Service, the Minnesota Department of Natural Resources, and the University of Minnesota. From August through December 1982, nine different groups of Minnesota landowners were surveyed by mail regarding their perceptions of landowner and governmental obligations for wildlife management on private land. A total of 821 landowners from the nine groups responded to the mail survey. Response rates for the subsamples varied from a low of 33 percent to a high of 70 percent. In response to a question concerning private landowner obligations for wildlife management, 18 percent felt little or no obligation, 11 percent saw the obligation as moral or social, and 23 percent thought wildlife management should be the option of the landowner. A majority of the landowners felt the government should provide incentives to private landowners for wildlife management. Of those responding to a question on the importance of having the opportunity to observe wildlife on their land, 90 percent felt it was important or very important. Most of the respondents (82 percent) said they did not want the government to be able to regulate private land for wildlife purposes.

841. Lee, Alexander, and Kellert, Stephen R. "Forest Landowners' Perspectives on Wildlife Management in New England." *Transactions of the Forty-ninth North American Wildlife and Natural Resources Conference* 49 (1984): 164–73.

Funding for this study was provided by the U.S. Department of Agriculture Forest Service, the Wildlife Management Institute, the American Petroleum Institute, the G.R. Dodge Foundation, and the R.K. Mellon Research Program of Yale University. Randomly selected private, nonindustrial forest landowners in Connecticut, Massachusetts, and New Hampshire were personally interviewed about their perceptions of wildlife on their land. The following specific topics were included in the interview: use of their land, personal practices to benefit wildlife, and perceived benefits from having wildlife on their property. The 204 landowners who completed the survey were also asked how they would respond to four scenarios with alternative courses of action for managing forest land and wildlife. The landowners indicated the three most important primary uses of their land were as a woodlot, an open space, and for recreation. The most important secondary and tertiary use of the land was for wildlife habitat. A large majority (88 percent) of the landowners said seeing or knowing wildlife existed on their property was a benefit of owning forest land. Using their land for hunting was not important to 82 percent of the sample, and 42 percent said they disapproved of hunting for sport. In one scenario, the landowners were asked how they would handle a situation where a developer wanted to buy their land to build a shopping center, but they discovered the land was considered a bird sanctuary. Only 10 percent indicated they would sell to the developer, and 20 percent indicated they would delay selling the land. Another one-third (33 percent) would sell to a conservation organization for half the price, and the largest number (37 percent) said they would never sell the land.

842. Adams, Lowell W.; Dove, Louise E.; and Leedy, Daniel L. "Public Attitudes Toward Urban Wetlands for Stormwater Control and Wildlife Enhancement." *Wildlife Society Bulletin* 12 (1984): 299–303.

   This article reports the findings of a survey developed to measure homeowner attitudes toward stormwater management basins such as lakes, retention ponds, and detention ponds. The study was conducted by the National Institute for Urban Wildlife with funding from the Richard King Mellon Foundation. In September 1982, a questionnaire was mailed to and returned by 360 randomly selected homeowners in Columbia, Maryland. Analysis of the surveys indicated the homeowners preferred permanent retention ponds to dry detention basins. Virtually all (98 percent) of the residents said they enjoyed viewing wildlife at the ponds, and 92 percent felt the benefits of wildlife outweighed any nuisance it caused. A large majority (75 percent) believed permanent retention ponds added to real estate values. Preferred wildlife species visiting the ponds included waterfowl, songbirds, shore and marsh birds, and frogs and turtles. The researchers recorded negative reactions to raccoons, muskrats, and snakes.

843. Wright, Brett A., and Kaiser, Ronald A. "Wildlife Administrators' Perceptions of Hunter Access Problems: A National Overview." *Wildlife Society Bulletin* 14 (1986): 30–35.

   In August 1984, chief executives of the 50 state wildlife agencies were sent a mail questionnaire about hunter access to private lands. The executives were asked to what extent they felt hunter access was a problem. If access was seen as a problem, the respondents were asked why they thought landowners denied hunting access and how hunters could be encouraged to allow access. Half of the administrators (52 percent) thought hunter access was a major problem in their state. Misconduct by hunters was rated as the most significant factor in landowners' decisions to deny access. Administrators felt increased law enforcement and prosecution of trespassers would be the most effective ways to motivate landowners to allow hunter access on their land.

Funding Wildlife Programs

844. Shaw, William W., and Mangun, William R. *Nonconsumptive Use of Wildlife in the United States.* Washington, DC: U.S. Department of Interior, Fish and Wildlife Service, Resource publication 154, 1984, 20 pp.

   The data presented in this government document were obtained from the

1980 National Survey of Fishing, Hunting and Wildlife–Associated Recreation conducted by the U.S. Bureau of the Census for the U.S. Fish and Wildlife Service. In that study, personal interviews were conducted with 5,997 Americans who participated in some form of nonconsumptive use of wildlife during 1980. The interviews included several questions about funding for the conservation of nongame wildlife species. Over 70 percent of the sample said they would support new sources of nongame funding. Those who favored nongame funding were also asked to rate the acceptability of various proposed alternative funding systems. The highest ranked funding source was voluntary conservation stamps, followed by income tax checkoff, general tax money, and a special tax on wildlife related purchases.

845. Connecticut Poll. *American Public Opinion Index: 1985.* Louisville, KY: Opinion Research Service Inc., 1986.

This poll was conducted by the Roper Center at the University of Connecticut during September 1985. A sample of 500 Connecticut residents were interviewed by telephone about support for state wildlife programs. Respondents were asked if they favored expanding the state's wildlife programs to study and protect nongame species and threatened and endangered species. The poll also explored attitudes toward alternative funding sources for wildlife programs including a tax on outdoor recreation items, state sales tax, real estate tax, and using unclaimed bottle bill refunds.

846. Moss, Mary Beth; Fraser, James D.; and Wellman, J. Douglas. "Characteristics of Nongame Fund Contributors versus Hunters in Virginia." *Wildlife Society Bulletin* 14 (1986): 107–14.

The authors of this article attempted to compare attitudes, values, and wildlife management preferences of Virginia nongame tax fund contributors with Virginia hunters and noncontributors to the Virginia tax fund. Income tax records were used to identify fund contributors and telephone subscriber lists were used for contacting both noncontributors and hunters. Mail questionnaires were returned by 302 contributors, 819 noncontributors, and 242 hunters. No differences were found between contributors and hunters on priorities for allocating nongame funds. Both groups chose endangered species programs as the top priority for spending the funds. Contributors and hunters did differ on three wildlife management issues: use of hunting and trapping licenses fees for nongame wildlife, whether the purpose of wildlife management was to benefit wildlife or humans, and whether the game commission should support wildlife rehabilitation. Contributors were much less likely than hunters to value wildlife for meat, furs, or sport. Sport hunting was, in fact, opposed by 42 percent of the contributors.

847. Indiana University Poll. *American Public Opinion Index: 1986.* Boston, MA: Opinion Research Service, Inc., 1987.

In November 1986, the Center for Survey Research at Indiana University interviewed 807 state residents by telephone. The sample was asked to indicate whether they would be willing to pay an additional state tax of about one dollar for local parks and whether they would be willing to contribute to a state fund for nongame and endangered species. While 73 percent said they would pay the extra state tax to fund local parks, only 46 percent of the respondents were willing to contribute to a nongame fund. Over two-thirds of those responding said the state should assist in acquiring and developing local and county parks.

848. Behrens-Tepper, Jean C., and O'Leary, Joseph T. *Southeastern Noncon-sumptive Wildlife Users and Their Support for Nongame Wildlife Pro-grams.* USDA Forest Service, Southern Recreation Research Conference, 1987, p. 53–66.

The research discussed in this report attempted to measure support for nongame wildlife management funding options and to explore the relationship be-tween funding preferences and level of nonconsumptive wildlife activity. Funding for the study was provided by a fellowship from the National Wildlife Federation. The sample for the study consisted of southeastern respondents to the 1980 Na-tional Survey of Fishing, Hunting, and Wildlife–Associated Recreation conducted by the U.S. Bureau of Census for the U.S. Fish and Wildlife Service. A total of 766 respondents were included in the study. And 555 of the respondents were also in-cluded in a subsample of those who supported new sources of nongame funding. A statistically significant relationship was found between level of nonconsumptive wildlife activity and support for new sources of funding. The most popular funding option was voluntary purchase of conservation stamps followed by income tax re-fund check-off, and general tax monies.

849. Kentucky Poll. *American Public Opinion Index: 1987.* Boston, MA: Opin-ion Research Service Inc., 1988.

The Survey Research Center at the University of Kentucky conducted this telephone poll during May 1987 with 746 residents of Kentucky. Respondents were asked who they thought paid for state wildlife programs and who should pay for wildlife conservation and protection. The amount of state spending on the environ-ment was seen as about right by 46 percent and too little by 40 percent of the sample.

850. *North Dakota Game and Fish Department Boat Poll.* Grand Forks, ND: Bureau of Governmental Affairs, 1991.

This poll was conducted by the University of North Dakota for the North Dakota Bureau of Government Affairs. During January 1991, over 1,000 residents of the state were interviewed by telephone about their opinion of state wildlife management programs. The survey asked respondents their perception of the seriousness of water pollution on fish resources and the seriousness of lack of understanding and respect for the value of fish and wildlife resources. A large ma-jority (83 percent) indicated they thought the loss of wildlife habitat was a "very serious" or "somewhat serious" problem. Hunter access to private land was seen as "very serious" or "somewhat serious" by two-thirds of the sample. The respond-ents were also asked to split Game and Fish funding between different game and nongame management programs. Supporting the Game and Fish Department with state tax dollars was supported by 55 percent of the residents.

APPENDIX A

Primary Bibliographic Sources

INDEXES

American Statistical Index
Bibliographic Index
Business Periodicals Index
Environment Index/Environment Abstracts Annual
NewsBank Index
Reader's Guide to Periodical Literature
Social Science Index
Statistical Reference Index

PROFESSIONAL JOURNALS

Environmental Education
Fisheries
Journal of Environment and Behavior
Journal of Environmental Education
Journal of Forestry
Journal of Leisure Research
Journal of Wildlife Management
Leisure Sciences
Natural Resources Journal
Public Opinion
Public Opinion Quarterly
Wildlife Society Bulletin

CONFERENCE PROCEEDINGS

Annual Conference, Southeast Association of Game and Fish Commissioners
Annual Conference, Southeast Association of Fish and Wildlife Agencies
Annual Conference of Western Association of Fish and Game Commissioners
Western Association of Fish and Wildlife Agencies
Transactions of the North American Wildlife and Natural Resources
  Conference

DAILY NEWSPAPERS

Chicago Tribune
The Christian Science Monitor
The Los Angeles Times
The New York Times
The Wall Street Journal
The Washington Post
USA Today

PUBLIC OPINION PERIODICALS

American Public Opinion Index
The Gallup Poll
The Harris Survey Yearbook of Public Opinion
The ABC News–Harris Survey
The Harris Survey
The Harris Poll

APPENDIX B

State Initiatives and Referendums: 1970–1992

GENERAL ENVIRONMENTAL FUNDS

Year	State	Issue/Result
1984	MI	Establish natural resources trust fund financed by revenues from resource leases (approved, 65 percent to 35 percent)
1988	MN	Create environmental trust fund for preservation and conservation (approved)
1990	NY	$1.9 billion environmental bond issue (defeated, 51 percent to 49 percent)

LAND OWNERSHIP

Year	State	Issue/Result
1970	FL	Require state owned land to be sold only in public interest (approved)
1982	AK	Claim state ownership of federal lands (approved, 73 percent to 27 percent)
1982	AZ	Abandon state claims to certain federal lands (defeated, 43 percent to 57 percent)
1990	AZ	Allow state to trade state trust land for public or private property of equal value (defeated, 55 percent to 45 percent)
1992	AZ	Allow state to trade state trust land for public or private property of equal value (defeated, 53 percent to 47 percent)

LAND ACQUISITION AND PRESERVATION

Year	State	Issue/Result
1972	NC	Create "environmental bill of rights" giving citizens a legal claim on ecological protection and allow state to acquire sensitive land for preservation (approved)

1972	NY	$1.15 billion bond issue for pollution control, solid waste management, and recreation land acquisition (approved)
1972	FL	$240 million bond issue for state acquisition of threatened shorelines and other recreational tracts (approved)
1989	RI	$74.5 million bond issue for environmental management and "open-space" purchases (approved, 66 percent to 34 percent)
1990	AZ	Establish $20 million Heritage Fund from lottery proceeds to maintain state parks, acquire natural areas, and purchase wildlife habitat (approved, 62 percent to 38 percent)
1990	CA	Ban sport hunting of mountain lions and spend $30 million a year for 30 years to purchase wildlife habitat (approved, 52 percent to 48 percent)
1990	WA	Mandate cities to conform to land use plans (defeated, 75 percent to 25 percent)

COASTAL MANAGEMENT

Year	State	Issue/Result
1972	CA	Place shoreline development control under a new state commission structure (approved)
1972	FL	$240 million bond issue for state acquisition of threatened shorelines and other recreational tracts (approved)
1972	WA	Place shoreline management under state control (approved)
1990	CA	Create plan to control pesticides, air pollution and offshore drilling (defeated, 63 percent to 37 percent)
1990	CA	Ban use of gill and trammel nets along southern coast (approved, 55 percent to 45 percent)

FOREST MANAGEMENT

Year	State	Issue/Result
1973	NY	Allow legislature to dispose of odd forest land parcels not part of Adirondack or Catskill parks (defeated)
1979	NY	Allow state and paper company to swap parcels of forest lands (approved)

| 1990 | CA | Restrict timber cutting (defeated, 53 percent to 47 percent) |
| 1990 | CA | Timber industry plan to authorize $300 million for trees (defeated, 71 percent to 29 percent) |

MINING

Year	State	Issue/Result
1980	MT	Limit uranium mining (defeated)
1980	SD	Prohibit nuclear waste dumping and ban uranium mining (defeated, 51 percent to 49 percent)
1988	SD	Require restoration of all big strip-mining operations (defeated)
1988	SD	Raise taxes on strip-mining operations (defeated)
1990	SD	Require permits for large-scale mining in Black Hills (defeated, 53 percent to 47 percent)
1992	SD	Restrict surface mining of gold and silver in Black Hills (approved, 59 percent to 41 percent)

POLLUTION CONTROL

Year	State	Issue/Result
1972	CA	Allow state loans to industry for pollution control equipment (approved)
1972	NY	$1.15 billion bond issue for pollution control, solid waste management, and recreation land acquisition (approved)
1990	CA	Establish plan to control pesticides, air pollution, and offshore drilling (defeated, 63 percent to 37 percent)

PESTICIDES

Year	State	Issue/Result
1990	CA	Establish plan to control pesticides, air pollution, and offshore drilling (defeated, 63 percent to 37 percent)
1990	CA	Set up pesticide panel (defeated, 70 percent to 30 percent)

WATER CONSERVATION AND TREATMENT

Year	State	Issue/Result
1970	FL	Finance construction of water treatment facilities (approved)
1972	WA	$340 million bond issue for sewage treatment, water supply, and recreational facilities (approved)
1974	CA	Stop the damming of the Stanislaus River (defeated)
1975	NJ	Bond issue for preservation of water resources (defeated, 54 percent to 46 percent)
1982	CA	Establish plan for water conservation and redistribution (defeated, 35 percent to 65 percent)
1986	CA	Restrict toxic discharges into drinking water (approved, 63 percent to 37 percent)
1989	TX	$500 million bond issue for water treatment (approved)
1989	WA	Allow local governments to finance private water conservation efforts (approved, 62 percent to 38 percent)
1990	MO	Protect 52 scenic waterways by banning new dams and restricting water use (defeated, 75 percent to 25 percent)

SEWAGE TREATMENT

Year	State	Issue/Result
1970	IL	$750 million bond issue for sewage treatment disposal system (approved)
1972	WA	$340 million bond issue for sewage treatment, water supply, and recreational facilities (approved)
1973	NY	Permit local governments to exceed debt limits for sewage treatment plant construction (approved)
1975	NY	Bond issue for financing the construction of sewers (defeated, 56 percent to 44 percent)

SOLID WASTE MANAGEMENT

Year	State	Issue/Result
1970	WA	Require refundable deposits on beverage containers (defeated)

1976	CO	Require refundable deposits on beverage containers (defeated)
1976	MA	Require refundable deposits on beverage containers (defeated)
1976	ME	Require refundable deposits on beverage containers (approved)
1976	MI	Require refundable deposits on beverage containers (approved)
1978	AK	Require refundable deposits on beverage containers (defeated)
1978	NE	Require refundable deposits on beverage containers (defeated)
1979	MA	Repeal law requiring refundable deposits on beverage containers (defeated)
1979	OH	Require refundable deposits on beverage containers (defeated)
1979	WA	Require refundable deposits on beverage containers (defeated)
1982	AZ	Require refundable deposits on beverage containers (defeated, 68 percent to 32 percent)
1982	CA	Require refundable deposits on beverage containers (defeated 56 percent to 44 percent)
1982	CO	Require refundable deposits on beverage containers (defeated, 76 percent to 24 percent)
1982	MA	Retain law requiring refundable deposits on beverage containers (approved, 59 percent to 41 percent)
1982	WA	Require refundable deposits on beverage containers (defeated, 71 percent to 29 percent)
1987	DC	Require refundable deposits on beverage containers (defeated)
1988	MT	Require refundable deposits on beverage containers (defeated, 79 percent to 21 percent)
1990	OR	Require recycling and ban on plastic foam packaging by 1993 (defeated, 57 percent to 43 percent)
1990	SD	Require legislative approval to build large garbage dumps (approved, 53 percent to 47 percent)
1992	MA	Require all packaging to be reusable, recyclable, made of recycled material, or reduced in size as of 1996 (defeated, 59 percent to 41 percent)

NUCLEAR/TOXIC WASTE DISPOSAL

Year	State	Issue/Result
1980	MO	Prohibit operation of nuclear power plants until federal government licenses waste storage facility in state (defeated)
1980	MT	Ban dumping of nuclear wastes in state (defeated)
1980	OR	Require permanent facility for nuclear waste disposal before consideration of new nuclear power plant (approved, 53 percent to 47 percent)
1980	SD	Prohibit nuclear waste dumping and ban uranium mining (defeated, 51 percent to 49 percent)
1980	WA	Ban importation and storage of nonmedical nuclear waste (approved, 75 percent to 25 percent)
1982	MA	Restrict building of new nuclear power plants and disposal of nuclear wastes (approved, 67 percent to 33 percent)
1982	MT	Remove present prohibitions against placing nuclear wastes in state (defeated, 76 percent to 24 percent)
1984	OR	Tighten requirements for approving nuclear waste disposal sites (approved, 55 percent to 45 percent)
1984	SD	Require voter approval of nuclear waste disposal sites (approved, 62 percent to 38 percent)
1986	MA	Limit hazardous waste disposal sites (approved, 73 percent to 27 percent)
1986	OR	Prohibit nuclear power plants until federal government licenses a disposal site (defeated, 64 percent to 36 percent)
1986	WA	Urge Congress to disapprove of a nuclear waste site in state (approved, 83 percent to 7 percent)
1988	MA	Stop electric power generation by commercial nuclear power plants that produce waste (defeated, 68 percent to 32 percent)
1988	NE	Allow state to withdraw from 5-state compact for coordinating facilities for nuclear waste; require voter approval of proposed sites for waste facilities (defeated, 65 percent to 35 percent)
1992	OR	Require shareholders to clean up nuclear power plant and ban operation of plant until permanent waste storage site found (defeated, 57 percent to 43 percent)

WILDLIFE MANAGEMENT

Year	State	Issue/Result
1972	SD	Ban mourning dove hunting (approved, 67 percent to 33 percent)
1977	OH	Ban use of steel-jaw traps (defeated, 63 percent to 37 percent)
1980	OR	Ban use of steel-jaw traps (defeated, 63 percent to 37 percent)
1980	SD	Remove ban on mourning dove hunting (approved, 58 percent to 42 percent)
1983	ME	Maintain annual moose hunt (approved, 63 percent to 37 percent)
1984	WA	End Native American fishing privileges (approved, 53 percent to 47 percent)
1990	AZ	Establish $20 million Heritage Fund from lottery proceeds to maintain state parks, acquire natural areas, and purchase wildlife habitat (approved, 62 percent to 38 percent)
1990	CA	Ban sport hunting of mountain lions and spend $30 million a year for 30 years to purchase wildlife habitat (approved, 52 percent to 48 percent)
1992	AZ	Ban most uses of steel-jaw traps on public lands (defeated, 62 percent to 38 percent)
1992	CO	Ban spring black bear hunts and use of bait and dogs in bear hunting (approved, 70 percent to 30 percent)

STUDY POPULATION INDEX

References are to entry numbers, not pages.
Entries not included in this index surveyed national, adult samples.

African-Americans 760; Denver, CO 760; Virginia, southeastern 56
American Association for the Advancement of Science members 798
American Sheep Producers Association members 745
Animals' Agenda subscribers 705
Anti-hunting organization members 643, 677, 679
Arboretum managers 551
Arboretum visitors 551
Audubon Society members 39, 474; Michigan 643

Backcountry visitors 725; Bridger Wilderness, WY 729; Cape Hatteras National Seashore, NC 606; Glacier National Park, MT 775; Grand Canyon National Park, AZ 565, 730; Great Smoky Mountains National Park, TN 726, 731, 817; Jewel Basin Hiking Area, MT 775; Kings Canyon National Park, CA 565; Monongahela National Forest, WV 566; Mt. McKinley National Park, AK 554; Rocky Mountain National Park, CO 563; Sequoia National Park, CA 565; Shenandoah National Park, VA 606, 723; Superstition Wilderness, AZ 729; Sylvania Recreation Area, MI 555; Uinta Primitive Area, UT 729; *see also* Hikers; Wilderness area visitors
"Backyard Wildlife Program" participants 771
Bear hunters: Michigan 819
Birdwatchers 710, 761, 806, 807
Boat owners: Dade County, FL 57
Boaters: Apostle Islands National Lakeshore, WI 733; Buckeye Lake, OH 534; Delaware Lake, OH 534; Deschutes River, OR 543; Lake Shelbyville, IL 605

Bureau of Land Management biologists 753, 759
Business leaders 151, 189, 285, 287, 490; Ohio, central 391; *see also* Industry executives

Campers 533, 542, 599, 607, 713, 715, 720, 721; Allegheny National Forest, PA 723; Colton Point State Park, PA 552; Gallatin Canyon, MT 721; George Washington State Forest, MN 718; Great Smoky Mountain National Park, TN 817; Hickory Run State Park, PA 552; Indiana state parks 572, 715; Leonard Harrison State Park, PA 552; Mt. Baker-Snoqualmie National Forest, WA 540; Mt. Hood National Forest, OR 540; Mt. Jefferson Wilderness, OR 541; Ottawa National Forest, MI 724; Pacific Northwest 715; St. Croix State Park, MN 718; Scenic State Park, MN 718; Unicoi Recreation Experiment Station, GA 719; Washington national forest campgrounds 717; Wenatchee National Forest, WA 540; Wisconsin campgrounds 715; Yellowstone National Park, WY 782; youth 686
Campground owners 561; Catskill Mountains, NY, 773
Camping club members 561
Canoeists 599; Au Sable River, MI 615; Boundary Waters Canoe Area, MN 676
Church organization members 473; Columbus, OH 593
City residents 265
Civic organization members 473, 475; Columbus, OH 593
College students 2, 502, 508, 526, 527, 528, 601, 675, 719, 743; African-American 28; biology 803; California State University 468, 469; Cornell

RESEARCHER/SPONSOR INDEX

SUBJECT INDEX